## The Cover

The artwork used on the cover is taken from a 60-foot mural created by seven Hawaiian 'ōpio (young people) in kumu (teacher) Meleanna Meyer's "Creating Treasures" art class during the 1994 summer program of Nā Pua No'eau: Center for Gifted and Talented Native Hawaiian Children. The students were: Kellee Anela Auna, Carly Ku'ulani Bolson, Samuel Kaimana David, Kamuela Hunter, Kimo Hunter, Tenneille Ieremia, and Nicole Waianuheake'alaopuakenikeni Tenn.

The mural depicts the Kumulipo, the most well known of the approximately ten Hawaiian cosmogonic genealogical chants that have survived to present day. Since ancestral times, the telling of Hawaiian mo'olelo (stories) and related literary forms began properly with earlier beginnings, with the hero's immediate antecedents or several generations further back along the ancestral line. In some instances, the telling would start at the very beginning of time, as in the Kumulipo, the birth chant of Kalaninui-'Īamamao, the Hawai'i island chiefly ancestor of the last two reigning monarchs of the Hawaiian Kingdom.

The Kumulipo starts in the distant, dark beginnings (kumu) of the world. From out of darkness (pō), primordial slime (lipo) emerged, then a male element (kāne) and a female element (wahine) were born, and from them the earth and everything in it would then unfold in genealogical sequence: from creatures of the sea to those of the sky to those of the land; from the land itself to human chiefs and gods; and from them to generations of their descendants until the present time.

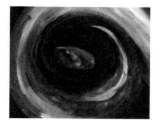

A chief's birth chant proclaimed him or her to be an inseparable part of an ancient procession of life, and defined the chief's relationship with the earth and the people.

The Kumulipo's essential lesson is that everything in the world is related by birth and, as such, together constitute a single indivisible lineage. Conceived in this way, the heavens, the seas, the land, the gods, the chiefs, and the people intertwine as myriad, intrinsically related aspects of the universe. For if someone were to ask a Hawaiian, Who are you?, he or she could only meaningfully answer by referring to his or her beginnings, to his or her genealogy, which is a map that guides each Hawaiian's relationship to the world.

Hawaiians customarily patterned their behavior after the ancestral examples found in their genealogy. Today, we Hawaiians use genealogical relationships to establish our collective identity via a social network of extended 'ohana (family). Our shared genealogy helps us define our lāhui (nation) as an entity distinct from the waves of foreigners that came to inundate and transform the face of our islands.

Thus, at this time of transformation from one epoch to another, the Kumulipo reminds us of our beginnings, ancient and new, and of our connections to each other and everything in this world.

# Kunihi ka mauna i ka lai e,

O Waialeale la i Wailua,

Huki i luna ka popoo ua o Kawaikini,

Alai ia ae la e Nounou,

Nalo ka ipu haa,

Ka laula ma uka o Kapaa e,

I paa i ka leo, he ole ka hea mai,

E hea mai ka leo—e."

*Steep stands the mountain in the calm*

*Wai'ale'ale there at Wailua*

*The heavy rain of Kawaikini*

*Reaches up to the heavens*

*Obstructed by Nounou*

*Kaipuha'a is hidden*

"Kunihi ka mauna i ka lai e

O Waialeale la i Wailua

Huki iluna ka popo ua o Kawaikini

Alai ia aela e Nounou

Nalo Kaipuhaa

Ka laula mauka o Kapaa—e

I paa i ka leo, he ole ka hea mai

E hea mai ka leo—e."

"Kunihi ka mauna i ka lai—e

O Waialeale la—e i Waialua

Huki ae la iluna ka papa o Anokawailani

Alai ia ae la e Nounou

Nalowale Kaipuhaa

Haa i ka laula

Haa ka ipu, haa makai o Kapaa—e

Haa ka ipu, haa mauka o Kapaa—e

Mai paa i ka leo

He ole ka heahea mai."

"Kūnihi ka mauna i ka laʻi ē

ʻO Waiʻaleʻale lā, i Wailua;

Huki aʻela i ka lani,

Ka papa ʻauwai o Kawaikini;

Ālai ʻia aʻela e Nounou,

Nalo Kaipuhaʻa,

Ka laulā, ma uka o Kapaʻa ē;

Mai paʻa i ka leo.

# He ʻole ka hea mai ē!"

"Kunihi ka mauna i ka laʻi e,
O Wai-aleale, la, i Wai-lua;
Huki iluna ka popo ua o Ka-wai-kini;
Alai ia aʻe la e Nounou,
Nalo ka Ipu-haʻa,
Ka laula ma uka o Ka-paʻa e.
I paʻa i ka leo, he ole e hea mai.
E hea mai ka leo, e!"

The broad plains above Kapaʻa

Humble in the expanse

The gourd is low, low below Kapaʻa

The gourd is low, low above Kapaʻa

If the voice is withheld,

No greeting will come;

The voice calls.

"Kunihi ka mauna i ka laʻi e—

O Waialeale la i Wailua

Huki ae la ka lani kapapa-ua Kawaiki

Alai ae la paa Nounou

Nalowale ka laula mauka

Makai o Kapaa e—

Mai paa i ka le—o

He ole ka hea ma—i."

# kūnihi ka mauna

## The Opening Pages

One of the most well-known and oft-per-formed *oli* (chants) in the hula world takes its title from its first line, *Kūnihi ka mauna i ka la'i ē* (Steep stands the mountain [Wai'ale'ale] in the calm), and comes from the *mo'olelo* (story) of Hi'iaka, the youngest and favorite sister of the volcano goddess Pele. The earli-est known version of "Kūnihi ka mauna" in print comes from *haku mo'olelo* (writer) J. N. Kapihenui in *He Moolelo no Hiiakaikapoliopele* (A Tale of Hi'iaka-in-the-bosom-of-Pele), published in the newspaper *Ka Hoku o ka Pakipika* (Star of the Pacific) in 1861. But the most well-known version is found in Nathaniel B. Emerson's *Unwritten Literature of Hawaii* (originally published in 1909), and in slightly different form in his later book *Pele and Hiiaka, a Myth from Hawaii* (origi-nally published in 1915). The popularity of Emerson's version undoubtedly has much to do with the fact that it was the only one translated into English. However, at least five other versions of "Kūnihi" were published in the Hawaiian language in the 19th-century newspapers. The chant also exists in at least 17 unpublished forms in various collections in the Bishop Museum Archives.

In the most well-known version of this *mo'olelo,* Hi'iaka is sent by her sister Pele from the island of Hawai'i to the island of Kaua'i to fetch Pele's beloved, the handsome chief Lohi'au. When Hi'iaka reaches the south bank of Kaua'i's Wailua River near the *muli-wai* (river mouth), she chants "Kūnihi" to the guardian *mo'o* (giant reptile or water spirit), also known as Wailua, asking to be granted passage across the river. When the *mo'o* rebukes her, Hi'iaka kills it, then crosses the river by placing stepping stones, and contin-ues on her journey. In different versions, Hi'iaka chants "Kūnihi" in other situations: when she first catches sight of the island of Kaua'i while she is still sitting in her canoe, both greeting the island and seeking permis-sion to step onto Kaua'i soil; when her canoe lands at Kapa'a before she continues on to Naue and then to Hā'ena; outside the home of the fisherman Malaeha'akoa and his wife Wailuanuiaho'āno when seeking permission to enter their *hale* (home). In yet another version Pele, not Hi'iaka, chants "Kūnihi" when she arrives at Hā'ena on Kaua'i's north shore and sees Lohi'au for the very first time.

Although the individual contexts of each of these versions vary, they all express the traditional Hawaiian attitude of not "barging in" where one does not have *kuleana* (privilege and responsibility), and of showing respect for the people, place, and culture where one is an outsider. Although Hiʻiaka is a goddess, she must still pay respect to the *ʻāina* (land) and to those who have *kuleana* over it, as well as to those who have traveled the path she now seeks to travel.

"Kūnihi" is also about confronting obstacles and challenges, such as those that obstruct Hiʻiaka's efforts to fulfill her *kuleana* to her sister Pele, and about deciding to whom greater *kuleana* is owed. Although at times the obstructions seem impossible to overcome, Hiʻiaka's bravery, cleverness, and fortitude—aided by her companions, *ʻohana* (family), and *ʻaumākua* (family gods)—enable her to reach her destiny.

Just as a growing number of Hawaiian scholars are now questioning and challenging Emerson's work on many levels, including his translation skills, we have chosen to include other versions of "Kūnihi" on the opening pages so as not to continue the problematic practice of privileging Emerson's text. The incorporation of these different versions also embodies the attitude contained in an oft-quoted *ʻōlelo noʻeau* (Hawaiian saying) which states, *ʻAʻole pau ka ʻike i ka hālau hoʻokahi*—Not all knowledge is contained within one *hālau* (school). And, finally, it embodies the *oli's* transition from the oral to the written form, demonstrating the strength and adaptability of our ancient traditions as we move into the modern world.

Esteemed Hawaiian scholar Mary Kawena Pukui once wrote that while there were

many *mele kāhea* ("calling" or "entrance" chants), "this Kauai one was well liked and commonly used," even by those from other islands. Centuries after Hiʻiaka first chanted "Kūnihi," the *oli* is still treasured by Hawaiians, even though the context has changed. Today it is regularly heard by *hālau hula* (hula dance troupes) seeking permission to ascend the stage for a rehearsal, performance, or competition; and its refrain is still sent echoing across the land by *haumāna* (students) and other cultural practitioners seeking permission to enter a classroom, forest, or *heiau* (place of worship).

"Kūnihi" is thus "chanted" in the opening pages of this second issue of *ʻŌiwi* on behalf of all those seeking permission to enter into the sharing of talent, *manaʻo* (expression and thought), and *mana* (spiritual energy) that follows. It is also chanted at the closing as a request from all seeking to enter into the new *wā* (epoch) of contemporary times as we confront its many challenges, ever mindful of our relationship to this *ʻāina* and to those who came before us and who will come after us.

Today when "Kūnihi" is chanted, proper protocol instructs that a *pane* (response) be given in the form of a *mele komo,* a chant that grants entry. The *mele komo* on the following page invites those who are sincere in their desire to hear and learn, to partake of the *mea waiwai,* the riches contained between these covers. As another *ʻōlelo noʻeau* states, which is associated with the area of Kauaʻi containing the places invoked in "Kūnihi": *Ua nani ʻo Puna mai ʻō a ʻō*— Only beauty is found in the Puna (Kawaihau) district, from one end to the other. Here then enter, and enjoy the beauty *mai ʻō a ʻō,* from cover to cover.

Kuʻualoha Hoʻomanawanui

*"E hea i ke kanaka*

Call the person

*E komo ma loko,*

to come in,

*E hānai ai a hewa ka waha;*

And eat till the mouth can take no more;

*Eia nō ka uku lā 'o kou leo,*

This is the reward, the voice,

*A he leo wale nō ē!"*

Simply the voice!

# *Kūnihi ka mauna*

(steep stands the mountain)

*'ōiwi*

a native hawaiian **journal**

puke 'elua (volume 2)

Kuleana 'Ōiwi Press
Honolulu, Hawai'i

# 'ōiwi

## a native hawaiian journal

**Rates**
**Volume 1:** $12.50 (domestic); $18 (foreign)
**Volume 2:** $16 (domestic); $24 (foreign)

Prices include surface mail (2-6 weeks delivery).
For air mail add $6 per volume.

Make check or money order payable to
KULEANA 'ŌIWI PRESS

**Correspondence**
'Ōiwi: A Native Hawaiian Journal
P.O. Box 189
Kāne'ohe, HI 96744-0189
tel:      (808) 237-1444
fax:      (808) 237-1445
oiwi@hawaii.edu
http://www.hawaii.edu/oiwi

When sending submissions, please include your
address, phone and fax numbers, e-mail
address, and a self-addressed, stamped envelope
for return of manuscript or for our reply. Payment
for submissions accepted for publication is in the
form of two complimentary copies of the volume
in which the work appears.

ISSN   1521-7329
ISBN   0-9668220-2-1

This volume is supported in part by grants from
Nā Pua No'eau: Center for Gifted and Talented
Native Hawaiian Children; The Native Hawaiian
Leadership Project; and State Foundation on
Culture and the Arts through appropriations from
the legislature of the State of Hawai'i and/or grants
from the National Endowment for the Arts.

The contents of this journal were developed in part
by a grant by the Department of Education.
However, those contents do not necessarily represent the policy of the Department of Education,
and you should not assume endorsement by the
Federal Government.

**Luna Ho'oponopono / Chief Editor**
D. Māhealani Dudoit

**Hope Luna Ho'oponopono /
Associate Editor**
Ku'ualoha Meyer Ho'omanawanui

**Nā Luna Ho'oponopono 'Ōlelo
Hawai'i / Hawaiian-Language
Editors**
Noelani Arista, Laiana Wong

**Nā Luna Kōkua Ho'oponopono /
Assistant Editors**
Mohala Aiu, Kimo Armitage,
Lisa Kanae, Michael Puleloa, Leslie
Keli'ilauahi Stewart, Māhealani Wong

**Hakulau / Graphic Artist**
'Alika McNicoll

**Mea Ulele Hua / Typesetter**
B. Kanai'akukui Nakamura

Design layout for this issue created by
Stacey Leong.

Photograph on pgs. ii, iii, 268, and 269 by
Ku'ualoha Ho'omanawanui.

Photograph on pg. 97 of 'Ualapu'e Fishpond
printed by permission of Marine Option
Program, University of Hawai'i.

William Akutagawa Jr.'s "'Ualapu'e Fishpond,
Moloka'i: Oral History from the East End"
is excerpted and reprinted in modified form
from Center for Oral History, et al., 'Ualapu'e,
Moloka'i: Oral Histories from the East End, vol.
1 (Honolulu: Center for Oral History, Social
Science Research Institute, University of
Hawai'i-Mānoa, and the State of Hawai'i
Department of Business, Economic
Development and Tourism, 1991) and is
reprinted by permission of the Center for Oral
History. Skippy Ioane's "Samuela Texas" was
recorded by Big Island Conspiracy on the CD
entitled Reflective but Unrepentent (Ka'a Ka'a
Records, 1999) and is reprinted by permission
of the record company and the songwriter.
J. Kehaulani Kauanui's "Homestead/Heart
Steady" first appeared in Moana: Pacific Islands
Student Publication (University of Utah) 2
(Spring 1999):13 and is reprinted by permis-
sion of the author. Leslie Stewart's "Legacy of
Music, Legacy of Love" appeared in part in Ka
Wai Ola o OHA (March 2002) and is printed
here in full by permission of the author.

# *mahalo*

Mahalo a nui loa i nā kānaka like 'ole i ko lākou kōkua 'ana i ka puka 'ana i kēia puke 'elua o 'Ōiwi. Many, many thanks to those who brought this second issue of 'Ōiwi into being:

To Pat Matsueda and Frank Stewart of *Mānoa* journal, you have always been ready and willing to share your vast experience in the literary arts of Hawai'i by answering our numerous and frequent questions of all kinds: A big mahalo for your friendship and for your support in helping us to stay afloat.

To Jason Kim and David Forman, mahalo for your much needed pro bono legal advice, given out of the kindness of your hearts and your belief in and support of the worthiness of our project; Wing Tek Lum and Betty Donery, for your much needed advice and help on bookkeeping and accounting; Kalei Kahā'ulelio, for your kind kōkua with grantwriting; Mehanaokalā Hind, for the sharing of your 'ike regarding the House and Senate bills on tuition waivers for Hawaiian students; and videomakers Sparky Rodrigues and Lillian Hong, for your expertise and time in documenting our projects.

To both the Center for Hawaiian Studies and to the English Department of the University of Hawai'i-Mānoa, mahalo for the much needed storage space!

To David Sing of Nā Pua No'eau: Center for Gifted and Talented Native Hawaiian Children, and Manu Ka'iama of The Native Hawaiian Leadership Project, a HUGE mahalo for your personal moral support and advice, and for the GENEROUS monetary support from your programs, and from State Foundation on Culture and the Arts. We could not have printed this issue without your help.

To Lee Tonouchi ("da Pidgin guerrilla"), congrats on da AWESOME new local journal *Hybolics.* Mahalo to you and your staff, and to Kyle Koza and da staff of *Hawai'i Review* too, for your friendship, moral support, advice, laughtah, shoulders fo' cry on, and general good vibes. *Write On!* (appropriated from Lee!).

To Nāpua Spock and her hui of supporters, mahalo for bringing 'Ōiwi to the island of Maui, and being such warm and generous hosts.

To Miki'ala Ayau and Kimo Armitage, mahalo for sharing your talent in oli and hana keaka to materialize 'Ōiwi as literary performance.

To "Uncle" and dear friend Calvin Hoe—Hawaiian instrument maker, composer, and musician—a very very special and warm mahalo to you for bringing our literary performances to a high level of art.

In regard to the inclusion of the oli "Kūnihi ka mauna" in the opening and closing pages of this issue, grateful thanks is given to all of the 19th-century mea kākau (writers) of the published versions of the mo'olelo (story) of Pele and Hi'iaka for your commitment to our language and culture in a time of great adversity: J. N. Kapihenui, Joseph Poepoe, Ho'oulumāhiehie (which some say is a pseudonym for Poepoe), S. Pa'aluhi and John E. Bush, and Moses "Moke" Manu. Thanks are also given to Mary Kawena Pukui and to you "living treasures" of today, who in your lifetimes committed yourselves to perpetuating our language and cultural traditions: Noenoe Silva; Noelani Arista; Ioane Ho'omanawanui; and Ipo Torio and the staff of the summer 2000 program of Nā Pua No'eau: Center for Gifted and Talented Native Hawaiian Children, especially to kumu Kēhaulani Kekua, as well as to Maka and 'Iwalani Ka'auwai-Herrod, kumu of Hālau Hula 'o Kamakaokalani. Mahalo also to Randy Wichman and Nā Kahu a Hikinaakalā, who generously supplied the aerial photograph of Wailua, Kaua'i, on page iv.

To our families and friends, and to our partners in this life—Ioane, Scott, Lilinoe, and Maluhia—(and not to forget our dogs Ala'e, Lilikoi, and Sistah, who bring us much warm companionship, happiness, and laughter... and headaches sometimes!), mahalo to you for putting up with all our personal and professional trials and tribulations, as well as for being there as confidantes, givers of much needed hugs and kisses, and as helpers in numerous ways (including carrying heavy stuffs!), and, not the least, for sharing in our joys. *Mahalo iā 'oukou me ka pu'uwai piha i ke aloha pau 'ole.*

To our readers, supporters, and contributors, mahalo to you for loyally sticking by us as we were struggling to get this second issue out long after the planned publication date.

Plus a personal mahalo from D. Māhealani Dudoit, luna ho'oponopono, to associate editor Ku'ualoha Ho'omanawanui for her conceptualization and carrying out of the compilation of the special feature "Notable Hawaiians of the 20th Century"; to graphic artists 'Alika McNicoll and Kanai'a Nakamura; and to all the editors of this journal, who generously and unselfishly volunteered their time, energies, 'ike, and personal resources to mālama *'Ōiwi* in its growth and development. You've done an awesome job in helping to revitalize Hawaiian artistic expression to a level that does honor to our past, our kūpuna, and our culture. *E ho'omau kākou.*

And finally, mahalo nui loa me ke aloha nui i nā kūpuna, nā 'aumākua a me nā akua no ko 'oukou mālama 'ana iā mākou, kā 'oukou pulapula, nā 'ōiwi o Hawai'i nei.

# 'ōiwi

a native hawaiian **journal**

## contents

*'Ōlelo Ho'ākāka*
*(Language Policy)*

'A'ole pau ka 'ike i ka hālau ho'okahi. I mākia maika'i kūpono nō paha kēia no kākou a pau e ho'omaopopo ai ke komo aku kākou i loko o ia māhele 'o ka ho'oponopono. I loko nō o ko kākou hānai 'ia a kula 'ia 'ana paha ma ka 'ike ē he 'ao'ao pololei a he 'ao'ao hewa ko nā nīnau a pau, ke 'ike nei nō na'e kākou i ka na'auao o ia 'ōlelo e kau maila ma luna nei, 'o ia ho'i, ua hānai 'ia kākou ma loko o nā hālau like 'ole he nui wale a ua 'oko'a ka mana'o o kekahi a 'oko'a ho'i ko kekahi. 'A'ohe hālau e kaena a'e i mua o ke ākea ua pau ka 'ike i lalo o kona kaupoku, no ka mea, ma kona kaena 'ana i ka pololei o kona mana'o, eia nō kā 'o ia ke kapa nei i ka mana'o 'oko'a o kona hoa i ka hewa. Mali'a o 'ike 'ia auane'i i ka lā 'apōpō ka pololei o ka mea e ho'okae 'ia nei i kēia lā ua hewa. Na wai ho'i e 'ole ka hilahila?

No ka hō'ike 'ana i ko kākou mana'o ma o ka palapala, 'a'ole ana paha e nele ke kū

We are living in exciting times: Hawaiian-language immersion schools from pre-school through high school have been established on all the main islands of Hawai'i; more and more high schools—both public and private—are adding Hawaiian-language classes to their curriculum; enrollment is up in Hawaiian-language classes at the college and university level across the state.

Despite the increased interest in and awareness of *ka 'ōlelo 'ōiwi* (the native language), or perhaps because of it, several points of contention regarding translations and the use of diacritical marks (the *'okina,* or glottal stop; and the *[kaha]kō,* or macron) have arisen in the past several years. This is not a new subject. Since the first missionaries sought to represent the spoken language using a standardized alphabet and written form, issues of "proper" or "correct" marking, vocabulary, grammar, and translation have been disputed by Hawaiians and mai o kekahi kanaka me ke koikoi ʻana mai e mālama ʻia kekahi kulekele kūmau ma ka pela ʻana i nā huaʻōlelo Hawaiʻi me ka ʻokina a me ke kahakō. E ʻōlelo mai paha kēlā ē ʻo ia ka mea e akāka ai ka manaʻo o ia mau huaʻōlelo ke heluhelu aku. A he manaʻo maikaʻi nō paha kēlā. Eia naʻe, e kūʻē mai paha auaneʻi ka manaʻo o kekahi kanaka ē he mea kēlā e paʻa ai kēlā manaʻo a ʻike ʻole ʻia ai hoʻi kona naʻauao ma ke ʻano laulā a hohonu paha. A no laila, ma kahi o ka hoʻokaʻawale ʻana i kēia mau manaʻo e like me ko kākou manaʻo he pololei a he hewa, e huli hou aku kākou i ka ʻōlelo a ko kākou poʻe kūpuna i hoʻoili maila ma luna o kākou, a no ka mea, ʻo ia ana ko kākou ʻike a mahalo hoʻi i ka naʻauao o ua mau hālau lā a ʻelua.

Mai nō a kuhihewa e ka mea heluhelu ē he pono kākau wale aku ka hana me ka nānā ʻole i nā loina kākau e laha nei i kēia wā a kākou e ʻike nei. ʻAʻole nō pēlā ka hana. ʻAʻole lā! He nānā ʻia nō e nā luna hoʻoponopono kēlā me kēia huaʻōlelo me ka loihape pono aku o ka maka ma nā ʻano a pau. ʻO ke ʻano naʻe o ia hoʻoponopono ʻana, ʻo ia hoʻi, ua waiho ʻia ka mana hoʻoholo i loko o ka lima o ka mea kākau e hoʻoponopono ai i kāna hana ponoʻī e like me kona manaʻo he pono.

non-Hawaiians alike. The disputes are not a matter of mere whim, but are seriously considered choices arising from different philosophies regarding language—its place in our lives; its power and its inadequacies in representing the oral; its ability and its limitations in capturing thought and feeling and in translating that thought and feeling into another, sometimes very foreign language.

In response to the diversity of perspectives, our policy regarding language use allows for broad individual choice. This policy applies to Hawaiian, English, Pidgin, and any other language. Translation of works between Hawaiian and English is also left to the discretion of the author, even though we have decided—not unanimously—to translate material from the past (such as 19th-century Hawaiian-language newspapers and other historical documents) into English in order to make them more accessible to those who can't read Hawaiian. This policy explains the seeming inconsistencies you may notice from piece to piece—why some have been translated and others haven't; why some include diacritical marks and some don't; why some names are marked and others aren't. The differences reflect the vitality of language.

**Some notes:** In keeping with normal publishing convention, the use or absence of diacriticals in quoted material, including the titles of works, remains true to the original (e.g. the name of the newspaper *Ke Aloha Aina*). Similarly, some personal names are not marked, depending on the preference of the person or family or on popular usage (e.g. David Kawananakoa). Finally, regarding the use of the term "native Hawaiian," unless otherwise stated, we do not adhere to the restrictive definition employed by the State of Hawaiʻi to refer only to those Hawaiians of 50% blood quantum or more, but are using that term instead as we do in our lived community to refer to *all* Hawaiians with pre-contact genealogical ties to this *ʻāina*.

# Editors' Note: Huliau

(from left to right) Michael Puleloa, Laiana Wong, Māhealani Dudoit, Leslie Stewart, Kuʻualoha Hoʻomanawanui, Lisa Kanae, Noelani Arista, Māhealani Wong

Welcome to our new editor, Kimo Armitage (da big guy)

# nā luna ʻōiwi

Nā Luna ʻŌiwi • Nā Luna ʻŌiwi • Nā Luna ʻŌiwi • Nā Luna ʻŌiwi

**KUʻUALOHA HOʻOMANAWANUI**

In a university class the other day, the first thing the instructor read was from the Editors' Note of the first issue of ʻŌiwi. It was a very wonderful experience, to be part of something we were not really sure how was going to be received, to it being incorporated into classrooms.

What has really amazed me since the first issue of the journal came out is that in traveling to different places—even if it's just going across island to visit family and friends, or going off island for different functions and coming across people who had a chance to see ʻŌiwi—it has been sometimes overwhelming to share people's enthusiasm about the project. Many people, particularly Hawaiians, are reacting to it in such a positive way because it has been so long in coming. Once upon a time our kūpuna had a number of Hawaiian-language newspapers to read and respond

to, but those newspapers disappeared. And then our parents' generation was so busy working to understand this new American system and to get us ahead. Now we are able to give something back. A lot of people appreciate that, and that's something for me that's been really exciting, the idea that we started with a vision and we put it out there. We weren't sure how people would respond and the response has been very positive and very encouraging.

One of the differences between ʻŌiwi and the typical journal is that the end goal isn't for our own glory—take these pieces in, publish them, and become a noted journal. We are opening a community dialogue in a new way. We are Hawaiians talking to other Hawaiians. And in working against the false stereotypes that Hawaiians don't or can't appreciate literature or literacy, the challenge is How do we maintain relationships while at the same time maintain a standard, and still encourage Hawaiians to keep writing, to keep submitting material?

**LAIANA WONG**
There are a lot of people who are talented. But my impression of Hawaiians is that they don't feel that they are as talented as they really are. On the other hand, you get a lot of people—and maybe I'm stereotyping, but a lot of them are non-Hawaiians—whose stuff isn't that good, but they really think it is. I seen that, especially when I was on the mainland.

**KUʻUALOHA HOʻOMANAWANUI**
That thought leads to the question of language. Having gone through three years of Hawaiian, I definitely relate to the idea of not feeling my Hawaiian is good enough in speaking, writing, or comprehension. But working in English or in Pidgin, I never question my ability to speak, write, or comprehend those languages.

**LAIANA WONG**
Pidgin doesn't have that tradition of prescriptivism, of right and wrong. Of course, that is an issue that could come up if Pidgin were to go more fully into the schools. People are going to be looking for objective ways to evaluate the performance of students. Pidgin could get like that, too. That would be weird, to have someone tell a local kid, "Your Pidgin isn't making it!"

**MĀHEALANI WONG**
I think they're already doing it. Not standardization yet, but they can judge if your Pidgin is good enough or not by using the criteria, Did the other person understand you?

**LAIANA WONG**
And then there's Pidgin as cultural marker,

Pidgin as language of resistance, and questions like whether a non-Pidgin speaker can come in and just pick it up. Like one of my professors says, they call it "broken English." Does that mean I can take my English, broke ʻum, and then speak Pidgin? It don't work that way.

If you were a native speaker of Hawaiian and somebody said your Hawaiian wasn't grammatically correct, you'd say, "Get out of here, I speak my language you know!" I not going let anybody tell me my Pidgin isn't any good or my English. That's the language I speak. But with Hawaiian I have this insecurity because I'm not there. Like when I interview a native speaker and I gotta listen to my voice right next to that person's voice, the difference comes out so clear. It's not just the voice, it's the manaʻo, how they make ʻum. Totally different. It goes back to that saying, "The more you know, the more you know you don't know." I think Hawaiian is like that for me.

**LESLIE STEWART**
Maybe we nurture the Hawaiian more. There is more of a sense of aloha and kuleana. We want to preserve and protect its integrity. We don't feel the same way towards English because it was forced upon us at the expense of Hawaiian. Maybe if Hawaiian had been allowed to continue and our kūpuna weren't beaten for speaking it, it would be a different story.

**NOE ARISTA**
Because the Hawaiian language still potentially could be lost, it's so important to pay attention. But because there's a written record in the Hawaiian newspapers of the last century, it can be passed down. Yet we don't know if there will be enough Hawaiian-speaking people who will have

the facility to read and understand Hawaiian. We don't know if those newspapers will be translated, because we are still debating that right now. It's uncharted water that is dangerous because of the crisis situation of the language. We are very worried. The worry makes you weary.

**KIMO ARMITAGE**

Therein lies this problem that we all acknowledge as writers: preserving the Hawaiian language while trying to integrate it into our everyday lives. Language is dynamic: it flies, it jumps, and it broods. But try writing a critique in Hawaiian of, say, social reformation where one would need to create a viable vocabulary, and upon doing it, not be criticized for the words that you have created by people who don't realize that we need to move the language.

**MĀHEALANI DUDOIT**

In Noenoe Silva's Hawaiian-language class this semester, we're doing the moʻolelo of Hiʻiaka. Most people are familiar with Nathaniel B. Emerson's version, which you, Kuʻualoha, in your guest lecture to our class one day, told us was a compilation of parts plagiarized from other sources put into writing earlier by Hawaiians. The version we're doing is by Joseph M. Poepoe, serialized in the newspaper *Kuokoa Home Rula* from 1908 to 1911. We were really surprised to find several things, one of 'um being that Poepoe's really conscious about the language disappearing. He says that the motivation for him and the newspaper editors working so patiently and so hard is that they are concerned about the loss of words, the loss of pronunciation, the loss of language use.

**NOE ARISTA**

One of the things I collect in my spare time

are articles on the loss of tradition, Hawaiians concerned with the loss of tradition. I have articles from people writing letters to the newspaper throughout the 19th century. As they're living, during their own time, they can feel the body of tradition withering and they start to say, "Oh, we're losing this. You know how I know this? Because we used to know that, now we don't." That's common.

**LAIANA WONG**

We're in a place and time now where we are trying to bridge a gap, and so we even have this added burden on us to project from that time to the present how it would have been if it had followed an unbroken course, then try to rebuild that bridge and make sure we make a strong enough link so that we can move on.

**KUʻUALOHA HOʻOMANAWANUI**

I think we are in a tough position for two reasons: One is that we know that something was severed and we're trying our best to link it up again as best as we can. But the other position which is equally as difficult is that we're fighting against all of the abuse and misuse of our traditions by non-Hawaiians that didn't just end with Emerson. And it's not only with written tradition. There are now websites that offer classes on "The Womb of Pele" in Sweden and as far away as Greenland. And then there are the "Hawaiian Lemurian Goddesses," which list includes Pele, Hiʻiaka, Hina, Kapo, etc. This website prescribes astronomical and New Age qualities to our Hawaiian goddesses, our ancestors!

**NOE ARISTA**

A lot of people are making a lot of money on Hawaiian traditions that never existed. Whenever I talk to students who are not from Hawaiʻi about Hawaiian tradition, the first thing I ask them is, "Well, what did you want to do when you came to Hawai'i? What was the first thing you wanted to do?" And the first answer I got from this class from Minnesota was, "Lie out on the beach and laze around." And I said, "Ya, I do that every day!" No, I never get to do that. And then one by one people will tell me about this image they have that the media has plastered throughout American culture—the Voice of Paradise, from Elvis movies in the '50s all the way to Real World MTV 1998–1999, to—

**EVERYONE**
BAYWATCH!!

**NOE ARISTA**
Not only does it make Hawaiian culture invisible and ignored right in plain sight, it eviscerates it. And the very horrible, rotten thing about it is that the natives are starting to complain, and yet people are like, "Well how dare you complain, darn it, you live in paradise? How dare you complain? I live in Nebraska. The snow in the winter is freezing. It's horrible. But shame on you natives. You shouldn't be complaining." This environment suppresses Hawaiian culture by supplanting it with glossy tourist images of Hawai'i as a paradise that people can run to to forget their worries and cares. This situation makes it hard to address problems in a place that's supposed to be problem free.

To drive my point home I always say to them, the governor of the State of Hawai'i said Hawai'i is the healthiest state in the nation...based on statistics for Asians! They actually said in the paper that Asian-Americans make up for the lesser than average life span of Hawaiians. I thought, gee, we can't even die properly, somebody is gonna make up for us when we die. We live

in paradise, right? Then how come we have Third World health statistics for Native Hawaiians? The worst in the nation. How is it possible that people in my family drop dead at a faster rate than anybody else in America? But look outside. I live in paradise. And that's the paradox I try to teach the students.

**LESLIE STEWART**
Going back to what you said about Hawaiians being concerned about the loss of tradition, just from the 1840s to the present there's this different outlook of worldview here and the mentality that the United States is "progress." What happened from the 1840s to now? We had railroads coming and all this technology and everything was moving "forward." Hawaiians from then to now are looking at everything that we are losing as the United States is progressing. Everything that we have has been run over, banned, corrupted, or lost. On one hand Hawai'i is celebrated as a health state, while on the other hand Hawaiians as a people native to this place have the worse statistics than everyone else in health, in education, in social services.

**NOE ARISTA**
There's an article by the 19th-century Hawaiian historian David Malo about the decrease of the Hawaiian population where he asks the question, Why is it that Hawaiians are dying? This is a question people keep debating all the way through the mid-1900s. What makes a Hawaiian is the common experience of all of those things that had happened to us. Maybe the suffering didn't happen to everybody, but out there is this pervasive sense of loss. The thing that blew my mind in editing pieces for 'Ōiwi was that that sense of loss was almost in every piece. Articulating, recogniz-

ing, and working past that sense of loss in a forum like this journal helps us to heal. The power of 'Ōiwi is that it provides a venue for seeing these things and bringing them to the surface.

### KIMO ARMITAGE

The power of 'Ōiwi is that it publishes, prints, and reprints not only normally accepted forms of prose like poetry, critical essays, short stories, and plays, but also mele, oli, and legislative testimony. This last thing is important because of a new generation of Hawaiian children whose identities will be based on grievances.

### LAIANA WONG

I keep thinking about Charlie Kupa [who was the kahu of Ka Papa Lo'i 'o Kānewai]. He said this Hawaiianness—or whatever it is we are trying to hold on to—it's like poi when it's really runny. You try to grab as much as you can, and because you cherish it so much, you squeeze it. But as you squeeze, it's coming out of your hand and you're losing it as you are trying to hold on to it. What a spooky thought. But, well, we are going to continue on...

### LISA KANAE

There is such a compelling need for a journal like 'Ōiwi, that I knew it would have to be successful. I have to admit, I had no idea how big that success was going to be. After the first issue of the journal came out, one of the many pleasant surprises for me was how we got word from a Maori community and a Samoan community who said that 'Ōiwi gave them the motivation to start their own journals. Talk about a satisfying feeling. Knowing that 'Ōiwi, a book filled with Native Hawaiian voices and vision, inspired other indigenous peoples to document their heritage, create contemporary art, and fur-

ther their legacy, well, it feels pretty good inside. We owe so much to the writers and artists from our first issue.

On a very personal level, 'Ōiwi has touched me the way no other kind of literary journal has touched me. Many of the pieces in the first issue taught me so much about my history, my heritage, and about who I am—my Hawaiianness, which is a part of me that I will admit to not knowing as well as I want to. Some of the pieces in the first issue brought me to tears. I didn't have to talk over whether or not the work met a particular publishable standard. I just knew that I was not going to be the only person who was going to be moved by these writers' words and pictures. Noe and Ku'ualoha called this feeling amongst the Hawaiian community a common loss, a common sorrow. For me, contributing what I can to the journal is a kind of journey of self-discovery. I want to play a part in rectifying that sorrow. This year I'm teaching English composition at Kapi'olani Community College. One of my personal missions is to use as much Native Hawaiian and local writers' works in my course. I've been eagerly waiting for this second issue of 'Ōiwi to come out! Granted, I have to choose the essays by Native Hawaiian writers that are written in English, but the students feel such a strong connection to these writings because they can identify with them. In fact, the response is overwhelming. "Miss Kanae," they always say, "We can really relate to this stuff!" "Good," I tell them. "Now write your own personal narratives, your own argumentative essays, your own compositions," and they do.

### KIMO ARMITAGE

Maika'i. That's the ultimate message, Lisa. Whether you write in Pidgin, English, or Hawaiian. You write and show us your own unique, valid Hawaiian perspective and we'll try to take care of you in the next issue. You're Hawaiian and what you say counts. There is power in your voice.

**KU'UALOHA HO'OMANAWANUI**
But it still goes back to that same problem: "Why aren't you natives out on the beach every day soaking up the sun? Don't you live in paradise?" It's because of economic issues, paying exorbitant rents or mortgages to live in their so-called "paradise," it's the "progress" of being American that has led to the loss of our lo'i lands and our fishponds, the pollution of our land and waters.

**MĀHEALANI WONG**
It's hard to go back, especially when you have influence from things like TV. But once we got rid of our TV, our children were able to sit still and listen to a story. Luckily my kids are old enough to read to themselves, but it's also taking the time to do that with them. Taking them to listen to kūpuna, making them practice their listening. Because that's a skill that is learned, and it's a big problem for our children, not being able to read.

**LESLIE STEWART**
That's so true. Part of it is having things for them to read, and stories to listen to that are part of their culture and heritage so they can have role models, so they can be proud of who they are and where they come from. Hawaiian children read very few Hawaiian writers, see very few Hawaiian artists, and aren't aware there are any Hawaiian editors or publishers. In other words, they don't get to see Hawaiians who are interested in books, art, literature, or Hawaiians who have been successful or who have achieved much.

**KU'UALOHA HO'OMANAWANUI**
That's why the Notable Hawaiians feature is so important in this issue. The idea for doing it came when I got caught up in that end of the century list of everything imaginable, and I couldn't remember anyone asking the question, "Who do Hawaiians look at as role models or mentors or people they admire?" particularly other Hawaiians, although a local newspaper did put out a list they came up with after we had put out the word for our feature. We talk about culture and tradition, but there hasn't been a lot of conversation about Hawaiian people we admire. Maybe the most interesting, unusual, fascinating part about the feature once it came together was that I had my own preconceived ideas of who would be nominated to that list and what actually happened was very, very surprising. For example, there were a number of Hawaiians who were nominated because of their military service, something some other Hawaiians might not think of as something to be proud of.

**LESLIE STEWART**
There's also Hawaiians of note who aren't on the list in this issue because we didn't get enough information about them from the people who nominated them. So we're going to continue the feature in the third issue to give people a chance to get us their material and also so that people who didn't see the call for nominations in the newspapers can have a chance to nominate, too.

**KU'UALOHA HO'OMANAWANUI**
We keep hearing about dismal statistics, how we're uneducated, we're in prison, we die young, and those things are all very true and they're serious matters. But there are Hawaiians in every profession who've "made it" in recognizable ways, too. There are a number of lawyers and judges on the list,

medical doctors, politicians, career military people. On one extreme we have a large number of Hawaiians who make up negative statistics, but we also have a number of Hawaiians who don't.

**LESLIE STEWART**
While that's really nice to know, on the other hand where's the kuleana to give back to the community, to help those who haven't made it? A couple of years ago was real controversial with the Bishop Estate Trustees issue and this whole idea of kuleana regarding those people who are successful in the Western system, who are in a position of power to help others who obviously need the help as a whole. Why isn't that gap getting bridged?

**NOE ARISTA**
I don't think that part of our history is really taught. There have been notable Hawaiians, but they haven't been noted as being part of a larger community. Stereotypes have prevented these leaders from being seen as both Hawaiians and leaders in their fields.

**KU'UALOHA HO'OMANAWANUI**
But one thing that concerns me is that people will look at the list and say, "Well, obviously Hawaiians can be successful, so if these Hawaiians can make it, why don't most Hawaiians make it?" There's the American idea of individualism where if you're successful it's because you pulled yourself up by the bootstraps, and if you're not it's because you didn't work hard enough.

One thing to keep in mind is that after everything that was done to our kūpuna throughout the 19th century—the onslaught of diseases, purposely or accidentally; the banning of the Hawaiian language; the overthrow of the government, our way of life, our religion—the fact that we are even still here

makes us all notable. Because we are survivors, not just victims. There are other native people in places like the Caribbean, for example, who don't have survivors. The aboriginal people were wiped out in the coming of the West to their shores and the "natives" there today are descendants of slaves and plantation owners. There are no native people to speak on behalf of that land base, that culture. Just the fact that we're still here is notable, I think.

One of the things I do for fun is try to track all the Hawaiian names in the phone book. I'm interested in going back in time and seeing how many names we've lost over the decades, how many Hawaiian names were in the phone book 20 years ago and aren't there anymore.

**LAIANA WONG**
And how many people don't even know how to pronounce their Hawaiian name and don't have a way to get at it either, even though meaning in Hawaiian names is so important. Even in my own family I don't know what some names mean. I feel minamina because I don't even have that link to my own. I can imagine how many others are like that, too.

**MĀHEALANI DUDOIT**
My own experience with this second issue of the journal is another aspect of that that's a little different, maybe the other side of the coin. Whereas you're talking now about a loss of identity to the point of names, when we constructed the second issue and we were thinking of identity and the future, I was thinking of the big scale, the historical level, as something to mark this end of—what's the Hawaiian word people are using for "millennium"?

**LAIANA WONG**
The word in the dictionary is "milenia."

**MĀHEALANI DUDOIT**
I think a more revealing word for this moment in history is "huliau," a turning point, a time of change. Even though this 1,000- or 2,000-year marker is artificial in a sense and based on a mechanical time clock, I think it was beneficial in that it gave us an opportunity to assess where we came from and where we're going.

So in conceptualizing this issue, I was thinking history as big events. But what happened is that the materials that came in were really focused on the individual life. The whole issue is like that. Seeing that developed views I already had about the relationship between the individual and history, how even though history is something that focuses on movement on a social scale, it really begins with and is constructed on the individual level, and history is made up of individual stories.

I think very much for us, for nā ʻōiwi Hawaiʻi, in our desire or need to bridge to the past, we reach for—maybe instinctively, maybe consciously—the individual life. And we see how nā ʻōiwi have survived in a very real way, and also how at the same time we've become remnants of the past, only remnants that you find here and there on an individual level.

**NOE ARISTA**
That's why the translations are important. In my own search for identity, I've found a lot of people are big on genealogies. One time I made the mistake of asking my grandmother, "What was our family ʻaumakua?" And she said, "We don't talk about that, we're Christian!" and she cut my line. And I

thought, Here's my grandmother who never really raised her voice towards me so seriously like that for anything before. I didn't understand at the time what that was about.

Then my grandmother had a stroke. I would spend time with her and I would try to practice my beginning Hawaiian with her. She would nod at me sometimes. But a lot of the time she was very unresponsive towards everyone.

Then one day, my great-uncle, her brother Rudy, came from Waimānalo. He looked at her from the doorway and started to cry and talk to her in Hawaiian. He started to kāhea from the doorway. I was shocked when she started to answer him in Hawaiian!

That turned *my world* upside down. And I thought, "How is it possible that my grandmother had ten children but none of them speak Hawaiian, not one of them?" That experience really charged me to learn Hawaiian. I agree with something Laiana said in the first issue—it's going to take my entire life, and I'm never going to be comfortable. But I'm going to always try in fits and starts to learn.

When the translations were submitted to us by Noenoe Silva, they gave me an opportunity to practice my skills at reading and at understanding the translation process. But more than that, when I read the manaʻo of the people who were writing back then, I am overwhelmed by their conviction. The materials that Noenoe Silva is bringing out shows that the majority of our kūpuna at the time of the overthrow and the annexation didn't have any question about what was right. They were convinced that they were heading down the same path together. They didn't have confusion. They were against those events. They were for reinstating the kingdom. It's important for those people who do not understand Hawaiian language enough, or those who do not value it at all, to understand the conviction of our ancestors. That's why I think translation is important.

The second reason has to do with family. My mother is in her 50s and she does the everyday grind. My father is in his 60s and he works six or seven days out of the week. They don't have the time to learn. So I do it for them, and also for my uncle who went to Vietnam and my other uncle who served in the Korean War who didn't have the opportunity to learn Hawaiian. It's a question of access. Maybe their lifestyle didn't afford them the opportunity to learn the language, but if we make English translations available, they will be able to learn about their history and culture. A lot of people have anxiety about learning a language, because they feel guilty about not knowing it, about not being able to pronounce words correctly, and they buy into the idea that after a certain age they won't be able to learn. I started learning Hawaiian when I was 25. I had that anxiety, and I still carry parts of that anxiety with me as I continue to learn and grow in the language. It's a common feeling. I think if you have the opportunity to learn, you should take it, because Hawaiian is a beautiful language. It's our 'ōlelo makuahine.

The translation medium *is* difficult, but my family is now able to appreciate and connect with their past, and that experience would not have happened had Noenoe Silva not undertaken the translation process. The translations will offer people who haven't learned language yet another avenue for reconnection.

From another perspective, engaging in the process of translation makes the translator always refer back to the Hawaiian. This concentrated back-and-forth between Hawaiian and English struggling to find the appropriate word strengthens your understanding of usage and deepens your insight into the language. Even though this process is difficult, the more translations we can make available to students, the more opportunities there are to compare translations and judge which ones are better or worse. To be able to exercise judgment will bring people again and again back to the Hawaiian.

The third reason is that the translations are bait for people who never had an interest in reading Hawaiian, or who thought they couldn't, to say, "My God, look at all the literature I'm missing *because* I don't know Hawaiian. Hawaiian literature is profound and interesting, something important that the world will miss if we don't make it available in translation. I think our kūpuna saw the world in a special way and they left us this enormous written record in newspapers, books, diaries, and letters to tell us about the experiences of their lives and the lives of those before them. Hawaiians are lucky enough to be the inheritors of the largest collection of written materials in a native language in all of Polynesia. Should we keep those works to ourselves? What is our place in this world as Hawaiians? As human beings? The world needs to have Hawaiian literature in its life, because Hawaiians have a lot to offer and teach. Literature is not only for the here and now, but for other places and other times.

**LAIANA WONG**
I agree with you that it doesn't necessarily have to be those words. I've heard many people using Hawaiian vocabulary and

grammatical patterns and saying very English things. And on the other hand, Charlie Kupa talking about the poi going through the hand like that was in English, yet it was very Hawaiian. I'm not saying that everything is incorporated in the language. I'm just saying that for political reasons at this point in time, until Hawaiian equals English in prestige and status, I want Hawaiian to be able to stand on its own.

The whole argument we had with *Ka Leo o Hawai'i*—the newspaper of the University of Hawai'i-Mānoa that calls itself that Hawaiian name but which did not allow us to put Hawaiian articles in there unless they had translations with them—was politically damaging to our situation. So my reasons are very political. If we have a situation where Hawaiian and English are really equal as competing languages, then the question is moot. But as much good as translation can bring to people, it also can give them misconceptions about how things are and a false sense about what was really said.

It's a tough issue. If I didn't have translations when I first started learning Hawaiian, there's no way I could have made the strides. I had to depend on that. But right now I'm in a position where I feel it's very important that if English is a crutch, then I need to get rid of that crutch. In evaluating our Hawaiian, the more we find out how much English we have in our thinking, the more we need to think about it. Because if we never have an impetus to question, we'll just keep on doing the same thing.

Legalese stuff is pretty straightforward, but when you get into literature there's so many levels of understanding, and we don't even have access to the meaning of some of that stuff. Remember in the story of Kawelo,

where there's the little pōhaku and the author is including information about how it represents the kanaka who was a kupua, who was an i'a? The pōhaku is in the shape of a shark, with a mouth and dorsal fin and tail, and one side is black and one side is red. What does that mean? It just opens up the question, What does color mean to us from the Hawaiian perspective?

## MICHAEL PULELOA
Whether we're talking about translations or not, about English, Hawaiian, or Pidgin, *'Ōiwi* offers Hawaiian people a chance to represent themselves in print. It's our hale, a house that we have built. You know when you read *'Ōiwi* that you will find real definitions for what it means to be Hawaiian today and what it meant to be a Hawaiian in the past. It also allows visitors the chance to find our hale and learn about who we really are. And it offers Hawaiian readers an opportunity to learn so much about themselves and about other Hawaiians, to see our diversity and our commonalities.

Ua ao Hawaiʻi
ke ʻōlino nei mālamalama.
(Pukui 1983:305)

*hakulau ʻōiwi*

ʻAlika McNicoll • ʻAlika McNicoll • ʻAlika McNicoll • ʻAlika McNicoll

*Graphic design is a system of visual communication. But whose system is it? Ever since foreigners first brought bookmaking to Hawaiʻi, graphic design in the islands has been approached in a Western manner. Is there a way to design books so that they speak of this place? What would an approach look like that uses Hawaiian cultural sensibilities perceptually and conceptually different from one guided by Western sensibilities? In this essay I explore possible responses to these questions, including ways that I have incorporated such an approach in this second issue of ʻŌiwi.*

The origins of bookmaking coincided with the advent of papermaking in China around A.D. 105, when some of the first books were printed using wooden blocks. By the 11th century, "movable" type made up of pieces of clay was already in use in China. By the 1400s, metal type was being cast in Korea. Soon after, in Europe, printing with movable metal type was developed by Johannes Gutenberg. Although a certain number of books had been produced during the Middle Ages, artists and scribes had had to create them painstakingly by hand. Gutenberg's invention made a tremendous impact throughout Europe, including the subsequent mass production of books to supply university libraries (Pipes 1998:14–16).

The printing press and the publishing of books eventually made their way to America in the early 1600s (16). Consequently, in the late 1800s, a need developed for a foundation of rules to determine the way in which

11

manuscripts were written, edited, designed into publishable form, and printed. One steadfast cornerstone of American publishing standards was, and still is, the *Chicago Manual of Style,* first published in 1906. The manual serves as a guide to punctuation, grammar, and style; as well as to bookmaking and publishing. As such, the manual sets the standard for good book design in America.

However, long before the creation of the manual, books were being published in Hawai'i. When the first missionaries arrived in the islands in 1820, Hawaiian was an "oral" language. But even though Hawaiians were not using an alphabet, they used petroglyphs (*ki'i pōhaku*)—precursors to ascribed alphabetic symbols—to communicate with the gods, spirits, and other humans (Kwiatkowski 1991:2). By establishing an alphabetic writing system, the missionaries intended to convert Hawaiians to Christianity by teaching the Hawaiian people how to read the Bible in Hawaiian. The Hawaiian-translated version of the Bible, along with Hawaiian-language primers, were the first attempts at bookmaking in Hawai'i. Later in the century, more than 70 Hawaiian-language newspapers emerged.

In Europe, the written word has had a long history as an important means of communication. Writing was originally used to record significant events, including the keeping of legal documents, land titles, and transactions of currency. Even though Western notions of communication possess characteristics of metaphor and imagination, on the whole they have nonetheless come to emphasize analysis, with an interest in defining absolute truths in order to accurately and straightforwardly communicate information to others.

In contrast, when Westerners arrived in Hawai'i, Hawaiian traditions and important events were still being preserved, maintained, and passed on orally through the memorization of cosmological narratives, genealogical chants, songs, and dances. An important element of verbal communication was the use of *kaona,* or the double or hidden meaning. If, for example, a child was thirsty and asked his or her *kupuna* (grandparent) for a drink of water, the reply would sometimes be in the form of a riddle or metaphor. Instead of directly telling the child exactly where to go or what to do, the *kupuna* would say, "He pūnāwai kau i ka lewa"; that is, "There is a fountain of water hanging in the air." In other words, a drink of water could be obtained by climbing a nearby coconut tree (Veary 1989:25).

But in 1896, three years after the overthrow of the Hawaiian monarchy by American expatriate and American-descended businessmen and politicians, a law was passed which made the use of Hawaiian in public schools illegal, both in the classroom and in the playground. With English as the sole legal language of instruction, schoolchildren on all islands, with the exception of Ni'ihau, were forced to abandon their native tongue (Schütz 1994:353). As a result, the way in which the Hawaiian language is spoken today is much more akin to the way in which English is spoken, where metaphor has largely been replaced by more straightforward communication.

When Gutenberg's development of movable metal type led to the realization that the publication of the printed word in the form of pamphlets or books would allow information to reach a much larger audience, a system of book design was developed in Europe. Book design is defined as the style and visual flow of a book's interior through the use of typography, illustration, and photography. A formally trained designer in the West will typically begin the conceptualization process with the principle of form following function. The book's specific content will guide the way in which the book will be structured and the way in which the information is organized with respect to its structural concept and theme. On the other hand, a traditionally Hawaiian cultural approach to design can also use frameworks existing in the larger culture of which the book is a part as structural concepts for the book.

The contemporary Maori art book *Mataora: The Living Face* is a good example. The book is the first of its kind in Aotearoa (New Zealand) to incorporate a Maori cultural approach to book design. The structural and visual flow of *Mataora* enacts the ceremonial entrance into a *marae,* or a fortified tribal complex. The book opens with a title page and a contents page, followed by a *wero* (a challenge by a warrior). The *wero* is followed by a *karanga* (a ceremonial call to enter), which is always performed by a Maori woman. Next is the *whaikorero* (the welcoming speech to the ancestors), which also incorporates a prefatory narrative, followed by an introduction, then the essays and artwork that make up the subject of the book, and concluding with a *poroporoaki* (a farewell speech), and a *waiata* (a song of closure). The editors of *Mataora* articulate their design intention as follows:

> We have often said we wanted to produce a book on contemporary Maori art by ourselves and in our own way. We wanted a book that would "feel" Maori. So we have adopted a layout for *Mataora* that recognises Maori protocols

of interaction, as when, for instance a takoha, offering, is taken onto a marae. Hence the format at the beginning of the book including the wero, challenge, the karanga, call, through to the end of the book with its poroporoaki, farewell, and waiata, final song. (Adsett 1996:167)

In another Maori publication called *Mana Tiriti: The Art of Protest and Partnership,* the protocol is similar, beginning with a *mihi* (a chant of welcome) on the very first page, and ending with a *poroporoaki* on the very last page. One reason the *marae* structure works well in Aotearoa is because it is widely practiced and understood by the majority of Maori people. There are slight differences in protocol from region to region, yet the overall structure is the same. Therefore, when such a framework is conceptually translated into another form—in this case into book design—it is readily understood.

There are many frameworks that could be conceptually translated into book design from a Hawaiian perspective. For example, the use of cosmological narratives and genealogy and its sequence of events; the protocol of entering a *heiau,* a Hawaiian temple; and the use of Hawaiian proverbs. The most well-known cosmological narrative of creation, the Kumulipo, could be used as a framework for book design. In *Hawaiian Mythology,* Martha Beckwith describes Hawaiian values at work in the Kumulipo as follows:

> He [the receiver] arrives at an organized conception of form through the pairing of opposites, one depending upon the other to complete the whole. So ideas of night and day, light and darkness, male and female, land and water, rising

and setting (of the sun), small and large, little and big, hard and light (of force), upright and prostrate (of position), upward and downward, toward and away from (the speaker) appear paired in repeated reiteration as a stylistic element in the composition of chants, and function also in everyday language, where one of a pair lies implicit whenever its opposite is used in reference to the speaker. It determines the order of emergence in the so-called chant of creation, where from lower forms of life emerge offspring on a higher scale and water forms of life are paired with land forms until the period of the gods (po [darkness]) is passed and the birth of the great gods and of mankind ushers in the era of light (ao). (Beckwith 1970 [1940]:3)

A second possible Hawaiian-based framework that could be conceptually translated into book design is the protocol of entering in a *heiau,* when one crosses over into the realm of *kapu,* or the sacred. Upon entering the *heiau* a series of *pule,* or prayers, would then follow, ending with a presentation of *ho'okupu,* or tribute or offering, with a strict observance of all protocol. Thus, the layout of the opening pages of a book could follow this series of protocol in its visual language, ending with a *ho'okupu* of some kind, either typographically or photographically, prior to commencing the actual content of the book.

A third possible framework is the use of Hawaiian proverbs. The book *'Ōlelo No'eau: Hawaiian Proverbs & Poetical Sayings,* compiled by Mary Kawena Pukui, is a wealth of Hawaiian worldviews that embraces metaphor and analogy. A collection of over 2,000 ancient proverbs and sayings provides an insight into the thought processes of Kānaka Maoli, or Hawaiian people. For instance, one proverb reads, "*E kaupē aku no i ka hoe a kō mai.* Put forward the paddle and draw it back. [In other words,] go on with the task that is started and finish it" (Pukui 1983:39). The metaphorical image of the canoe paddle could serve as a structural theme for the entire book.

A perhaps more familiar framework is the protocol used by *hālau hula* (Hawaiian dance schools) upon entering the dance studio. The *haumāna* (students) will gather in front of the entrance to the room and chant an ancient *mele noi komo (*also called *mele kāhea),* an admittance or calling song, such as "Kūnihi ka mauna," as a request to enter the room. The students are then acknowledged with a *mele kāhea (*also called *mele komo),* an acceptance to enter, by their *kumu* (teacher), who is already inside the room. Thus, the students are reminded that it is important to memorize in order to learn, and that humility in addition to effort underly the sources of knowledge (Johnson 1980). This widely practiced protocol among *hālau hula* has been conceptually translated into a ritual that is used upon entering any room in general, and its incorporation into the design of a book could theoretically be readily understood by both Hawaiians and non-Hawaiians.

Once a particular framework has been adopted for a structural concept, design principles with respect to layout and composition must be defined. According to Philip B. Meggs' book *Type & Image: The Language of Graphic Design,* formal design principles that frequently appear in a Western approach to layout and composition include: the principle of the human factor with its relation to visual, horizontal, and vertical orientation, alignment, continuation, proximity, completion of relationships, symmetry and asymmetry, modular relationships with respect to the underlying structure or grid of a design, field of tension, repetition and rhythm, visual continuity, foreground and background, scale and visual hierarchy, motion and implied motion, and, finally, unity through correspondence, such as color, shape, and form. Meggs explains the complex process of organizing a graphic space: the vitality of contrast must be weighed against the unity of correspondence. Decisions about symmetrical versus asymmetrical organization, establishing a grid system, or creating a field of tension with forms in dynamic equilibrium should evolve from the designer's analysis of content and message, for communication and composition should be viewed as an organic and inseparable whole (Meggs 1989:116).

The choice of font usage is based on the mood or function of the piece. The use of text and image juxtapositions provoke thought and feeling through the power of word and image association. Robert Jahnke, in "Design Principles in Maori Art," defines a Maori perspective to design with respect to *whakairo rakau* (Maori carving) by adapting Western formal qualities of art—such as scale, proportion, balance, movement, and space—and redefining them in relation to a Maori worldview. These Maori principles are similar to Hawaiian principles of design and provide a basis for composition priorities from a Kanaka Maoli perspective. With respect to design aesthetics, the same importance is placed on the design principles, such as the value of symmetry or balance and duality, the monumental scale and sense of urgency in Hawaiian carvings, the negotiation of space upon entering a *heiau* or any sacred space, and the proportion of the human body with an emphasis on the

lower body. The choice of font usage should also be based on the mood or function of the piece, and not have to look particularly "tropical" or "native." The traditional use of metaphor would allow for a wealth of imagery and the power of juxtaposition to be included in the design. In addition, dedication rituals in which Hawaiian implements were imbued with *mana* (spiritual power) could also be used, consequently taking book design to a deeper, spiritual level (Jahnke 1998).

The following is an example of a *pule malu ko'i*, a ritual dedication chant that was used to impart *mana* to a newly sculptured image:

> E Kane uakea
> Eia ka alana,
> He moa ualehu,
> He moa uakea,
> He moa ula hiwa.
> He alana keia ia oe [e] Kane,
> No ke koi kalai,
> Koi kua,
> Koi kikoni,
> Koi lou,
> He koi e kai e kalai ai [i] ke kii,
> He koi ou e Kane ke akua ola.
> Ke akua mana,
> Ke akua noho i ka iuiu,
> Ke akua i ke ao polohiwa.
>
> E ike iau ia...
> Ke kahuna kalai kii,
> A ku ke kii o Lana-i-ka-wai,
> O ka wai ola loa a Kane.
> E Kane eia kou hale la, o Mauliola.
> . . .
> [U]a noa...
> Amama.

O Kane [God of the forest],
white as mist
Here is the offering,
A chicken ash-white,
A chicken mist-white,
A chicken red and black.
These are offerings for you, O Kane,
For the carving adz,
For the striking adz,
For the smoothing down adz,
For the rotatable adz,
An adz to direct, to carve the image,
Your adz, O Kane, god of life.
God with mana,
God dwelling in the unfathomable
heights,
God in the glistening clouds of darkness.

Look upon me...
The carver of images,
Let the image of Lana-i-ka-wai stand,
The water of eternal life of Kane.
O Kane, here is your house, life-
that-lives.
. . .
The taboo is lifted.
The prayer is said.

(Cox 1988:34; Malo 1951 [1903]:180)

Perhaps a treatment of type could also be devised so that the viewer of the book would be compelled to enunciate Hawaiian words or phrases, thus incorporating the oral tradition into the physical design of the book.

The change of a Hawaiian oral culture to a written or visual culture can be compared to the current state of change in Africa. In "The graphic design challenge in Africa," Amrik Kalsi writes of a shift in communication paradigms in Africa:

In communication terms, transmission of information is changing from oral to written. In perceptual terms, an ear culture is changing into an eye culture. In social terms, an egalitarian tribal society is changing into a stratified hierarchical structure. In economic terms, a natural economy is changing into a socialist/capitalist economy. In psychological terms, previously involved and integrated individuals are now feeling alienated. In political terms, the distribution of power is centralizing in bureaucracy and dictatorships. In environmental terms, harmony with nature is changing into domination and destruction of nature. (Kalsi 1990:114)

According to Kalsi, in terms of communication, graphic design in Africa will be based on the needs of the people in Africa in order to cope with these drastic changes, perhaps to reinforce African cultural values and beliefs, as well as to advocate issues that concern the well-being of the African people through visual communication (116).

Not all individuals of Hawaiian ancestry will recognize the structural concepts and design sensibilities that are indeed their own, or be familiar with the cultural practices to which the design refers. Still, the application of Hawaiian principles toward design could help to inform the viewer of Hawaiian values, thus benefiting not only Hawaiians, but non-Hawaiians as well. Adopting such principles allows for more innovations in graphic design. But more important, it provides an opportunity to advocate for issues concerning the welfare of the Hawaiian community, as well as the general population in these islands. Issues such as Hawaiian culture and language awareness, dire health conditions, lack of education, substance and alcohol addiction, domestic violence, and teenage pregnancy are of concern to the general public, but moreso to native Hawaiians, who statistically rank the highest in every negative, and lowest in every positive, socio-economic category. An ideal indigenous cultural perspective to graphic design would be intrinsically sensitive and responsive to the needs of the host culture.

Western notions of graphic design have dominated visual and verbal communication in much of the world. Although the application of Hawaiian sensibilities to book design as discussed here are possibilities for creating a contemporary form of books more attuned to the native culture of Hawai'i, a further exploration into Hawaiian design could embrace "interactive design." Traditionally, Hawaiians communicated through various media: hula, music, oratory, prayers, ritual, etc. As Hawaiian graphic design develops, it need not restrict itself to print media or to multimedia communication as we know it today. In any case, the creation of a new system of communication that links tradition with contemporary Hawaiian expression will include a new vocabulary that speaks through art from the native culture of Hawai'i.

## References

Adsett, Sandy, Cliff Whiting, and Witi Ihimaera. 1996. *Mataora: The Living Face.* Auckland, New Zealand: David Bateman.

Beckwith, Martha. 1970 [1940]. *Hawaiian Mythology.* Honolulu: University of Hawai'i Press.

*Chicago Manual of Style.* 1993. Fourteenth Edition. Chicago: University of Chicago Press.

Cox, J. Halley. 1988. *Hawaiian Sculpture.* Revised Edition. Honolulu: University of Hawai'i Press.

Haeata Collective. 1991. *Mana Tiriti: The Art of Protest and Partnership.* Wellington, New Zealand: Daphne Brasell Associates Press.

Jahnke, Robert. 1998. "Design Principles in Maori Art." Unpublished essay.

Johnson, Rubellite Kawena. 1980. "A Brief Introduction to Hawaiian Poetry." Unpublished essay.

Kalsi, Amrik. 1990. "The graphic design challenge in Africa." *Graphic Design, World Views: A Celebration of Icograda's 25th Anniversary.* Ed. Jorge Frascara. Tokyo: Kodansha.

Kwiatkowski, P. F. 1991. *Nā Ki'i Pōhaku: A Hawaiian Petroglyphs Primer.* Honolulu: Ku Pa'a.

Malo, David. 1951 [1903]. *Hawaiian Antiquities.* Second Edition. Trans. Nathaniel B. Emerson. Bernice P. Bishop Museum Special Publication 2. Honolulu: Bishop Museum.

Meggs, Philip B. 1989. *Type & Image: The Language of Graphic Design.* New York: Van Nostrand Reinhold.

Pipes, Alan. 1998. *Production for Graphic Designers.* Second Edition. Upper Saddie River, New Jersey: Prentice Hall.

Pukui, Mary Kawena, comp. and trans. 1983. *'Ōlelo No'eau: Hawaiian Proverbs & Poetical Sayings.* Honolulu: Bishop Museum Press.

Schütz, Albert J. 1994. *The Voices of Eden: A History of Hawaiian Language Studies.* Honolulu: University of Hawai'i Press.

Veary, Nana. 1989. *Change We Must: My Spiritual Journey.* Vancouver and Calgary, Canada: Water Margin Press.

E Kāne uakea

Eia ka ʻālana,

He moa ualehu,

He moa uakea,

He moa ʻula hiwa.

He ʻālana kēia iā ʻoe e Kāne,

No ke koʻi kālai,

Koʻi kua,

Koʻi kīkoni,

Koʻi lou,

He koʻi e kaʻi e kālai ai i ke kiʻi,

He koʻi ou e Kāne ke akua ola.

Ke akua mana,

Ke akua noho i ka ʻiuʻiu,

Ke akua i ke ao polohiwa.

E ʻike iaʻu,

Ke kahuna kālai kiʻi,

A kū ke kiʻi ʻo Lanaikawai,

ʻO ka wai ola loa a Kāne.

E Kāne eia kou hale lā, ʻo Mauliola.

ʻĀmama, ua noa.

O Kāne, God of the forest, white as mist

Here is the offering,

A chicken ash-white,

A chicken mist-white,

A chicken red and black.

These are offerings for you, O Kāne,

For the carving adz,

For the striking adz,

For the smoothing down adz,

For the rotatable adz,

An adz to direct, to carve the image,

Your adz, O Kāne, God of life.

God with mana,

God dwelling in the unfathomable heights,

God in the glistening clouds of darkness.

Look upon me,

The carver of images,

Let the image of Lanaikawai stand,

The water of eternal life of Kāne.

O Kāne, here is your house, Life-that-lives.

The prayer is said. The taboo is lifted.

# No nā Pua
## (For the Children)

# keala-o-ānuenue
Sally-Jo Keala-o-Ānuenue Bowman • Sally-Jo Keala-o-Ānuenue Bowman

I have been a writer since I first could form words with a pencil one of my parents sharpened with a kitchen paring knife. My earliest work were letters, sent from my home post office, Lanikai, Oahu, T.H.—Territory of Hawai'i—to my mother's Swedish immigrant mother in North Dakota. And then letters to my Hawaiian-haole father at Lanikai, when my mother took us to visit her family 5,000 miles away in a place that sometimes had snowbanks taller than a full-grown man.

My professional writing has been mostly journalism. The first published pieces were short news articles, and, later, newspaper features. Encouraged steadfastly by my husband, David, I have included in my freelance magazine work in the last 15 years a bigger and bigger proportion of articles on Hawaiian culture and issues. My style, perhaps a natural result of the subject matter, has grown ever more personal and poetic.

Lately a number of people have asked me what early influences propelled me to be a writer. At first I pointed to my mother, who read to my brother, Peter (the late *Star-Bulletin* writer Pierre Bowman), and me a lot when we were children, and who made us write all those letters to and from Lanikai, T.H. I mentioned my answer to my son, himself a poet. He said, "What about your father?" Indeed my father—and his brothers and sisters—often sat together at one of their homes, drinking and talking story, my brother and I and miscellaneous cousins lurking nearby, ears wide open. In my new answer to the question of influence, I now credit both my parents—my father for being a model of a storyteller, my mother for reading us published stories and insisting that we write our own on paper.

I also credit the later influences of my children: Rolf Kaleohanohano, the poet, for showing the way for me to be a poet too; and Tamara Leiokanoe, another poet and a painter, to whom I complained recently that a friend who had read a lot of my current work, especially the Hawaiian pieces, had wrongly observed that my business as a journalist is information. Tamara commented that of course that made no sense, for I was not a purveyor of information, but a storyteller.

To me, a storyteller accepts a sacred trust. In all primal cultures, stories are the means of both entertaining and teaching. The two functions go hand in hand. People, especially the young, learn from whatever stories they meet. The storyteller who accepts the sacred trust entertains while teaching that which is pono. The storyteller who ignores or even deliberately violates the sacred trust—such as those who make most of today's movies—abdicates the

teaching responsibility. The listener or viewer still learns, but what he learns is not pono.

I hope my work is that of a storyteller who accepts a sacred trust. I hope my work affects readers in the naʻau, where we really remember, where we can feel another person's happiness or anguish as well as our own. I hope my stories help readers share the lives of those they cannot know by reason of time or distance, for such stories, honorable stories rendered by a sacred storyteller, help us understand, and help us learn how to behave properly.

And so I thank those who encouraged me and who pointed out the storytelling path to me. I find it especially comforting that they are my parents, Moffett Bowman and Ida May Larson Bowman, ahead of me on life's journey; my husband, David Walp, at my side; and my children, Tamara Moan and Rolf Moan, behind me on the path. I am surrounded with their inspiration.

## No nā Pua
## (For the Children)

The day you wed
The time was high tide
When you stood on the beach
In ceremony.

You asked me to accept a lei
For Peter, my brother
For Dad, you said.
Oh, and that's not all.
You know where he is
Will you please deliver it?

Ten, no eleven years now
He's been in the sea
Where we lifted his ashes
From a pū'olo at dawn
To spread them in swirling waters
To live where we had always lived.

And so it was
At your wedding's end
I took your charge.
Your father's friend Lopaka
Nodded at me, and I knew it was time.
I handed him
My own lei from my neck
And took your lei
In a new pū'olo in my hand
Your bridal lei for Dad.

Lopaka said, No, wait.
Another lei, from me
Fragrant white ginger twined
With the green power of woven ti.
This one from Lindsey
Feather blaze of 'ohai ali'i.
He laid these, and my lei
Over my wrist
And enveloped me in his arms
And we sobbed and sobbed.

I know you could see our
Great gasps of weeping,
But did you hear
Us whisper ragged,
"We loved him so much"?

And then we parted,
I into the sea at your request
A slow march
To the high tide bursting.
I held nā lei high on my arm
Your pū'olo up in my other hand
The water dimming green and gray
The last-light sky translucent blue
Clouds gold-rimmed
In the waning sun of Kāne.

I shouted to the sea
Mahalo no kēia lā
Thank you for this day.

At last I marched past break line
Into the blue neck-deep
Gave up my footing
Swam free.
I turned landward with the current.
I saw you on the beach
You and John and nā pua
All our children.

I released my own lei
As on the day we strewed his ashes.
I let loose the 'ohai ali'i
Then the ti.
Swells rose and fell
And I with them.
You waited, and watched.
The sea throbbed
Like the beat of our hearts
And pulse of our blood.

I unwound your pū'olo
Unwound your lei within.
The procession of nā lei

Danced west upon the current
West to the setting sun
West in the time of long-shadowed day
When sometimes
Peter and I—
Were we eight and twelve
Or just a little older?—
Could not ignore the call
And we'd dash into the sea
Wearing all our clothes.

Nā lei danced west
And still you stood.
I surfed a fine swell in
Praying I wouldn't tumble
To the bottom
But knowing if I did
Peter would be laughing.
As it was, this run
Would have won a nickel bet
In those yesterdays so long ago.

I caught the wave
And I was with him
Your Dad
Whose one wish
In the long weeks of the last summer
Was just to go to the water.
I was with him
And with the rest of them
In the sea
And with all of you
On the sand, all of you
Nā pua.

And then in the windward twilight
I came from the waters
Of Peter and family gone on
Into your smiles
Blotching you wet with salt
And knowing then our truths:
Hawaiian hearts last forever.
The sea is our refuge, our peace, our bond.

So go to the sea, my dears
Nā pua, my children
All of you, go to the sea
To heal all wounds
To cure the heart
To share the soul
For the sea holds all
The past
The now
The yet to come.

Go to the sea, my dears
And know to say
Mahalo no kēia lā
Thank you for this day.

*'Awapuhi, Hawai'i*
*Peoples' Tribunal 1993*

*Homestead / Heart Steady*

# kehaulani

J. Kehaulani Kauanui • J. Kehaulani Kauanui • J. Kehaulani Kauanui

At *Tita's* Hawaiian restaurant in
San Francisco, September 1999

In 1968, I was born in southern California to
Carol Lee Evert and Joseph Kauanui III. As
one can guess by my surname, I am Hawaiian
through my father's side. Our Kauanui line
(through my grandfather) links us to Molokai
and through my Tūtūwahine's lines (Kane
and Kauahi), we connect to Maui. My closest
relations are now Kaua'i-based, on Anahola
Hawaiian Home Lands (where my father grew
up), a place with which I have always maintained contact. I consider myself part of
Hawaiian communities both in and outside of
Hawai'i and actively support Hawaiian sovereignty and decolonization. I am currently an
Assistant Professor of American Studies and
Anthropology at Wesleyan University in
Connecticut. In 2000, I completed my disser-
tation titled "Rehabilitating the Native:
Hawaiian Blood Quantum and the Politics of
Race, Citizenship, and Entitlement." I am
particularly interested in genealogical reckon-
ing as our indigenous mode of contesting this

colonial race classification. I also write about Hawaiian presence in America and, recognizing that Hawaiians migrated there as early as 1788, I hope to develop a framework to historicize multiple Hawaiian diasporas. In Hawai'i, I have met many Hawaiians who once lived outside of Hawai'i yet have never told me so themselves. I encourage them—and all Hawaiians who have had experiences outside of Hawai'i—to incorporate those movements into their genealogical recitations as part of their personal heritage and to reclaim those travels as part of their Hawaiianness.

## 'Awapuhi, Hawai'i Peoples' Tribunal 1993

I make my way to the lua, slowly
drained from the day
of long testimonies
where nā 'aumākua linger
and catch glimpses of my torn spirit

As I remember all of it
I prepare myself for this bath
hoping for relief by the wash

Lei, she knocks on the door
offers me unlit torch ginger
I inquire, for shower? my hair?
—Whatevah you like

I climb into the tub
hold the bud to my nose
never having held it unopened

But I have seen this flower before
in Gramma's quilt stitch
and still ask myself
What more have they kept from me?

Still holding my breath I squeeze
and clear gel cleanser
like my own tears
washes over me
as I yearn for that
and more

# Homestead / Heart Steady

U.S. Congress 1921
Hawaiian Homes Commission Act:
lease lands for Hawaiians
with fifty-percent
quantified and certified
Hawaiian blood
with fifty-percent
quantified and certified
Hawaiian blood
Hawaiians waiting
Hawaiians waiting on list for leases
Hawaiians waiting for Home
Hawaiians waiting on list for leases
Hawaiians waiting for Home
Hawaiians leaving without land
Hawaiians leaving without land leases
Hawaiians leaving Home
Hawaiians waiting on list for leases
Hawaiians waiting for Home
Hawaiians waiting on lists
Hawaiians transplanting to another Home
Hawaiians transplanting with broken hearts
Hawaiians waiting on list for leases
Hawaiians waiting for Home
Hawaiians waiting on lists
Hawaiians waiting with heart disease
Hawaiians waiting on list for hearts
Hawaiians waiting on list for transplants
Hawaiians waiting on list for Home
Hawaiians at heart living on Home/Lands
Home Lands and heart
Hawaiians at Home
Hawaiians searching hearts
Hawaiians searching for Home/Lands
Hawaiians waiting for land leases
Hawaiians waiting for heart transplants
Hawaiians waiting for leases
Hawaiians waiting for a lease on life
Hawaiians waiting for hearts
Hawaiians waiting for Hawaiians at heart
Transplanted hearts
Transplanted Hawaiians

Immunosuppressants try to protect
Transplanted hearts
Immune repressants try to reject
Transplanted Hawaiians
Hearts pump the blood to qualify
Hearts pump the fraction to quantify
Heart is where the home is
Hurt is where the home is
Home is where the heart is
Home is where the hurt is

David J. Imaikalani Wallace • David J. Imaikalani Wallace • David J. Imaikalani Wallace

## *Papa's Mango Seed*

Growing up in the Hawaiian Homestead community of Ho'olehua on the island of Moloka'i was an exercise in creativity and imagination. Most of the grocery stores on the island—like Misaki's, Friendly Market, and Kualapuu Market—usually carried just the bare necessities of rice, spam, corned beef, and other local staples. There were no McDonalds or Jack In The Box where french fries and burgers could be bought. So when the craving for a hamburger or some other treat overwhelmed us, we went to our kitchen and made it.

Our family spent many Saturdays cooking up a wide variety of goodies, some really "'ono," but some really "pilau." Of all the treats we created during my childhood, none stirs my memories of small-kid time like making Papa's mango seed. Much of the fun associated with making mango seed was the joy of working together with my Dad, my Mom, and my brother and three sisters. Making mango seed also meant that school was almost over and summer break was just around the corner.

Making Papa's mango seed began just as the mangos were turning orange-yellow on the trees. Everyone kept a vigilant eye on our neighbors' trees from the time the mangos flowered to the time of harvest. Harvest day was signaled by Dad's frantic search for containers. Burlap bags, empty five-gallon paint buckets, and the open trunk of our '57 Chevy were used during the annual harvest. Nothing had to be said. By the time Dad had loaded all of the equipment into the car, we would have already warmed up the engine.

We would then drive around the island community for three to four hours, first traveling to Kualapu'u, then to Kalama'ula and Kaunakakai, and finally to Kawela, stopping all along the way to talk to families who owned mango trees. No one turned us away. Sharing was a way of life on Moloka'i. Of course, when we picked mango, we wouldn't bolo head the tree. We always left enough fruit so the owners could enjoy them too. Showing respect guaranteed a fruitful harvest the following year. Besides, we always shared Papa's mango seed with the people who gave us fruit.

Picking mango was like celebrating Easter. Dad, Mom, and my brother would take long bamboo poles and knock the mangos to the ground as we little ones scurried after the fallen fruits like they were Easter eggs. Often, we would play a game by seeing how many mangos each of us could pick. The winner of the game was the person who picked the most mangos. For the first couple of years, I easily won and teased my sisters, making them cry. Then suddenly one year, a spark of inspiration hit me. Why should I bust my 'ōkole picking all the mangos when I could make my sisters do it for me? While giving the appearance of playing the game, I found myself losing by a *huge* score. Everywhere we stopped, my sisters would pick almost all the mangos by themselves while I cruised along. No matter how hard my sisters teased me for losing the game, they had absolutely no effect on me...until Mom and Dad saw what I was doing to them. That year, Dad taught me another way a bamboo stick could be used. His adjustment to my attitude made me a better mango picker, for that day at least.

After the burlap bags, buckets, and car trunk were swollen with their fruitful bounty, a fond mahalo was given to the people who had shared their mangos with us. As we traveled home, visions of the tart, succulent, crimson prize were already fixed in our consciousness.

When we got home, the mangos were unloaded and placed in a large tub called a "pā kini" that contained warm water. We all sat around the pā kini with scrub brushes and washed the mangos. Then we put the clean fruit into a larger pā kini. There Dad sat with a huge cleaver, chopping each mango in half and removing the seed. With a flick of his wrist, the chopped, seeded mangos were tossed into a third pā kini, where they were peeled.

Peeling mango could never be mistaken for a game. If the acid from the fruit didn't burn your hand, the sharp blade of the peeler would cut you. Most of the time Mom and Dad finished the peeling by themselves, while, one by one, we children found ways to sneak away. Mom and Dad never really minded. A lot of times we just got in the way.

After the mangos were peeled, then rinsed for the final time, Dad took out a large package of Hawaiian salt and started stirring it into the fruit. Round and round he mixed in the salt with his bare hand. After all the fruits were salted, two cups of vinegar were added and the mixing continued as before. Finally, a large white cloth was tied securely around the pā kini and the mangos were allowed to marinate for two days.

For the next two days, it was absolute torture to awake in the morning to the aroma of salted mangos and vinegar. Every one of us was tempted to risk our delicate bottoms just to sample a slither of the marinating mix.

Late one night, after everyone had gone to bed, I slipped out of my room and headed to the kitchen to sneak a piece of mango. There to my surprise, in the light of the kukui hele pō, was my Dad, kneeling over the pā kini. He was munching on a big juicy piece of fruit. As I stepped into the kitchen, I startled him. To cover up, he said, "Just testing to see if it's ready or not..." He gave me a huge chunk of mango to make sure I didn't say anything to anyone, then sent me to bed. I ate all of the meat on the seed, then sucked on the husk like it was a pacifier.

If a few pieces of mango disappeared during the marinating stage, even more vanished when the mangos were placed out to dry. There is nothing finer than the flavor of half-dried, vinegar-laced, salted mango. Da bugga is 'ono!!!

Since I was the runt of the litter, I came in handy when the mangos were put out to dry. Early in the morning, I climbed to the top of our garage and carefully lined up the fruit on strips of wood. When I came home from school, I climbed back up and turned the fruit over. In the evening, I returned to pick up the fruit and bring them to the kitchen.

I loved climbing to the rooftop of our garage and house. I could see over the trees and down through the pastures and pineapple fields. I often fantasized while visiting my lofty perch. Mountains of bellowing clouds conjured up herds of wild mustangs or giant buffalo as I sat and hurled imaginary lassos or fired imaginary 50-caliber rounds into their ranks.

Sometimes things got pretty weird. Once, after watching *Superman*, my favorite TV series, I donned my Superman costume, cape and all, and went up to the roof to bring in the mangos for the night. As I turned to come down, an exciting idea raced through my mind. Instead of climbing down, why

didn't I *fly* down? Mustering all the strength of a six-year-old, off the roof I leaped. Time seemed to slow as I soared into the air...and fell into the hibiscus bush below. That was the last time my parents allowed me to play on the roof. But that never stopped my teeming imagination or acts of weirdness.

Once the mangos were dried by the sun, they were gathered up and put into a huge military-surplus cooking pot. Water was added and the fruit was brought to a rolling boil. Following instinct and aroma rather than a recipe, Dad began adding the ingredients to the mix: mounds of brown sugar, a touch of lime juice, a smidgen of five-spice, a fistful of lemon rinds, a comb of honey, and a squirt of red food coloring. Once all the ingredients were blended, the flame would be reduced and the bubbling concoction was allowed to simmer for just over an hour. The scent of the brewing delight permeated our home with an aroma that broke your jaw. Often, we risked burning our fingers trying to get a taste of the sizzling treat, but snagging a fresh morsel of mango seed was always well worth the sorrow and pain.

After the new batch of mango seed cooled, it was portioned out into jars of various sizes, ranging from pints to gallons. Each container was labeled, dated, and sealed, then stored to marinate for three weeks. Like clockwork, relatives would begin showing up around our home just about when the first gallon of mango seed was about to premiere.

When the time was right, Dad got the first gallon out and popped open the lid, releasing the familiar sweet-and-sour odor of vintage mango seed. Saliva filled our mouths, making our jaws ache in anticipation. Using an old wooden spoon, mounds of precious mango seed were spooned out to each of us as we savagely and joyfully feasted upon the long-awaited delicacy.

As the days wore on and the novelty of having all the mango seed we wanted wore off, we quickly turned our good fortune into a lucrative business. Every night before going to bed, we opened a container or two of mango seed and carefully weighed and packaged four-ounce servings. The next morning, we collected our packages and headed to school. Once there, we were surrounded by classmates who quickly bought up all of our supply. By morning recess, our pockets were filled with quarters and fifty-cent pieces, more than enough to buy cinnamon toast and milk from the school cafeteria. We felt like millionaires.

In a few short weeks, all the mango seed was gone and school was done for the year. For the rest of the summer, our family spent lots of time at the beach, fishing and swimming, resting and waiting for another mango season to come along.

The memory of mango seasons long since past still lingers with me. When our family is together now, usually during reunions or funerals, we still take time to recall those times with fondness in our hearts. As we reminisce, we realize how we have changed, just as our Hawai'i has changed, and we wonder if our children's childhood will be as memorable as ours. I guess now would be a perfect time to make some mango seed. Now if I could only find a mango tree...

*Pehea lā e pono ai? (How are we to make right?)*

*Time Will Cry*

*Ka Pūnohu (Night Rainbow)*

*E Pele Ē*

*'O Wākea Noho iā Papahānaumoku*

*The Sky Is Falling*

*Ke Ō Nei Nō*

# meleanna

Meleanna Aluli Meyer • Meleanna Aluli Meyer • Meleanna Aluli Meyer

My work is about a life in process—my own. A continuous visual commentary on all that goes on about me in my day to day. The process of making art is as important as the consolidation of thoughts that arrange themselves into a finished form, either on canvas or paper, layers of interaction and dialogue with those around me about my passion for all that is creative, for all that is divine.

Art is the most natural extension of one's soul, the ultimate application and expression of one's relationship, both inner and outer—and to all living things. An amalgam of intimate visual experiences, stories that, once worked into reality, become part of a personal history—vignettes animated, ephemeral, provocative...

Collaged, multilayered, painted over, photographed, xeroxed, cut-out, sewn, worked and worked again until there is singing. Not only the surface, but the core, the foundation of the work, like a scaffolding—everything considered in its time. Preceding layers added and worked one by one, tied together by pain and joy, by design elements, by threads of a visual history, my story—like notes to a song. This work speaks for me in a language that is unique to its calling, in a tongue that gives voice to the way I see, intuit, and hold the world.

*Pehea lā e pono ai?*
*(How are we to make right?)*
1993
collage-mixed media, acrylic, and color pencil
24 x 30 in. (private collection)

Uncle Sam, demon juggler of stolen spoils,

of lives laid to waste.

You've tried to break our spirits but we

remain steadfast—

How will this be made right?

## Time Will Cry
1986
cliché verre
15 x 12 in. (collection of the artist)

Tears flow towards all that pains,

all that causes suffering—

loss, grief—and time too will cry.

*Ka Pūnohu (Night Rainbow)*
1998
paper and acrylic on wood panel
24 x 60 in. (private collection)

Hō'ailona, precious night visions

luminescence as rare as the murmur

of our kūpuna asleep in the mists.

## E Pele Ē
1998
paper and acrylic on wood panel
24 x 12 in. (private collection)

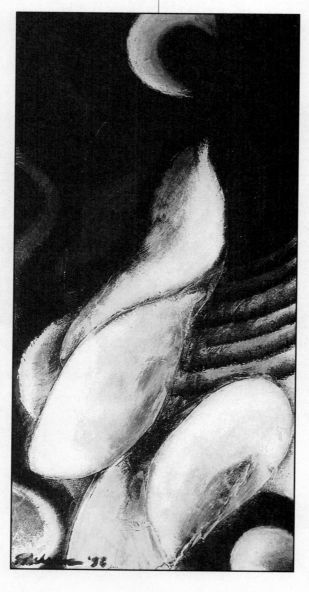

Living, from the
earth your scent,
your heat,
your mana exudes
life—fertile, fecund.

## 'O Wākea Noho iā
## Papahānaumoku
1997
foam core on painted black acrylic
48 x 24 in. (collection of the artist)

The mists settle atop the mountains,

a tease of wet as Wākea settles atop Papa.

Union as divine as any mingling of

the waters.

*The Sky Is Falling*
1996
color pencil
36 x 6 in. (private collection)

The burden each carries is great and
sometimes the sky does seem to be falling.

## *Ke Ō Nei Nō*

2000
acrylic on kapa
84 x 36 in. (private collection)

This space and time and echo,

as before—present—

as tomorrow binds us, one to the other.

Generations, a continuum.

We go together, naue pū.

always Hawaiian

*Ua Lohe Au*
*Manu Kani*
*Time for Sovereignty*
*Kahikinui*
*ʻO Puʻu Māhoe Uʻi*
*Lānaʻi City*
*ʻIke Au iā Kahoʻolawe*

# *walaka*

Walaka Kanamu • Walaka Kanamu • Walaka Kanamu • Walaka Kanamu

Today we trample over native plants just because our shoes don't know the difference. We fail to experience the soft cushion under our feet that the native understory affords us. We never notice the cooling sensation of soft mud that's oozing up between our toes as we pass near a gentle stream of fresh water. We never take time to walk the forests and enjoy the playful game of the ʻiʻiwi and ʻapapane as they battle over ownership of a certain ʻōhiʻa lehua tree. We never notice the tiny droplets that form and run down the koa tree as the thick, moisture-filled clouds pass the trees. We never work the loʻi of the kalo lehua during harvest and witness the blood that flows from the hā when the lāʻalo is cut or broken off. We never sit in the surf and call the waves that take us sliding along with them and give us pleasure. We never take time to lie alone in a lava tube and wonder who was there before and listen to their voices. We never stop under a kiawe tree with the full moon above us and notice the leaves and branches like arteries and veins of the heart pumping life through the tree and returning it back to the ʻāina.

We never give our mana to those we touch so they feel and experience our essence.

Yet we call ourselves "HAWAIIAN."

Well, it's time to kick off the shoes and walk the ʻāina. Live each step and feel with all that surrounds you. Hear what you've always seen. Touch what you've always heard.

IF WE DO NOT SEE LIFE IN EVERY-THING AROUND US BESIDES OUR-SELVES, WE ARE NOT "HAWAIIAN."

## Ua Lohe Au

Ua lohe au i nā leo o nā kūpuna—
Kāhea lākou ia'u—
E ho'i 'oe i Kahikinui
Ka 'āina o kou kupuna
E ho'i 'oe i Kahikinui
Ka 'āina o ke aloha a ke Akua.

Makemake au e nānā i kou maka
Makemake au e pili aku me 'oe
A 'ike i kou mana
Makemake au e lohe
I kou pu'uwai e kāhea ana ia'u.

Ma 'ane'i, eia au, i kēia lā!
Ma 'ane'i, eia au, i kēia lā!
E mālama wau iā 'oe
A mālama mai 'oe ia'u—
Ma 'ane'i, eia au, ua hiki mai!

(1998)

## Manu Kani

*In search of the meaning—*
*I found myself on top the pu'u 'o Manu Kani—*
*All alone I sat and waited—*
*The reward for waiting was the sound of a*
*    thousand birds singing, chirping, and screeching—*
*Only, there were no birds and no trees—*
*The Hawaiians call it—Manu Kani*

On top the pu'u 'o Manu Kani
Looking out into the sea
On top the pu'u 'o Manu Kani
The birds begin to sing to me.

At first I'm sitting all alone
It feels like there's nobody home
The Kona winds come from the sea
The clouds are all surrounding me.

I feel a chill run through my bones
It seems to say I'm not alone
And as the clouds fly over me
I hear the song of Manu Kani
I hear the birds of Manu Kani
The Hawaiians call it Manu Kani.

On top the pu'u 'o Manu Kani
Looking out into the sea
On top the pu'u 'o Manu Kani
The 'amakihi screeches from the tree
The 'i'iwi sings to me
The chirping 'apapane in the tree...oh yeah.

(1997)

## Time for Sovereignty

Well everybody thinks it's funny
Say we're the laugh of the town
Well keep on laughing, yes,
    keep on laughing
You're going to take us all down.
Humpty Dumpty sat on the wall
Humpty Dumpty had a great big fall!

Well all the soldiers on the land
And all the sailors at the seashore
And all the fighters in the sky
Tell me, Is there going to be...war?
Is there going to be war?
Humpty Dumpty sat on the wall
Humpty Dumpty had a great big fall!

Kaho'olawe, Pōhakuloa, Kāne'ohe,
    and Ni'ihau
Pearl Harbor, Diamond Head, Bellows Field,
    and Kahuku
Schofield Barracks, Moanalua, Barbers Point,
    and Mākua
Wheeler Field, Fort Shafter, Punchbowl,
    and Hickam
Mokulē'ia, Haleakalā—House of the Sun or
    The House of Star Wars?
Do you want any more? We cannot give you
    any more!
Is there going to be war?
Humpty Dumpty sat on the wall
Humpty Dumpty had a great big fall!

It's time for action to STOP THE FACTION!
The desecration of our LAND!
We're just like magnets in the ocean
Attracting missiles from all foreign lands.
In the middle of the deep blue sea.
Just set your sites on me.
Do you want any more? We cannot give you
    any more!

Is there going to be war?
Humpty Dumpty sat on the wall
Humpty Dumpty had a great big fall!

Well everybody, STILL THINK IT'S FUNNY?
HAWAIIANS ONLY WANT TO BE FREE!
GET BACK THE LAND, DO WHAT YOU CAN!
IT'S TIME TO HELP YOURSELF BE FREE!
IT'S TIME FOR SOVEREIGNTY, IT'S TIME FOR
    SOVEREIGNTY!

# Kahikinui

*Once a thriving community of 10,000 Hawaiians, the moku of Kahikinui sits on the south slopes of Haleakalā. When the early trading of sandalwood began, the decline of the Hawaiian settlement and the complete abandonment of the 'āina followed.*

*Through the efforts of many Hawaiians and non-Hawaiians, the moku of Kahikinui was given over to Ka 'Ohana o Kahikinui when the Department of Hawaiian Home Lands approved the resettlement of Hawaiians in Kahikinui utilizing a newly established "kuleana" system of self-sufficiency. "The land will be the way it used to be, Kahikinui."*

On the south side of Maui is a moku on
  the slopes of Haleakalā, Kahikinui
Some folks come from miles and miles away,
  to the place that used to be, Kahikinui
Oh, they come from miles and miles away,
  they work all the night and all the day
To bring back the land that used to be,
  Kahikinui.

When you come around the mountain
  you've reached your destiny
From the cloud tops down to the sea,
Kahikinui, Kahikinui
The pastures are green below the forest,
The lava is hard, as hard as it can be,
Kahikinui, Kahikinui
The old goat that lies upon the land,
The wind that blows his hair as white
  as sand,
Can you bring it back the way it used to be,
Kahikinui, Kahikinui.

Well, the old man that lies upon the land
Will rise up again to take his stand
The nation will have its sovereignty
The land will be the way it used to be,
Kahikinui, Kahikinui, Kahikinui.

# 'O Pu'u Māhoe U'i

*Pu'u Māhoe, located in Kanaio, Maui, was selected as the site for the ahu and regreening ceremony to call for the nāulu to return to Kaho'olawe.*

*My mother told me of how the women of the area would notice the growing breasts of a younger girl—u'i pu'u māhoe: the breasts that would eventually nurture a newborn infant, "Kaho'olawe." As in the old days, the clouds would form a lei over the islands of Maui, Kaho'olawe, Lāna'i, and Moloka'i, causing adequate rainfall for all.*

E ho'ōla iā Kaho'olawe.

E nānā 'oe i ka pu'u
'O Pu'u Māhoe u'i
Kū ana i ka uhiwai
I luna a'e o ke kai

'Ākoakoa mai kākou
E kāhea aku i ka ua
E ho'ōla iā Kaho'olawe
Aloha au i ka uhiwai

He aloha nō ke Akua
Uhaele mai kākou e pule
No ke kilikili noe
I luna o Kaho'olawe
Ua mau ke ea o ka 'āina i ka pono.

E nānā 'oe i ka pu'u
'O Moa'ula a me Mōiwi
Kū ana i ka uhiwai
I luna a'e o ke kai
Mahalo ke Akua

Ha'ina 'ia mai
Ana ka puana
E ho'ōla iā Kaho'olawe
Aloha au iā Kaho'iwai.

## Lāna'i City

There is a place not too far from me,
  Lāna'i, Lāna'i City.
Not too long ago they came to taste and see
  the pineapples of Lāna'i City.
Big and juicy as sweet as can be, like the aku
  swimming in the sea
And the deer as free as free can be in Lāna'i
  City, Lāna'i City.

Oh the BOSS MAN he says I'm coming, you
  will see progress in Lāna'i City
We'll build you homes affordable, they say,
  until the day when you cannot pay!
In the name of progress I offer you new life,
  in the name of progress I will employ
  your wife.
In the name of progress I'll take you from
  the fields—this is real—from the fields.

People of Lāna'i open up your eyes,
  in Mānele tell me what you see
The ROCK RESORT overlooking the bay
  where the deer and the children used
  to play.
Oh if the tourist do not pay—
Oh if the tourist do not stay—
Oh if the tourist run away—
HOW WILL I PAY? HOW WILL I PAY???

Known for pineapples and aku in the sea
The axis deers underneath the trees
Now people come from all around to see
What's going DOWN in Lāna'i City, What's
  going down in Lāna'i City.

THERE WAS A PLACE
NOT TOO FAR FROM ME
LĀNA'I, LĀNA'I CITY...

(1996)

## 'Ike Au iā Kaho'olawe

*Similar to the plight of the Hawaiians—
Kaho'olawe is now experiencing a new life.*

'Ike au iā Kaho'olawe
Aia i ke kai
Kūlia ho'okahi wale nō
E kāhea ana ia'u.

Ua mau ke ea o ka 'āina i ka pono
Ua mau ke ea o ka 'āina i ka pono
Ua mau ke ea o ka 'āina i ka pono

A no Kaho'olawe
Makemake au i ke ea
Kūlia ho'okahi wale nō
Kū'oko'a! Kū'oko'a!

Ua mau ke ea o ka 'āina i ka pono
Ua mau ke ea o ka 'āina i ka pono
Ua mau ke ea o ka 'āina i ka pono

'O kēia ka manawa
O ke ola pono
Ola hou ko kākou 'āina
E ho'iho'i 'ia mai ka 'āina
I ko kākou lima.

Ua mau ke ea o ka 'āina i ka pono
Ua mau ke ea o ka 'āina i ka pono
Ua mau ke ea o ka 'āina i ka pono.

Photo by Jo Giubilato

*Legacy of Music, Legacy of Love: The Gifts of Aunty Martha Kaumakaokalani A'oe Poepoe Hohu*

Aunty Martha and author,
great-great-grandniece
Leslie Stewart

# keli'ilauahi

Leslie Keli'ilauahi Stewart • Leslie Keli'ilauahi Stewart • Leslie Keli'ilauahi Stewart

Someone once asked me what I remembered most about my childhood, and I replied, "music." When I close my eyes and imagine my kūpuna, I can still hear their voices harmonizing the upcoming Sunday choir selections, Aunty Martha playing her piano, the scent of Aunty Leila's fragrant ginger blossoms wafting through the air. On the corner of Rooke Avenue in Nu'uanu, the soothing melodies of Hawaiian music had a home in the Stewart, Poepoe, Hohu, and Kiaha 'ohana.

Despite the numerous disappointments and challenges my kūpuna faced in their lifetimes, there had always been a sense of hope and resilience that allowed them to persevere. The cornerstone of their lives was their faith in God, and music, which were inextricably tied to one another. Music, as my grandfather once said, "nurtured your soul and reminded you that your life has a purpose."

I never had the chance to record the life stories of my two heroes, my father's parents, Harry Kaonohiaweaweokala Stewart Jr. and Wilhelmina Peleaumokukalunaholoholo Ludloff Stewart. Like many Hawaiians, they passed from this life long before their time. As their granddaughter, I have learned that despite the weight of their physical absence, their presence lives on through their love of music. One woman who shared this love was my father's great-aunt, Martha Kaumakaokalani A'oe Poepoe Hohu. This is a story about one woman's life and the thousands of people that she has touched over the last nine decades.

# Legacy of Music, Legacy of Love: The Gifts of Aunty Martha Kaumakaokalani A'oe Poepoe Hohu

Martha Kaumakaokalani A'oe Poepoe came into this world on January 7, 1907, the ninth child out of a family of 11 children, the sixth daughter of Henry and Lucia Poepoe. "Aunty Martha," as she is known to the 'ohana, attended Ka'iulani Elementary School until the sixth grade, where she then entered Kamehameha Schools, graduating as class salutatorian in 1925. From there she went on to the Territorial Normal and Training School at the University of Hawai'i, where she trained to be a teacher. She graduated in 1930 with an education certificate and then went on to the University of Hawai'i, receiving her bachelor's degree in education in 1932.

Upon graduating, she was employed in the music department at Kamehameha Schools, where she served as a music teacher, accompanist, composer, and arranger, a job she held for over 40 years until retiring in 1972. Besides her regular career as a music teacher at Kamehameha Schools, Aunty Martha served as choir director and organist of Kaumakapili Church from 1930 to 1997. During these years, she also flew to Kalaupapa, Moloka'i, every Saturday morning for ten years (1955-1965) to teach the patients there how to sing Hawaiian songs. She spent 25 years making weekly trips to Hāna, Maui, to direct the Hotel Hana Maui Choral Group, while at the same time directing the Hawaiian Electric Choral Group. In addition to her musical career, Aunty Martha spent 18 years as a docent at Washington Place and worked with Hawaiian-language scholar Mary Kawena Pukui at the Bishop Museum.

Besides teaching music, Aunty Martha is also known for her contribution to the preservation of Hawaiian hīmeni (Hawaiian hymns). She spearheaded the compilation of two well-known Hawaiian hymnals. The first, *Leo Hoonani* (Beautiful Voice), was published with revisions as *Leo Hoonani Hou* in 1953. The second, *Na Himeni Haipule Hawaii* (Religious Hymns of Hawai'i), was published in 1972 and has come to be a standard Hawaiian hymnal throughout the islands. Aunty Martha served as chairwoman of the committee that gathered the songs from Hawaiian churches, translated many traditional hymns from English to Hawaiian, and saw the hymnal to press. She also served as consultant for the 2001 revised edition of *Nā Hīmeni O Ka Ekalesia* (Church Hymns), first published in 1821; and the new edition is dedicated to her.

For her diverse work, Aunty Martha has won numerous awards, including Mother of the Year in 1959, Director Emeritus of Kaumakapili Church in 1977, Nā Hōkū Hanohano lifetime achievement award in 1995, the Kamehameha Schools–Bishop Estate Order of Keali'i Pauahi in 1998, and Honpa Hongwanji Mission Living Treasure.

Aunty Martha had a solid musical foundation long before she was born. Her father, my great-great grandfather Henry Keli'ikuniaupuni Poepoe, was the pastor of Kaumakapili Church from 1903 to 1950. A few years ago, I had the great pleasure of "talking story" with Aunty Martha as she reminisced about her father and her first job as the organist for Kaumakapili Church in 1924, when she was a senior in high school. "We never missed a Sunday. All 11 of us [children] spent every Sunday with Daddy up at the pulpit. Back then Daddy never carried any notecards or pieces of paper to remember his sermons; he could quote passages from the Bible by heart. When he spoke or sang, he put his whole heart into it, and if you were sitting in the congregation, you could feel the power of what he was saying."

Aunty Martha credits her musical foundation to her fourth-grade teacher, Mrs. Sally Trask of Ka'iulani Elementary School. She said that it was Mrs. Trask who taught her how to read music and to play the piano: "Mrs. Trask laid the technical foundation of understanding music which has allowed me to expand my knowledge and to share it with others."

Sharing her knowledge and aloha with others is perhaps one of the things Aunty Martha is most famous for. For over 60 years, she arranged many of the award-winning compositions sung at the Kamehameha Song Contest. Arrangements such as "Kamehameha Waltz," "Wailana," "Uluhua Wale Au," and "Ua Kea o Hana" are considered standards which have stood the test of time. She has a commanding knowledge not only of the technical aspects of music, but also of the history of the evolution of Hawaiian music.

"No one likes to credit the missionaries with anything good," she said. "You young kids like to only point out the negative side to what the missionaries brought with them. Let me tell you, the missionaries gave us the foundation of the [modern Hawaiian] music you hear today. I am living proof of that. The Mākaha Sons of Ni'ihau are living proof of that, and so are the Brothers Cazimero, as well as many others. The Hawaiians had and still have a very beautiful musical tradition which preceded the arrival of the missionar-

ies. You just need to watch the first night of Merrie Monarch kahiko competition to see that. But what the missionaries brought with them was a different style of singing: choral singing [hīmeni], instead of chanting. The Hawaiians took what they learned from them and made it their own. Don't you think that Hawaiian church music sounds different from what you hear on the mainland?"

As a small child, my favorite part of attending Kaumakapili Church was listening to and singing some of my favorite hīmeni. Later, when I was a young woman attending college in Oregon, I distinctly remember how different the church services were there. Everyone seemed so austere and remote; their voices were singing sacred songs but they seemed so detached. Perhaps it was my homesickness which shaded my opinions. Or maybe it was the fact that Hawaiians have always rejoiced in singing, chanting, and dancing. I laughed as my aunt took me back to a time when the simple joy of singing reinforced the love that we all felt for each other and our community.

With her musical foundation firmly planted by Mrs. Trask and her father, Aunty Martha went on to Kamehameha Schools. For every child growing up in Hawai'i, Kamehameha Schools are synonymous with their annual song contest, a musical showcase of talent and competition between the high school classes. Aunty Martha was among the first students of Kamehameha to participate in the Kamehameha Schools Song Contest. During our conversation, Aunty Martha reflected on some of the changes in the contest over the decades:

"I believe the Song Contest began in 1922. Originally the students wrote their own songs and poems to sing in a friendly competition. Over the years students began to choose songs to sing by other composers instead of writing original compositions. I honestly don't know why the song selections have changed. When I was a student there—keep in mind that was over 70 years ago—we composed our own songs as a way to unify our class. Today when the children sing, they sing songs that don't belong to them; they sometimes just sing the songs without understanding the depth of their meaning. And I don't mean that they can't sing other people's music—heavens no! I sing a lot of other people's music. I just like the fact that when the students composed their own songs it allowed them to be creative, it allowed them to learn the Hawaiian language and the beauty which is so evident in the words."

Aunty Martha hit upon an intriguing point in our conversation—the intrinsic connection between language, culture, and music. That concept, which appears to be such an ele-mentary one, is actually at the forefront of many debates in Hawai'i today surround-ing Hawaiian culture. From the issue of "Jawaiian vs. Hawaiian" music, to the perpetuation of Hawaiian language, to the classification of who or what is Hawaiian, one fact remains: As with all other living cultures, the Hawaiian culture has always been and will continue to be in a state of evolution. The fact that culture changes is a sign of its vitality. "Jawaiian music was inevitable," Aunty Martha claimed. "There is so much mass communication today that it would be impossible for Hawaiian music to exist in isolation. And who would want Hawaiian music to be isolated? I suppose there are those people out there who would like Hawaiian music to be 'pure,' but what I would like to know is, Who gets to define what Hawaiian music is? Like I said earlier, the missionaries brought choral signing to the islands, and we adopted it. The Portuguese brought the 'ukulele [which predecessor instrument they called the "*braguinha*"] and the Spanish brought the guitar. Do you really think guys like Israel Kamakawiwo'ole and Gabby Pahinui would be able to produce the kind of music they did if it wasn't for the introduction of those instruments?

"Musicians like Gabby and Israel are artists; they feel their music and the audience feels it right along with them. If you want to compare it to another artistic form, it's sort of like watching hula. When the dancer knows the meaning behind the song that she is dancing you can see it in her face,

Aunty Martha
at Kaumakapili
Church

her movements, her expression. You can feel what she is feeling without question. It's like that in singing and music. When you understand the words that you are singing, the expression and the depth of the song comes out in your performance. It is something that is felt, and the audience knows it."

Two years ago I had the opportunity to backpack across India, a country with an ancient and thriving civilization. One evening while I was attending a classical Indian dance performance in Bangalore in southern India, I was struck by my emotional response to the dancer's performance, a beautiful and passionate interpretation of a story of Rama and Sita from the classical Indian epic *Ramayana*. I couldn't help but cry as the dancers portrayed the two young lovers being separated from one another and struggling to overcome numerous obstacles in order to be reunited. As I've traveled around the world, I've come to understand that one does not always have to be a student of the culture to be affected by it.

Since Aunty Martha mentioned Gabby Pahinui, I asked her about the Hawaiian Renaissance and the new interest in Hawaiian music in the 1970s. She laughed and had this to say: "The Hawaiian Renaissance went a long way in reviving cultural pride. With Nainoa [Thompson] making his first voyage [on the *Hōkūle'a*], George [Helm] and Kimo [Mitchell] protesting for Kaho'olawe, and the many young Hawaiians getting elected into political office, I feel that it was a great thing for Hawaiians to gain a greater interest in their cultural roots. You notice that I say a 'greater' interest. I say that because I don't really believe that Hawaiians ever lost interest in their music, their culture, and their traditions. Perhaps the Hawaiian Renaissance helped to popular-

ize Hawaiian music in a way that was different from the Hawaiian music and the hīmeni that I sang in church, but Hawaiians have been making music since the beginning of time and we always will—in one form or another."

Throughout the past nine decades—for almost the entire 20th century—Aunty Martha could have kept her many gifts to herself. Instead she chose to serve the Hawaiian community with her talent and intelligence. As I sat in awe of my great aunt's life, I asked her why she had taken on the responsibilities that she did. In a response that is so typical of Aunty Martha she said, "God gave me many gifts. I must share these gifts with people who want to listen and learn. If I kept all of my knowledge to myself, what would the younger generation have? I would not be worthy of all of the blessings that God has bestowed upon me if I didn't share it with everyone."

My brother and his family now live on my grandparents' property on Rooke Avenue. The original house and Aunty Leila's ginger hedge are long gone. Aunty Martha hasn't lived next door for many years now. And the neighbors have rebuilt, covering the entire property in concrete. Yet, when I return, I still recall the lush gardens, and the two homes divided only by the fragrant ginger hedge. In my mind, I still hear Aunty Martha on the piano, practicing Sunday's choir selection, and my grandparents in their home on the other side of the hedge, singing along in perfect pitch, in perfect harmony, their legacy of music, and of love, blessing our family for generations to come.

*The Flute of the ʻOhe*

*Kona Kai ʻŌpua*

*Ruins*

Speaking at the ʻOnipaʻa sovereignty
march and gathering on the ʻIolani
Palace grounds on 17 January 1993,
the centenary of the overthrow of
the Hawaiian nation

# *haunani-kay*

Haunani-Kay Trask • Haunani-Kay Trask • Haunani-Kay Trask • Haunani-Kay Trask

Poetry is a kind of song from the deeper part of human beings. Beyond the constraints and entanglements and sufferings of our lives, there is that light of nourishment which leads us toward beauty and the wonder of creation.

## *The Flute of the ʻOhe*

The flute of the *ʻohe*
   filters our music:
      notes of the burning
         the jeweled, the tender
            dead.

Here, in our wanderings,
   disembodied islands
      turn yellow, rotting
         in a human forest.

Over the ancient roads,
   muddy waters are
      rushing, anthills
         moving inland,
            a twilight horizon closing.

In the anguished
   hours, loud-voiced foreigners
      ravage the land at will.

## Kona Kai ʻŌpua

Across a fathomless horizon,
　koa voyaging canoes

　　　plumed Kanaloa,
　　　　provocative summer clouds

　　　　gilded by the god:
　　blue pearl, green
　olivine. In the Kona

noon, a lone *naiʻa*—
　sea-sleek *kinolau*
　of divinity.

　　　Between coastal *heiau*
　　　castrated *niu*, shorn

　of fruit and flower,
　　fawning. From the ancestral
　　shore, tlack-tlack

　of lava stones, massaged
　　by tidal seas: eternal
　　*kanikau* for long

　　　forgotten *aliʻi*, entombed
　　　beneath grandiose hotels
　　　mocked

by crass amusements
　Japanese machines
　　and the common greed

　　of vulgar Americans.

## Ruins

To choose the late noon
　　sun, running barefoot
　　　on wet Waimānalo
　　　　beach; to go with all

　　our souls' lost yearnings
　　to that deeper place
　　　where love has let
　　　　the stars come down,

　　　has let my hair, shawled
　　　over bare shoulders,
　　　　fall in black waves
　　　across my face;

there, at last,
　escaped from the ruins
　of our nation,

　　　to lift our voices
　　　over the sea
　　　　in bitter songs
　　　　　of mourning.

# kekeha

Ron Kekeha Solis • Ron Kekeha Solis • Ron Kekeha Solis • Ron Kekeha Solis

Aloha kākou! ʻO Ron Kekeha Solis koʻu inoa, a no Oʻahu nei nō au. A ua nui koʻu mahalo i kēia puke nei ʻo ʻŌiwi kahi e heluhelu ai i nā moʻolelo like ʻole a nā Kānaka Maoli o nēia pae ʻāina. A ma muli o ka ikaika a me ka hoʻomanawanui ʻana o nā limahana e paʻi ʻia nei kēia puke a laha. Ke lana nei ka manaʻo, e hoʻonanea ʻoukou i ka heluhelu i kēia moʻolelo ma lalo nei.

## He Moʻolelo Pōkole

Aloha ʻoe, e ka puke hiwahiwa a ka lāhui Hawaiʻi, e ʻike ʻia nei ma neia pae ʻāina a puni. Eia ma lalo nei kekahi moʻolelo o Oʻahu nei. ʻO Kona ka moku, a ʻo Honolulu ke ahupuaʻa.

ʻO Kū ka makuakāne, a ʻo Hina ka makuahine. ʻO ko lāua wahi e noho nei, aia ma Waialamoʻo ma Nuʻuanu. He mau makahiki ko lāua o ka noho ʻana he kāne a he wahine, ʻaʻole naʻe i ʻike ʻia ka hiʻohiʻona o ke keiki ma luna o Hina.

Noho ihola lāua a ʻaʻohe wahi mea a loaʻa o ke keiki, ʻo ke kāhea akula nō ia o Kū me ke kaumaha ʻai ʻana i ke akua i keiki na lāua. A ua loaʻa nō i kou mea kākau he hapa o ia pule, a he pule ia mai kahiko mai, a penei ia,

> E hoʻohāpai mai i keiki
> I hānau mai auaneʻi he keikikāne

I mahi'ai
I lawai'a
I kūkulu hale
A i ho'ohiki inoa no 'oukou e ke akua.

A i hānau mai ho'i he kaikamahine
He kuku kapa
I kuku malo
I kuku pā'ū
I kuku 'oloa,
I ulana moena
I hāli'ili'i hale
A i ho'ohiki inoa no 'oukou e ke akua
'O ia ho'i ka waiwai a ka pulapula.

A 'o ke ola ho'i āu e ke akua
A kaniko'o a palalauhala kolopūpū
a haumaka'iole
'O kā 'oukou ola ia e ke akua.

Noho lāua a 'ono ihola 'o Hina i ka hilu. A
'o ia ka i'a ho'okahi a ua Hina nei i 'ono ai.
'O ka ho'opuka kā Hina i kāna mea e 'ono
ai, a 'o ka ho'okō aku kā Kū. He mau malama ma hope mai o ka ho'omaka 'ana o ka
'ono a Hina, 'ike akula 'o Kū he keiki ko
Hina e kōkō ana. Hau'oli ihola lāua nei i ka
'ike 'ana ē ua loa'a ka mea e ola ai nā lā
hāpauea. A i ka puni 'ana o nā malama,
hānau maila na lāua he keiki kāne, a ua
kapa 'ia ihola kona inoa 'o Kapa'ahana.
Mālama nō 'o Kū lāua 'o Hina i ua keiki nei
a nui, a a'oa'o maila i kā lāua keiki aloha,
"'A'ole 'oe e pi'i aku i uka o Nu'uanu."
'A'ole na'e lāua i hō'ike aku i ke kumu
o kā lāua 'ōlelo pēlā.

'O ke kumu, e ka mea heluhelu, i pāpā 'ia ai
'a'ole e hele ua wahi keiki nei ma ia wahi,
'o ia ho'i, aia ma laila he kupua, 'o Maui
ka inoa. 'Eā, 'a'ole kēia 'o ka Maui nāna i
ho'ohei i ka lā, i wahi e kaula'i ai a malo'o
ke kapa a kona makuahine a Hina. 'O kēia
kanaka 'o Maui, he kupua; he kino kanaka

a he kino 'īlio. Ke lilo kēia wahi kupua i 'īlio,
he keu nō a ka weliweli ke nānā aku, a he
hana ho'omāinoino wale kāna. 'O kēia
kupua 'o Maui, he hana 'o ia i nā kānaka
o ia wahi e like me kona makemake. 'A'ohe
wahi kanaka a mau kānaka paha nāna e
hō'a'ano aku i ua kupua lā o ia 'āina. I kēia
manawa, e waiho aku kākou i ua kupua lā
'o Maui, a e nānā hou kākou i ka hana a
Kapa'ahana, 'oiai, he ho'olohe kāna i ka
'ōlelo a kona mau mākua, a 'a'ole 'o ia hele
iki i kēlā wahi. A i ia manawa a ua keiki nei
a Hina mā lāua 'o Kū e ulu ana a kanaka
makua, ua a'o nō 'o ia nei a mākaukau ma
nā mea a pau e pono ai ka nohona, 'o ia
ho'i, ka mahi'ai, ka lawai'a, a me ke kūkulu
hale.

I kekahi lā, hele aku nei 'o Kapa'ahana i ka
he'enalu ma kai o Waikīkī, a pau, ho'i mai
ana kēia i kauhale. A iā ia nei ma ke alahele
e naue ana, 'ike akula kēia i kekahi wahine
u'i a ka launa 'ole i ka 'ohi hua 'ai o ka
nāhelehele. A i nānā mai ka hana o ua
wahine u'i lā a 'ike iā Kapa'ahana, ho'ohihi
maila i ka maika'i o kēia kanaka e kā'alo
akula i mua o kona maka. 'O Wa'ahila ka
inoa o ia wahine. No Luakaha kēia wahine
maka onaona. Nīnau akula 'o Kapa'ahana,
"E aha ana kāu o kēia lā mōlehulehu?"

Pane maila ua wahine lā, "Ke 'ohi maila i
hua 'ai na mākou me ka 'ohana e 'ai ai. He
mau lā makapehu i'a 'ole ko mākou, a 'o ka
hua 'ai wale ihola nō paha ka mea e ola ai
ko kauhale."

"He aha lā kā 'oukou o ka 'ai wahi i'a 'ole?"
wahi a Kapa'ahana i nīnau aku ai i kahi
wahine me ka ho'omau 'ana aku, "'A'ole o
kana mai o ka i'a ma ke kai lā, he ulua a me
ke āhole nō ho'i paha."

"Auē! 'O ka ulua a me ke āhole, he mau i'a

loa'a wale. Ua pōpilikia mākou e noho akula ma uka lā, he kupua 'ino ke 'ai nei i ka i'a ke loa'a iā mākou. Ke loa'a kahi i'a ma kahakai a huli ho'i ana i kauhale, 'o ka hālāwai nō ia me kahi 'īlio nui weliweli. Lālau ua 'īlio nei i ka i'a a pau koke i ka 'ai ia. A ho'i nele ka lawai'a i kauhale, a i kekahi manawa, pau nō ho'i ke kanaka lawai'a i ka make i ua 'īlio weliweli nei," wahi a ka wahine i pane mai ai me ka ho'omau 'ana i ka 'ōlelo, "a 'a'ole 'o ia wale nō, pau iho nei nō ho'i i ua wahi kupua 'ino nei nā pua'a, ke kalo, ka 'uala, a me ia mea 'ai aku ia mea 'ai aku o ko mākou wahi."

'Ī akula 'o Kapa'ahana, "Ke lewalewa nei kahi houpo, e ho'iho'i hā kāua i ko'u hale, e 'ai ai."

Iā lāua i hō'ea ai i kahi o nā mākua o Kapa'ahana, pā ana kāhea a Hina, "Mai, mai 'olua, ma loko mai e noho pū ai."

Komo akula 'o Kapa'ahana i loko o ka hale, komo pū aku nō me kona kōko'olua o ka hele 'ana, a noho ihola lāua nei i lalo o ka papahele.

"Ma hea mai nei 'olua?" i nīnau mai ai 'o Hina.

Pane akula 'o Kapa'ahana me ka 'ī 'ana aku, "I Waikīkī aku nei au i ka he'enalu a ho'i maila. A ia'u e naue mai ana, 'ike aku nei au iā ia nei i ka 'ohi hua 'ai. 'O ko'u kono aku nō ia e ho'i māua i kauhale, a ho'i mai nei māua."

Nīnau akula 'o Hina iā Wa'ahila, "No hea mai 'oe, e ke kaikamahine?"

'Ī akula 'o Wa'ahila, "No Nu'uanu nei nō, ma uka aku na'e o ko 'oukou wahi e noho mai nei."

I ia manawa, komo maila 'o Kū, a kau iho ana i ka mea 'ai ma ka papa 'aina, 'o ka i'a 'oe, 'o ke kalo 'oe, ka pa'i 'ai me ka poi, ka lū'au, 'o ka 'uala 'oe.

Mea a'ela 'o Hina, "E pā'ina wahi 'ai kākou a mālō ke 'eke." Kaumaha akula 'o Kū i nā 'aumākua, a pau, 'o ka 'ai ihola nō ia o lākou. 'Ai a mā'ona, puka a'ela 'o Kapa'ahana me Wa'ahila i waho o ka hale, hele ana no ka nāhelehele, he wahi kahawai ma laila. 'Au'au ihola lāua. 'A'ole i li'uli'u ko lāua nei 'au'au 'ana, ho'i akula i kapa kahawai. A 'o ua wahine lā, 'o Wa'ahila, he keu nō a ka wahine maika'i, e like nō ho'i me ia moku 'o Maunaloa, "kīkala nui," peia nō kahi kaikamahine o Luakaha. A 'o ka launa ihola nō ia o lāua, a ua hele nō a "wela ka nuku o Nu'uanu i ka hole 'ia e ke āhole." Ho'āo ihola lāua i ia pō, a noho kāne a wahine ihola lāua nei. A ma ia hope mai, he hele pū nō 'o Kapa'ahana lāua me Wa'ahila i Luakaha me ka nui pū'olo, he wahi mea 'ai e pā'ina ai nā mākua o kāna wahine. 'A'ole na'e o lāua hele ma ke ala i ma'a iā Wa'ahila. Ma uka o Kapālama lāua e hele ai, a hiki i uka loa o laila, huli ana no Luakaha. Pēlā e hō'alo ai i ka maka o ua kupua 'ino lā o Maui.

Noho ihola lāua nei a hānau maila he kaikamahine, a ua kapa iho nā mākua i kona inoa 'o Kapunaola a 'o ka lilo akula nō ia na nā kūpuna e mālama, a e hānai a nui, e like me ka ma'a mau. 'Oiai, he hana kā Kapa'ahana me Wa'ahila i nā mea e pono ai ka nohona. Noho ihola nō 'o Kapa'ahana mā, a hāpai hou ihola 'o Wa'ahila. A i ka puni 'ana o nā malama, hānau maila he keiki kāne. Ua kapa 'ia ka inoa o ua keiki kāne nei 'o Kupanihi. A e like nō ho'i me kona kaikuahine, hānai pū 'ia 'o ia nei e kona mau kūpuna. I ka ulu kā'ala'ala 'ana o Kupanihi, he mea ma'a mau iā ia nei ka 'anau 'ana aku ma 'ō a ma 'ane'i e 'anau wale aku ai.

I kekahi lā, naue aku nei 'o Kupanihi i kahi o Maui e noho ana. Ua pāpā 'ia nō ua keiki kāne nei, 'a'ole e hele i laila, o pō'ino auane'i ke ola. 'A'ohe na'e he wahi mea a maliu aku i ka 'ōlelo a kona mau kūpuna. I kona hiki 'ana aku i laila, 'ike aku nei kēia i kahi 'īlio maka hae e haka pono maila iā ia nei. Kau ka weli o ua keiki nei, 'o kona huli a'ela nō ia, a naholo akula. He makehewa na'e ka holo 'ana o nei keiki, 'a'ohe nō i 'emo, po'i maila kēlā wahi kupua, a nahu ana i ua keiki nei. A he mea ho'omāna'ona'o nō i ka no'ono'o ke 'ike aku i ka hana a ia 'īlio. Pau ke keiki i ka make, ho'i akula 'o Maui i uka, i kona wahi noho. 'O Kupanihi ho'i, e waiho wale ana kona kino make. I ia manawa o Kupanihi i make ai, hā'upu ihola 'o Kapunaola i kona kaikunāne. A no laila, 'imi a'e ana ma 'ō a ma 'ane'i i kona kaikunāne aloha. A li'uli'u, loa'a ihola iā ia ke kino o ua Kupanihi nei, ua pau loa i ka make. Ho'omaka kēia e uē i kēia make 'ana o kona kaikunāne. 'Oi uē 'o ia nei a lohe maila ke kupunahine, 'o Hina, i kēia uē 'ana a me ka makemake o Kapunaola, e ola hou kona kaikunāne. Ho'okolo mai ana kahi kupunahine i ka leo o ka mo'opuna. Hiki kēlā i kahi o ka mo'opuna kāne, ua make. Nīnau maila ke kupunahine, "E ku'u mo'opuna, ua aha 'ia mai nei kō kaikunāne?"

"'Akahi nō a loa'a ia'u, na kēlā kupua nō paha 'o ia nei i pepehi."

"Mai uē, e ku'u mo'opuna, e ho'i aku 'oe i kauhale, 'ānō, a ma hope aku nō māua me kou kaikunāne."

Ua kāhāhā iho ka no'ono'o o kahi kaikamahine i ka 'ōlelo a ke kupunahine, 'o ka ho'i akula nō na'e ia no ka hale.

I ia manawa nō, hana ihola 'o Hina i ke kino o Kupanihi a ola hou kēia. Iho akula lāua a 'elua i kai, 'au'au iho la a pau ho'i i ka hale.

He anahulu ma hope mai o ia manawa i make ai 'o Kupanihi a ola hou, komo ihola i loko ona ka mana'o e hō'a'ano hou aku iā Maui, kēlā kupua 'ino e noho ana ma uka aku o ko lāua nei hale. Hele akula nō kēia keiki me ka pa'a nō o ka ihe ma kona lima. Hiki akula i kahi o Maui, 'imi ana kēia i ua kupua 'ino, 'a'ohe wahi mea a loa'a iki. 'O ia 'imi nō o Kupanihi a 'ike akula i kekahi kanaka e noho ana ma kapa o ke kahawai. Hele nō ua keiki nei a i mua o ke kanaka, a nīnau akula, "Ua 'ike aku nei paha 'oe i kekahi 'īlio pī'alu o nei kaha?"

"He aha maila kāu e kēnā wahi keiki ma'i lewalewa? 'A'ole 'īlio pī'alu," i 'ōlelo mai ai kēlā. "E aho kāua e hopu i kēlā 'oau e holo ana ma kahawai. E hō mai i kāu ihe, a na'u e 'ō aku a pa'a.

"'A'ole 'o ka ihe ka mea e pa'a ai kēlā i'a, e hāhā aku nō ka lima, a e pa'a koke," wahi a Kupanihi i pane aku ai.

"'A'ohe nō e pa'a i ka lima, 'o ka ihe ka mea e pa'a ai.' 'Eā, e ka mea heluhelu, 'o kēia kanaka a Kupanihi e kama'ilio aku nei, 'o ia nō 'o Maui, ua kū a kanaka ihola na'e. A ke 'imi nei 'o Maui i wahi e waiho iho ai 'o Kupanihi i kāna ihe i lalo. A ua ho'okō 'ia nō kona makemake. "'Eā, e hō'ike mai paha i kou akamai, e kēnā keiki, ma ka hāhāmau. E aho paha, e hō mai i ka ihe, a na'u kēlā i'a e 'ō, a pa'a."

Ua pa'a loa ka mana'o o Kupanihi, ma ka lima nō e pa'a ai kahi i'a. Waiho ihola i kāna ihe ma lalo, a lēkei akula i loko o ke kahawai. A hāhā ana, 'a'ohe 'emo, hāpai ana 'o Kupanihi i ka 'oau momona. I nānā aku ka hana o Kupanihi i kahi o ua kanaka lā e noho ana, aia hoʻi, ʻo Maui ke kū ana ma kona kino ʻīlio, a e kahe wale iho ana nō ka hāʻae. Lele ua Maui nei ma luna o Kupanihi, a pau ihola ʻo Kupanihi, a pau pū nō me ka ʻoau. ʻAi ihola ʻo Maui i kahi iʻa a māʻona, hoʻi akula i kona wahi noho, hāʻule ihola hiʻolani. I ia manawa nō i make ai ʻo Kupanihi, hāʻupu hou ihola ʻo Kapunaola i kahi kaikunāne ona. Huli hele ana ma ʻō a ma ʻaneʻi, e like nō me kēlā manawa mua, a loaʻa ke kino kupapaʻu o kona kaikunāne. Kāhea akula kēia i kona kupunahine, iā Hina, me ka ʻōlelo pū aku i ka makemake, ʻo ia hoʻi, e ola ke kaikunāne. ʻOi kāhea aku ʻo Kapunaola, a hiki maila ke kupunahine. A ʻōlelo maila ʻo Hina i kahi moʻopuna wahine āna, "E hoʻi aku ʻoe i kauhale, ʻānō, a naʻu nō e hana aku e like me ka mea i aʻo ʻia mai iaʻu. I ia hoʻi ʻana aku o kahi kaikamahine, ʻaʻole i liʻuliʻu, ola hou aʻela nō ʻo Kupanihi, iho akula lāua me kona kupunahine i kahakai.

ʻAuʻau ihola a pau, hoʻi ana no ka hale. Hauʻoli ihola ʻo Kapunaola i ka ʻike ʻana i ua kaikunāne aloha nei ona. Aʻoaʻo hou ʻia kahi keiki kāne hoʻolohe ʻole e nā kūpuna, "ʻAʻole ʻoe e hele hou aku i kēlā wahi o Maui."

He anahulu ma hope mai o ia make ʻalua ʻana o Kupanihi, hele hou ana e kolohe aku i kahi ʻīlio, iā Maui. I kēia manawa, hahai aku ana kona kaikuahine ma hope ona me ka ʻike ʻole ʻia e ke kaikunāne. Lawe pū ʻo Kapunaola i kekahi mau ihe ʻekolu. I kēia hele ʻana o Kupanihi, hālāwai hou akula me ke kanaka āna i ʻike ai ma kapa o ke kahawai. Nīnau akula ʻo Kupanihi, "Ua ʻike aku nei paha ʻoe i kahi ʻīlio pīʻalu o nei kaha?"

Pane maila kahi kanaka, "ʻAʻole ia ʻīlio ma ʻaneʻi. Akā he manu nui momona naʻe i luna o kahi kumu kukui. E pahu aku ʻoe i kāu ihe a kū ua manu momona lā, ola kāua iā ʻoe."

ʻĪ akula kēia, "ʻAʻole nō e kū ka manu i ka ihe, aia ka pono o ka hoʻopaʻa ʻana i ka manu ʻo ke kau ʻana i ke kēpau ma ka lālā. A ke paʻa ka manu i ka lālā, he hopu wale aku nō ka hana."

Koi ana naʻe kahi kanaka, "ʻO ka pahu ihe nō a kū ana kahi manu momona, ola ai kāua. Inā he kēpau, pehea auaneʻi e piʻi ai i luna o ke kumu lāʻau?"

Hele akula kēia i ke kēpau, a hoʻi mai, waiho ihola i ka ihe i lalo, a pinana akula i ia kumu kukui. A hiki aku i kahi lālā, hāpala ihola i ke kēpau, a kali ihola ʻo ke kau mai o ka manu. ʻAʻole i liʻuliʻu, paʻa ihola ka manu i ka lima o Kupanihi, iho ihola ua Kupanihi nei. Iā ia nō a hiki i lalo o ka honua nei, ʻike akula ʻo ia i ka ʻīlio nui weliweli e kahe ana ka hāʻae. Kau ka weli o ua keiki nei. Hoʻomaka ihola ʻo Maui e lele ma luna o ua ʻo Kupanihi. I ia manawa nō, lele ʻo Kapunaola, a hou akula i kekahi ihe, kū ka ʻōpū o ua kupua lā. Lālau hou akula kēia i ka lua o ka ihe, a hou akula. I kēia hou ʻana, kū akula ke poʻo o ua kupua lā. A laila, lālau kēia i ke kolu o ka ihe, pahu pololei akula i kona kaikunāne, kū ka manu e paʻa ana ma ka lima o kona kaikunāne. Hoʻi akula lāua nei i kauhale, a haʻi akula i kahi kupunakāne o lāua, e hoʻā i ka imu, he ʻīlio nui ma ka nāhelehele, ua make.

A ʻo ia ihola kahi moʻolelo o ia ʻāina i kapa ʻia ʻo Nuʻuanu. E hoʻi ana kahi keiki o Mānoa, ua ahiahi.

(mother and children, from left to right) Douglas John,
Phyllis Coochie, Josy Leipūpū, Nicholas Kāwika

*He Lā i Kapu-a*

*Ka ʻŌhiʻa Lehua*

*Echoes of Kuamoʻo*

*He Mele no Kaʻala*

*Ancient Walls*

*Haikus for the Days of
the Voyaging Canoes*

*Tūtū Mikala*

# cayan

Phyllis Coochie Tanodra Cayan • Phyllis Coochie Tanodra Cayan • Phyllis Coochie Tanodra Cayan

Most of my writings emerge from memories of special people, places, and events. Sometimes I jot down impressions and feelings and later develop those into haiku or other forms of poetry... Often words come to mind and I have learned to immediately write them. Those poems are the ones where I rarely change a word... It seems they simply hānau ʻia from my thoughts after a significant day.

I like to use specific sounds and words to evoke a particular moment. This is why I like to work in a haiku format and use both Hawaiian and English words. Most of us mix both languages when we speak to each other. My poetry is pretty much a way of preserving special moments and evoking that memory every time you read it.

Most of my childhood was spent growing up on Lānaʻi when it was still a plantation town. I was very blessed to have known my great-grandparents TūtūMan and TūtūLady Cockett. My memories of TūtūMan were his blue eyes, kind smile, and white hair of his later years. I always thought of him as a large man, and TūtūLady as a very gracious lady. I grew up interacting with all my grandparents, aunties, uncles, and a great assortment of cousins on both sides of the family, as well as my siblings. My parents were divorced when I was about six years old, so my large extended ʻohana was a major influence. Even today, most of my socializing is with my cousins and their ʻohana. Both of my grandparents had ten children, so you can imagine the number of cousins and cousins and cousins...

Growing up on Lānaʻi is unlike any other place. Children were nurtured, sometimes spoiled, but always loved and cared for. We literally had the run of the island—hiking in the forests and the mountains, going to the beaches, fishing and diving off the harbor pier, swimming every weekend at Mānele. As we got older, our adventures became more daring. I recall one time there was an enormous winter storm pounding at Mānele Beach and my grandma told us not to go into the ocean. We promised that we were just going to look at the waves. Well, the five of us drove to Mānele in the jeep, looked at those huge 10–15 foot waves and—yep!—we decided we would go in and just catch one wave and get out! Well, cousin Rosemond got caught in the backwash, and thank goodness there was a safety equipment ring to throw to her and pull her out! We knew what would have happened if we came home and she was injured! Now that story will get back to my oldest son, who longboards, and all my warnings to be careful will be negated!

I have three grown children—DJ, Josy, and Nicholas—and one moʻopuna, Laʻakeaomaunalei. They've all spent time and continue to visit Lānaʻi and know their roots and our ʻohana there. I've tried to emphasize a love of reading books with each one. They have all been brought up to be independent. Maybe sometimes they get too outspoken and radical! I guess that's in the koko. My ancestors Ohua and Keliihananui were the last konohiki of Lānaʻi.

My community activism manifested when the desecration at Honokahua escalated to more than 1,000 remains being disturbed. That lead to working on a legislative bill to protect traditional Hawaiian burials and burial sites, now part of Chapter 6E HRS. From that effort, the Island Burials Councils were formed. It is an honor to continue to serve over ten years on the council since its inception. My current community work includes working with the Waiʻanae community groups in the Ukanipō Heiau Advisory Council. That heiau is adjacent to Mākua Valley, so both are interwoven. Certainly Mākua is another version of Kahoʻolawe—we seek to protect and restore our access and gathering rights to all of ka

ʻāina and nā wahi pana. Last, but not least, when there's quiet moments, I continue to jot down impressions and these eventually emerge as poetry to remember people and places.

## He Lā i Kapu-a*

(for Baba)

A day at Kapu-a,
waves pound along the shore,
whitewash swirls in the blue.

Niu tidepools fill with foam,
we dip into the whitewash,
savoring the salty sea spray.

Cool breeze lingers at Kaupō,
we nap beneath kiawe shade,
the sun warms our backs.

Waves pull north of Oea,
sets of rolling blue ocean
crash upon the white sand.

Ha'ina mai ana ka puana,
'a'ole e poina 'o Kapu-a,
a place for the many gods.

*Mahalo for sharing, Kapu'a.*

*I am retaining the older hyphenated
spelling of "Kapu-a" over the more current
spelling "Kapu'a" because my experience
there has also been through an old map and
one South Kona kanaka who spelt it in the
old style.*

## Ka 'Ōhi'a Lehua

(haikus for the lonely warrior)

The 'ōhi'a tree
Tall, strong branches reach out above,
Liko lehua.

***

Many warriors
Stand with scarred spears at their side—
Ho'olehua.

***

Yellow lehua
Blossoms reach for the blue sky,
'Alohi ka lā.

***

Misty fog lingers
In the 'ōhi'a forest,
You walk in silence.

***

He lei lehua,
He makana nani nei
O kou aloha.

***

The tall 'ōhi'a
Watching over the 'āina
For those yet to come.

*These haiku are for 'Ōhi'a...and for the many
warriors past and present who lead the path
towards Hawaiian justice.*

## Echoes of Kuamoʻo

There near the blue shimmering sea,
A ferocious battle took place long ago.
Kanaka against kanaka,
ʻOhana against ʻohana,
To keep the kapu and traditions
Or to follow the white man's ways.

Chiefly bloods clash in combat,
Of kin and cousins,
Of sister and brother,
Of warriors elite and strong,
A fight to stay true to Hawaiʻi,
To resist the changing times.

Kekuaokalani stands firm,
The image of Kūkāʻilimoku held high,
Manono at his side until the end.
The loyal warriors continue to fight
For nā aliʻi, for the kapu beliefs,
For the life of the land.

The stillness of silence echoes loudly:
    canoes landing, feet running ashore,
    two armies advancing and fighting,
    the cries of pain, of dying by the gun,
    last calls to loved ones—auē! auē! auē!
    the red and yellow cloak has fallen.

There are many hōʻailona in the gathering
clouds:
    a chief wearing a mahiole,
    a kāne and a wahine stand together,
    a pueo looks upon Kuamoʻo,
    a honu hovers above the ocean,
    some restless spirits linger behind.

Today, I gaze upon black ʻaʻā lava fields,
Burial platforms and stacked stone walls,
And sense the sadness of that battle—
The loss of mana, the fighting ʻohana—
The beginning of despair for nā kānaka,
The struggle to control our own ʻāina.

The quiet spell is pau, time to leave.
Two black birds fly overhead,
The waves are rising offshore,
The pule has been offered:
    *E hō mai ka ʻike*
    *E hō mai ka ikaika*
    *E hō mai ke akamai.*

E aloha nā kūpuna koa,
E aloha mai, e aloha mai, e aloha mai...

*This is for my ancestral chief...mahalo nui loa
i kou manaʻo.*

*Kuamoʻo is a point and battleground with
burials near Keauhou, Hawaiʻi. Kekuaokalani
was the favorite nephew of Kamehameha
and heir to the war god, Kūkāʻilimoku. His
chiefess Manono remained with him until
they both were killed by their ʻohana using
the new weapons brought by foreigners.*

## He Mele no Ka'ala

Here is a song for Ka'ala
The majestic mountain of Wai'anae
Where the water flows to Pōka'ī.

There in the shadow of Ka'ala,
A breeze stirs the morning air
And the sun warms ka 'āina.

The beauty of Ka'ala lingers
With the scent of maile lau li'i,
A sweet reminder of you.

This is a song for Ka'ala
Where the water flows
to the kalo fields below.

## Ancient Walls

Kihawahine looks below,
tall chiefly clouds gather at her ridge,
bringing the waters of Kāne,
to the valley below
where ancient walls are hidden.

Offerings are laid at the ahu,
to Kāne and the life-giving waters,
to Lono for a good harvest,
to Hāloa the elder brother,
to the ancestors who once lived.

Strong backs bend in the sun,
removing the 'ōpala,
revealing old walls and 'auwai,
restoring the lo'i kalo,
nurturing ka 'āina.

Kihawahine teary eyed blinks,
a raincloud covers the ridge,
ancestral spirits descend again
into the lush valley,
bringing rainy blessings.

The konohiki stands on the hill
watching rainclouds gather,
soft raindrops fall on the 'āina,
the 'auwai flows and flows,
feeding the ancient lo'i kalo again.

E mahalo nā kini akua,
e mahalo nā 'aumākua,
e mahalo nā kūpuna...


*He mele inspired by Ka'ala and all who
mālama 'āina—past and present, and yet
to come.*

59

## Haikus for the Days of the Voyaging Canoes

The tall cloud rises high
Above the green Ko'olau,
A chief is present.

Blue waves swell to shore,
The kōlea leaves footprints,
Petroglyphs in sand.

Your goodbye honi
Lingers in my memory,
Sweet 'awapuhi.

Voyaging canoes
Follow the stars, swells, and wind,
Seeking ancient routes.

All around we see
Deep blue water meet the sky,
Merging their mana.

Lying on the deck,
Looking for Hōkū above,
The sky shifts slowly.

The ho'okupu,
Green specks in waterworn stone,
Offered by moonlight.

Makali'i rises,
Looks upon a lone canoe,
Sail to Tahiti.

Soft Hilo raindrops,
Mauna Kea hides her face
In a misty veil.

Crossing the channel,
You brave the pounding waves,
Stroking to the shore.

*This mele is for nā keiki o ka 'āina o Lāna'i: DJ, Leipūpū, Kāwika, Kealoha, Leilani, Kanani, Makalani, Kaipo, May Kanani, Keoni, Mikala Lehua, Mailelauli'i, La'akeaomaunalei, Kalāonāwa'a, and Lokelauli'i...they link the past with the future. E ola mau!*

## Tūtū Mikala

(for Annie Mikala Cockett Enfield,
1905–1994)

O Tūtū, who will gather our 'ohana
After you are gone?
Like the many stars above,
We have scattered afar.

Tūtū, what was your horse's name?
All the old folks remember
How well you rode with bright bangles
And a smile for all.

Tūtū, how did you know
Where the squid hides after the rain?
And is it true, TūtūLady, folks
Wen' catch squid on horseback?

O Tūtū, the white ginger are in bloom
Beneath your bedroom window.
They remind me of you and Grandpa,
Are you with him now?

Aloha nui loa e Tūtū...
A hui hou.

*...sweet ginger in the pink vase, the poi bowl
always on the kitchen table, kids running in
and out, plenty of scoldings if we pick on
the younger ones, we pile up in the old Willy
jeep and go riding, watching her find all the
he'e after the heavy rains, worn knobby
hands weaving lauhala, much much too
late we begin to ask questions...aloha 'oe
e Tūtū...*

# *keala-o-ānuenue*

Sally-Jo Keala-o-Ānuenue Bowman • Sally-Jo Keala-o-Ānuenue Bowman

In my novel-in-progress *Nā Koa: The Warriors,* protagonist Kanaka Jack, after 17 years sailing the world, reluctantly returns to Hawaiʻi with his Missouri-born friend, Cracker. They expect to stay two weeks, just long enough to cash in on a sweet money-making deal. They arrive in Honolulu in January 1893, the day after white businessmen overthrew the Kingdom of Hawaiʻi and deposed the Queen. While the city is under martial law and the port is closed, they meet Lehua and Uncle, then become embroiled in plans for a counterrevolution. When Jack commits himself to the Queen's cause, he learns that the meaning of life lies in pono relationships with people, the ʻāina, and heritage, values that doom him to destruction under a new, foreign political regime. This excerpt, Chapter Seventeen, about two-thirds into the story, takes place in January 1895, during the opening battle of the counterrevolution.

## *Chapter Seventeen*

Cracker followed Jack along the back way to Waikīkī. They kept their horses at a walk. At Kapiʻolani Park, white buildings and fencing gleamed sharper than the high moon. From the dark beyond the buildings, five other horsemen joined them, and a dozen men followed on foot. At the beach junction Cracker saw two bands of men coming up Waikīkī Road.

The army was forming! The Queen's secret army! At last he would be fighting on the right side. He thought of the night he had seen the Queen at Washington Place, of hearing her piano music drift through the open window. He thought of all Sammy and Lehua and Jack had told him, how the sugarmen had stolen Hawaiʻi. Now he felt big, strong. And proud, to stand for the Kingdom.

The pointed peak of Diamond Head at the end of Waikīkī towered flat and black and sharp-edged. He and Jack had climbed it, twice. It was as dry as Punchbowl, its steep outer slopes sliced by ravines.

They rode closer and closer to Diamond Head, until, at its foot, they could no longer see the top. Their destination sat in the shadow of the peak: a secret weapons depot. A place he had not been told of until just now—Bertelmann's. Jack said Bertelmann was not quite so important as Wilcox and Nowlein, but he was one of the leaders the *Pacific Commercial Advertiser* called "half-castes." It didn't sound nice, Cracker thought.

In twos and threes, men carried rifles in and out of Bertelmann's sprawling house. A lamp glowed through the front downstairs window and Cracker saw furniture, a piano, and two guitars hanging on the wall. Two men stood leaning over a table.

Jack motioned to dismount and they led the horses around the house and tied them to coconut trees on the beach side. Beyond the yard, Cracker saw surf breaking, frothing white in the moonlight. He and Jack joined dozens of men in a large canoe shed. They had moved the outriggers out onto the grass to make room for cases of rifles, which they were now cleaning. The sharp, metallic clatter of actions being tested drowned out any sound of the night surf.

Cracker followed Jack's lead and joined the labor. Talk was that the men would be ready in about two hours, then they would march for Honolulu, picking up forces along the way at other secret stations, other homes that had volunteered to hide weapons. By the time they reached town at daylight,

they should be 600 strong. Six hundred! More than enough to occupy all the government buildings. The troops that had backed the overthrow had numbered less than 200.

The lantern hanging from the top beam in the canoe shed sputtered. Smoke curled under the leaf-thatched roof, its oily stink mixing with the cleaner smell of solvent rubbed over rifle barrels. The lamp flickered its last and went out.

"Eh!" A Hawaiian nudged Cracker. "Haole boy. Try go inside, get one can kerosene."

Cracker knocked on the back door. No answer, though he could hear voices. He stepped into the entryway and peered into a large kitchen. He wished someone would come. It didn't feel right, barging into Bertelmann's house without someone answering the door. After long minutes, a man strode to the sink and began to work the pump handle.

"'Scuse me," Cracker said.

The man looked up. "Eh, I never went see you. You like?" He held out a glass of water.

"They sent me for kerosene. The lamp in the shed is out."

"Come-come." The man led the way through the kitchen, down a hallway that smelled of new wood, and into the front room, where three men sat around the table.

"Henry," the man said. "Where you get—"

The front door slammed open and the doorway filled with enormous uniformed figures.

"Police!" one of them shouted.

The first two moved farther into the room and Cracker stared into the black hole of a gun barrel.

"Search warrant! No one move!" The police fanned into the room, scanning it with their revolvers.

Like the rest of the royalists, Cracker froze. All he could hear were the sergeant's boot heels on the wood floor.

Outside, a shot cracked. Then another. Then a volley. Inside and out, the air burst with shouting, running, the zip of bullets flying, the ominous thump of lead shattering wood.

And the icy jingle of breaking glass. Cracker's face stung and he put his hands to his cheeks. The wetness smeared red in his palms. Another shot rang through the broken window and the top part of one of his legs turned into a rolling wall of pain.

Cracker fell into the shards of glass. Boots and bare feet ran over him and he choked on gunsmoke and his own blood.

*****

Cracker tried to move, tried to pull himself along the floor. The glass under his hands glittered in the lamplight. He pulled himself as far as a table leg, gripped its fat foot and pressed his face against it, breathing hard, sweating.

No one else was in the room. The shooting had stopped, though shouting and running continued outside.

He lay under the table on his side, on his good leg. He reached for the wound. With the slight movement, the broken bone splintered into his flesh and pain stabbed his thigh.

His pant leg was soaked, but the blood wasn't puddling on the floor. *Missed the big vein*, he thought. He pressed his fingers gingerly along his thigh, along the throbbing muscle, and came to a ragged hole in his pants near the hip. Busted good.

*Water. I need water.* He licked his lips. *Salty. Blood. Still-wet blood. Stop the blood. Stop. Stop it.* He moved his hand from his thigh slowly, slowly. In the top of his pocket. *Don't move the leg. Don't move it.* He pinched the corner of his handkerchief, sneaking it from the pocket as if stealing it from a dozing guard dog.

Darts of pain shot up and down his leg, firing into the flesh, beyond the flesh, firing into his mind. The guard dog's teeth slashed lines of pain up and down his body, until Cracker's clothes and skin hung in tatters and shreds, and his bones burst with red and black blood that spurted in fountains from the sharp and dreadful ends of the break in his leg.

And then a blanket of black soaked up the pain and closed off the room. In the dark blank he saw the Queen, and under her crown her face changed. His mother's face. Lehua's. Then the faces blended, so the Queen was all of them at once. He could feel them touching his face, blotting it with something soft, stroking his hair away from his forehead. Their fingers seemed like the tips of angel's wings.

He opened his eyes. Dark shapes moved dimly, and he concentrated to think of what they were. *Feet. Yes, feet. Feet with boots. But why would the Queen wear boots?*

"They'll be back," a man said. "Get him out of here. In the kitchen for now."

Hands and arms burrowed under him. And when they lifted, the pain seared again, bright and hot and sharp.

He squeezed his eyes shut and clenched his jaw and neck and swallowed a scream. In the trough between new waves of pain, he opened his eyes. This time the face he saw was real. *Kanaka Jack.*

\*\*\*\*\*

In the dark before dawn, Jack splinted the leg with the shafts of two canoe paddles, wrapped long rags around the leg and the splints until the whole thing was as thick and rigid as a mast. Another Hawaiian pumped a basin of water at the sink, then set it on the floor. Jack mopped the drying blood from Cracker's face. Two of the cuts reopened, and he bandaged them, winding strips of torn sheet around Cracker's head. Blood seeped through over the left eye.

"Easy now. Easy," he said to three Hawaiians ready to move Cracker onto a litter laid beside him on the floor. "Wait." Jack adjusted the makeshift stretcher, a blanket wound around two poles. He wanted to be sure Cracker's weight would keep the litter together. "Now."

As they lifted Cracker a few inches and moved him sideways, Jack heard a low groan and a stifled whimper. They settled Cracker on the blanket, and Jack knelt on the floor, cradled Cracker's head in one hand, and put a cup of water to his mouth. Some of the water dribbled down Cracker's chin.

"Jack," Cracker whispered.

"Don't talk. Save your strength. We're getting you out."

"The Queen's army..."

"A little setback. None of our men were killed. Our forces will regroup. Be ready when the Republic comes back. Now hush." He checked the litter, the bandage, the splints, his canteen on his belt, his binoculars, his pocket of cartridges.

"Ready." Jack and the other men squatted, two at each end of the litter.

"Hāpai!" They lifted in one smooth motion and moved through the kitchen door.

The litter carriers wended along the foot of Diamond Head. They would start with the rest of the army, then continue to the end of the crater, the most direct route back to Pālolo Valley. The other men from the canoe shed hurried past them, Winchesters in their hands, their bodies hung with cartridge belts. By the time the sky grew light, they had taken positions in ravines, looking down on the Bertelmann house.

"The buggahs never goin' come back," a soldier yawned.

"But if they do, we going pick 'em off. They going wave the white flag. We nevah even have to march."

And then a shower of dirt and rocks exploded on the ridge above the ravine, and from the sea came a loud *whump*!

"Set him down!" Jack ordered. He leaned on a rock to steady his binoculars. A tugboat lay offshore, just outside the reef. He couldn't make out exactly what field piece was mounted on the deck. Two gunners fired. Fired again. The slopes of Diamond Head rained sand and dirt and rocks.

Jack trained the glasses on Bertelmann's house. A formation of uniforms swarmed through the property. Not police. Militia. What they called the Citizens Guard, same bastards who backed the Committee of Safety. Hatred rumbled in Jack's gut.

Jack knew the leaders had taken every precaution against a tip-off, and yet something had clearly gone very wrong. He raised the glasses to look at the tug. Maybe the Hawaiians could do some damage before the field piece fired again.

Next to him two royalists crouched. They fired, and two Republic soldiers fell. Their comrades scurried for the house, the outbuildings, the canoe shed.

Jack dropped the binoculars around his neck. "Rifle!" he called to a shooter nearby. The man tossed the weapon and Jack caught it by the gun's forearm.

He reached down to pull Cracker's cap over the bandage to shield his face from flying dirt. Then he stood, laid the rifle stock against his cheek, fixed his sights against the Bertelmann house, and fired. Fired again. And again.

It looked to Jack that the Republic forces numbered perhaps a hundred. It would only be a matter of time before they positioned more field pieces to shell the slopes. The Hawaiians better make the best of the Winchesters now.

A shell from the tugboat burst twenty feet below Jack and two Hawaiians tumbled

down the slope. Jack dug his remaining cartridges from his pocket, reloaded, and fired.

He called to the other litter carriers shooting from behind a natural rock wall. "When you're out of rounds, we go."

He crouched next to Cracker and gave him more water.

Cracker swallowed. "You got 'em, Jack."

"Shh."

"You're a sharpshooter." Jack laid Cracker's head back down. "The Queen's sharpshooter."

*****

"Rest," Jack ordered. The men lowered Cracker's litter to the ground under a tree, his head near the trunk, his trussed leg stretched into the meager shadow of midday, looking like a piece of duffle. They found patches of shade themselves, lying on their backs and shielding their eyes with their hands.

Jack held the canteen to Cracker's crusted lips, moistened his handkerchief with a few drops of water, and sponged Cracker's face below the bandage, then wiped his own forehead with his sleeve. It seemed unduly hot for January.

With his eyes closed and his body still, Cracker looked to Jack like a little boy playing soldier. Sweat beaded on his upper lip, and the sheet bandage was bright with new blood. Beneath the makeshift vise locking Cracker's leg in place lay a wound Jack knew would change the rest of Cracker's life. A life that should be years, but might be a few days. Or a few hours.

Some justice. He signs up to fight for the Queen and he gets it going after kerosene for the lantern. Jack wearily leaned on his elbows, covering his face with his hands. Justice. Loyalty. Right. What did it come to?

Nothing much was going right just now. The Queen's forces probably were scuffling up the harsh ravines of Diamond Head under the shelling, to take better cover at the summit rim. And what of the other squads at the other posts? Had they marched on to the city? Had any Republic forces been dispatched to Hālawa?

Jack peered through his fingers. Cracker's freckles seemed especially prominent against his pale, drained face.

If the Bertelmann attack was a fluke, the Queen's forces could win. If not... Jack didn't want to think of it. Either way, Cracker lay here. For what? Jack knew the answer. And he knew that answer was the reason he loved his friend. To Cracker, life was simple and clear, people were good, worth his loyalty and effort. He trusted too much and questioned too little. And stood for what he believed.

*Don't die!* Jack almost spoke aloud. *Don't die, you freckle-faced ninny!* He touched his fingers to the stained bandage. His own eyes seemed to sweat, and he wiped at them with the back of his hands.

"Let's go," he said. "He's got to get to a doctor."

*****

Jack and the others toiled on, from shade to shade, arriving at the Pālolo house in midafternoon. As they carried Cracker up the steps, Jack heard horses coming fast. "In

here," he said to the men, and they ducked into the front room.

Jack stepped to the side of a window, peered cautiously around the edge, realized the laua'e baskets prevented someone outside from seeing in, and he took a longer look.

"They're our people," he said to his helpers. "Take him in the bedroom by the kitchen."

Uncle and Lehua hurried up the steps, and Jack saw Sammy leading the horses around the back. They wouldn't be expecting him. He stepped toward the door as they crossed the porch.

"It's me, Jack," he said, pushing the door open.

"We came back for some extra horses and provisions," Lehua said. "What are you doing here? What happened at Bertelmann's?"

"A rout."

"Auē." Uncle's voice sounded as if it came from a dark hole. "Where are the men? How many losses?"

"Up Diamond Head. No dead, some wounded. Cracker's the worst. He's in the bedroom. Got to have a doctor."

Uncle moved through the front room to the back of the house, Jack and Lehua crowding behind him. A good man to have in charge, Jack thought. A man who had counseled well before. Jack watched Uncle survey the tiny bedroom.

"Mahalo," Uncle said to the Hawaiians who had carried the litter. "Thank you. Go in the kitchen. Eat. Rest."

Uncle stood above Cracker's motionless form, the stretcher still under him, one of its poles hanging over the side of the narrow bed. Uncle moved slowly from Cracker's face to his feet, leaning to look. Lehua knelt next to Cracker's head, her fingers barely touching the lank hair lying over the dirty bandage. Her eyes followed Uncle.

Long minutes went by, silent, heavy minutes. Once Cracker sighed, a tiny, pitiful sound that, in the thick silence, filled the room to the rough board walls. Yet Uncle only stared. He's wasting time, Jack thought. Time that could mean the difference between life and death. And Lehua! Sitting there doing nothing when Cracker needed a doctor? His chest tightened, and he hoped Sammy hadn't unsaddled the horses. When he opened his mouth to interrupt the oppressive silence, Uncle spoke instead.

"Auē," he lamented again. "For us, and for our friend here, the haole boy with the good heart."

"Compound fracture." Jack faced the door, ready. "Where do I go for a doctor?"

"No. No doctor."

"He's going to die! He's got to have a doctor!" Jack's voice seemed to shake the little room.

Lehua put her hand on his arm. He shook it off. "Die! Because we didn't get him a doctor! We got him into this and it will be our fault! He doesn't deserve it!" The hysterical voice seemed to belong to someone else, but Jack felt his own arms flailing, and his hand stung when he struck the doorframe with his open palm. "Get him a doctor!" He wiped

the back of his smarting hand across his face, and he knew he was crying.

Hands were on him, soft hands, strong hands.

"The boy, he won't die." Uncle sounded again as if he were somewhere else. "But no doctor." Jack flinched against Uncle's grip on his arms. "He must have a kahuna."

*****

Lehua looked directly into Jack's face, where weariness and worry showed in his red-rimmed eyes.

"Sit," she said. "Sit by your friend, and I'll bring water to wash his face."

She hurried out back and found Sammy in the shed, coiling rope. "Cracker needs 'awa," she said in Hawaiian.

"Cracker? For a ceremony? In the middle of the war?"

"He's in the house. Shot in the head. Uncle has gone for a kahuna lapa'au. It'll be at least two hours before he gets back. Can you brew some 'awa? At least it will ease the pain."

"I can get some in Mānoa. Over the ridge. How bad is he?"

"I don't know. His leg is broken for sure." She blinked her eyes against welling tears. Under her hand Cracker's cheeks had flushed and burned. His eyelids had flickered, but the eyes themselves were rolled back, white and dead as boiled eggs.

Sammy moved closer to her. "Eh," he said. "What?"

"Jack thinks he might die." She closed her eyes and rested her forehead on Sammy's shoulder for a moment, then straightened herself. "Get the 'awa."

She returned to the room with a basin of water and kukui bark and ti leaves to make a poultice. Jack sat on the floor next to the bed, his arms folded along the edge of the mattress.

Lehua set her water bowl on the chair seat. "We'll clean the head wound," she said. "How did this not kill him?" She touched the bloody bandage over Cracker's eye.

Jack turned his face up, his brow furrowed. "It was glass," Jack said in a monotone. "Window glass. Not a shot."

Cracker turned his head on the pillow and a deep growl came through his closed lips.

Maybe Uncle should have gone for a haole doctor. And yet, she knew the haole doctors couldn't set bones any better, had nothing better than 'awa for pain, nothing more to help a healing wound than the poultices she'd known all her life.

"Help me," she said, unwinding the bandage from Cracker's head. Jack pushed himself slowly from the floor and took the wadded sheet she held out.

"Don't hurt him," Jack said. "He hurts enough already."

As she worked the torn sheet free, the dark blood stains grew brighter and bigger. Her nostrils flared with fear, yet she saw that the blood was dry, and she hoped. The last layers of bandage stuck to Cracker's forehead, and she sponged carefully, until she could

peel them slowly from his skin.

Cracker groaned again, and blew through his mouth. A few foul saliva bubbles burst on his lips.

"You're hurting him! Stop!" Jack pushed her sideways.

"I..." Lehua clamped her teeth together. She wanted to scream at Jack. Instead, she rinsed the sponging rag, wrung it nearly dry, and handed it to Jack. "There's one more spot."

She watched Jack dab at the last bit of bandage, then loosen it, his thick fingers working so delicately he might have been tying an ancient cloak one tiny feather at a time. Then he grasped the strip of sheet and lifted it from Cracker's face.

Lehua bit her lower lip and the taste of warm and salty blood filled her mouth. Blood, like the caked blood marbling Cracker's face. His left eye was swollen shut, purple and black as rotted fruit. A large, scalloped cut ran from the outside corner of the eye along his temple. A spot in the center of it opened, bright with new blood.

Jack rinsed the rag and pressed it on the reopened wound. "Wash the rest," he said. "I'm sorry I was sharp with you. He needs you as much as anybody."

She pounded the herbs to a mash, mixed them with a little poi, and anointed the wounds, careful to paint just along the edges of each cut. Jack lifted his cloth. Lehua traced the feathery gape of the big cut with her mixture.

"This one will scar," she said. "It will stay with him forever. Like your tattoo."

"What—" Jack began, but Cracker cried out, a sharp bark, and he tried to sit, but Jack forced him back against the bed. "He's bleeding again."

Lehua pressed a rag against the blood. Her hair fell over Cracker's chest. Cracker sighed, stretched his neck, and opened his eyes just long enough to speak a single word: *Mama.*

*****

To Cracker, his Mama had never looked more beautiful. He'd never noticed before that she had tea-colored eyes, that her black hair wisped around her face like a special dark halo.

If he watched her without blinking and never once glanced away, she would stay with him, he knew she would, he just knew it.

Concentrate. Concentrate. Don't blink. Don't think about anything, just Mama, Mama's beautiful face, don't think about the long pulsing ache down the side, don't think, don't think, the pain just wants you to look away and if you do, she'll be gone.

*Water, Mama,* he thought. He forced his eyes to stay open. *Please give me some water. Please.* She had taught him it was always best to say please. And she lifted his head and held a cup to his lips and he drank.

The water tasted like, like, like what? Like magic warm medicine that stayed in his mouth and oozed down his throat and rushed through his arms and his legs, his legs, legs, why did his leg hurt? And then the magic water came and it didn't hurt so much anymore. He tried to move the hurting leg and he saw that it wasn't a leg at all but a huge bundle of sticks and rags, and he couldn't lift it, and then he was mad, mad, mad, because the leg had made him look away, and Mama's face was gone.

But she had given him the water, and now the leg-bundle floated where he couldn't lift it and he thought he'd sleep and when he woke up later he'd look for Mama and she'd be there.

But when he woke up, there were lots of faces all around, stranger faces, dark, and they spoke and spoke but not in English, so he couldn't understand, but the sounds were soft in his ears and he looked and looked to find Mama and he called to her, *Mama!* and she came and he saw her face with the tea-colored eyes, and he tried to keep his eyes from blinking, but he must have blinked because then there were just men all around, Uncle and Jack and a man with a dark face in a white cloud.

He tried to call out. *Jack! Jack! Where were we Jack? Why did you carry me?* But when he did call out, he heard growling and groaning and crying, as if these sounds were supposed to be words.

And he looked and looked for Mama but instead darkness fell over him and the magic water drained away and his leg became light as a wisp but shot with pain, shot! shot! not shot! *Leave me alone!* he tried to cry, and the dark face in the white cloud breathed in his own face, and the cloud man held his leg and tore it apart and laid it back together and pain burned and raced, wild like a prairie fire, and the man wound the fire around around and around with fence posts and wire and slapped it with pig dung and rotten leaves and he tried to cry out, *I want my Mama!,* but all that came was the yelping shriek of a dog.

And then the man named Jack lifted his
head and put to his lips another drink of
magic water and it ran down through his
body, down, down, down all the way to the
leg, the enormous leg bound in wire and
posts, and the leg lay itself down to rest, and
the man named Uncle came up to the ear of
the man named Jack and said, *Go now, go
fast, they are after you.*

*Traffic Hour*

*Aī Kā Pāpio*

*And there she goes*

# kaleokealoha

Kathy Dee Kaleokealoha Kaloloahilani Banggo • Kathy Dee Kaleokealoha Kaloloahilani Banggo

I am Hawaiian/Filipino and was born and raised on the island of Oʻahu, Hawaiʻi. My mother's family originates from the North Shore (Haleʻiwa, Waialua, Waimea) of Oʻahu and the island of Molokaʻi. My father is from the Philippines.

I was raised in Hawaiian ways by my mother, from whom I have gained an understanding of and love for huna; a sprinkling of the language and metaphor; food; dance; haku mele; spiritual beliefs and more. I have some memories of my father, who passed away when I was seven years old. I mostly remember my parents together as "extremely passionate."

My Hawaiian grandmother and my father were close. They often talked to each other in Hawaiian and Filipino, and sometimes a strange mixture of both with standard and pidgin English thrown in. I thought "baño" (which is "bathroom" in Spanish and I'm not sure what dialect of Filipino) was English until I was in the third grade or so. I was at school and I told this teacher I had to go to the "baño" and she said, "What?" like I was crazy or something. So I said, "lua," and then I peed in my pants because I felt nervous and stupid about her not understanding me. She caught on when I wet my favorite royal blue May Day muʻumuʻu. By the time I got home I had it all figured out that our house was a mixture of different spoken languages and that we weren't supposed to understand any one of them thoroughly except for English, which we were to master as best we could. I really worked at it. I was a bookworm and extremely shy. At recess, I preferred the library. I dreamed a lot. I haven't stopped dreaming.

About the poems: The focus of these poems are movement and rhythm, the fluidity of loosely connected images that are not necessarily completely comprehensible. This is because I hope to engage the reader in that which is sensual. I also want to share my understanding of and experience with Hawaiian water—the surrounding Pacific, waves, streams, waterfalls, ponds, rain—as a source of sustenance and nurturing for body, mind, and spirit. My faith in water comes from teachings of my Hawaiian mum and her sisters; also learning to crab, fish, pick limu, swim, catch waves, heal sicknesses, nurture the body, grow things, etc., with water, sweet, salty, fresh water not bottled or sold.

# Traffic Hour

she stuck in that box of a room used to be her body. no alphabet. no dial tone. in late afternoon, the corner spaces deepen. used to take her dolls there. used to sit in mama's rocker. watch the paint stick to the walls. what grace.

out there, at every street corner light turned red for waiting she see them. woman come forth of the rib of somebody whose name she don't remember. woman carry baby low on the hip. woman return to the dirt and fallen rain.

now she a mud woman. once a mud child. came feet first from its cold weight. made dark cakes. topped off with stones. fistful of clover to taste. she call herself *starry-eyes-raised-up-from-the-mud.* a good name.

## Aī Kā Pāpio

How come you shake da leaf, Pāpio?
Az why da mynah fly away.

Bye-bye, black bird,
da maddah tell da faddah.

Bah-bye, Pāpio,
da faddah tell da son.

Aī kī you fullahs no shame?
Jus hemo da Pāpio.

Boy kā 'ono fo da milk an den
but Henehene she no mo;

aunty's nipples stay all raisin,
aunty's plumbing stay all broke.

Bumbye you spread your wings, Pāpio.
Bumbye 'ale kēlā mea.

'A'ole kenikeni.
'A'ole maka le'a.

"'Ale kēlā mea" is used mostly metaphorical-
ly by the kūpuna in my family, usually in a
teasing manner. "'Ale" is a shortened form
of "'a'ale" (a spoken form of "'a'ole").
"Kēlā" refers to the "thing" (mea)—one's
lover or sweetheart ("mea nui" or
"haumea") or to the lover's genitalia.
"Kēlā" also refers to panipani (intercourse).
The entire phrase refers to both the joy of
having the lover—for love and sex, which
is expressed by spoken teasing, facial
expressions, and gestures—as well as the
pain or loss caused by the absence of the
lover. "Bumbye you spread your wings,
Pāpio / Bumbye 'ale kēlā mea" shows the
kupuna teaching the child that his time will
come to leave. Just as his parents left him,
he will in turn leave his parents and a mea
or two. This loving and leaving is part of the
natural order and not to be feared, but
experienced.

## And there she goes

following you (again) up and down up and
down another muddy trail, barefoot and
afraid of falling, the wish list done up in the
head while the fingers cross:

you & her at the piano bench, your
fingers loose and flying, a cadence of kisses
softly counting octaves, 8—the lucky
number, up and down up and down, you
eat her out underwater, how tangible, like
midnight, a darkness of days and loving,
love, the smell of sex. Tangible, you bleed
her fruitful so some months later later she
hold her belly out to you round.

there he goes again, jazz boy grin, svelte
and always on key, this one takes his shoes
off, leave something behind so he come
back to her later, later, whistling, the notes
so pure, like rain, cool rain rap tap tapping
tin roof in Mānoa. They make love to the
sound, match rhythms, breathing stones and
fresh water.

He want to leave his old shoes with her
when he go. He come all the way from a
view of Harlem highrise in Manhattan, the
East River, only to leave a girl, say Honolulu
is a romantic city, all hips and sweet kisses,
'ahi poke, limu, wet trails and salt water.
Clean air and salt water. All of this. All
of this.

*I Never Knew*
*Where?*
*A Navigator's Purpose*

‘Auli‘i Ka‘ōnohiokalā George • ‘Auli‘i Ka‘ōnohiokalā George • ‘Auli‘i Ka‘ōnohiokalā George

My chief interest is in preserving the Hawaiian culture and its environment. I am now a freshman in Environmental Studies at Evergreen State College in Washington State. And at Kamehameha Schools I was privileged to participate in Hui Lama, the school's environmental club, which does service projects in the community, such as cleaning and restoring heiau. One summer, club members flew to Rapa Nui to plant seeds in a reforestation project.

As far as my poetry is concerned, I write when I'm really inspired. "I Never Knew" is about an imaginary person, but is based on my great-great grandmother Julia Hoa‘ai. She was born in Kohala and according to my grandmother was wonderfully wise and full of fun. Her favorite food was fish and poi. She ate with her fingers and could delicately strip with her teeth an entire baked fish—right down to its skeleton! In the poem, I try to imagine what it was like to be a Hawaiian in her day.

"Where" was inspired by Rapa Nui, so different from O‘ahu in its open space with the people living off the land and ocean.

"Hiwa" was inspired by a legend told by a native of Rapa Nui, saying we all are brothers and sisters. I also thought of Nainoa Thompson, Hawai‘i's foremost navigator, trying in his voyages to reunite us with the past and the native people of all Polynesia.

## I Never Knew

I dream the dream of my great grandmama...
Big brown eyes like a curly koa bowl
Long silvery Hawaiian hair like limu in the sea
Wrinkles like the ripples of the ocean current
Pink and red lush lips like a blooming 'ōhi'a
Nose like a kalo, round and perfect
Teeth white and strong from biting coconut husk
Arms tan and built from pounding kapa
Legs like a warrior, old yet strong
Feet, wide and delicate, move to the hula
I dream the dream of my grandmama...
The one I never knew.

## Where?

Large buildings, Where's the ocean?
Electric lights, Where's the stars?
Pollution, Where's the clean waters?
Alienation, Where's the native birds?
Tourists, Where's Waikīkī?
Hawai'i in 2004, Where's the HAWAIIANS?

## A Navigator's Purpose

Hiwa was born
Hiwa was broken
Hiwa is Polynesia
Hawai'i, Tahiti, Rapa Nui
Constellations
Humu, Keoe, Pira'etea
Going back to Hiwa
Part of our culture
Reunite with the past
Brothers and sisters of...
HIWA

# *piilani*

Patricia Piilani Ono Nakama • Patricia Piilani Ono Nakama • Patricia Piilani Ono Nakama

Piilani pauses for a moment with Grandpa Paleka and Grandma Keahi in 1951

The school bell sounded. It was the end of the first period at Waimea High School. As a 14-year-old freshman student, I was part of the shy minority among the hundreds of older students.

I squeezed my armful of books as I walked through the throng of talking and laughing students in the dimly lit hallway of the administration building. Lockers banging shut were part of the familiar sounds in our school community during the morning recess. I had a few more minutes to get to class, but it didn't slow my determined walk to get there as soon as possible. The classroom was my haven of safety.

As I approached Mrs. Doris Crowell's English class, I noticed a large group of older boys, the football players, hanging out near the lockers on the lānai. I had to pass them to get to my English class, which was at the Kekaha end of the building. I felt a moment's hesitation and fear. Those boys are so huge, I thought. My 110-pound frame could easily be overcome by one of them. As my steps took me past the football players, I heard one of them say, "Ey! She's n-i-c-e. Okay, you guys, she's mine." Then, out from the mass, a short, dark-complexioned, local boy emerged. He wanted to know my name.

Almost simultaneously, a tall, lanky older boy from the back of the group commanded. "Hey! Leave her alone. She's Paleka Ono's girl."

I saw the hesitation as the short stranger looked at me, then turned with a questioning look on his face towards his football brother. "What?" he asked.

"She's off limits, brah. No lies. Unless you want to end up in jail. Nobody fools with her and gets away with it. She's Paleka's grand-daughter, the policeman from Kekaha."

I looked at the tall lad who had come to my rescue only long enough to imprint his face in my mind. Then I quickly turned and continued on my way to class. A feeling of relief and gratitude swept over me as I thought about Tūtū. Once again, his protective reputation had saved me from an embarrassing situation.

My grandfather, Paleka Ono (nui), was my hero since childhood. He helped parents teach their children to walk the law-abiding path. Tūtū was known in Waimea Precinct on the island of Kaua'i as the Sherlock Holmes of his day. He managed to solve all the cases that he was asked to look into by the Chief of Police. He was the first officer to use white gloves for directing traffic at night on Kaua'i in the

1940s. He was called upon by parents who needed help in disciplining their children. He became a friend to teenagers who hung out at Long's Pool Hall in Kekaha, and he coached baseball and basketball teams after school. He counseled the teens he caught playing hooky from school. After the long talks with truant youths, he found that very few of them skipped school anymore for a day at the beach.

He was called upon many times to act as translator between the Hawaiian, Japanese, and Filipino plantation workers of Kekaha Sugar Mill Company. He made it his business to get to know the newcomers to the plantation town he lived in. They in turn would call on him for advice on filling out applications, buying property, getting permission to bring wife or family to Kaua'i, applying for a job, etc.

Tūtū was a priest in the Kekaha Mormon Church, but he quit that position and going to church when a visiting priest from Utah told the congregation that Negroes would not be accepted into heaven. Tūtū told me that if Negroes weren't accepted, what made him think he would be since he was so dark complexioned. About ten years later, and three months before he died, Tūtū was "born again" in the Pentescostal Church.

My grandfather inherited kuleana land acquired during the Great Mahele, upon which he built four homes. When my father was 20 years old, together he and my grandfather built a skating rink, invested in 200 pairs of metal skates, and opened a skating rink. (This is where my parents met.) Several years later, the two men built the Bamboo Restaurant that served lunch to tourists on their way to Kalalau Lookout and Waimea Canyon. In the 1940s, my grandfather used his financial wisdom to buy several pieces of property in Kōke'e (a mountain cabin), Waimea Valley, Kekaha Beach Lots, and Hanapēpē Heights Subdivision.

My grandfather once said, "As Hawaiians, we must be very cautious. We should never sell our land. The white men are smart. They know the value of land. I can remember when the white men came knocking on our doors, offering to let us live in our house until we died and promising us free food and clothes for the rest of our lives if we gave them our land deeds and allowed them to plant cane on our land. Some of the lazy Hawaiians agreed because they didn't want to work hard."

Shaking his head sadly, he went on. "That was the beginning of the pilikia [trouble] that the Hawaiians face today. When the father and mother of the homes that made this kind of agreement died, the white men who had the land deeds kicked the keiki [children] and mo'opuna [grandchildren] out of the house. The children had to live with their aunties and uncles because they no longer owned the land.

"That is how the Robinsons in Makaweli got some of their land. The Hawaiians who wouldn't give up their deeds, like us, were surrounded and trapped because the white men planted cane all around our plots of land. Then they refused to give us the right of way to build a road to our land. After a few years, the land was absorbed into the plantation fields. Now, we still pay taxes on land that Robinsons plant cane on. And I will not stop paying the taxes, because that is the only way I can say I own that plot of ground.

"Piilani, someday you become educated and fight for the land that is ours. My great-grand-father, Pikinene, owned a whole valley in Makaweli. His name is on the old maps. Someday, you get it back."

Near the end of my freshman year in high school, Tūtū died of a heart attack. He lived from May 1888 to May 1956, sixty-eight years.

I kept a promise I had made to myself and worked my way through college. I graduated from Southern California College in 1966 and received a B.A. degree in English Literature and Elementary Education. I met my husband in 1971 while teaching on Kaua'i. We were married two years later. In 1984, I received my Professional Degree in Secondary Education from Chaminade University.

I now teach Secondary English at Farrington High School. The tall lad who had come to my rescue in the ninth grade is now my brother-in-law, William "Longy" Gonsalves. Longy is also the son of Manuel Gonsalves in "Scarred for Life."

For years, my grandfather shared stories of his experiences as a Hawaiian and a policeman. He asked me to write these stories so people would remember.

## Stolen Lands and Other Stories of Paleka Ono (nui)

### Stolen Lands

Tūtū Paleka Ono (nui) was my hero since childhood. It was an exciting trip accompanying him to town to run an errand, or just to buy a snail pastry for four cents from Nitta Store. I would stand nearby on a store porch and listen to his conversations with a store manager, or a plantation luna, or an unmarried Filipino plantation worker who wanted a wife.

One day, I noticed the fear on the face of a teenage boy when he saw Tūtū standing on the front porch of Kuramoto Store. He quickly hid behind his father, who smiled and greeted Tūtū cordially as they walked into the store. I looked at my grandfather's dark brown, lined face. Why would anyone be afraid of him? I wondered. He was so gentle and caring. Even though he was retired from the police force, he still protected me and the people of our town. He would never hurt anyone. Maybe he was mean and ugly looking to that boy. I shook the thoughts from my head as Tūtū Paleka indicated he was ready to leave and led the way back to our 1948 Buick Sedan.

Tūtū didn't turn homeward that day. Instead, we headed for Waimea, which was three miles away and the last town tourists passed through en route to Waimea Canyon and Kalalau Lookout. The Waimea Police Station was a rectangular wooden building with an A-shape roofline located at the southwestern corner of Waimea High and Elementary Schools campus, facing the main road through town. After parking his car in the almost empty, unpaved parking area next to the station, he opened the passenger side door and quietly said, "Come." I followed him up four wooden steps onto the porch, then past a counter facing the doorway, through the two bar-type swinging doors, and into a large room with several metal desks, file cabinets, and three doors leading into two small offices and a large back room. A policeman was seated at a desk with several manila folders, working on papers. He stood when my grandfather introduced me to him. "This is my granddaughter, Piilani." Then, after a pause, he continued, "Piilani, this is Sgt. Buddy."

The sergeant had a big smile on his face as he reached out to shake my hand. I didn't understand his gesture, and quickly looked up at Tūtū Paleka's face to find out if Tūtū approved of this man touching me. His eyes and the slight nod of his head told me it was okay. I shyly allowed this friendly stranger to give me a first-hand lesson on how to grasp a person's hand and give a "firm" handshake. I noticed that his hands were large and soft, not tough-skinned like Tūtū's hands.

After the hand-shaking lesson, Tūtū showed me around. He pointed out that one of the two small rooms was the Chief of Police's office. Then he led the way to the back of the office into a storage room, which was about the same size as the first one. Inside, there were file cabinets and books, and near the middle of the room were large sets of hanging blueprint maps of the Hawaiian Islands next to a brown varnished counter similar to the one at the front of the station facing the doorway. Tūtū pulled out a set of maps and placed them on the countertop. After pointing out the names and the numbers on the maps, he told me why he had brought me here.

"Two weeks ago," he said, "I was looking through these maps of Kaua'i and noticed that my great-grandfather's name—*Pikinene*—was written on Makaweli Valley. My father told me that during the Great Mahele, Pikinene claimed the land we are now living on in Kekaha and Makaweli Valley, where he raised his herds of cows and a few horses. He said he hid the deeds while he was living in the house that Levi rents from us now for $25 per month. We have never been able to claim the land because of the lost deed. When I saw his name on the map, I knew I had proof that my great-grandfather owned it. I was so excited. I showed it to the Chief, who was in his office. I considered him my friend. I knew I couldn't take the map with me because it was county property, but I figured with the Chief's help I would be able to get a copy and make a claim. Two days later, I came to work and looked it up again. The map was gone. I looked everywhere, through all the other maps in the room, but it was gone. I asked the Chief about it, and he said, 'It should be there.'

"I left the station very upset that day. During the following days, I recalled all the details of this incident and I figured out what had happened to the map.

"I know the Chief *ho'omalimali*s people like the Robinsons. Right now, our valley is in the middle of a field that the Robinsons are planting cane on. I think the Chief called the Robinsons and told them what I found. I think he took the map out of the set and destroyed it or gave it to the Robinsons. I went to the Līhu'e County office to look for it; but, no, it wasn't there either. I tell you all this, because someday you can go to college and learn how to fight for the land that is rightfully ours."

## The Jailhouse Experience

We walked back to Tūtū Paleka's car, which was parked in the grassless large open area between the station and a long, skinny wooden structure built on the back edge of the property.

"What's that?" I asked, pointing to the wooden structure with eight to ten wooden doors with metal padlocks facing us. The long, dilapidated building stretched almost the full width of the mauka property line. It was about six-feet wide, with a corrugated iron roof.

"This is our jailhouse," Tūtū Paleka answered as he unhooked one of the padlocks. "We used to have 16 cells, but the termites ate the wood of the other building, so this is what is left." Swinging the door open, he allowed me to step into one of them.

A putrid smell hit my nose and darkness overwhelmed me. I stepped back out. After a few seconds, my eyes became accustomed to the small room and my curiosity drew me back in. The noon sun shone through the doorway. The smell faded as the Waimea Valley breeze blew in through the open doorway. I noticed there were no windows, and a wide wooden shelf was built on the left wall of the jail. On it was a dusty old mattress with several torn holes on its outer edge. Straw, like the ones on the broom we used to sweep our wooden floor at home, was sticking out of the dusty, torn cotton mattress cover. The faded gray design was covered with stains, dust, and dirt marks. I put my fingers on it and felt the hard, lumpy texture. This is a hard bed to sleep on, I thought.

"That's the toilet," my grandfather said, pointing to a gallon tin can half filled with sand.

"They have to use that to make shi-shi?" I asked.

"Yes. Remember," he said, "the men and one or two women who were locked up in one of these jailhouses were here for one or two days."

"What was the longest time someone stayed here?"

"I think it was about four days," he replied. "Most of them were transferred to the jail in Līhu'e before that. This is just a temporary place for us to keep prisoners while we investigate their cases."

"Tūtū, close the door. I want to see how dark it is." Tūtū obliged me by pulling the door shut with a rope looped through two holes in the wooden door.

The unfamiliar darkness gripped me with a moment of fear. It was like midnight with no moon or stars shining on my familiar blue-black night world at home. Then my accustomed-to-the-dark eyes saw the bright sunlit, threadlike lines shining between the ten-foot wooden planks that made up the back wall of the cell. A few pinholes of light shone in an irregular pattern through the corrugated iron ceiling. None of them were large enough to allow me to see my hand in front of my face. I leaned back to feel the comfort of my grandfather's presence. "Okay, Tūtū," I whispered. "Open the door."

The door swung open and the darkness disappeared as the streaming sunlight shone on the dirt floor of the jailhouse. Relief swept over me. The dark world of a jailhouse would never be my fate, I thought. I'm never going to break a law that will put me there. Thus, my morals were being

cemented into my being as I learned of the real-world consequences of breaking the law.

**The Ungrateful Pig Farmer's Son**

The "jailhouse experience" added meaning and understanding to my mind when Tūtū Paleka told me the story of one of the boys who lived in our neighborhood.

Taka Arashiro, a pig farmer, who lived at the west end of our neighborhood, came walking along the side of the two-lane Kekaha Road, which ran through Hawaiian Camp. He walked into our dirt driveway and greeted Tūtū. I watched him as I sat under one of the mango trees, playing with my favorite baby doll. Tūtū stopped hoeing the weeds from the inner edge of the stone wall separating Kekaha Road and our yard and they shook hands, exchanging the smiles and greetings of old friends. Then I saw a frown on Mr. Arashiro's forehead. I couldn't hear his conversation with Tūtū, but it was a serious concern. After a while, he smiled and thanked Tūtū. They shook hands again and Mr. Arashiro walked back up the road toward his farm. I wondered why he was walking instead of using his white pickup truck. Tūtū must have helped him somehow, I thought. At least he's not mad anymore.

After hoeing up the weeds for a short while, Tūtū put away the tool in the garage and went into the house. A few minutes later, I decided to follow him, since there was no one to play with. As I entered the front door to the living room, I saw that Tūtū was almost fully dressed in his police uniform. "Where are you going, Tūtū?" I asked, confused that he was wearing his uniform on his day off.

"I have work to do," he answered. I knew that whatever the problem was, I would have to wait until he came home to hear about it. I followed him out the door and stood on the porch, watching him drive out and turn northwest. That's not the direction of the police station, I thought. Maybe he's going to help Mr. Arashiro with the problem.

Late that afternoon, Tūtū came home with a big smile on his face. I overheard him talking with Mama about Mr. Arashiro's son. After many days, Tūtū told me the story:

Toshi was one of seven children in Taka Arashiro's family. The older children were taught early to help on the pig farm, for there was a lot of work to be done. But Toshi, the baby of Taka's family, was over-looked when assignments of work were handed out. He was not noticed until Mr. Arashiro's two oldest children were married and moved into their own homes. Now Toshi was 12 years old and capable of helping out on the farm. But Toshi had other interests. He was part of a group of neighborhood boys that he went to school with. They played baseball, went fishing or swimming, or just hung out at Long's Pool Hall. He got home after dark when all the work on the farm was done. At five in the morning, he was too tired to get up and help with the early morning chore of picking up slop from neighbors who had set aside leftovers that Mr. Arashiro boiled in 100-gallon drums for eight hours or more.

One day, a neighbor told Mr. Arashiro that his son and some other boys had stolen man-goes from his orchard. Mr. Arashiro decided that his policeman friend, Paleka, might be able to talk some sense into his stubborn son's head. How many times had he warned his son, "The jailhouse is where bad boys go"? Now he had to take action. A visit to Paleka's house and a handshake sealed the agreement that Paleka could do whatever he saw fit to teach Toshi a lesson about respecting his parents' and other people's property.

An hour later, Paleka drove into the Arashiro's driveway and announced he had come for Toshi Arashiro. Toshi went meekly with this tall, dark policeman because his father said he had to. From the front seat of the policeman's car, he glanced up at his mother's sad face. She wiped her eyes with a towel she held in the hand that was holding the kitchen screen door half open. His moth-er's face made him want to cry. Suddenly he regretted all the times he had argued with her. He remembered the many quiet, but urgent, talks she had with him about help-ing his father on the farm, and growing up to be a good man. He realized now he was going to jail for stealing mangoes from Mr. Lee's orchard, and that he might not see his mother for a long, long time.

Policeman Paleka was quiet as they drove onto Kekaha Beach Road and turned east toward Waimea town. Toshi waited for this policeman to yell and call him a thief. But, instead, he began to tell Toshi about his hard-working grandfather who had come from Okinawa so his children would have a better life. He heard how his grandfather ate only potatoes for his three daily meals in Okinawa, and how he never ate potatoes while he lived in Hawai'i. At 17, he came to Hawai'i to work for Kekaha Sugar Plantation. He worked hard and, after many years, he had enough money in the "Tanimoshi" saving system to start a pig farm. Toshi's father helped Grandpa Arashiro on the farm from the time he was a young boy. He saw tough times when all the pigs died of cholera and Grandpa Arashiro had to borrow money from his friends to buy more piglets. Toshi's father dreamed of his sons growing up and going to college and becoming a store manager or bank manager or working for a big company in Honolulu. But, no, Toshi had chosen to steal. Now he had to pay the consequences and go to jail, maybe for a long time.

The policeman turned into a driveway behind a big building. Paleka got out of his car, walked around it, and opened the car door for Toshi. Then he led Toshi to a long wooden building nearby that had many wooden doors. He flipped the padlock on one of the doors and pulled it open. Toshi faced a small room with a dirt floor that smelled like an outhouse. The policeman made him sit on the old mattress that was only wide enough for one person to lie on, and said, "You stay here." Then the door closed and darkness invaded his world.

After waiting for a long time, Toshi's imagination created fearsome creatures in the dark with him. "Help! Get me outta here!" Toshi screamed.

Sgt. Buddy looked at Paleka, who sat on the wooden armchair in front of him. The officers exchanged knowing looks that the next few hours would be filled with heart-rending cries, pleas, words of repentance, calls for mama or some loved one in the family.

The sergeant had seen Tūtū lock teenage boys in the jail before. This Hawaiian old-timer had succeeded in turning around the lives of some of the worst kids in their towns. Most of them now worked in the community and taught their children the lessons on respect and hard work they had learned from him.

When silence returned, both men knew that the dark jail had taught another teenager the pain and fear of being cut off from society.

After another hour or so of silence, Paleka opened the jailhouse door. He led the worn-out youth to an outdoor porcelain sink next to the men's restroom. He allowed him to wash his face and drink some water. Then Paleka took the boy into the police station for booking and fingerprinting. Another police officer told the youth that he would be given "one more chance" to do things right. In Toshi's case, he had to apologize and work for Mr. Lee to pay for the mangoes he stole. He was warned that if he was ever caught breaking any law, he would end up in jail again, but the next time the policeman would "throw away the key."

Tūtū Paleka's smile, as he ended his story, made me wonder if he really meant what he said. "What about Mr. Arashiro, Tūtū? Has he talked to you about his son?"

"Yes. He is so amazed at the change in his son's behavior. He is a good boy and a hard-working son now."

In December of that year, Mr. Arashiro gave Tūtū a pig for Christmas, with another warm handshake and the words, "Thank you for changing my boy."

**Scarred for Life**

I loved following my grandfather around our plantation town of Kekaha. Everyone, the men folks especially, seemed to know him and greeted him whenever we went to the post office or Kekaha Store or the park, where he loved to sit and watch the young guys play baseball. He was a tall, very dark, and slender man and I knew in my heart he would never let anything bad happen to me. I can recall, when I was about ten years old, how Mama, Tūtū, and I used to sit down for dinner each evening at the rectangular table in the kitchen covered with a red-and-white checkered vinyl tablecloth. I would sit facing Tūtū, while Mama sat on the mauka (mountain) side of the table, next to the kerosene stove. Our daily diet was made up of fish and poi for lunch; and eggs, beef, or pork with rice for dinner. We had a garden of lettuce, beets, beans, mangoes, papayas, and corn that supplemented our meals—depending on what was full-grown and in season.

Each evening, Tūtū would finish his meal, pick up a toothpick, and lean back in his chair. I knew I would be hearing a story of his days as a young cowboy on the Knudsen Ranch or of his hunting trips with his friends into the Kōke'e Mountains, or of one of his experiences as a young policeman on the Kaua'i County force. That night it was about the scar he had on the left side of his face.

One Saturday afternoon when Tūtū was off duty, a call came over the car radio for help from officers in the Kekaha vicinity. A Filipino man was chasing another man with a cane knife. Almost a half-hour later, our home phone rang. It was the Waimea Police Station. None of the other officers had been able to disarm the angry man with the cane knife. Did Paleka think he could do something about this?

Grumbling under his breath about being called on duty on his day off, Tūtū buckled his gun belt and drove about three blocks to the back road of the St. Theresa Catholic School campus. As he drove slowly towards the school, he saw a small Filipino man walking on the side of the road. Two policemen stood talking on the other side of the

road. Tūtū parked his car a short distance from the officers.

"What's going on?" he asked them.

"He's crazy, he's drunk, and we can't speak Filipino," said Officer Aipolani. "I tried to talk him into putting the cane knife down, and he chased me with it. Good thing he's drunk. He can't run too fast and straight."

Tūtū nodded his head. He had befriended many of the plantation workers, but this was a new arrival. He didn't know this man. He decided that a gun belt was not the thing to be wearing if he were to approach the man, so Tūtū unbuckled his belt and left it on the front seat of his black jalopy.

"Hey, manong!" he called as he tried to catch up with the man. "What happened?"

Just as he caught up with him, the man turned and glared at him like an angry bull ready to charge. All the words in the world did not seem to penetrate those angry eyes. Without warning, he ran towards Tūtū, holding his cane knife high over his head. He swung it, and Tūtū raised his left hand to block his face. Too late! Blood spurted all over the place as the cane knife found its mark, slashing Tūtū's left cheek and his left hand. Utilizing his judo training, Tūtū caught hold of the man with his right hand and threw him onto the ground. The other officers held the man down and handcuffed him. Bleeding profusely, Tūtū ran into the closest plantation cottage, the home of Manuel Gonsalves. Backup and the hospital was called. After tying a tourniquet around the bleeding arm, Mr. Gonsalves rushed Tūtū to Waimea Veterans Hospital.

Tūtū ended up with a four-inch scar on his left cheek and a slanted scar on the edge of his palm and little finger that doesn't bend anymore. All because of a gambling game, liquor, and a fight between two single plantation workers.

**The End of the 'Ohana Era**

It was a quiet Saturday afternoon on the west Kaua'i town of Kekaha. Tūtū Paleka raked the mango tree leaves into a pile next to his 35-year-old home. The sun had begun its travel into the western skies over the Pacific. All seemed so peaceful, until—

"Paleka! Paleka! Hūūūi!!" Walking around the side of his home, Tūtū saw his good friend Joe Kiluano from across the street. The young man had a look of urgency. When Joe saw Tūtū, he paused and nodded a greeting of respect, then walked over to Tūtū.

As a policeman, Tūtū was always called on to take care of the most dangerous situations. On his left cheek and left hand, he wore the scars of the cane knife swung at him by an angry Filipino plantation worker whom no one had dared to stop. The younger police officers were not so brave or willing to be heroes. That was over ten years ago. Since Tūtū had retired, there were very few dangerous situations to face. Now he smiled. "Joe! Pehea 'oe? (How are you?)"

"Maika'i nō (I am fine)... But your horse is not... Someone shot your horse..."

"Whitey shot? No..." His voice trailed into nothingness. Who would want to shoot his horse? The horse was tame and not a danger to anyone. He had been loosely tied to a tree in the kiawe tree grove next to Kekaha Baseball Park, and he was trained to avoid people.

Whitey was his pride and joy. He had bought the colt from Mr. Knudsen of Grove Farm, a former employer. Tūtū loved animals. He could sense their fears, uncertainty, and stubbornness about being tamed. While working on the farm as a cowboy, he had learned to tame the horses brought to the farm for Mr. Knudsen. Then he heard about a new police station opening up in Waimea, three miles from Kekaha, where he grew up.

Tūtū Paleka patrolling Kekaha Park during a baseball game

Recruitment ads had appeared in the *Garden Island* newspaper. If he got a job as a policeman, it would mean he would be working for the City and County of Kaua'i. It would mean security and retirement when he was old. He went for it. His application was processed and he passed the tests.

Tūtū's mode of transportation in those days was a horse. He had not yet been able to afford the Ford jalopies that Mr. Knudsen owned. His Brownie had been getting old. She needed to pasture instead of going to work with him every day. He needed a colt that he could train to do what he wanted it to do.

Whitey had been born several weeks before Tūtū started working as a policeman. He had helped the colt through the birth canal; otherwise the mother and baby would have died, since breach births are not usually successful. Mr. Knudsen offered to sell Whitey to him because the colt was unusually small and weak, and he felt he had more horses than he needed. So Whitey became Tūtū's. The extra care he gave the colt bonded them, and soon the colt was neighing and pricking up his ears every time Tūtū came into sight.

When Whitey was nine months old, Tūtū knew it was time to "break him in." A blanket was the first object tied to Whitey's back. Then came a saddle. Whitey's trust in Tūtū made him a fast learner. It didn't take long before they were taking long rides into other towns and hunting in Kōke'e Mountain.

Tūtū brushed Whitey's coat almost daily, talking to Whitey about his day's activities. Whitey would stand very still and look at Tūtū with big brown eyes that understood his master's affection for him. After a brisk brushing, when Tūtū turned to put the grooming brushes away, Whitey would nudge him with his nose, as if to say, "Let's play."

Tūtū taught Whitey to do tricks. He would say, "Whitey, this is Piilani," and Tūtū would bow to me. Whitey mimicked Tūtū by lowering his head in a deep bow, which surprised me the first time he did that.

Then Tūtū tapped Whitey under his left leg pit saying, "Can you count to three, Whitey?" The white horse lowered and raised his head with a snort, and tapped his hoof on the ground three times. "Good boy, Whitey!" Tūtū would pat Whitey on his back with long strokes or give him a treat.

"Can you count to six?" he would ask, tapping Whitey under his left leg pit twice. Again Whitey would raise and lower his head and tap his hoof on the ground six times.

The play-acting would go on between Tūtū and Whitey as the white horse learned to roll over, play dead, say hello, walk on two legs, and turn on a water faucet to fill a bowl with water, which he had placed under it himself.

Everyone in the neighborhood knew of Tūtū's talented horse. At a Fourth of July celebration in Kekaha Park, Tūtū and Whitey performed in a local talent show, delighting the youthful crowd and winning the respect of the Japanese and Filipino plantation workers, as well as the older crowd of Hawaiian grandmas and grandpas.

The tall buffalo grass and sweet kiawe beans in Tūtū's yard were a part of Whitey's daily diet. During the summer, hundreds of ripe mangoes and guavas lay on the ground waiting to be picked. Whitey was usually the first one up each morning, and we would find him standing under one of the trees munching on a ripe fallen mango, with a stripped mango seed or two lying at his feet. In the evening, Tūtū would release Whitey to run free on the canefield roads nearby.

I remember a time that a call came to Tūtū from Police Chief George Crowell himself. A complaint had been called in because Whitey had gone into a neighbor's property and turned on the faucet to drink water. The problem was that Whitey hadn't turned off the faucet. He knew how, but after having his thirst satisfied, Whitey seldom remembered to turn off the faucet unless Tūtū was nearby to remind him. It was this problem that had angered a neighbor who lived next to the kiawe tree grove near Kekaha Park.

A couple of teenage boys were in the park playing ball when the shot rang out. They turned in the direction of the sound and saw Whitey fall down on the narrow dusty road near an open water faucet.

When I got to the park with Tūtū, Whitey was standing in the middle of the kiawe tree grove. His ears perked up and he turned to welcome us. He looked fine, except for a slightly lifted foot. He had been shot in the front leg and a bone was shattered.

A veterinarian was called, and he looked Whitey over carefully before pronouncing his verdict. "He must be put to sleep," he said. "A horse sleeps standing. He is in pain and the leg will never heal if he continues to use it."

"No! No! No!" I cried in protest. My grandfather stood silently next to Whitey, his eyes downcast. "Why can't we just try to give Whitey's leg time to heal? Please, Tūtū!" I kept begging, until I was taken home, protesting and mourning a verdict that my child's mind could not accept.

At home, Tūtū sadly shook his head. Stories of his days as a cowboy flashed through my mind. I remember the time he had to shoot one of Mr. Knudsen's horses when it stepped into a pothole and broke its leg. Now a man had shot Whitey because Whitey was on "private property."

"The law has changed," Tūtū reasoned with me. "Once upon a time, horses, cows, chickens, and all our animals were not caged. They were free and all the neighbors knew which livestock was theirs. At feeding time, our chickens and animals came home and were waiting for us to feed them. If one of Kawika's hens ate at our house, it was okay. I am sure some of my chickens ate at his place sometimes. If it bothered me because his hens began to make it a habit, I would chase them away and block the way back to our feeding ground. Eventually, the hens would catch on and go home.

"Your great-great-grandfather Pikinene claimed this land under the Great Mahele, when the King signed it over to him for $10. The Great Mahele was good for us as landowners, and now we have to respect each other's property rights. I know who shot Whitey, but I cannot do anything about it because the law is on his side. Maybe I shouldn't have taught Whitey how to turn a faucet on…" he paused. A sad look was on his face. Then he said. "No, I taught Whitey how to do that after he pawed the front lawn faucet one day and broke it because he was thirsty."

I stared at Tūtū's brown creased face. The wisdom and respect he felt for the law he defended as a policeman exuded from him to me. "With privileges come responsibility," he reasoned sadly with a final note in his voice that I knew meant "This subject is closed."

Forty-eight years have passed since this incident. Time has changed the face of the land and the people who live on it, but many laws remain the same. I am grateful for wise ancestors who claimed the land and passed it on to their keiki and mo'opuna. Through income derived from enterprises on the land we inherited, I was able to pay for my children's private school education. Maybe one day one of my grandchildren or great-grandchildren will find a new way to work the land to benefit his or her descendants.

NOTE: WITH THE EXCEPTION OF FAMILY MEMBERS, ALL OTHER NAMES HAVE BEEN CHANGED.

# Tūtū
## (He Hoʻouēuē no Keola)

# mikiʻala
Mikiʻala Ayau • Mikiʻala Ayau • Mikiʻala Ayau • Mikiʻala Ayau • Mikiʻala Ayau

E ke Akua, nā kūpuna, nā ʻaumākua, nā hoa aloha a me koʻu ʻohana pili mau i kuʻu poli, he aloha nō. This hoʻouēuē is an excerpt from a hana keaka entitled ʻĀkia, winner of the 1998 Kumu Kahua Theatre/University of Hawaiʻi at Mānoa Playwright Competition, Pacific Rim Division. ʻĀkia was written by a dear friend, Kimo Armitage, who gave me the privilege of composing this portion of the play. I am very proud of Kimo's own accomplishments in the Hawaiian language, a no laila, nāu kēia makana, e kuʻu pōkiʻi.

In ʻĀkia, Keola was always Tūtūʻs ukali, the one who was there by her side, to listen, absorb, and appreciate. Keola was the punahele. But he was also the one who was puni by all the other tūtū in the other realm, and when they beckoned him, he went bravely, knowing what was waiting on the other side.

This is dedicated to all my tūtū, especially Ahiona, Kamohoaliʻi, Haleaniani, and Kaleialohaokalāhui. Also to my dear friends who have departed suddenly, Jared Elia and Jason Keo, and every person who left this world bravely to fulfill the master plan God has laid out for us. E moe iho ʻoe, e moe mālie. Sleep in peace, but know that your ʻohana has never forgotten you.

He pua kukui ʻo Mikiʻala Ayau ma ka lei hiwahiwa o Lanikāula. Mahalo aku ʻo ia i kona mau kumu a pau, kona ʻohana, ka Hui Nunui, Keliʻionāpua a me tona mau tamariki, ʻo KūkahiaKeliʻi me Tamaʻāina.

## Tūtū
### (He Hoʻouēuē no Keola)

E aloha e kuʻu pua ē, e kuʻu kama,
Kuʻu pua, kuʻu moʻopuna ē.
He pua makamae no Hawaiʻi nei.
He pua hiwahiwa, pua onaona ē.
Pua i ka lei mae ʻole.
Pua o nēia ʻāina hānau.
Hānau ʻia e ke aloha, lua ʻole.
Hānai ʻia me ke aloha, ke aloha pau ʻole.

Auē! Mehameha kuʻu poli i kou hele ʻana.
Auē! Mehameha kuʻu naʻau i kou hala ʻana.
E kuʻu pua ē, e kuʻu pua ē...

Ma Haleʻiwa, ma kāu lua heʻe punahele,
Kahi āu i kiʻi ai i ka ʻai kamahaʻo na kou
  ʻohana,
Kēlā lua, piha i nā ʻawe lālau wale.
Auē! Heheʻe akula nō, lālau ʻia ē!

Ma Kāneʻohe mili ʻia e ka ua ʻĀpuakea.
Kahi āu i hahai ai i nā puaʻa ʻāhiu!
Kēlā ʻāina kuauli, ka nāhelehele lālau wale.
Auē! Hele akula nō, lālau ʻia ē!

Aloha ē, kuʻu pua ē, aloha ē!
E hoʻi i ka poli o Milu.
Ua māmā kou kaumaha!
E moe, e moe, e moe mālie ʻoe...

Love to my beloved, my dearest child,
Beloved, dearest grandchild.
Precious flower of Hawaiʻi.
Cherished flower, fragrant flower.
Flower in a never-fading lei.
Flower of thy birthland.
Born from love, unequaled.
Raised with love, love never-ending.

Alas! My arms are empty because you left.
Alas! I am alone to my very core because of
  your passing.
My dearest beloved...

At Haleʻiwa, at your favorite octopus hole,
Where you caught the best meal for your
  family,
That hole, full of those tentacles grasping.
Alas! You have slipped away, been snatched
  away!

At Kāneʻohe, land caressed by the
  ʻĀpuakea rain.
Where you loved to hunt wild pigs!
That lush verdant land, the entangling
  bushes.
Alas! Youʻve gone, snatched away!

Cherished, hear me calling out to you!
Return to the bosom of Milu.
Your burdens have been lifted!
Sleep, sleep, sleep peacefully now.

'Cause
Ka I'a

Photo by Danielle's mother, Dalani Kauihou

# *ka'iulani*

Danielle Ka'iulani Kauihou • Danielle Ka'iulani Kauihou • Danielle Ka'iulani Kauihou

*Aloha mai e nā hoa makamaka mai ka lae 'o Kepuhi a hiki i ka lae 'o Lahilahi.*

Mākaha, on the west side of O'ahu, became my home at the age of seven. We lived between the ocean and the mountains and considered all of it our playground. Mākaha Stream ran through our backyard, and although it was considered an extinct, dry bed, there were winters when the rains gathered and fell and flowed from the base of the mountain to the sands of Mākaha Beach. With the uncertain permission of wary mothers, we kids would grab bodyboards, surfboards, rubber rafts, plywood...anything that would float, and we would vanish into our own world. Dams and waterfalls were constructed...boundaries and kingdoms established. Fishing poles were made of branches, purple yarn, and kiawe-thorn hooks, and we usually caught more laughs than fish. At night you could hear the toads singing away, and when the stream was nothing more than a big, stinky pond, we would gather buckets of the tadpoles that had hatched there and raise them in our own backyard nursery. Even when their legs grew out, they were still so tiny one could sit on your fingernail. Months later, there were toads all over our yard...singing their songs at night. I miss the river. I wonder if my kūpuna grew kalo by that river...did they pound kapa near its banks...did the children swim and bathe and catch 'ōpae...did they tell stories about it when they grew up...?

93

## 'Cause

Sometimes I do tings jus' 'cause I like

I go beach in da middle of da night
    swim till I feel good
    and walk home soaking
    jus' 'cause I like

Da house always dirty
    so I clean 'um
    not fo' my mom
    jus' 'cause I like

I make fun of some people
    not fo' be mean
    not fo' make me look good
    jus' 'cause I like

I take care of my cousin dem
    and my braddah and sistah
    not 'cause I 'posed to
    jus' 'cause I like

Plenny stuffs I do
    not fo' you
    not fo' dem
    jus' 'cause I like

## Ka I'a

Another day in paradise. Blue skies above with rays of light sparkling through every now and then. I wander sleepily out of my dark hole and take a look around. Most of my neighbors are already up and searching for food.

I keep close to the ground, looking for the pink limu that is so 'ono to eat. I soon find it, swaying to and fro as if being blown by a gentle breeze. I nibble on the little tree and eat till my 'ōpū is full. I never eat all the way to the root because if I do, that pink limu will never grow back. Back in my grand-parents' days, there used to be so many different types of limu. But because humans were careless and tore the limu out by their roots, those kinds of limu grow no more.

Not knowing what to do next, I go holoholo for a little while. Aaaah! I run and hide in the nearest cavern available. The brown and white spotted eel slithers out from behind some rocks, looking for prey. I surely don't want to be his dinner, I'm too young to die! I hope he goes away soon 'cause I don't want to stay in here forever! In a short time he leaves, finding a small squid to chase. I hate eels! All they want to do is munch on little fishies like us. They can be just like humans sometimes. Once when I was small, I got caught on a fisherman's hook. It hurt my mouth a lot, but I was so panicked that I hardly felt a thing. Lucky for me though, the fisherman said that I was too small and threw me back. Now whenever I see a silver sparkle in the water, I stay as far away from it as I can get.

Last night, I was talking to my Aunty Uhu, and she told me that in Ke'anae, not one eel can be found living in its reef. She said that once there was this big fish who got tired of watching so many baby fish lose their lives to eels that he became an eater of eels. Well, he cleaned out that whole place and even though he's long gone, no eels have ever dared to return. I just might take a vacation there one time. I've never been outer island, but my friends tell me it's the greatest.

The other day, my friend Humu told me that there was a northwest swell coming in. I thought that there would probably be a surf contest, so I journeyed down to the shore-break to see what was up. Sure enough, Manini and Hīnālea were wrestling in the shorebreaks. Sometimes I just sat under the rolling waves and watched wave after wave pass me by. It's always entertaining to see someone get caught in the bowls and watch them tumble over and over with the waves. Watching the playful humans is also fun. They look so funny trying to ride waves like us. They always fall off their boards. The dolphins were always the best surfers. They ride so gracefully and make surfing look so easy. They're the most beautiful creatures I've ever seen. I'm just a small Mamo—a flicker of blue and silver in the vast blue sea.

But I don't care if I'm small, just as long as I'm a big fish in Kole's eyes. She's a beautiful combination of gray, white, and black. We met on New Year's Eve. Every year, the humans come out to Mākaha beach to catch the first wave of the year. They wear glow-in-the-dark necklaces and bracelets, making it seem as if there were such a thing as swimming fireflies. Anyway, there must have been a surfer who lost his bracelet, because there it was, lying on the ocean floor. Kole was near it, and the glow that reflected off her face awed me. She seemed to be radiating some beautiful form of light,

and this drew me to her. Well, eventually we "hooked" up (maybe "hook" is a bad word, but you get the point). There are a lot of people who are against us being together, but we don't care. I guess that's because we were raised to mate only with our own kind, but this is LOVE!

Sometimes I wonder why there are so many different types of fishes in the sea. Then I realize that there must have been fishes like me, willing to risk their reputation to be with a fish of another species. Their children came out as hapa fishes, and that's where we all came from. I wonder why everyone doesn't know that?

Being a fish in these modern days is difficult. It's always a "survival" thing. I know I'm part of the food chain, but come on. There are a lot more good foods to eat. Besides, we have millions of tiny little bones that can kill you (hint, hint).

All right, so maybe we are delicious. But we deserve a break. We deserve rights too. We deserve a say in who gets to be eaten and when. I just want to live, maybe even travel. So please, remember that we're people too!

## 'Ualapu'e Fishpond, Moloka'i: Oral History from the East End

# *akutagawa*

William M. Akutagawa Jr. • William M. Akutagawa Jr. • William M. Akutagawa Jr.

William (Billy) M. Akutagawa Jr. was born 18 February 1948, on Moloka'i. His late father, William M. Akutagawa Sr., was the son of Japanese immigrants. His mother, Katharine Hagemann Akutagawa, is the daughter of a German immigrant father and Hawaiian mother.

William grew up in Kamalō and visited his grandparents in 'Ualapu'e often, spending much of his youth fishing the waters off of 'Ualapu'e Fishpond. He attended Kilohana School and Moloka'i High School, graduating in 1966.

He is presently the Executive Director of Nā Pu'uwai—a Native Hawaiian health care sytem serving the islands of Moloka'i and Lāna'i—and currently director of Hui O Kuapa.

The narrative that follows is edited from an interview of William Akutagawa, Jr. that was conducted on Moloka'i by Warren Nishimoto on 12 December 1989. All attempts were made to retain the oral style as much as possible.

Billy Akutagawa at time of interview (1989)

*The following introduction (written by Warren Nishimoto, director of the Center for Oral History at the University of Hawai'i-Mānoa) is reprinted in modified form from Center for Oral History, et al.,* 'Ualapu'e, Moloka'i: Oral Histories from the East End, *vol. 1 (Honolulu: Center for Oral History, Social Science Research Institute, University of Hawai'i-Mānoa, and the State of Hawai'i Department of Business, Economic Development and Tourism, 1991.*

'Ualapu'e Fishpond (1998)

'Ualapu'e Fishpond is one of many ancient Hawaiian fishponds on the East End of Moloka'i. It is one of only four or five fishponds which, when restored, have the capability of commercially producing large quantities of food to help elevate the island's depressed economy. Presently owned by the State of Hawai'i, the 18-acre fishpond is being restored by Hui O Kuapa, a non-profit organization consisting of Moloka'i residents, and the State of Hawai'i Department of Business, Economic Development and Tourism (DBEDT). In addition to its potential to stimulate economic development for Moloka'i and its people, the pond is valued for its cultural and histor-ical significance. In 1966, it was declared a National Historic Site.

Between 1989 and 1991, interviews were conducted with 13 individuals who possessed knowledge of the area's past or who were actively involved in the restoration of the fishpond. The oral history project was conducted under a contract between the Center for Oral History of the Social Science Research Institute at the University of Hawai'i-Mānoa (which has been conducting such projects since 1976), and the DBEDT for the purposes of: (1) documenting firsthand historical information on 'Ualapu'e Fishpond and the surrounding community to both preserve the cultural integrity of the fishpond as restoration takes place and to provide educational materials relating to fishpond culture and East End, Moloka'i, community history; (2) making this informa-tion available to those planning to restore other fishponds in the future; as well as to researchers, students, and the general public needing information on Moloka'i's social and cultural history; and (3) obtaining from community residents input and reactions regarding the fishpond's restoration.

'Ualapu'e Fishpond is located in 'Ualapu'e, an East End rural area approximately 13 miles east of Kaunakakai, Moloka'i's main town, and 11 miles west of Hālawa Valley. It is one of the larger and historically one of the most productive of about 58 shore fish-ponds once utilized on the southern coast of the island (Summers 1964:1). In the 19th century, 'Ualapu'e Fishpond was noted for the "fatness" of its mullet, and in 1959, a report noted that it was "one of the best fishponds on Moloka'i because there are several freshwater springs in the pond which seem to benefit the raising of mullet and clams" (Summers 1971:123). In 1960, it was one of only four fishponds on the island still being used commercially. Other ponds were Ka'opeahina Fishpond, Keawanui Fishpond, and Kūpeke Fishpond (Summers 1964:12).

Like the majority of Moloka'i's fishponds, 'Ualapu'e Fishpond is a loko kuapā, or walled pond, built in ancient times by commoners for the benefit of the ali'i, or royalty. The wall of basalt rock and coral runs from two places on the shoreline to form a semicircular enclosure (3). Built into the wall are mākāhā, or sluice gates, leading to the open ocean. The mākāhā, usually one to three, regulate water circulation and serve as areas to stock and harvest fish (Bigelow 1989:86). The fish best suited for Moloka'i's loko kuapā are mullet and awa (milkfish). These fish, which feed primarily on algae thriving in brackish water, benefit from streams leading into the pond from underground springs and nearby taro patches. 'Ualapu'e Fishpond has suffered from many years of neglect and exposure to the elements, such as the 1960 tsunami which damaged part of the wall and mākāhā (Summers 1971:123). The encroachment of bulrushes and mangrove, introduced to Moloka'i from New Zealand, has become so severe that the pond's useable acreage has decreased significantly (121). The wall was also damaged by a previous lessee who broke down a portion of it to gain easier access to the open ocean.

Hawaiian fishponds were once held by ali'i, who relied on commoners to build the ponds and on the konohiki (land stewards) to watch over and maintain the ponds. After the Mahele of 1848 and the Kuleana Act of 1850, the fishponds became private property.

No longer a community endeavor, most fishponds fell into disrepair as many private owners lacked the knowledge and motivation required for fishpond maintenance and cultivation. The concept which encouraged communities of Hawaiians to share resources and take care of the land and water from the mountains to the sea was abandoned in favor of a system emphasizing individual land and water rights (Wyban 1990:25).

'Ualapu'e Fishpond was unique in that it eventually came to be owned by the Territory and then the State of Hawai'i. The pond was maintained and cultivated by individual lessees, who often hired caretakers to oversee day-to-day duties (e.g., maintaining the wall, keeping poachers away, and giving permission to residents who wanted to gather clams, limu, fish, etc.). Edward Kekuhi Duvauchelle, a prominent Pūko'o resident, leased 'Ualapu'e Fishpond in the 1920s. An avid fisherman himself, Duvauchelle hired a Japanese man named Sakanashi as the pond's caretaker. The fishpond's lease was later taken over by another Moloka'i resident, Harry Apo, who managed the pond until the 1960s. Duvauchelle, Sakanashi, and Apo are the three individuals remembered well by the 13 people who were interviewed.

The town of 'Ualapu'e was once the major municipal center of Moloka'i. The hospital ('Ualapu'e County Hospital), courthouse, and tax office were located where Kilohana School stands today, across the road from 'Ualapu'e Fishpond. In 1935, the hospital, courthouse, and tax office were moved to Kaunakakai. Kalua'aha School in nearby Kalua'aha, together with Hālawa School, served East End children until it was moved to 'Ualapu'e and became Kilohana School. The post office was located in nearby Pūko'o.

'Ualapu'e was home to fishermen, farmers, county workers, homemakers, and others, mostly Native Hawaiians who grew up on kuleana lands owned by their ancestors for generations. Many fished the open waters of the East End and gathered clams and limu, and fished for mullet, awa, 'ō'io, 'ōpae, and crab in the East End fishponds. Many also remember the freshwater streams that fed into 'Ualapu'e Fishpond. One of these streams, Lo'ipūnāwai, has been the subject of legends.

'Ualapu'e was selected by the DBEDT to be a model aquaculture project. While profit and economic development utilizing modern aquaculture techniques are major long-term goals, equally important goals are the revitalization of traditional Hawaiian fishpond practices and the preservation of the history, culture, and values associated with 'Ualapu'e.

William Akutagawa Jr., current director of Hui O Kuapa, updates the preceding introduction as follows:

Today 'Ualapu'e Fishpond is still under the control of Hui O Kuapa, but management has been given to Hui director Billy Kalipi and his 'ohana. They have repaired part of the mākāhā system, dug a small adjacent pond to raise mullet and awa fingerlings brought in from Oceanic Institute on O'ahu, and expanded the artificial cage system within the main pond for later transferrance of the growing fingerlings. They are also conducting experiments there on the cultivation of the seaweed limu 'ele'ele.

Recently, the fishpond restoration project called Project Loko I'a was begun at Kahinapōhaku Fishpond on the East End of Moloka'i. The project is under the direction of the Pacific American Foundation through a grant from the Environmental Protection Agency (EPA). The office of Hawai'i Senator Daniel Inouye has been successful in sponsoring the efforts to obtain these funds for fishponds on Moloka'i and Maui. The objective of the project is to monitor water quality before, during, and after the restoration of the fishpond. Results from the project will help to successfully meet the water quality permit requirements for rehabilitating Native Hawaiian fishponds. Moloka'i residents have been hired for the project and a partnership has been established to use the workforce to assist other fishpond projects.

Another aquaculture initiative soon to begin is the Moloka'i Finfish Hatchery at Keawanui. Lease agreements are being finalized and construction and operations will be done by Oceanic Institute. The hatchery will be built with federal monies secured through the office of Senator Inouye. A match from private non-federal sources has also been secured. The hatchery will produce the fingerlings that eventually will be put into the restored fishponds on Moloka'i. After operations have stabilized and proved profitable, the hatchery will be turned over to the Moloka'i Ice House, a community-based fisheries cooperative.

**References**

Bigelow, Keith A. 1989. *Assessment of the Mangrove Ecosystem of West Moloka'i, Hawai'i, with Additional Site Surveys of Moanui Beach Park and 'Ualapu'e Fishpond.* Honolulu: Marine Option Program.

Summers, Catherine C. 1964. *Hawaiian Fishponds.* Honolulu: Bishop Museum Press.

_____. 1971. *Moloka'i: A Site Survey.* Honolulu: Bernice P. Bishop Museum.

Wyban, Carol Araki. 1990. *Master Plan for 'Ualapu'e Ahupua'a: Blending Tradition and Technology.* Kaunakakai, HI: Department of Business and Economic Development.

# 'Ualapu'e Fishpond, Moloka'i: Oral History from the East End

One of the things that I remember about 'Ualapu'e Pond as I was growing up, we used to do a lot of diving, fishing. In the front of the pond is an extension of coral reef that runs out almost to the breakers. This is like a bunched coral, or like table coral, but it runs out in a pattern, straight out. Those used to be the favorite diving places for us because the fish, the *kūmū*, would run in and out along that coral reef that extended out from in front of the pond. We used to go help these Filipino guys lay net. They would lay what was called "bull pen" before, in which the main circular part where the fish go in and get trapped inside was made of heavy *aho* cordage for retain the fish inside. They would never gill in the main pen. They would just swim inside, and they would stay for two, three days in there just swimming around. All kinds of fish. Some of the main wings that go out from this pen that drives the fish into the pen were gill nets, so the fish could get caught if they ran into the net. They used to harvest a lot of fish out on the reef. The reef area used to be real productive in front of 'Ualapu'e. Perhaps one of the best reproductive areas.

I remember, young time, we used to go out to several places they call "*hoaka*"—like blue holes—and go dive over there for *kala,* the unicorn fish. I never did see *kala* inside the pond. The only things I used to see in the pond before was small *pāpio* and a lot of barracuda. Mullet used to be inside of the pond. At night that pond was just one of the best places to go pick up what we call "half-breed crabs"—'ala'eke crab. And in the middle part was kūhonu.

At that time I think the original owner, Harry Apo, had kind of given up the lease. He was getting old already. He used to have the pond up there, but he used to live on the homestead down in Kalama'ula. So we used to venture up that side and go back home.

One of the favorite pastimes we used to do before was go in and take fish out of the pond, usually at night. We used to go in various ponds on the eastern end of the island, late at night, go lay net across, and just pull the net and either gill the fish or drag them into one smaller area. I remember doing several of the ponds, but we never did do 'Ualapu'e Pond. I always remember 'Ualapu'e Pond, being told that the pond was like a sacred pond. You go fool around inside there you might get, you know, mo'o might get you, eh. Before, people always talk about mo'o and ponds as going together. They synonymous. One and the same.

'Ualapu'e, get kepalōs generally around the area—you know, ghosts. They always talk about 'Ualapu'e being a spooky place inhabited by ghosts that travel—malicious kind, mischievous ghosts. They come out nighttime, the whole area—Kilohana School, under the school, around the school. As a matter of fact, there were teachers that used to talk to us about it. They said that they hear singing at night that come out of the area behind the school.

Down by my house used to be spooky area. I guess 'Ualapu'e people who really lived there, they're not too afraid of it. It was just that there was a mo'o that live in the pond. The mo'o usually was in the form of a white

puhi. They call him puhi ūhā, I think. That was the guardian eel of the pond. Moreso, they said women shouldn't be going inside that area when they menstruating. They'd be attacked by the barracudas or something like that.

The pond must have gone to somebody else. I can remember young, growing up, going in the pond. Harry Apo let people go inside and take clams, and we used to dig on the western part of the pond, close to the wall itself—the sandy area. I remember going in with about nine, ten people, and they'd be digging for the clam. Part of that area we cleaned up, but there's more extensive growth going toward the road area. That area had clams, too, inland. But, we haven't really touched that. Still get mangrove out there.

I remember digging for clams with people, and this was in the '50s. I think we probably seen the clams before the 1960 tidal wave. When the 1960 tidal wave came, I remember that one day, not too long after the tidal wave, going up that end (we always used to go to Ah Ping Store). I noticed that the walls was broken in sections. Before, the wall used to be nice and straight and level.

At the time of the 1960 tidal wave we was living down Kamalō. But the funny thing about Kamalō is that, before, in those days, never had siren. So they used to dispatch the police to go up in the whole Mana'e area, or East End, to go around the neighborhood and ask everybody to go to Kilohana School—not to take too many possessions, just a blanket, or whatever, and get up to the school area. But soon as the policeman leave our area, everybody go back to sleep again.

I remember also growing up, that there was a pending tidal wave that was coming in. I forget what year it was. It was during the daytime. And we all went down to the road to go look at the tidal wave. There were so many people standing on the road in front Kamalō, looking, waiting for the water. All we seen the water do is just recede a little and come back up. So we used to ask, "How come nobody run?" As we got older, we said, "Eh, we better listen to the policemen and run and hide." And the folks always used to tell us, the tidal wave no going bother them. The fringing reef is so far out that even I thought it was interesting that we just stood there and waited for something to happen.

When I was growing up there, I didn't see any houses adjacent to the pond like you see today. It was a cleared-out area. People lived across the road. There were one family that lived close to the pond in an old house. I think it was Kaauwai. Other than that, I didn't see anybody else living there. The lower portion of the pond used to be nice. There were no mangrove on the bottom portion. There were two *mākāhā,* one on the western side, and one on the eastern end of the pond. The *mākāhā*s was clean. There was no break; the walls were intact. There was some grating—steel grating, old mesh kind steel.

Then in 1967 or '66, Oceanic Institute came here to Moloka'i and they worked Ali'i Pond down in the Kamiloloa area. I had a friend who was working there with the pond people. They also went up to 'Ualapu'e Pond and fixed the *mākāhā* at that time. The cement that you see today, they went out and built the *mākāhā* up again.

The Oceanic Institute is associated with the Sea Life Park. They did extensive work on Ali'i Pond. Whether they did with any other pond, I don't know. I remember the pond manager. His name was John Crouch. I met John recently, about two months ago. He's working on the Big Island now, and he sells wind energy, like wind turbines, windmills. The pond that Oceanic Institute was working on down here belonged to the Department of Hawaiian Home Lands. So they may have had a research grant or something. I remember asking John about the pond, How did they do on the experiment? He said they'd start with 180,000 small fries; try to cultivate the thing outside of the pond and then introduce it back into the pond system. Half would die within so many months, and then the rest would grow kind of big. Before got to 'ama stage, another half would die, so you really was left with something like 20,000 or 10,000. And out of that another half died through predation or other causes.

It's interesting. I always thought that mangroves was the culprit of ponds. When I was growing up on the eastern end of Moloka'i, there's a lot of ponds, so we used to go in and out of different ponds. Even if the walls were wrecked and completely submerged, we'd know where the ponds were. I remember seeing the mangrove growing in the pond walls and kind of disrupting them. But someone told me that the interesting thing about mangrove is that it provides refuge for the small *pua* to hide in. Chee, it seems awfully funny to me that you have a foreign thing in there. I think there must have been another system with Hawaiians, as far as raising the fries, without the mangrove itself, because mangrove is foreign to Moloka'i.

I don't think barracuda would take as much of a toll. I remember—this was years after I came back from the service—I had some good friends still living on the East End, in 'Ualapu'e. I used to go up to see them. That time, I stayed up that place already, just a stone's throw. I'd walk down their house. At that time I don't think anybody leased 'Ualapu'e Pond, but I used to watch them, how they catch fish in 'Ualapu'e Pond. I think they waited till either an outgoing tide or an incoming tide. They'd wait on the wall. One guy would be close to the opening [i.e. *mākāhā*]. Another person would be on the upper portion, toward the East End side of the wall; one on the west and one on the east. They'd wait and throw net blind on *pāpio* that were coming out of the pond. I asked them how did they do it. What they said they did was, they'd watch all the small mullet *pua* running and jumping out of the water, either going with the outgoing tide or incoming tide. They would know that following behind would be the predators; the school of *pāpio.* One would throw inside, one would throw outside of the pond, right where the *mākāhā* stay, right where she either pouring out or pouring in. I did that one time and I just threw blind. I caught good-sized *pāpio*, maybe about five or six.

They don't have any fish now. The water just free flow—go in and out of the pond. The grills probably rotten away, or the last pond owner (and this would be probably around '67, '68, as far as I can remember, when I left here for the service), whoever was the last owner just let it rot away. The fish go in and out, free-flowing.

Recently I took a look at the pond wall. I walked with Marion Kelly and some people to look at the wall. It's been broken in three

or four places. There weren't any *mākāhā*s there, but the guy (whoever had the pond before that just did a terrible job) just opened up the wall like that. The encroachment of mangrove is so heavy and dense, it has covered half the opening already. So in order to restore that *mākāhā* back to its original state, there's going to be extensive cutting of mangrove. The mangrove has just proliferated. That area is real bad.

I remember the two *mākāhā* when I was growing up in the '50s. I don't know if they were on the inside or ocean side. Hard to remember. I didn't see any heavy wooden slab or metal slab. All I saw was the grating. It was like a slide-type grating—you could slide, pull it right up. It ran in cemented slots. I don't know how they did it, but they must have done it with one-by-twos or something. Pour the cement molding during very low tide around that one-by-two, and then remove that, and then you get the slot to run your metal grating down. They must have had two grills because it's wide

mākāhā (sluice gates) (2000)

mākāhā (grating showing in-flowing tide) (2000)

enough. They must have opened the incoming tide or outgoing tide, lift up one side and just drop it back down to trap anything in the middle. Or they may have done it another way, which would have been just using a small-eyed net and go surround the inside during the incoming tide. I guess the fish would run against the tide, and then they would catch it like that.

There was another pond right adjacent to 'Ualapu'e Pond. It's called Halemahana Fishpond. I remember growing up, I used to see some guys used to go catch mullet in there. Even though the wall is broken and can only be seen during the low tide, the mullet still ran in particular areas in there. There were about three *mākāhā*. Even on the high tide I'd see the big *'anae* [mullet] running. I used to go throw net on that lower pond, and I used to see the school of mullet running in and out—real big ones, big like your forearm. On the upper side today, I've seen big mullet. The people who live adjacent to 'Ualapu'e Pond, on the eastern end of the property, in front of Pedro's Place, we can just be sitting in the afternoon, talking story, drinking beer, and look right out and one big *'anae* would just jump right up in front. But nobody can catch them. We used to surround them, try to figure out how the old-timers did it.

The only guy I remember who could catch *'anae* over there was Jack Kalilikane, one old man, old fisherman. That, perhaps, is another guy that should be talked to, 'cause he lived in 'Ualapu'e for a while. He lived on Moloka'i, and he can tell you about fishing, 'cause if there ever was a fisherman who did it for a livelihood, that was Jack. We didn't use hook and line. Hook and line take patience, eh? We rather go with throw net. If you cannot go with throw net, then you gotta

go dive for fish. That was our philosophy. The 'Ualapu'e area is noted until today for abundance of fish; it is noted for *he'e*—squid [octopus]. Those are one of the prime squid grounds. You can talk to a lot of Moloka'i guys today and it's surprising because a long time ago, when we were growing up, never had too many people come around fish. There was enough fishing for the local people around that area. Today, and I'm probably guilty of it, I live in Kaunakakai, but I have a flat-bottom boat and I run to East End, outside of my parents' place. 'Ualapu'e for me is one of the prime areas that I go to launch my flat-bottom and go out and fish. Dive beyond the reef. Inside the reef I lay net. I recently laid net about a month ago. Outside of 'Ualapu'e Pond, I went in the area called "*hoaka*" and laid gill net. Caught mullet, *'ō'io,* and *weke.* She still run in that area. But, like people said, "You gotta know." Sometime we lay close to the shore below the pond and we catch a lot of *pāpio* certain times. Certain times we catch big *'anae* mullet. So, they still get fish.

The grills looked like about half-inch to one inch apart. When I seen the grills they were kind of old and had almost like sludge or *limu* on top. You can tell nobody was cleaning. Every once in a while you gotta take the grating out and either wash 'em down, scrub 'em down, or dry 'em out. Small *pua* probably would run inside there and they cannot get out. The area in front of the pond is real muddy. You sink a lot in front. It's built up from before. It wasn't too much like that before. I don't know if it's over-fishing or whatever, because I don't see too much *kūmū* anymore that run in front of the pond. The previous owner (previous to the Hui O Kuapa getting the pond) sealed up the last *mākāhā*, the one on the western end. He piled up rocks, so there wasn't a natural outflow. And he opened up the middle part of the pond. Whatever he did affected the Halemahana Pond, on the western end, because that pond started to fill up right after they closed the *mākāhā* on that side.

All I remember about agriculture in the area is my mom growing sweet potato. It's interesting because "*'uala*" means sweet potato and "*pu'e*" means "to heap, to pile"—and so "sweet potato hill." My mom grew for *kaukau*, for home use. The thing was really growing well up there until she had a fight with the mongooses. They would come and dig out the sweet potato and eat it themselves. The soil there is rich— 'Ualapu'e soil. I don't know if it's a consequence of flooding from the Kahananui Stream.

I think Kahananui Stream might be the western boundary of 'Ualapu'e. The eastern boundary is...when you go past Ah Ping Store, there's a hill that you climb. There's a church on the top of the hill, when you level off. Before the church, there's a long stone wall running inland. You can see the stone wall from the highway. That's supposed to be the boundary marker for 'Ualapu'e—the eastern boundary. After that begins the land of Kalua'aha. The boundary supposed to go straight down. But my friend live in the area. There's three houses. They own that land running down. His house is on the top; his grandfather is right below him. His lot is considered Kalua'aha; and his grandfather's house, right below him, is considered 'Ualapu'e. So, till today, I no can figure the thing out. They must have made a boo-boo.

Panila Kapuni used to have *lo'is* west of 'Ualapu'e Fishpond. The eastern part of 'Ualapu'e, the Pedros used to have. And this guy, Masashi Otsuka, "Cowboy," he using his wife's family plot, Puailihau. Edward Kaupu had *lo'is*, but I don't know who used to work them. Those are *lo'is* that's right inside of the bulrushes and part of the mangrove thicket area, but that's abutting the pond. I don't know where the springs of Lo'ipūnāwai stay. Used to have one Hawai'i Visitors Bureau marker. But people used to laugh. They said the sign point, but nobody can find the thing. Because the legend was, if you looking for it, you died of thirst; when you found it, you drank too much and you died anyway. So nobody lived to tell where the *pūnāwai* was.

I always believed that in a straight line from my grandmother's house to the pond, there were old *lo'is* inside there. And, even till today, there's still water that seeps up, and you can see where the *lo'is* used to be. It must have gone into the pond itself. Otherwise, the water could not escape out into the ocean, and it was like bubbling up and going out. It was a swampy area. By the time when I went in the back there exploring, it was not in use already. I don't remember a caretaker's house being there. That time there were some shacks out there, but I didn't see anybody living in them.

I guess Hui O Kuapa really got started with Walter Ritte, although, some years back, community development monies were supposed to come down, and the federal people were gonna get in on the project. It was going to be given to Alu Like to run a fishpond demonstration project on Moloka'i. At that time, five ponds were identified. One of them was 'Ualapu'e. 'Ualapu'e belonged to the state, but it was leased out to a private person. There were three major projects for Moloka'i. One was the icehouse, one was the cooling plant, and the other

main wall prior to repair (1990)

main wall after restoration (2000)

one was the fishpond demonstration project. But the monies didn't come down for a fishpond project. So the thing just went on the wayside. This happened in the early '80s.

After that, utilization of the ancient fishpond was put on a back burner. Nothing was being done about it. But I guess when the Department of Planning and Economic Development eventually became the Department of Business and Economic Development, and Walter became the economic development coordinator for Moloka'i, he looked into the fishpond project and tried to find out where some monies could be gotten. Maybe some dialogue with Carol [Araki] Wyban took place or with Jim [Wyban] and some other people, and it was decided that, "Eh, maybe the fishpond, it could be a go."

When Walter started calling people and asking them if they wanted to be on the fishpond planning committee, he called me. I said okay, although I was going school at

the time, and still am, and I couldn't be heavily involved in it. Barbara Hanchett [Kalipi] was asked to serve also. She said, "Well, why don't we just see what we can do?" and that she would try to do as much of the work as possible.

Then we tried to delve into the issue of How do you get the federal monies? How do you get the state monies and the country monies to run that? First of all, the state couldn't be the one to run the project. We were told earlier that the state couldn't lease something to itself and become an entity to run the thing. The lease had to be given to someone. So we said, okay, we needed to become a non-profit organization. Carol did a lot of work at that time. Walter too.

I don't know where the term "Hui O Kuapa" came from, but that was the name that we took. I don't know who thought it up. "Hui" is a group. "Kuapā" is always associated with the pond: "to build, to erect a wall." And "loko"—on the East End of the island, most of the ponds that I know are called "loko kuapā"—enclosed rock wall, sea wall." Although there are many ponds on Moloka'i, I think only on the eastern end of Moloka'i they are called "loko 'ume iki"— those are "fish traps," as opposed to "fishponds." There's quite a number of them on the eastern end of Moloka'i. But I guess "loko kuapā" is an appropriate term for us.

Our principal aim is: one, revitalization of the pond—to document the process of getting permits—state, county, or federal—to use the pond; rebuild the pond; if it's a historic site, to make sure that we take the proper steps and procedures in getting it restored, and also using it as an educational tool while we're in the process of developing the pond culture—get it down on tape, or whatever, so people in our school system can take advantage of it. Finally, what's the marketing economy for the type of fishes and crustaceans that we're going to raise in the pond? Is there a market? Is it viable to get a pond back into a working condition? How long does it take?

Hopefully, when we do it in this manner, and it's a non-profit organization that's doing it, some of the areas of operations and procedures that we come up with—like the process of doing the permits—will help ease the way for people who own private ponds to see it as a lucrative way, besides getting 'em back into production, of maintaining a culturally historic site.

I think you have to get some state permits, like conservation district use application permits, because it's in conservation area. You have to apply for usage of that particular site. And to the Historic Site Office of the State Department of Land and Natural Resources because it's a historic site. If it's on the Federal Register, they're really picky that you take the proper procedure. I remember seeing something that said, "You can build, but you cannot tear down or remove." What does that mean? Removal of the rocks that form the wall itself? You cannot remove any rocks; you can only build? I don't really know. We really haven't gotten down into the practical aspect of getting the wall back into its former state. That's why Carol is doing a historic plan, documenting all the information on how the wall was prior to all these changes.

Physically, perhaps the most important thing to be done is to stop the breaking down of the walls, and that would probably mean getting rid of as much of the mangrove as possible, and in such a way that it doesn't

tear apart the walls, cutting it in such a manner that it'll die upon itself. I don't know if chemicals can be used on the plant itself. Second is to restore the pond wall to its original state. Third might be to clean the pond once or twice, might be with *huki* net. Next is to get the flow of the pond back into its former state, and that may mean they might have to furrow. Real extreme tides can help flush out the pond. Then, work on the gates itself. After that, you probably have to clean adjacent areas around the pond, clean back the vegetation. At least get it to a point where you can see into the pond itself. While all of this is going on, you probably have to have a building there for storage of equipment. A pond manager has to be picked up, and equipment. The person has to be innovative enough to use whatever help he can.

I guess in the early stages you might have a certain inflow of cash or money, but after that it's gonna kind of taper off. So if you can, get as much free help as possible. It may mean going to federal programs that have youths working during summers. Get the youths to participate and help in cleaning the pond. You write some kind of education plan in which, at the same time as they clean in there, they're given education about how the pond usage was in ancient times and why are they cleaning these particular areas. The promotional aspect of the whole pond project might be to inform the community, as much as possible while we're working on the pond, on what's going on. I think that's being done, one, through the newsletter *The Fishpond News.* It might be community presentations later on. We've completed the first year of the pond restoration project, and we'd like the community to know what's going on there. It might be to get the 'Ualapu'e community actively involved.

I believe in the concept that in ancient times if you want something done—and the Hawaiians probably did it this way—they got the whole community to work behind the project. If you wanted the *kapu* system to be kept enforced for the good of everybody, in keeping the resources, then you would have to let everybody have a sense of ownership of that particular pond. Then they would watch and say, "Now if somebody goes inside there and takes something out of that pond, he is actually taking a portion of what I have inside there. That's no good." The actual censure would come from the people from that particular community. And ownership can take many, many forms. The best way to promote ownership is to work through the young people.

I think there's support, so far, from the community. One thing we gotta remember, it's a new community inside that area. I see some of the old-timers have gone away. Not too many of the young people have come back, and we have, in fact, different kinds of people coming back to live in that particular area. There's a lot of fluctuation, because people move from one district into the next district. I myself may be an example. I moved from Kamalō into 'Ualapu'e, and then I'm out in Kaunakakai now. I've seen some people who used to live in Mapulehu. Now they live in 'Ualapu'e. Some people who lived in 'Ualapu'e moved up onto the homestead area. So there's a lot of movement, but I think if you fix the pond in such a way, and you promote it to the general Moloka'i community, they will take some pride in knowing that it's a part of them already.

It's funny how Moloka'i people always, always have that sense of "Well, I'm Moloka'i." When I'm facing anybody outside, I'm Moloka'i. This still happens. It

used to be more territoriality, before, when Kilohana School went till the tenth grade. Lot of rivalry with the other people on the outside. That would be mainly the East End (Mana'e) people against the Kaunakakai and the Ho'olehua and the Maunaloa people. There was a sense of rivalry at that time. But now everything has changed. It's mandated now that there is only one high school. Everybody gets on the bus and goes to the [Moloka'i] High School, except when you have a private car or whatever. A long time ago, there was no busing for us kids from East Moloka'i, from 'Ualapu'e and up, Kamalō and up. We had to catch our own ride down to Kaunakakai to catch the bus to high school. We'd get on cars, six or seven people to one car. It used to be Why come to Kaunakakai on the car and catch the bus? Why not, in fact, go on the car all the way up to the high school, and pay those people for the gas? So that's how we did it. About three, four cars came from the East End of Moloka'i and went all the way to the high school. We still felt, at that time, a sense of

Kilohana School (1990)

Ah Ping Store (1991)

territoriality. We came from there. Nobody gave us any concessions being East Moloka'i people. We young people only went to the high school for the last two years—11th, 12th grades—so we didn't really make too many friends there. It was such a short term.

When we were going to Kilohana School, they had two periods of ag work up there. There was an indictment against the program there that, "Hey, nothing is too heavy on education over there, on academics. Everything is on farming." But we used to raise our own vegetables, and a bunch of us, depending on what ag period you was working in, would plant all our vegetables: corn, lettuce, cabbage, eggplant, bush beans. What would actually happen is that the principal would send us down, harvest, wash all the crops down there, put it into bags, and a portion of us would walk up to Ah Ping Store to sell it, and walk back to school, give them the money. Then it would go into an ag fund. And every year, there would be a farm party, because at Kilohana School we also raised pigs and chickens with our vegetable crops. We would have a boys' *lū'au*, in which we'd invite all the families. I remember killing pig, *kālua* the pig, doing everything for the families that would come up to the school and enjoy the *lū'au.*

The school (at that time, it went to the tenth grade) was little bit more community support, I feel, because they had a lot of programs that ran in the school that benefited the community: the May Day pageant, scouting. More of it was utilized. Today they have a community center, and I don't know what goes on in the community center, but it's just like it's just there for parties. Well, I've been out of touch with Kilohana School for some years now.

There were more Japanese in the area, too, in East Moloka'i, truck farmers. Their kids used to really take advantage of the ag program and many of them today are living on O'ahu. They have not come back to Moloka'i. I remember the other people talking about those Japanese families. A lot of Japanese in Mapulehu. Mapulehu was good farming. All those areas around the mouth of big valleys—like Mapulehu Valley, Kahananui, 'Ōhi'a—get good farming land. Kamalō used to have a big farming area.

While I was growing up, the main wharf was Kaunakakai. Pūko'o was broken already, broken down. When I grew up, you could ride down to Kamalō Wharf on a vehicle, right on the causeway going down. There was a building there. The wharf was intact, and nets were on the wharf itself. I remember going down to the wharf to go look for mullet. You could see almost three or four schools of fish, different kinds of fish, layers of it, under the wharf itself. But not anymore.

Well, about the fishpond project, at the beginning the hardest part was probably getting the permits and getting the non-profit status. And then securing funds, because the funds had to be gotten out of the legislature, earmarked for a certain period of time, and you had to use it up, and then reapply again for funds. It's like, you get a lot of money, but they telling you to hurry up and use the money. Then there's no guarantee that you gonna get it in the next session, so it's just like *pohō*. You went use all the money.

We decided that the important thing was to get the permit process going within at least a year's time. Try to clear up all of that mess. Then, hopefully, by the second year, to get a pond manager onto the project and then to get some kind of building laid out there to store needed equipment. Then to get the pond to a state of productivity at the end of the fourth or fifth year, where it would mean some kind of income, however small, and that might be the sale of fishes itself, or crustaceans.

That might be the plan, to get it self-sufficient, but I don't think it can be totally self-sufficient. It can be used as an education tool. But if we talking total self-sufficiency, we talking about whatever income derives out of the pond has to pay for the manager, has to pay for the utilities—electrical, water, and the maintenance of equipment. I'm not too sure if can go total self-sufficiency. It has to be tied into something else. Maybe we looking at the concept of a series of ponds run by a manager and maybe a staff person, or two staff persons or three. A series of ponds that produce so much fish that can be sold outside, and support all. Maybe all three or four of the ponds could then be self-sufficient, with limited use of bodies [staff persons].

I think in ancient times, maybe one *ahupua'a* get about one or two fishponds. They could sustain that particular community. But they have to take the time and effort to go in and clean the pond. The specialists will do that with the help of the community. Subsistence-wise it could be okay. But for sell, you gotta get one good marketing arm, and that might seem to be the problem, because I noticed here on Moloka'i, we have mullet in our stores. Some of those mullet come from the West Coast [U.S.A.] and Australia. Frozen. It's an awful thing to say we have the same species here but we can't sell it. But what's gonna drive this guy to buy the mullet that we produce in the

pond? We have to go and sell the idea to him that we can provide him with mullet on a year-round basis. If we can't do that out of the pond that we have, we can't make it self-sufficient.

The other concept that might be helpful is to look at the fishing industry in Moloka'i. Look at the fishing industry and say to those fishermen that mullet is *kapu* on the open ocean from December to February 28. You cannot net or any other way. However, in the pond it's year-round. If you can get the fishermen that lay outside on the reef to see the pond as a source to tide you over the winter months, they'll have year-round supply to market. During certain periods of time, he takes it easy on the reef resources and comes in, work on the pond. Then, when everything is going fine on the pond and the season is lifted, go back out on the reef and fish on the outside. But, then, fishermen are a funny group. You talk to them and they're not always in agreement with you.

We can learn something from the Hawaiian culture. Hawaiians had a culture where at certain times of the year—if you look at the *aku* and the *'ōpelu*—*aku* would be *kapu* and *'ōpelu* would be open, so they fish for *'ōpelu*. Then *'ōpelu* would be closed and they would open *aku* or go on the outside for the deep-sea *aku*. That kind of dual purpose would be real good for them.

Fisherman would be part of the pond system, too. They would have to put their time and effort into the pond and look at it as a resource, a fallback. Hui O Kuapa is trying to work on this pond concept. It might open up the way for another way of thinking to take place, instead of fishermen always grumbling, "I don't know why they *kapu*."

Like now, there's a big issue over here about *akule* with the state. They're yelling at the state people, "Have you done a study on *akule*? Why can't we go surround *akule* inside the harbor? You folks don't even know when they spawn, why they spawn, how come there's fluctuations [in the amount of schools]. You folks don't really know that and you guys telling us ease up on the *akule*." The fishermen might be able to fall back on another product besides *akule*.

For the privilege of using the pond, I would say they have to get their hands dirty. They have to go inside and work a particular pond. With their hard work, the resources can belong to them in the pond. Because, fishermen, while they patching net and everything, you could get them to go in. It's the same concept, work on the pond. Let them do like animal husbandry. Our commercial fishermen are our harvesters, but not particularly farmers. They just harvest off the ocean, but they have never learned the concept of "I gotta propagate; I gotta let 'em grow."

I see Hui O Kuapa as a demonstration project for now. If you really want to run something on a viable, commercial, economic basis, it has to be run by the private sector. Because we set up as a non-profit, it defeats the purpose of trying to push economic development to the point where it becomes viable. For us, it's to maybe show the way to others who want to get involved on a private basis and make money. Maybe you can utilize this fishpond scheme for economic development, then form a fisherman cooperative or fishing association, or a pond association run strictly along profit-making lines. That's it. Culture and profit.

I always looked at the pond when I was growing up. I saw all these ponds, and I kind of wondered, Wow, who built them? Who was able to pile so many rocks? Sometimes I would go out on the pond area and look at the rocks and say, These rocks must have come from inland. It's kind of surprising, 'cause in order to get the rocks—and rocks not usually found all along the beach—they had to form lines to go way in to get these rocks out. Who commanded a vast project like that? What was really amazing is that although a majority of the ponds are broken, some below high tide, the fish still run in the same pattern. They still utilize the *mākāhā*. It's broken down. They can swim right over the pond wall, but they seem to congregate in these openings. How did they do it before? There must have been a specialist who knew about how to develop the pond, who understood how fishes ran in particular areas.

It's amazing, because almost all of the ponds that you see utilize the freshwater springs to mix with salt water. But some of them are built in such a way that there are channel openings that come from the reef into these areas, so fish traveled in these areas. It kind of made sense how they built it. There are channels on both sides of the two *mākāhā*. If you go further outside, you can see there is some sand area coming in, breaks in the fringing reef leading toward those two areas. Somebody had to know where to put the *mākāhā*, the best use of the land from point to point.

I don't know if anybody made a compilation, but there's a tremendous amount of literature on the ponds. What really is amazing, too, is that the fisheries people [the U.S. Commission of Fish and Fisheries] back in the 1900s did a study on the Hawaiian reefs and fishponds. It's just amazing that it was done even during that time. Ponds are intriguing. I've seen pond walls outside of pond walls, but one pond wall is below the high water mark. I don't know why it's like that.

I don't know if there are any *kūpuna* living today that would know how to help us in the restoration—there might be on other islands. I know there's some. I can recall Alika Cooper. There was a Japanese man who was a commercial fisherman here. He died about three years ago. He and the brother had a pond on the East End. They leased the pond. I think it was Kūpeke Pond. It's a nice pond today. He was one of the guys that I remember talking to one time. He learned the cleaning of the pond from an old-timer from before. These guys had it in their heads. If you think about it now, he may have told someone else. So if there's somebody who has this knowledge inside of their head but has not put it to practical use, if we can just hit on people like that before it's all lost, that can help.

This Japanese guy said he learned from this guy how to clean the ponds in the ancient way. The only modern thing is, instead of canoe, use the power boat now to clean the pond—dragging, almost like a rake. And instead of maybe a bamboo rake, they can use a steel rake along the bottom to create the furrow to clean the pond itself.

I remember stealing fish out of Kūpeke Pond with a net. About three of us. The two guys that I went with at night to go get the fish, they knew how the fish ran in the pond. We'd go at night and they'd take so much net and they tell me to wait close to the *mākāhā* on the side of the pond, on the bank. Then they would go up along the pond wall, jump in the water, and they

would come down. With a prearranged signal—maybe two whistles or something, or yell, two yell—we would start moving already with the net. I would run with the net in the water, right from the shore to an anchor on the other end, and the pond wall would be about four or five feet away from me in a parallel pattern. A tub of *'ō'io* would be stuck inside the net. The fish would all be fighting against the net, because they against the wall—they trying to go back into the net. We'd lay net at one *mākāhā*, pick up the fish, put 'em in the tub, leave 'em there, then go up to the next *mākāhā*. But the farther up you got, you're closer to the caretaker's home of the pond. On the extreme end, when we catch that, when the fish would hit, we would run around and break the heads, along the net, to stop the fish from making a lot of noise inside. Break 'em, break 'em like that. And then we would take the net and we would bring 'em back down.

Now I regret doing something like that, because we'd come home at night, maybe about one o'clock in the morning, and we get too much *'ō'io*. I remember coming back down to 'Ualapu'e from where we were in the district of Pūko'o, bringing the fish down into the 'Ualapu'e area to people we know, and going to their house in the morning and asking, "You folks like *'ō'io*?" One thing you gotta remember about *'ō'io*, it's called "bone fish" but it's one of the best fish for *lomi*. They would scrape the *'ō'io*, and then just *lomi* and take out all the bones and add in *'inamona* and chili pepper, and sprinkle salt water inside. Just eat 'em like that. Japanese would take the *'ō'io*, too, make fish cake. They used to catch big *'ō'io*. *Pohō*, though, wasting during that time. That's how much fish had. You know fishermen tell tales, yeah, but two guys carrying home a tub overloaded with *'ō'io* is just…

It might not be a selective process where we say we going raise. It might be that fish just come in. We may initially have to stock fish from the outside. I noticed, when I went to the pond to check, there was a lot of jellyfish in there—huge jellyfish. They said that's the stinging variety, so that has to be cleaned out. No telling what you got in there. You might have Samoan crabs, anything.

I remember one pond that we went to in the night, Kāinā'ohe Pond in Ka'amola. We went at night to go lay net, and we'd walk, and there would be about five of us carrying each section of the net. Walk, walk, walk. We'd say, "What we gonna do?" I said, "We going take the net on the far end—the eastern end—we going walk up to the eastern end, spread out, and we going bring the net down and come back." So we would walk, walk, walk. Warm inside the water. But all of sudden, the water turned cold. That was a spring. I said, "Oh, it's cold, spring, spring. Keep going. Fast." Coming from underneath. We can feel the spring, the cold water running. Oh, boy. Then, we get to the other end and we say, "Okay, we going turn around. Okay, we going bring net down." Ho, we gotta cross that cold water area again.

I think there's several springs along the shore area. All the eastern end of the island, I noticed that even some areas where we'd go hunting, the water would flow on the mauka portion, like in Kamalō. It would never come out through the stream. There was not enough force behind it to push it all the way out into the stream. The water would sink under the stream bed. All along the Kamalō coastline, there will be springs bubbling up in those ponds.

In 20 years I hope to see the pond back into working condition—some of the ponds, not all. I discussed it with somebody else who was into ponds. He's no longer on the island. He and I took a different view of ponds. I looked at ponds as being the visual monuments to the Hawaiians' past. You can look at it from an economic standpoint and say, "Yes, it's a viable thing. We can work the ponds." But I look at it also from a historic point of view. If I'm taking the perspective that, historically, you want the thing to be preserved, then we're saying that we gotta stop the natural destruction of the pond by the elements, to save what's left of the ponds, whether it be for economic purposes or historical purposes. We gotta save. So the idea might be that, as much as possible, we'll use the ponds that are economically viable today, to get them in working order. That's hope for Moloka'i.

The other thing is the visual beauty of the ponds, to restore them to a state that may not be economically viable, but kept in a state of preservation. That would be one of my principal aims.

Ponds and Moloka'i are, to me, synonymous as a cultural element, cultural value. I come from the East End of the island, and what we say, the minute you get into the lowlands of Moloka'i and you go along the coast, you're gonna see ponds. A whole lot of ponds. They must have been built by some people who had the strength and who utilized a system that could feed so many people. I look at 'Ualapu'e Pond as one of the better ponds. It needs work, but there are many more in a worse state of disrepair. The pond was very, very important, and I think we should preserve it, historically and economically.

Grandma Betty, Keoki, me, and Grandpa
George at our family home in Haleʻiwa

*E Tūtū-Kāne, ʻAuhea ʻOe?*

*Ka Manawa*

*Awawa o Waimea, Oahu*

*Mahch Fye*

# *kimo*

Kimo Armitage • Kimo Armitage • Kimo Armitage • Kimo Armitage

*I kēia manawa:* Kimo Armitage has written children's books: *Limu, The Blue Turtle; Manuliʻi and the Beautiful Cape;* and *Mahalo e Grandpa,* which are beautifully illustrated by Scott Kaneshiro. He has co-authored with Tūtū Lilia Wahinemaikaʻi Hale two Hawaiian-language books: *ʻŌlelo Noʻeau No Nā Keiki* (illustrated by Solomon Enos) and *Nā ʻAno O Nā Leo* (illustrated by Kupihea Romero); and, with Keliʻi Kiʻilehua, a Hawaiian-language primer called *Hoʻomālamalama* (illustrated by Mark Furuya). His play *ʻĀkia* won the Pacific Rim Division of the 1998 Kumu Kahua Theatre/University of Hawaiʻi-Mānoa Playwriting Contest and was produced in the fall of 2001 under the title *Ola Ka Lau*. He was nominated for a Poʻokela Award in Playwriting for his contribution to a series of plays based on indigenous peoples' folktales produced by Honolulu Theatre for Youth in 2000. He also wrote and co-produced the Hawaiian-language video series *Kanu Pono*.

*I kuʻu wā ʻōpiopio:* I was raised in Haleʻiwa, Oʻahu, by my maternal grandparents, George Poepoe Kaulalena Akina and Beatrice Bo Inn Lau Akina. As the last of their children, I had no curfew, my own car, and generous allowances. Weekends and school holidays were spent spearing fish, harvesting wana, collecting rock salt, pickling mangoes, cooking huli-huli chicken, and picking limu. My pet pig, Noname, and my pet (surfing!) dog, Hanalei, also occupied my time. Harvests were usually followed by informal jam sessions, the sound of my grandpa's voice floating from beneath his favorite mango tree and into the humid night while my grandmother prepared ʻono pūpū for all their guests.

*Ko Kākou Leo:* Mahalo i kuʻu mau kumu: ʻo Keaweʻaimoku Kaholokula, ʻo Kamanaʻo Ku, ʻo Liko Rogers, ʻo Hailama Farden, ʻo Hauʻoli Busby, ʻo Mikiʻala Ayau, ʻo Kalama Cabigon a ʻo Kamehaʻililani Waiau. Holomua wau i ka ʻōlelo Hawaiʻi ma muli o lākou.

114

Na Miki'ala i ho'olālā i ka huaka'i no kāna papa 'ōlelo Hawai'i i ka Hula Piko ma Molokai i ka mahina 'o Mei, 1998. Iā mākou i nānā ai i nā mea hula i ke kakahiaka nui, ua lohe 'ia ke kani o ka pahu a me nā leo e oli ana. Ua kupu ko'u leo maoli i ia kakahiaka ma luna o ka pu'u 'o Kā'ana, no ka mea, ua mana'o wau: eia nō ku'u piko, eia nō ko nā kūpuna leo, a eia nō ko'u pana pu'uwai. Ma mua, ua hūnā 'ia nā mo'olelo i loko o nā mele e nā kūpuna. I kēia manawa, he leo ko'u: 'a'ole wau pono e hūnā i ko'u mana'o. 'Ae, laki loa wau.

Ma mua, ua kaumaha nā kānaka maoli a poina. Akā, i kēia wā, he leo ko kākou a ikaika loa kēia leo. Hiki iā kākou ke ho'one'e i nā mauna me kēia leo. Hiki iā kākou ke ho'ona'auao i kā kākou mau keiki me kēia leo, a hiki iā kākou ke kūkākūkā i mea e poina 'ole ai ke alanui pono. *E kanu pono kākou i nā kukui me ko kākou mau leo!*

## E Tūtū-Kāne, 'Auhea 'Oe?

E Tūtū-kāne, 'auhea 'oe?
Pono mākou iā 'oe
'A'ale maopopo ka lawai'a 'ana
Ua poina nā lua he'e
A wīwī ka'u mau keiki

Ua malo'o nā kalo a pau
Ma kāu lo'i
A 'a'ale maopopo ke kanu 'ana
A wīwī ka'u mau keiki

'A'ale hiki ke pule
Pono e nānā i ka puke wehewehe,
I nā hua 'ōlelo
Nui loa kēia hana
A wīwī ko'u 'uhane

115

## Ka Manawa

E TūtūMan
'O'ole'a kou leo.

'Ae. Nui nā pōhaku i 'ai 'ia.

## Awawa o Waimea, Oahu

Barren is Kailiilii,
her monkeypod is gone, fallen.
Kaneaukai, this strong rock shrine,
attracts *uhu* and *kumu*.

The fertile *ha* of Kane
blows her moss womb wide open.
Rain slicks her thick *hapuu*,
red mud beads over her banks.

Touch this gulch Kamanaiki,
from that gulch Kamananui.
Ending in Waikakalaua
thirsty for the next rain, blowing.

Her smell is *pakalana*
blooming tiny random pearls.
Sheathed *maia*, peppered black,
engorged, bursts pockets of ripeness.

For the expert is Puulu,
thick, covered by *palapalai*.
Punakai the freshwater spring,
gushes into Kukuiee.

In June, *kuawa* and mango
satisfy honeycreepers.
While *lau* chop slanted sunlight
into blocks of purple shade.

## Mahch Fye

"Honey, you read the paper?"
"Yea. I red 'um."
"You going?"
"No. Wa foa?"
He's your *father.*"

Stahted smaw keed time fo' me. My fahdah used to bus' me up wen' I no lissen. My Mahdah dem had fowa keeds. Too many keeds. She work hod, her. In da mo'ning befoa we get up fo' sku, she stay alredy cook breakfes', wash klos, feed da chikens li'dat. My fahdah go werk fye in da mo'ning, so she mek his breakfas' and pak his kaukau fo' heem. He yuse to werk luna at da konstruk-shen site.

Auwa haus befoa no moa elektrik so my Mahdah gotta wash klos by han. An I can see sumtimes right hea by da nukles all blahd. And my frenz tell me: Wot, Jimmy? No moa respect, you. All dey yoa mahda werk hahd. Look her fingas stay bleeding from da washbohd. Why no kōkua yoa mah-dah? But, us keeds ah, only like play. So my fahdah com back hale—noting pau. We get likens. But, we only keeds. Das' wot I tink. Keeds is keeds.

He peel, befoa, da guava steek. Kos hod da steek. Hu! Da ting some soa man. He geev us likens all da time. Won time he wen trow my hed to da brik wall. Da wall wen puka my hed. Whyt wall wit all my blahd on top. My Maddah stay crying tell him no do dat—too soa da likens. But, he too mad. He no listen. I stil get da ska. She tol me, if my Grandfaddah ask, tell heem I wen bang my hed to da ka dowa. She tink nobody no. She tink my Granfaddah stoopid. He fite fo' me. He tell my Maddah he take me, hānai me. I go liv wit him an my Grandmaddah. Dey liv Hale'iwa side.

Afta dat, my life good. I go beech. I help my Granfaddah dem. I no family—reel kine family dat no moa fea. Sumatime we pick pa'akai from da beech. Lay 'um out dry. We all go togetta. Pik mangos off da tree mek mango seed li'dat. He liv off da 'āina. He take me diving, li'dat. He drink wit hees frenz, dey sing Hawaiian kine songs come float into da haus wea me an my Granmaddah stay waching t.v. My Granmaddah make pūpūs foa dem. An, owsie, my Granfaddah pūlehu kala, manini, kūmū, anykine.

But, I get pilikia in my na'au 'cause I no kan help my sistah and my braddahs dem. My dad, he stay drunk bern my sistah fase. He stay drunk and kookin' hibachi. He wen go fo' trow lieta fluid on da fiya. He no notise she stay too clos. Da fire bern beeg, tsā! Bern her face. She only smaw so da scars go away. But, she remaba an tell me.

My braddahs, two of dem no work now. Won stay jail 'cause he steel an do batu li'dat. Da oddah one smok pakalolo leev wit one strippah. Him an da strippah always beef. He call me up fo' go get him wen she fiyo domestiks fo him fo go jayl, but I tiyed alredy. He ol' enuf. He no lern. But, I stil sad. Dey boat brek my hot.

I da lahky won. Cuz I had luv from my Granfaddah dem. I die fo' dem. Wen my Granfaddah make, I wanted fo' die too. Dis' time I no feel noting—'cept *finally.* All yoa frenz goin see dat none of yowa keeds cum fo' pay respek. Cuz non of dem get fo' yu. Yu die wit shame! Mek ass dat kine.

My maddah wen leave heem. But, too late. Damage stay pau alredy. Twenty-fye yeas alredy. He neva give kālā fo' supot hees kids. He live hees life witout us. Den why I gotta go? I no moa aloha for heem. Pau alredy. Jus' *pau.*

"Look like won good day fo' go holoholo, honey. Maybe get kala and manini today."

*Translations of Articles from
the Hawaiian Nationalist
Newspaper* Ke Aloha Aina

# *noenoe*

Noenoe Silva • Noenoe Silva • Noenoe Silva • Noenoe Silva

## *Translations of Articles from the Hawaiian Nationalist Newspaper* Ke Aloha Aina

*Since not many of us are fluent enough
in Hawaiian to understand the words of
our kūpuna (ancestors), I have chosen to
translate the following articles in light of
their importance to us today. These articles
help us to understand who our kūpuna
were, their concerns and goals, and the
nature of their struggles during a critical
time a hundred years ago when Kānaka
Maoli—the people indigenous to the
Hawaiian islands—consciously and purposefully attempted to exercise their political
will within the United States system. They
were published in 1900 in the Hawaiian
nationalist newspaper* Ke Aloha Aina, *the
organ of the political group Hui Aloha ʻĀina.
In the protests against annexation, the* lāhui
Hawaiʻi *(Hawaiian people or nation) had*

united in unprecedented numbers under the banner of "aloha 'āina"—love for their land, their nation, and their people—to draw on the strength such feelings had given them collectively over the previous seven years since the overthrow of the monarchy in 1893. Their actions should not be construed as nationalism in which the people see themselves as superior to other races but, rather, as resistance to the loss of land, identity, culture, and political power. And their love for the land was based on the traditional familial relationship to the 'āina.

The excerpt from the series of articles entitled "E Hoomau i ke Kupaa no ke Aloha i ka Aina" (Persevere in Your Steadfastness for the Love of the Land) was written by Edward Kekoa, and ran from 20 January 1900 to 28 April 1900. At the time, Robert Kalanihiapo Wilcox was in Washington, D.C., with other Kanaka Maoli delegates, attempting to overturn the annexation of Hawai'i to the United States. The Newlands Resolution had been passed by both houses of Congress but had not yet been signed into law.

This was a time of great mourning for the lāhui. At this same time, Hawai'i was beginning to be overwhelmed by soldiers and settlers from the U.S. An editorial in Ke Aloha Aina entitled "Ko Kakou Noho Ana Kanikau" (Our Living In Mourning) (Ke Aloha Aina 1 July 1899) was also published around then. Its subject was the mourning practices of Kānaka Maoli and the lack of understanding on the part of the settlers who, for instance, often wrote to their compatriots about the strange ways of the natives. Since no specific person is mentioned in the editorial as having passed away at this time, it is quite probably the passing of Lili'uokalani's government that is being mourned.

The language of mourning is contained in another article written by Kekoa entitled "Ka La Kuokoa" (Independence Day, celebrated until 1895 in commemoration of the recognition of the restoring of Hawai'i's sovereignty by Great Britain and France in 1843), which is described as being "ma kona kino aka wailua" (in its shadowy corpse) (Ke Aloha Aina 2 Dec. 1899). In his articles, Kekoa attempts to comfort his fellow mourners, urging them to continue in their love for their nation as instructed by the great Hawaiian leader Joseph Nāwahī on his deathbed in 1896: "E ho'omau i ke kūpa'a no ke aloha i ka 'āina." He also urges them to pray to the Christian God. Through such articles, Kekoa is keeping the flame of resistance burning in Hawai'i while the nation awaits the results of the work of Wilcox and other Kanaka Maoli delegates in Washington.

The mass protests against annexation by the lāhui Hawai'i could be seen as unimpressive to a huge nation such as the United States, since the entire lāhui consisted of merely 40,000 people. Nonetheless, the political efforts of the Kanaka Maoli delegates, along with the protest petitions, succeeded in turning the vote against the treaty of annexation. However, soon after, the U.S. entered into war with Spain. Because of the militarily strategic position of the Hawaiian islands, Hawai'i was annexed through a joint resolution of Congress—the Newlands Resolution—despite the resolution's illegality under international law.

Although not reconciled to annexation, many Kānaka Maoli were relieved that the era of the oligarchy of haole businessmen who had overthrown the Queen appeared to be over, and it seemed that political power for Kānaka Maoli—on the local level at least—was possible under the U.S. system. In "Hewa i ka Wai na Kanaka" (Crowds of People), Wilcox reports that he was successful in lobbying for universal male suffrage for Hawai'i (under the oligarchy only the wealthy could vote). This would give Kānaka Maoli substantial power in territorial politics, provided they voted as a bloc. Wilcox believed that establishing a separate political party for Kānaka Maoli was the means to political power, and he envisioned a merging of Hui Aloha 'Āina with the other large Hawaiian nationalist political party, Hui Kālai'āina.

Before the leaders of this plan took any action to establish the party, they sought Lili'uokalani's blessing. They were no doubt concerned that she or others in the lāhui might think that they were betraying their commitment to aloha 'āina, and so explained to her their intent to keep aloha 'āina alive by taking control of local government. In "Ka Leo Alii i Mua o na Elele a ka Lahui" (The Ali'i's Voice Before the Representatives of the Nation), Lili'uokalani makes a simple statement of support for the leaders of the two Hui. It is notable that these representatives address Lili'uokalani by the traditional terms "Kalani" and "Ali'i." Even as they are moving into the U.S. political system, they remain rooted and draw strength from their traditional culture and language. Also notable is how the language of aloha 'āina is still in full use in these articles. They continue to be kūpa'a ma ke aloha i ka 'āina—steadfast in love for the land.

Although it may appear that the relationships between the Queen, the two Hui, and Robert Wilcox were harmonious, they were in fact complex and are still being researched. Wilcox and the Queen had had

public disagreements on more than one occasion in preceding years, and there was some bitterness between Wilcox and Hui Aloha 'Āina in 1896-97, after Wilcox failed in his bid for the Hui's presidency. In spite of their serious political disagreements and personal conflicts, these leaders made great efforts to establish a united front to reach their common objective. Even while Wilcox served as a delegate to the U.S. Congress, the lāhui continued to honor Queen Lili'uokalani as Ke Ali'i 'Ai Moku, and we continue to honor her today.

The events described and discussed in these articles express a time of hope for the lāhui, hope not yet crushed by the reality of being a numerically powerless minority within the U.S., nor by the oligarchy's looming metamorphosis into the Big Five, the alliance of large corporations that would come to monopolize Hawai'i's economy and politics for the next century.

Wilcox died in 1903, at the age of 48. The Home Rule Party continued to exist and its candidates remained active for many years. But it was eventually overpowered by the Democratic and Republican Parties, who were supported by the large national committees in the U.S. Within a few short years, Kānaka Maoli would no longer be a majority in their own land, and the promise of U.S. democracy would turn out to be the means not to prosperity and equality for Kānaka Maoli, but to loss of culture and nation.

# E Hoomau i ke Kupaa
# no ke Aloha i ka Aina

Edward Kekoa • Edward Kekoa • Edward Kekoa • Edward Kekoa

KE ALOHA AINA
Honolulu, Poaono, Maraki 3, 1900 ('ao'ao 4)

EDWARD L. LIKE,
Lunahooponopono
JOSEPH K. LIKE,
Luna Hoohana
HOGAN E. KALUNA,
Luna Hoopuka
EMMA A. NAWAHI,
Puuku o KE ALOHA AINA.

(Helu 4.)

E hoomau i ke kupaa i keaha? Pane: "I ka hoole aku, aole loa e hoohui ia aku na Paeaina o Hawaii nei me Amerika Huipuia kela hoohui aina a Kakina ma i halihali ai i Amerika maluna o ka moku Kalaudina, i ka malama o Ianuari, 1893."

2. E hoomau i ka hoole ana, aole he pololei o kela olelo hooholo hoohui aina a Nulana, no ka mea, he olelo hooholo pakaha maopopo loa ia o ke ano aihue hilahila ole, i hana ia a hooholo ia iloko o ka Ahaolelo o kekahi o na aupuni nui a naauao o ka honua nei, oia hoi, o Amerika Huiia.

3. E hoomau i ka hoole ana aku, aole loa he kuleana o ke aupuni Amerika e hana mai ai i aupuni no kakou e ka lahui Hawaii, me he mea la, he lahui aupuni aole kakou mai mua [sic], i kohu ai oia e hana mai i aupuni no kakou, elike me kana lauwili a e pauaka kolohe mai nei.

4. E hoomau kakou i ka hoole aku, aole kakou ka lahui Hawaii i mahalo iki i na hana kolohe me na hana hoopilikia wale a ke aupuni Amerika ia kakou, oiai kakou ka lahui Hawaii, aole i hana hewa aku i ke aupuni Amerika.

5. E hoomau kakou i ke koi ana, e hoihoi mai ke aupuni Amerika i ke aupuni kumu o

Hawaii, a me na pono a pau elike me ia i ka la a kona Kuhina kolohe i kokua ai i ka poe kipi ino naau keleawe hilahila ole, a ku hou me kona kilohana a pau, elike me ia mai mua mai.

6. E hoomau kakou i ka hoole ana, aole o kakou makemake i ke aupuni kolikoli a lakou i manao ai, oia ko kakou ano aupuni a lakou e haawi mai ai no kakou. Hele pela.

7. E hoole aku kakou i na kanawai hoomali-mali a lakou e hana mai nei, e pili ana i ke koho balota, a pela aku. He hookamani a he hoomalimali maalea a ka nahesa ia ano hana. E kipaku aku kakou, elike me Iesu i kipaku aku ai ia Diabolo me ka olelo ana aku. "E hele pela oe e Satana." Mat 4:10.

Pela kakou e hoole aku ai me ka ikaika ia mau hana maalea a lakou e hana mai nei, oiai, ua naauao no ko kakou lahui, a e hiki no ia kakou ke hooponopono i ko kakou aupuni, a heaha ke kumu o ka waiho aku na lakou e hana mai ke ano o ke aupuni, na kanawai a me na luna aupuni? Hele pela.

8. E hoomau kakou i ka olelo aku ia Amerika, ua hana hewa loa oe ia Hawaii lahui uuku, lahui palupalu a nawaliwali, a e holoi koke oe i kau karaima ekaeka i hana mai ai maluna o makou.

9. E hoomau kakou i ka hoole ana, aole he kupono iki o ko Amerika lawe lima nui ana ae, a hoomalu kumu ole ia kakou, he pakaha a me ka powa ia ano hana, he hana i kohu ole loa e hana ia e ke aupuni o Amerika. A oiai oia e noho hoomalu kohu ole ana ia Hawaii nei, puhi ia ke kino make o ke kanaka i ke ahi a puhi wale ia na hale a me na waiwai o kekahi poe he nui wale, aole o kana mai ka pilikia i loaa i kona wa e noho hoomalu kohu ole ana, he poino hoi i ike ole

ia mai mua mai ma keia aina a ka maluhia i luakaha ai.

Ma keia mau kumu a me na kumu aku i koe, e hoomau ai kakou i ke kupaa ana.

# Persevere in Your Steadfastness for the Love of the Land

## kekoa

Edward Kekoa • Edward Kekoa • Edward Kekoa • Edward Kekoa

*Ke Aloha Aina*
Honolulu, Friday 3 March 1900:4.

Edward L. Like, Editor
Joseph K. Like, Managing Editor
Hogan E. Kaluna, Publisher
Emma A. Nāwahī, [Owner and] Business
Manager of *Ke Aloha Aina*

[The following excerpt is number 4 in a series regarding continuing to protest the annexation of Hawai'i to the United States of America.]

(Number 4)

Persevere in your steadfastness for what? Answer: "Protest that the Hawaiian Islands should never be annexed to the United States, that [treaty of] annexation that Thurston et al. carried to the U.S. on the ship Claudine, in the month of January 1893."

2. Continue to protest that the Newlands Resolution is not right, because it is clearly a resolution of shameless robbery, made and passed in the Congress of one of the great and enlightened governments of the world, the United States of America.

3. Continue to protest that the U.S. government has absolutely no authority [*kuleana*] to create a government for us, the *lāhui Hawai'i* [Hawaiian people or nation], as if we were a people without a government already, so that by twisting words around and proceeding in a flagrantly unprincipled way it might therefore seem justified in creating a government for us.

4. Let us continue to protest that we the *lāhui Hawai'i* do not appreciate in the least the unethical actions and the actions that have caused great distress that America has done to us, the *lāhui Hawai'i*, who have not

123

done anything wrong to the American government.

5. Let us continue to demand that the U.S. government restore the original government of Hawai'i and all of the conditions [*pono*]* as they were on the day that its unethical Minister [John L. Stevens] aided the shameless, steel-hearted, evil conspirators, so that Hawai'i will stand again in all its excellence as it did before.

6. Let us continue to protest that we do not want the pared-down government that they have planned; that is, the type of government that they would hand to us. Get out!

7. Let us protest the laws they are making that are meant to appease us concerning voting and so forth. This is the hypocrisy and deceitful flattery of the snake. Let us drive them out, just as Jesus drove out the Devil, saying, "Get out, Satan." Mat. 4:10.

That is the way we should vehemently protest these deceitful actions that they are making, since our people are educated, and since we are able to administer our own government; why should we defer to them to create a form of government, laws, and government officers? Get out!

8. Let us continue to say to the U.S.: You have done very wrong to Hawai'i, a people small in number, frail and weak [militarily], and you should immediately clean up the dirty crime you have perpetrated on us.

9. Let us continue to protest that the U.S.'s forcefully taking and confining us without reason is not proper in the least. These kinds of actions are greed and robbery, actions completely illegal for the U.S. government to do. And while it is illegally ruling as the government over Hawai'i, corpses of people are being burnt in fires [because of the outbreak of bubonic plague], and the houses and valuables of many people are being burned up as well. There has never been so much trouble [in Hawai'i] as there has been since the U.S. has illegally governed. [We have experienced] misfortune never before seen in this land that once enjoyed peace.

For these and other reasons, let us continue to persevere.

---

*The word "*pono*" includes material welfare and well-being, with the *ali'i* and *maka'āinana* in proper balance, and also evokes the line from the song "Mele Aloha 'Āina" (also known as "Mele 'Ai Pōhaku" or "Kaulana nā Pua"): *Ma hope mākou o Lili'ulani, a loa'a ē ka pono o ka 'āina.*

TRANSLATED BY NOENOE SILVA

124

*Ka Leo Alii imua o
na Elele a ka Lahui*

Nā Luna o *Ke Aloha Aina* • Nā Luna o *Ke Aloha Aina* • Nā Luna o *Ke Aloha Aina*

Honolulu, Poaono, Iune 9, 1900 ('ao'ao 2)

EDWARD L. LIKE,
Lunahooponopono
HOGAN E. KALUNA,
Luna Hoopuka
ALEX NAWAHI,
Luna Hoohana
EMMA A. NAWAHI,
Puuku o KE ALOHA AINA.

Mahope iho o ka hoomaha ana o ka halawai
a ka Aha Elele o na Ahahui Aloha Aina a me
Kalai aina, ma ka hora 11:30 o ke awakea
Poakolu nei, ua hele aku la na Elele a pau e
ike i ke Alii ka Moiwahine Liliuokalani ma
Wakinekona Hale.

I ka akoakoa ana aku o na Elele, na
Kalauokalani i hoolauna aku i ua Elele i ke
Alii, a wahi a ka leo Alii i panai mai ai.

"Aloha oukou: Aole au i manao eia no

oukou ka lahui ke hoomanao mai nei Ia'u,
oiai, he umi makahiki i hala ae nei e ku ana
Au he Makuahine no oukou ka lahui, a i keia
manawa, ua noho mana mai la o Amerika
Huipuia maluna O'u a me oukou Kuu lahui,
he mea ehaeha no Ia'u na haawina i ili iho
maluna o kakou, aka, he mea hiki ole ke
pale ae, ua hoohamama ia mai Ko'u manao,
mamuli o na haawina a Amerika i hana mai
nei no ka lahui Hawai'i, a oia pono Ka'u e
a'o aku nei e nana mai no ka lahui i na
alakai ana a na alakai o ka lahui, oia o Mr.
Kaulia a me Mr. Kalauokalani, ua ili maluna
o laua ke koikoi no ka nana ana i ka pono o
ka lahui elike me ke Kanawai a Amerika i
haawi mai nei, a o ka loaa ana i ka lahui na
pono a me na pomaikai no na hanauna aku
a kakou o keia mua aku, o ka loaa ana no ia
Ia'u oia pono hookahi.

Aole o kakou kuhi'na [kuhi 'ana] aku i koe,
koe wale ae la no keia pono akea i haawi ia
mai e Amerika ia oukou ka lahui, e hopu a

paa, a na oukou e hooponopono no kakou no keia mua aku.

Me keia mau wahi hualelo [*sic*] pokole, a hookuu mai Ia'u, me ka haawi pu aku i Ko'u aloha i ka lahui, aloha oukou."

Na J. K. Kaulia i pane ma ka aoao o ka Aha Elele, wahi ana:

E Kalani: Ma ka aoao o na Elele a me Kou lahui, ke lawe nei makou me ka manao laahia loa i ka leo Alii a omau iho maluna o ko makou umauma a me Kou lahui, a e lilo hoi ia mau huaolelo Alii i pae mai nei i mea e alakai ia ai Kou lahui no na pono a me na pomaikai ma keia mua aku, a me ka pono o na hanauna o Kou lahui e hoea mai ana.

## The Ali'i's Voice before the Representatives of the Nation

Editors of *Ke Aloha Aina* • Editors of *Ke Aloha Aina* • Editors of *Ke Aloha Aina*

Honolulu, Friday 9 June 1900:2.

Edward L. Like, Editor
Hogan E. Kaluna, Publisher
Alex Nāwahī, Managing Editor
Emma A. Nāwahī, [Owner and] Business
Manager of *Ke Aloha Aina*

After the meeting of representatives of the 'Ahahui Aloha 'Āina and Kālai'āina at 11:30 a.m. last Wednesday, all the representatives went to meet with the *Ali'i*,* Queen Lili'uokalani, at Washington Place.

After the representatives assembled, Kalauokalani introduced them to the *Ali'i*, and the voice of the *Ali'i* said:

"Aloha to all of you: I did not think that you, the *lāhui* [people or nation] still were thinking of me, since ten years has passed since I became a Mother to you, the *lāhui*, and now the U.S. sits in power over me and over you, my dear [*Kuu*] *lāhui*. What has befallen us is very painful to me; however, it could not be prevented. My mind has been opened because of the [unrestricted vote] the U.S. has given to the *lāhui Hawai'i*. This is what I advise: that the *lāhui* should look to the guidance of the leaders of the *lāhui*, Mr. Kaulia and Mr. Kalauokalani. A great responsibility has fallen upon them to look out for the welfare of the *lāhui* in accordance with the laws that the U.S. has handed down, so that the *lāhui* will receive the rights and benefits for our future generations, and I will also receive that one benefit [i.e. the welfare of the *lāhui*].

"We have no other direction left to pursue, except this unrestricted right [to vote], given by the U.S. to you the *lāhui*, grasp it and hold on to it. It is up to you to make things right for all of us in the future.

"With these brief words, please excuse me,

# I KA LAHUI ALOHA AINA.

## Aloha Alii a Makee Alii.
## E Ala.    E Eu.

E hoike i ko oukou aloha a makee Alii ma ka haawi ana i na wahi kokua e hiki ana no ka hookipa ana mai Iaia e like no me ko kakou ano mau he mea nui na 'Lii ia kakou na makaainana mai kahiko mai.

E ike i ko kakou Makuahine Alii!  E ike i ko kakou Moiwahine aloha, LILIUOKALANI !!

      O KAMAKAEHA,
      O LILIU-O-LOLOKU,
      O WALANIA-I-KE-KII-ONOHI,
      O KA-ONOHI O-KALANINUI,
      O KE-KAHIWAULI-O KAONOHI-LANI,
      O KA-ONOHI IA-E-KOKONI-AI-O KA-EHA,
      E LOKU-AI-O KA-MAKA-I KA-PUUKAI,
      O KA-MAKA-IA I-HEA-IA-I-KAPA IA-AI,
      HE INOA—E,

Ina aku a hoea mai, ma ka Aukekulia o ka Poakolu ae nei, Iune 6, 1900, ina nae aole he mau kuia.

E moe ka oo i kai o ka uwapo i ka ike malihini Alii, a ike Mele pu hoi.  O ka ike aku ka paha i na maka o Kalani, he ma-u ia.  O ka wa hoihoi no ia o ka malihini o kinohi, ua lluliu wale keia mau la o ke kaawale ana.

E OLA!  E OLA!!  O LILIUOKALANI I KE AKUA!!!

---

Notice in *Ke Aloha Aina* on Friday 2 June 1900 to "the People Who Love the Land" on the event of Lili'uokalani's return to Hawai'i from Washington, D.C. The body of the text begins, "Show your love and great affection for the Queen by giving your help, as has always been our custom, as the day of welcoming her home draws near; the *Ali'i* have always been important to us, the *maka'āinana*, since ancient times."

give my aloha to the *lāhui*, and aloha
to you."

J[ames] K. Kaulia answered on behalf of the
representatives, saying:

"Your Majesty, on behalf of the representatives and Your *lāhui*, we reverently carry
away with us the message of the *Ali'i*, and
we bind it to our hearts and the hearts of
the *lāhui*, and these words that have been
heard will become something by which Your
*lāhui* will be led, for well-being and prosperity
in the future, and for the benefit of the
generations of Your *lāhui* yet to come."

*I chose to keep the original word "*Ali'i*" rather
than translate it as "Monarch" because it brings
to mind certain cultural connotations of
Hawai'i nei that link Lili'uokalani to Kalākaua
and to their entire genealogical line of ancestors.
"Monarch," on the other hand, evokes
European associations.

TRANSLATED BY NOENOE SILVA

*Hewa i ka Wai na*
*Kanaka, Hookui ka Ia*
*i ka Makaha*

*Uwa ka Pihe a Haalele Wale i na*
*Haiolelo a ka Aoao Kuokoa*

*He Mau Tausani i Hiki Ae*
*i ka Halawai Makaainana Nui a*
*ka Aoao Kuokoa ma ke Ahiahi*
*Poaono Nei, Iune 9, 1900.*

# ke aloha aina

Nā Luna o *Ke Aloha Aina* • Nā Luna o *Ke Aloha Aina* • Nā Luna o *Ke Aloha Aina*

Honolulu, Poaono, Iune 16, 1900
('ao'ao 5)

EDWARD L. LIKE,
Lunahooponopono.
HOGAN E. KALUNA,
Luna Hoopuka.
ALEX NAWAHI,
Luna Hoohana.
EMMA A. NAWAHI,
Puuku o KE ALOHA AINA.

Ma ka hora 8 o ka po Poaono nei, i malama io ia ae ai ka Halawai Makaainana Nui a ka Aoao Kuokoa, a mamua ae o ka hoea ana mai o ka manawa e wehe ia ai o na hana oia po, ua hoopiha ia ae la ke kahua mamua iho o ka hale paikau me na kanaka Hawaii me na haole, na kane, wahine a me na opio, e hoike maopopo mai ana, ua ohohia ko lakou manao e hele mai e hoolohe i na haiolelo oia po.

O D. Kalauokalani ka lunahoomalu oia halawai, a ua ku mai oia a hoakaka mai la i ke kumuhana i kahea ia ai keia halawai, e noonoo ana i ke kumuhana kupono e pili ana i ke aupuni a Amerika i haawi mai la no ko Hawaii Paeaina. A mahope o kekahi mau hoakaka ana no ka hoolohe ole ana mai la o Amerika Huipuia i ke koi kumu a ka lahui e hoihoi i ke Aupuni Moi, ua lawe ia mai la ka noonoo koho balota, a malaila hoi ka manaolana hope o ka lahui, me ka hoike pu mai ana [sic], aohe elele e ae a ka lahui e koho ai no ka holo ana aku i ka Ahaolelo o Amerika Huipuia, aka, o R. W. Wilikoki wale no, a ua apono ia e ke anaina me ka lokahi, a mahope o ka pau ana o kana haiolelo i ohohia nui ia, ua hoolauna mai la oia i ka elele R. W. Wilikoki.

Ia wa i ku mai ai o R. W. Wilikoki a hoike mai la penei:

E na lede a me na keonimana, na kupa

130

teritori. Owau ka Elele a ka Hui Kalaiaina i hoouna aku ai i Wasinetona, a i kakoo ia hoi e ka lahui, ua haalele iho au ma ka la 25 o Novemaba, maluna o ka mokumahu Coptic, a hoea aku la i Kapalakiko ma ka la 1 o Dekemaba, 1899. Mailaila ua holo aku au no ka akau no ka huipu ana me Caypless, ma Seattle, ua hoomaka maua i ka hana malaila no na mea e pili ana no ka hoihoi Aupuni Moi, a ua loaa ia maua he kakoo ana malaila mai ka nupepa Times mai, aka, i ko maua hiki ana ma Kikako, ilaila hoole ia mai aohe wahi pono i koe, no ka mea, puka ka olelo hooholo a Nulana, ua paa ia. Hiki maua i Wasinetona i ka la 31 o Dekemaba, a i ka la hapenuia ae hui me ka Moiwahine a launa aloha me Ia. Malaila ua hele aku maua i na nupepa oia wahi, ua hoole ia mai, aohe pono i koe, ua iho aku oia no ka wa mau loa, no na hewa i hana ia mai. I ka ike ana aohe wahi pono malaila, ua holo maua i Nu Ioka, aka, ua nele pu no ma ia wahi, a ua a'o ia mai aia iloko o ka Hale Ahaolelo ka pono. I ka maopopo loa ana, aohe hoihoi Moi i koe, ua hooholo iho la e hooikaika ma ka ae ia ana mai e loaa ka pono koho balota i ka lahui Hawaii, ua hele aku la au imua o ke Komite Teritori, ma ka la 22 o Ianuari, o Knox ka lunahoomalu, he hoakula no Hakawela, komo au iloko o laila, a ike aku la i na hana hoohaiki mana koho a ke Komisina Hawaii i hana ai, oia hoi, aole e loaa ka mana koho i kekahi mea ke loaa ole iaia he ana waiwai o $600, a o ka manao o keia no ka hoonele i na Hawaii, i ka mana koho ole, a o poe [sic] waiwai wale no ke loaa ka mana koho. I ke komo mua ana o ka Bila Hawaii iloko o ke Senate, aole au malaila.

Ua lawe ia mai keia bila i ka hale olalo, a ua nui ka paio i hanaia, a na Moon o Tenesi i lawe mai ka olelo hooholo e hoopau ana i ke ana waiwai, a ua apono ia. Mamuli o keia hoololi, ua lawe hou ia aku la ia i ke Senate. Ua nui ka'u mau hooikaika ana me ke komo aku iloko o na Senatoa i ke ao a me ka po, e hooikeike [sic] ana i na hana hoohaiki i hanaia aku i na Hawaii. Ua nui ko Callom [sic] a me Mogana hooikaika ana e hoomau ia keia kanawai, aka, ua haule nae a loaa ka [sic] eo ia kakou. O kekahi mea a'u i hooikaika ai, oia ka hoopau ia ana o kahi e olelo ana, e ukuia na auhau ma ka la 31 o Maraki o ka makahiki e koho balota ai, ma ke kokua ikaika a Petiguru, ua haule keia kumuhana. Ua hoakaka pu aku o Petiguru i ke ano o ka hana ia ana o na poe i uku ole i ko lakou mau auhau ma Hawaii, e hopu ia ana lakou a hoopaa ma ka hale paahao, he mea i hana ole ia e Amerika i kona lahui, a na ia mea i pepehi loa aku i ka bila a Collum. Ma Amerika, he 50 keneta wale no ka uku auhau o kekahi poe, a o na poe ilihune e like me na poe e hana nei ma kai o ka uwapo, aole o lakou uku auhau.

Nolaila e na Hawaii, e ku kakou me he pa pohaku la, a hina hoi i ka wa hookahi, e hooi aku i ko kakou kupaa ana, a e koho i ka Aoao Kuokoa. O ke teritori he elele wale no kona ma ka Hale Ahaolelo, aka nae, he mana kona. O kana mau hoike ana, oia ka ka Peresidena o Amerika e hoolohe mai ai, a he manaolana ko'u iloko o ka manawa pokole e loaa mai ana ia kakou ka Mokuaina (State), a ia wa e nana aku ai kakou i na aoao kalaiaina ikaika o Amerika. Mamua o ko'u haalele ana aku ia Wasinetona, ua loaa iho la ia'u he mau ao ana mai na hoaloha, e hoi mai a ao aku i na Hawaii e kukulu i Aoao Kuokoa no lakou, a mai kokua hoi i ka aoao Demokarata a i ole i ka Repubalika, no ka mea e hoehaeha ana ia i na hoaloha malaila, oiai, ua kokua like keia mau aoao kalaiaina o Amerika ia kakou. E mau ko kakou kupaa ana me he mea la eia no [o] Liliuokalani ke noho nei ma ke kalaunu. O ka mea aloha i make e waiho i ka noonoo ana nona, aka, e nana aku no mua. E hoomau i ko kakou kupaa ana, a pela wale no e loaa ai ka lanakila. Haawi ia na huro.

Maanei i hoolauna ia mai ai o James K. Kaulia, a nana i heluhelu mai ke kumuhana a ka Aoao Kuokoa e hooikaika ai no ka pono o ka lahui, a ua aponoia me ke ohohia nui ia. O keia ke kumuhana i hoopukaia ai maloko o KE ALOHA AINA. Ua waiho pu mai oia he wahi haiolelo pokole, e hoike ana, i ka noho ana o ka lahui iloko o na makahiki wi ehiku, aka, ua hala aku la nae ia, a eia ka lahui iloko o na makahiki momona e hele nei, me ka hoakaka pu mai, ua kukulu mua ia ae nei he elua mau aoao kalaiaina, oia ke Demokarata a me ka Repubalika, aka, o na poe no nae o loko oia mau aoao, oia no na poe hoohui aina. "E pepehi i ka moo," wahi ana i hooho mai ai.

O ka haiolelo hope oia po, oia o John Wise, a nana i haawi mai i kekahi haiolelo mikioi loa ma ka olelo Enelani, e kue ana i na olelo hakuepa a kekahi poe haole manao ino e olelo nei, he poe kue haole na Hawaii, wahi ana.

Ua kapa ia makou he poe kue haole (anti-whites), aka, e nana aku kakou ina he ekolu mau Hawaii palupalu e hanai moa ana, a e kanu ana hoi he mau wahi pue uala, i ka wa e hoea aku ai o kekahi ili keokeo malaila, aole e nele e kii ana lakou e pepehi he wahi moa me ka hue ana i na pue uala nana. E na keonimana e nana aku i hope i ka wa e hoea aku ai kekahi haole ma ka home o ka Hawaii, e haawi ana oia i kona wahi moe no ka haole, me ka moe aku iluna o ka papahele. I ka makahiki 1820, ua hoea mai he mau misionari kakaikahi a alakai aku la i na Hawaii no lakou ka huina lahui he 200,000, aka, aole nae lakou i kue aku i na haole. I ka

1890, ua koho ia na Alii o ka Ahaolelo he 9 haole a me 8 kanaka, e hoike maopopo mai ana aohe mau manao kue o na Hawaii no ka haole, aka, i ka hoea ana mai nae i ka 1893, i ka wa a na haole i lawe ae ai i ka mana hookele o ke aupuni, ua kipaku aku la na haole i na Hawaii mailoko aku o ka oihana aupuni, a hoonoho mai la i ko lakou mau ohana malaila, no ka ai ana i ka momona o ke aupuni. Mai ka 1893, o na haole e hoea mai ana iloko o ka manawa pokole e ku ana ko lakou mau hale nani, me na kaa nani e kalaiwa ia ana e na kahu kaa, mai hea ko lakou waiwai i hoea mai ai, mai Hawaii ae nei no. Ke hooiaio aku nei au, he hoaloha na Hawaii a pau no na haole e hana aloha mai ana ia lakou, a aole hoi lakou e hoopoina aku ana ia poe a e ike ia aku ana no he mau haole no kekahi e holo balota pu ana ma ka aoao o ka lahui. Aole i kue aku na Hawaii i na haole, elike la me na haole i hoouna aku ai i kekahi poe malalo o ka lilo o ka waihona o ke aupuni no Wasinetona, no ka hoopilikia ana i na Hawaii. Aole loa makou e hookau aku ana i uku panai no ua poe hana ino wale mai, aka, na na Lani no ia e haawi mai i kana uku hoopai kupono.

Ina he moa wiwi kai hoopakele ia mai kahi pauahi o Kinatona mai, a e hoololiia na dala a pau o ka waihona i mau hua kulina, a hanai aku iaia aole no e loaa ana iaia ka momona, pela no na haole.

Mahope o keia haiolelo i hookuu ia ai na hana iloko o leo huro, a hoi aku la na poe a pau me ke ohohia nui. Ke hauoli nei makou mamuli o ko makou ike ana aku ua hoopiha ia keia kahua holookoa e na Hawaii, e hoike maopopo aku ana i na aoao kalaiaina e ae, eia ka lahui Hawaii makee alii a aloha aina ke kupaa nei he hookahi aoao me ka mahae ole, a ua lilo ia i mea e hookomo aku ana i ka weli iloko o ko lakou mau houpo.

*Crowds of People; The Fish Unite at the Sluice Gate*

*People Shout Until Hoarse at the Speeches of the Independent Party*

*Several Thousand Attended the Grand Mass Meeting of the Independent Party on Saturday Evening, June 9, 1900*

Editors of *Ke Aloha Aina* • Editors of *Ke Aloha Aina* • Editors of *Ke Aloha Aina*

Honolulu, Friday 16 June 1900:5.

Edward L. Like, Editor
Hogan E. Kaluna, Publisher
Alex Nāwahī, Managing Editor
Emma A. Nāwahī, [Owner and] Business Manager of *Ke Aloha Aina*

At 8:00 on Saturday night, the mass meeting of the Independent Party was held, and prior to the commencement of the evening's events, the grounds in front of the military drill house [*hale paikau*] were filled with Kānaka Hawai'i[1] and *haole*, men, women, and young people, clearly showing their enthusiasm for coming to listen to the speeches that night.

D[avid] Kalauokalani was the presiding officer at the meeting, and he rose and explained why the meeting had been called: to consider the appropriate actions [the people should take] concerning the government the U.S. had handed to the Hawaiian Islands.

And after some clarifications about the U.S. not heeding the original demands of the *lāhui* [people or nation] to restore the Queen's government, the issue of voting was taken up, and [he said that] that was where the last hope of the *lāhui* lay. There was no other representative that the people had chosen to travel to the U.S. Congress but R[obert] W. Wilcox, [whose selection] had been unanimously approved by the people. After his speech, which was very enthusiastically received, he introduced the representative R. W. Wilcox.

Wilcox rose and spoke:

"Ladies and gentlemen, citizens of the Territory. I am the representative that Hui Kālai'āina sent to Washington, supported by the people. I departed on the 25th of November on the steamship Coptic and arrived in San Francisco on the 1st of December 1899. From there I traveled north to join up with [E.] Caypless [another delegate to Congress from Hawai'i] in Seattle. We started work there towards the restoration of the monarchy. We received support there from the Times newspaper; however, when we arrived in Chicago, it was unsupported [*hoole*] there. There was no hope because the Newlands Resolution has passed and it was final. We arrived in Washington on the 31st of December, and on New Year's Day we met together with the Queen with aloha. We went to the newspapers there [but our side] was unsupported; there was no hope left. It [or he or she] went down forever for the wrongs that had been committed.[2] When we saw that there was no hope there, we went to New York, but we were also unsatisfied there, and we were advised that the best thing was to go to Congress. When we realized that the restoration of the Queen was impossible, we decided to work towards getting voting rights for the *lāhui Hawai'i*. I went before the Territorial Committee on the 22nd of January [1900]. Knox was the chair; he was a classmate of Hartwell. I went in there and witnessed the actions of the commissioner of Hawai'i [Hartwell?] to restrict the voting rights; that is, a person would not have the power to vote unless he had property in the amount of $600. The purpose was to deprive Hawaiians of their voting rights so that only the rich would have voting power.[3] When that Hawaiian bill was first introduced in the Senate, I was not there.

"This bill [the Organic Act] was taken to the lower House [House of Representatives], and there was a great debate there. [Rep.] Moon of Tennessee introduced a resolution to end the property requirement and the resolution was passed. Because of this change, the bill was then taken back to the Senate. I made great efforts, going to the Senators night and day, talking about the restrictions that have been put upon the Kānaka Hawai'i.

Cullom and Morgan tried very hard to have this law remain in effect, but it failed, and we won. Another thing I strove for was to delete the section saying that taxes had to be paid on the 31st of March of the voting year, and with the active assistance of Pettigrew this measure also failed. Pettigrew also clarified [to the Senate] what was done to people who did not pay their taxes in Hawai'i, that they were arrested and imprisoned. This is something the United States does not do to their people, and it was this that killed Cullom's bill. In the U.S., some folks pay only fifty cents tax, and poor people, such as those working on the wharves, do not pay taxes.

"Therefore, Kānaka Hawai'i, let us stand like a rock wall, and fall all at once, and continue in our perseverance by choosing an Independent Party. Territories have only a [non-voting] representative in Congress, but he has some power. What he says is what the President of the U.S. heeds, and I hope that in a short time we will have statehood, and at that time we will look to the strong

Robert W. Wilcox as a delegate to Congress for the Independent Home Rule Party

political parties of the U.S. Before I left Washington, I received some advice from friends that I should return and suggest to the Kānaka Hawai'i the establishment of an independent party for themselves, and not to assist the Democratic or Republican parties, because that will hurt friends there [in those parties], since both of those parties helped us equally. Let us continue to be persevering, as if Lili'uokalani were still on the throne. Of the thing that has died, let us put aside thoughts of it and instead look to the future. Let us continue persevering; through that we will achieve victory." The crowd cheered.

Here James K. Kaulia was introduced, and it was he who read the platform of the Independent Party that was striving for the benefit of the people, and it was approved with great enthusiasm. This is the platform that was published in Ke Aloha Aina. He also gave a short speech, saying that the people had lived through seven years of famine, but that had passed, and the people are now in a time of future prosperity. He explained also that there were already established two political parties, the Democratic and the Republican, but the people in those parties were the annexationists. "Slay the mo'o!"[4] he shouted.

The last speech of the evening was given by John Wise.[5] He made a skillful speech in English, protesting the deceitful words of some evil-minded haole people who had said that the Kānaka Hawai'i were against the haole. He said:

"We have been called anti-whites, but let us look: if three old [palupalu] Hawaiians were raising chickens and planting some sweet potato hills when a white-skinned person came there, it is certain that they would go and kill a chicken and dig up some sweet

potatoes for him. Gentlemen, look back at the time that a certain haole [Caucasian foreigner] came to the home of the Hawaiian; he would give his bed to the haole and sleep on the floor. In 1820, a mere handful of missionaries arrived to lead the Hawaiians, who were 200,000 in number, but they did not go against the haole. In 1890, nine haole were elected to the House of Nobles and eight Hawaiians, which shows that the Hawaiians had no thought of going against the haole. But when 1893 came, when the haole took the executive power of the government, the haole fired the Hawaiians from their government jobs, and put their own family members there to eat of the fat of the government. Since 1893, the haole who have come within a short time have beautiful houses erected, with their pretty cars driven by chauffeurs. Where did their wealth come from? Here from Hawai'i. I am testifying that all the Hawaiians are friends to all haole who behave with aloha towards them, and they will not forget those people, and it will be seen that there will be haole who will vote on the side of the people. Hawaiians are not anti-haole, like the haole who sent people at the expense of the government to Washington to cause trouble for the Hawaiians. We will not levy vengeance on those people who do such evil; it is Heaven [na Lani] that will give the proper punishment.[6]

"If a skinny chicken escaped the fire of Chinatown and all the dollars of the treasury were made into corn seed and fed to it, it still would never get fat; such is the haole."[7]

After this speech, the event ended with cheers, and everyone left feeling enthusiastic. We were happy to see the whole field filled with Hawaiians, clearly showing the other political parties that the ali'i-desiring, land-loving Hawaiian nation is still determined and is one party, with no factions, and this will become a thing that will strike terror in their hearts.

## Notes

[1] Although "Kānaka Hawai'i" could be translated as "Hawaiians," I prefer not to use this English term and to instead use a term from our heritage language in order to stress our ancestral identity.

[2] This is a literal translation of what may be a biblical saying.

[3] The first draft of the Organic Act establishing the Territory of Hawai'i in 1899 indeed contained the property requirement that no one would be allowed to vote unless that person "possessed...property in the Territory of the value of not less than one thousand dollars, and upon which legal taxes shall have been paid...or shall have actually received a money income of not less than six hundred dollars." As Wilcox reports, this provision was taken out.

[4] This is translated in the English papers as "Slay the dragon!", a threat that elicits a war of retaliation by the English press against Kaulia.

[5] John Wise was *hapa Hawai'i* (half Caucasian, half Kanaka Hawai'i). He helped establish the Independent Home Rule Party, and shortly thereafter joined the Democratic Party. He was an editor for *Ke Au Hou* and *Hawaii Holomua* in the 1910s, as well as the first Hawaiian-language teacher at the University of Hawai'i.

[6] The text reads "*na na Lani no ia e haawi mai i kana uku hoopai kupono.*" In the

English newspaper article on Wise's speech, the text reads "vengeance belongs to God." The Hawaiian text "*na Lani*" evokes images of the *ali'i*, who are often called "*Ka Lani*" in the singular and "*Nā Lani*" in the plural.

[7] Following here is John Wise's speech as it appeared in the *Hawaiian Gazette* (12 June 1900:7) and in the *Pacific Commercial Advertiser* (11 June 1900:12). The gist of his speech was translated into Hawaiian for the readers of *Ke Aloha Aina*. The two different language versions give us some idea of the different worldviews of the respective cultures, as well as of some of the limitations of translating from English or from Hawaiian.

Wise Speaks in English.

"In justice to the cause for which we stand, in justice to the Hawaiian people, I will try to speak to you tonight in the English language.

"We have been called anti-whites, we have been named the anti-haoles. I will relate to you a few facts that are history, to show you that the assertion on the part of our enemies is not a true one.

"Picture to yourself away out in the country somewheres in the woods may be, long ago, or at any time for that matter, a humble grass hut. An old Hawaiian is working about the little garden. All he has in the world to keep himself alive is one last, poor chicken and a hill of potatoes. Along comes Mr. White Man, hungry and tired through long travelling. I tell you what, that poor Hawaiian gives his last chicken and his last few potatoes and his only bed to Mr. White Man.

"Does that show an opposition to the haoles?

### What History Shows.

"Have the Hawaiians ever treated the white men in the manner in which the white men have treated the Hawaiians? Any white man who has travelled at all in the Islands knows that the Hawaiians will even surrender his bed to the haole." [Cries of 'that's right!' 'every time!' and general applause.]

"To say that we are anti-haole in our political sentiments is the weakest kind of an argument. Our enemies cannot produce a bit of evidence to substantiate the foolish charge.

"I will dig up a little past history to show you how generous and friendly the Hawaiians have always been to the white men.

"In 1890, I believe the Hawaiians commanded the ballot box from Hawaii to Niihau. And whom did they elect to the House of Nobles? Nine white men and only eight Hawaiians. I tell you the Hawaiians were not against the haoles in those days. Nor are they against them today.

### The Other Side.

"In 1893 the white people controlled the Government. What did they do? They fired every Hawaiian from office who did not hold the same political opinions as they did themselves. The 'family compact' was in and was intending to stay in and the 'family compact' was fed until it grew fat on money that you had paid. Did you ever know of a Hawaiian who came out of the legislative halls with money in his pockets?"

Loud and prolonged cries of "Aole! aole! aole!" "No! no! no!"

The crowd at this point cheered the speaker enthusiastically, and was for a moment wild with enthusiasm.

### From Gripsack to Mansion.

"White people come to these Islands one day carrying their entire belongings in hand-bags; they look around for rooms, or else they hire a house. In a few days they are rolling around Honolulu in swell carriages with footmen and living in Roman mansions.

"You know where they got the money from. You know how they suddenly became rich. You don't suppose they had their wealth in their bags all the time, and went around saying nothing about it, do you? So much for anti-haoles.

### Cannot Tell the Future.

"We cannot comprehend the future. But the Hawaiians know their friends. A few white men there are who have stuck to us in the past, who are still standing by us, and we are not forgetting them. We will never forget them.

"We have been accused of looking for revenge. Revenge comes to every man who has been injured. There will be vengeance. Vengeance on those who have wronged us. I will try and make a picture for you of the make-up of the kind of white man who has done us wrong.

### The Bad Man.

"He is of medium height and stoops in his walk. He wears an old black hat down over his eyes and a big, loose coat, the pockets bulging with papers and slates. And these papers stick out of his pockets and on them are written sentiments like these: 'Anti-haole,' 'race-prejudice' and 'anti-white.' On his shoulders he carries a great bundle. Kids are chasing him around the streets all the time. He comes to where there is a grindstone by-and-by. He dumps his big load on the ground and it bursts open. It is full of old blunt axes. He heaves a great sigh and says: 'Old folks used to come to me to turn my grindstone, but now I have only little boys.'

"Now this is the kind of man we fight. Men like this have employed men to go to Washington to deprive us of our right to vote, and I defy the opposition to deny it. Do you expect we are going to be led by such men?

### Don't Seek Spoils.

"We have also been accused by our enemies of seeking spoils. If the poorest chicken saved from the ruins of the burned Chinatown were fed on the money in the treasury turned to corn, it would never get fat."

Cheer upon cheer greeted this emphatically delivered assertion. After quiet was restored the speaker wound up his speech in the following language:

"Who robbed the treasury? The Hawaiians know who the spoil-seekers are."

"Find them and get hold of them and punish them!" called out somebody at the back of the crowd.

"Yes, we will find them," went on the orator. "We will find the guilty ones. But vengeance is not ours. There is a Being high above us who knows all things, who watches all things, and who holds vengeance in the hollow of His hand. When the guilty ones are down, do not touch them, for vengeance belongs to God."

As Mr. Wise sat down the assembled enthusiasts lifted their hats and flourished their arms, cheering lustily and long.

### They Knew Him.

A half-drunken white man, well known in town, who speaks the Hawaiian language fluently, was very loud in his demonstrations of approval of what the different speakers said. Some native in the crowd called out to him after a while: "Oh, be still; we know you!"

The evening could not have been more pleasant for the mass meeting. It was cool and clear. The meeting was altogether most enthusiastic and interesting, though many of those who attended sat around on the grass at the edge of the crowd and held private conversations.

[Note: The article in the *Hawaiian Gazette* does not contain the subtitles "Don't Seek Spoils" and "They Knew Him," but it is otherwise identical to the version in the *Pacific Commercial Advertiser*.]

TRANSLATED BY NOENOE SILVA

Kekuewa standing next to the large *pōhaku* called "Ka U'i o Mānoa," located in Mānoa Valley on the island of O'ahu, at Wailele, on what is known today as Mid-Pacific Institute. Ka U'i o Mānoa is thought by some to be the famous Kahalaopuna.

# A 'Ōlelo Hawai'i Speaking Nation

## 'O Haukani, He Kumu Hina 'Ole; Ke Ola Nei i ka Makani

# kekuewa

Kekuewa Kikiloi • Kekuewa Kikiloi • Kekuewa Kikiloi • Kekuewa Kikiloi

I was born in 1975, in Honolulu, and most of my childhood was spent on the windward side of O'ahu and in Mānoa Valley at my grandparents' house. In my *wā kamali'i*, I understood that I was Hawaiian, but my interest in traditional Hawai'i and things of the past did not spark until my first few years of college.

At the University of Hawai'i at Mānoa, I double majored, getting one B.A. in Hawaiian Studies and the other in Anthropology in the spring of 1998. Today I am a graduate student in Anthropology pursuing an M.A. degree in Archaeology. I hope to one day take an active role in the preservation of Hawaiian cultural sites and burials. My interests, however, are diverse, spanning from traditional to modern. These interests range from the propagation of native plants, *'ōlelo Hawai'i*, *mo'olelo* and literature, geography and place names, *mo'okū'auhau*, etc....to hip hop/rap music, computers, and basketball.

As Hawaiians we all struggle to maintain *pono*...a certain degree of balance; to remain *pa'a* and rooted in our beliefs and values and to fulfill our ancestral *kuleana*, while at the same time living in a world that is changing at an incredible pace, one that penetrates and threatens our cultural space. This balance of living in two worlds is perhaps our greatest challenge as *kānaka maoli* in this millennium to come. I feel that it is important that we remain *kūpa'a*, standing firm and maintaining our traditional knowledge. At the same time, however, we must look forward and come up with new ways of being innovative...expanding *our* scope of influence, as *'ōiwi*. So what I submit here today are two pieces that I've worked on in the past few years. One is written *ma ka 'ōlelo makuahine*, a story situated in a time past about the land I love, Mānoa. The other is a *mele pāleoleo*, politically written to promote our struggle today, to reclaim our cultural space and extend it beyond.

## A ʻŌlelo Hawaiʻi
## Speaking Nation

KeKz up on da mic, to take a lyrical fight
 For a peepo oppressed
  And a language kept outta sight
   Hundred plus years of racism and colonization
   Concepts wit no representation
     Disadvantaged cuz a ʻōlelo HaoLe based education
    That teached da kamaliʻi political lies
      To Devalue culture, and forget ancestral Pride
       Heads filled wit knowledge irrelevant
       That STILL don't make no sense yet
       Hell u recite tha names of 37 dead presidents,
       Cuz I don't give a dayum bout dis shet...
       Secondary status is what makes me maddest
       ʻŌlelo Hawaiʻi marketing is tha definition of what a fad is
        Decoration for tourist signs, over usin mah aloha a thousand times
      Prostitutin n pimpin mah mother tongue
    Ain't no way of keepin a language alive
   So u gotta strive... To keep this reality real
  Get past tha raw deal and go with what u feel
 Just free yo mind wit these conscious rhymes
That give rise to innovations
Tah save a ʻōlelo Hawaiʻi speaking nation

140

## 'O Haukani, He Kumu Hina 'Ole; Ke Ola Nei i ka Makani

He mea ma'amau ka 'ike 'ana i ke ānuenue i ke awāwa 'o Mānoa, a he lua 'ole ka nani o ia mea ma O'ahu. E ho'omaopopo 'ia, 'eā, e ka mea heluhelu, 'o ia 'o Kahalaopuna, ke kaikamahine a Tuahine lāua 'o Haukani. He kamāli'i wahine 'o ia no Mānoa i ka wā kahiko, akā ua 'ai 'ia 'o ia 'oiai 'o ia e 'au'au ana ma Waikīkī, e Kauhi, he manō ia no ia wahi. Ua pau kona kino i ka 'ai 'ia a ua lilo 'o ia 'o ke ānuenue o ia 'āina uluwehi. Ma muli o kona hala 'ana, komo maila ka 'eha i loko o kona mau mākua. Ua lilo a'ela 'o Tuahine 'o ia ka ua o Mānoa a ua lilo nō ho'i 'o Haukani 'o ia ka makani o Mānoa a pēia nō ko lāua kūlana a hiki i kēia lā.

Ua kaulana 'o Mānoa i ka ho'opulu mau 'ia e ka ua Tuahine. He nui nā mele oli a me nā mele hīmeni i haku 'ia no ia ua, a pēia nō me Haukani, ka makani e pā ana mai Kailua mai a i Wa'ahila. Akā, eia kekahi mea a'u i lohe 'ole ai e pili ana iā Haukani, ia'u ho'i i hele ai i ka hale hō'ike'ike o Kamehameha a lohe i kekahi lola, i ka mana'o ho'i o kekahi wahine i pa'a iā ia nā 'ike a pau e pili ana i nā hi'ohi'ona o Mānoa. 'O Maka Woolsey kona inoa a he kupa 'o ia no ia 'āina. Eia ihola kāna mo'olelo.

'Elua 'ano o Haukani. He makani kekahi 'ano ona a he lā'au kekahi 'ano. Aia kēia kumu hau ma Kaho'iwai, kahi a Kahalaopuna i noho ai. Ua ulu 'o Haukani ma laila no ka manawa lō'ihi. 'A'ole 'o ia he lā'au ma'amau. He lā'au kūpaianaha na'e ia no kona uē leo nui 'ana a kohu leo kanaka ke lohe aku. Ma mua, 'a'ole i 'ike ka po'e o Mānoa i ke kumu o ia uē 'ana, aia ka ho'omaopopo 'ana a holo maila kekahi kūkini me kāna 'ōlelo. Aia

ho'i, ua hala ke ali'i! Aloha 'ino! Mai kēlā manawa mai, ua maopopo pono i ka po'e o Mānoa he mea hō'ailona ia kumulā'au, 'o Haukani, a ua mālama 'ia e lākou. I ka pauaho 'ana o ke ali'i wahine Emma, i ia wā, uē ihola nō 'o Haukani. 'A'ole i 'emo, hō'ea maila ke kūkini me ka ha'i pū mai i kāna 'ōlelo pilihua. I ka wā i lele ai ka hanu o ke ali'i Ka'iulani, 'o ia hō'ailona like nō. 'O ka hele ia a kaulana ia kumulā'au mai 'ō a 'ō.

I ka wā i māhuahua ai nā mahikō, nui nā Kepanī i ha'alele i ko lākou 'āina hānau ma Iāpana no ka 'imi 'ana i ola ma ka 'āina 'ē. Ua kū'ai 'ia ka 'āina 'o Kaho'iwai e kekahi 'ohana Kepanī me ka mana'o i 'āina ia e mahi'ai ai. Kua nui ihola lākou i nā kumulā'au o ia wahi i loa'a he 'āina māla'ela'e e kanu ai i nā meakanu, akā aia nō 'o Haukani e kū ala ma laila. Ua 'ōlelo kānaka Hawai'i, "Mai kua i ke kumulā'au. 'O ia nō 'o Haukani ke kumulā'au kaulana o Mānoa!" 'A'ohe aloha o ia kanaka Kepanī i nā mea Hawai'i, a no laila, ho'i akula 'o ia i Kaho'iwai a kua wale akula 'o ia iā Haukani. 'O ia ihola ka hina 'ana o ia kumulā'au kaulana. Ua pū'iwa ka po'e Hawai'i i ka 'ike 'ana i kā ia ala hana a i ka pō 'ana iho o ia lā, hao maila ka 'ino a loa'a pono ua kanaka Kepanī lā, a pau 'o ia i ka make. A no kona hewa ho'i i make ai. I kēia mau lā, 'a'ole ke kumulā'au 'o Haukani, akā 'o ia mau pā mai nō 'o ka makani Haukani i mea ho'omana'o no ia lā'au kūpaianaha.

Ua pau.

The artist and his beloved father, David Michael Kaipolauaʻeokekuahiwi Inciong

*a fresh start in the morning*

*let the party begin!*

*canoe race*

*at the waterfall*

*Don't you love it!?*

*Jump for Joy*

*begin and end the day*

*sorbet polynesia*

# inciong

Henry S. P. Inciong • Henry S. P. Inciong • Henry S. P. Inciong • Henry S. P. Inciong

The drawings shown here (which I call "Time Released Art©") are reflections of life at its simplest and basic best. Stripped away are the modern-day factories, stores, gas stations, etc. Here you may see the old-time factories (a kapa house), grocery store (the ocean), gas station (the paddle for a canoe), etc.

Life at its basic best...

Your movie screens are the stars and the surf, birds in the forest and sky, the people passing by...your radio is song and laughter. You can imagine the rest...

These are some of the things I see or feel when I do an art piece. It's a location frozen in time, just for that moment, when nothing is going wrong...and everything is going right...no heartache, no heartburn...no pain...no problems... It's what I wish for its viewers: for the drawing to bless you with everything that is

right and joyful in life...with all the good mana that I can emit...

The original intent of these artworks was to be an outlet for emotion...to express everything good about being alive and to exist at least for a moment with nothing going wrong. To put this down on paper was to cheat life on my own terms...to control the emotion and misfortune that we face every day...to wish all of us innocent creations of heaven to have good luck, happiness, and appreciation between life, land, the ocean, the universe...and each other. Because life is hard enough...and we all deserve to be loved...ALOHA!

a fresh start in the morning   (1994)

let the party begin! (1995)

canoe race  (1995)

at the waterfall  (1995)

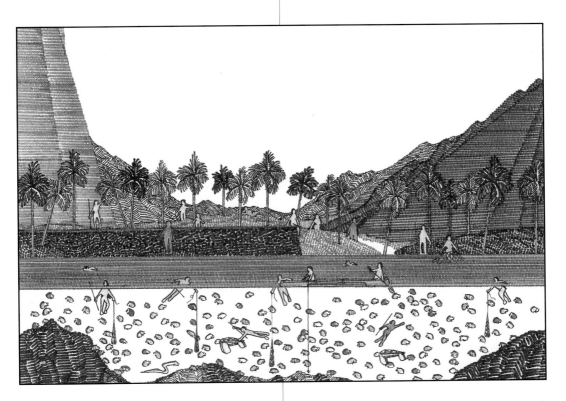

Don't you love it!?   (1995)

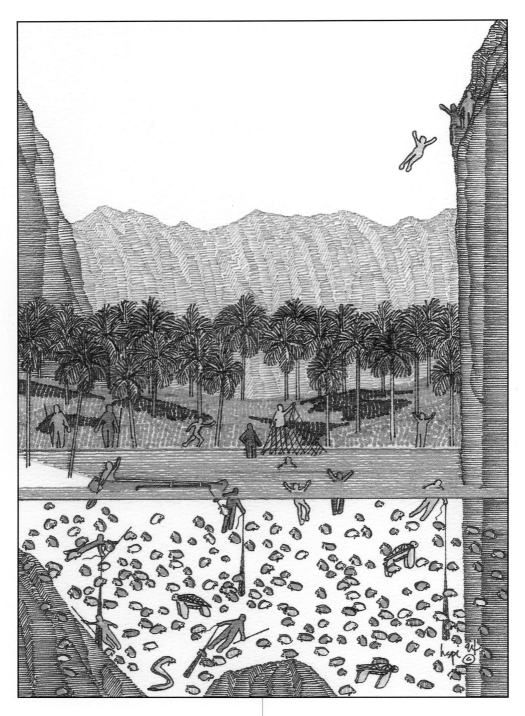

Jump for Joy   (1994)

begin and end the day   (1995)

sorbet polynesia   (1992)

# Calling All Mo'o!

Lōkahi Antonio • Lōkahi Antonio • Lōkahi Antonio • Lōkahi Antonio

I was in a dark place. I looked around, but all I could see was pitch blackness. I could not even see my hand in front of me. Then I saw something in the distance. It was shimmering. It seemed as if the moon was shining on rippling water or on chain-mail armor. I looked up and all around me. There was no moon, only blackness. "Where is that light coming from? How is that thing reflecting light?" Then that shimmering thing started to move toward me. Although it was pitch black, that thing moving closer to me was even blacker. "How can that be?" It kept coming closer. It started to take shape. I saw that it was a Mo'o. A big Mo'o. And it kept coming closer. It stopped right in front of me, this black, shimmering Mo'o. Its huge head turned slightly to the side and it looked at me with a big eye. Then the Mo'o stuck out its tongue and it began to lick my face. It licked my eyes, working its tongue under my eyelids. Then its tongue worked its way into my ear and down

into my na'au. I woke up. It was a dream. But it was more than a dream.

The next morning I went outside. I saw things in another way. The world was the same, but it looked different. The Mo'o had brought me out.

"Calling All Mo'o" was written for the Mo'o Family, especially for the younger Mo'o Brothers and Mo'o Sisters. Stand tall. Keep moving forward. Let no one step on our tails. Protect the Family. Protect our Places. Always be proud of the heritage we have received *mai ka pō mai.*

Lōkahi Antonio was born and raised on O'ahu. In 1988 he moved to Hawai'i island with his wife, Kapulani, and his parents, Roger and 'Iwalani. He and Kapulani attended the University of Hawai'i at Hilo and taught in the Hawaiian Studies Department. In 1998 they moved with their two children, 'Iolani and

Helekūnihi, to Maui, the island of their kūpuna. Lōkahi presently teaches at Maui Community College in the town of Kahului.

*Mahalo e Maui Nui a Kama. ʻO ʻoe nō ka ʻOi!*

## *Calling All Moʻo!*

(Dedicated to Aunty Marjorie Keoʻahu Costa and all other Moʻo who carry the Family)

Calling All Moʻo! Calling All Moʻo!!

You are wanted on the surface!

You are wanted ON THE SURFACE!!

Come on guys, let's go! We have work to do!
You know who you are.
Come out, come out,
Wherever you are!

Stop acting, you know who I'm talking to.
Yes you, Moʻo man! And you, Moʻo lady!

I know you know who you are.
'Cause you wen' ask Gramma
And Gramma told you, eh?
She did, eh?
Moʻo.

I know, I know.
When you wen' look around,
All you saw was those little guys
On the wall, in the corner, in the yard...
Eating bugs.
Or smashed in the door frame, or the
    window...
Not exactly your picture of what you like
    be, eh?
You know why?
You looking with somebody else's eye.
Put on those Moʻo eyes and take a closer look.

Look good.
Look deep.
Into the waters.
The dark waters.
Into the valley,
The dark valley.

Into the forest,
The dark forest.
Into the mirror,
The dark mirror.

I know you wen' try talk to other people
   about it.
I know you was looking for other Mo'o.
And when you found one,
You found out,
Very little.
Just that you was one,
And that he was one, too.

But that's something, eh?

You never notice get plenty of us?
Get plenty!
More than you can imagine.
We everywhere.
And everywhen.

Mo'olelo.

Mo'o 'Ōlelo.

So come on guys,
Don that lenalena suit!
Come on girls,
Comb that hair!
We're on.

What?
You think I just playing around?
Making fun?
Yeah, it can be fun.
Why not?
You rather I do the other thing?
And get ugly?
You sure you like see that side?
I no think so.
'Cause you know what the other side look like.
Spooky.

Goodness!
We seen people get futless
Looking at those 2-inch mo'o.
You can imagine what they would do
If they saw us
As we really are?
Goodness!

No, no...but you got a point.
It's not funny.
And it's not cute.
Mo'o are not cute.

But if we not scaring the shit out of you,
We're charming the love out of you.
And damn, we're good at it!

*Auē ka Mo'o!*

And speaking of mo'olelo,
Stop looking for one mo'olelo
On just Mo'o.
No more!

You gotta look deep.
Read the other guy's mo'olelo.
You'll see us there.
Look in our language.
You'll see us there.
We're there, and yet, we not there.
But's that's how we are, get over it!
We blend in.

That's why you gotta look good.
We in every valley you hike up.
We in every pool you swim in.
We under every waterfall you find beautiful.
We behind every tree you pick flowers from.
We on every ridge they bulldoze.
(We *are* every ridge they bulldoze!)
We in every house.
We in every *room* in every house.
(That's why you get such a thing as the
   mo'o ali'i.

Only Us could walk in the presence of the
   chief,
Without permission.)
We everywhere. And everywhen.

Mo'o Kū'auhau.

By the way,
I know you don't find it funny,
'Cause I don't.
But will somebody tell that guy
To stop making those stupid gecko t-shirts?!?
You seen 'em, right?
The gecko *himself* is wearing one t-shirt.
And one baseball cap.
That's not funny.
I tell you, one day some Mo'o is gonna walk
   up to that guy,
And poke out his two eyes
With his split tongue.
And then our turn laugh.

No make that kine, brah!
If you like make money on our picture,
Do it right!
Show us in all our Mo'o glory!
You think you can handle that?
And no think we joking.
'Cause one of our tūtū going visit you in your
   dreams.

And since we talking about that guy,
Maybe I should bring up something
That maybe shouldn't be brought up.
You know, 'cause we all *Hawaiians*.
Or is it Po'e Hawai'i?
Or Kānaka Hawai'i?
Or Kānaka Maoli?
Or just Maoli?
(How's about, the Po'e Kānaka Hawai'i Maoli?)
Anyway, you know what I mean,
The people of this land.
The originals.

But getting back on track,
It has to do with the Fire people.
The Pele people.
Don't get me wrong, I love Tūtū Pele.
She has style. There's nobody like her
And her family.
But you know what, Mo'o?
They're Fire.
We're Water.
The two don't mix.
We can cheer for them,
Watch *their* show.
I heard it's a good show.
But that's their show.
Never mind that they in the spotlight.
When Pele erupts, she take center stage.
Right?
And it's good to get excited.
Eruptions do that.
But don't jump on their bandwagon.
That's *their* bandwagon.
Let's just start up our own Mo'o Mobile,
And start rolling down the road,
Looking cool, and slick.

And no worry that Hi'iaka
Was bus'ing up the Mo'o from Hawai'i
   to Kaua'i.
(Except Maui.)
She'll never kill us.
Even if she could, she never would.
She's too smart for that.
What would fire be without water?
What would happen if she killed the Mo'o
   for good?
She's too smart for that.
She needs us.
So do the Kānaka of these islands.
After she beat up that great Mo'o, Pana'ewa,
The Kānaka didn't change
The name of the place to
Hi'iaka-ville.
Right?

The Kānaka need us.

When you get too hot,
You no run for get one nice glass...
Fire!
No. That's not how it is.
So make no mistake.
Mo'o are somebody.

Mo'o are the back-bone of these islands.

Iwi Kua Mo'o.

Well, we know what we gotta do.
So let's go do it.
Just keep on the lookout for each other.
Give each other the secret handshake.
Wink those beautiful eyes.
Keep making more Mo'o
And Mo'o Puna.

And...

COME OUT!

When everybody sees us,
As who we are,
The picture of Hawai'i will be complete.

And it's gonna be a beautiful picture.

But it ain't gonna happen,
Unless we come out,
And get in the picture.

SMILE!

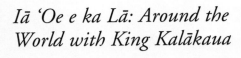

*Iā ʻOe e ka Lā: Around the World with King Kalākaua*

At Washington Place after receiving the Kilohana Award for Excellence in Public Service from the Governor in 1997, beside a portrait of Queen Liliʻuokalani.

# *hōkūlani*

Arnold Hōkūlani Requilmán • Arnold Hōkūlani Requilmán • Arnold Hōkūlani Requilmán

I would like to say a big Mahalo nui loa to *ʻŌiwi* for giving our people back their voice so we may tell our tales of our land.

I was born and raised on the island of Oʻahu. My ancestry links me to the Bays of Piʻilani to the green steppes of Asia to the blue mountains of Europe to the pounamu (jade) islands of Aotearoa. But first and foremost, I am Hawaiian.

When writing this I was reminded of how in elementary school we would have to pledge allegiance to the flag and read about things that happened in Pennsylvania and Vermont. Even at that age, I never quite understood why we had to learn those things or why my *naʻau* never felt comfortable saying the pledge of allegiance. Those history books tried to make it seem that we Hawaiians were a people without history. As if our history began with Captain Cook.

But then 1993 came with the ʻOnipaʻa sovereignty march and gathering at ʻIolani Palace. I soon realized why I never felt comfortable. I realized that we were a people with history. A long one at that. A history thousands of years older than America, in fact. Since then I've dedicated myself to learning all I can about our country's past. After all, a nation with no past is a nation with no future. This dedication has led me to become a docent at ʻIolani Palace and to pursue a degree in education at the University of Hawaiʻi at Mānoa.

Both "Iā ʻOe e ka Lā" and my other piece in this issue, "A Hundred Years after the Pīkake Princess," were originally written for the event called "Sacred Times Sacred Places," which was dedicated to the Kalākaua Dynasty (1874–1893) and which took place on the anniversaries of King Kalākaua's World Trip and Princess Kaʻiulani's passing. People and history books often remember the shortcomings of the Kalākaua Dynasty and forget that the reigns of King Kalākaua and Queen Liliʻuokalani saw the birth of the truly modern Hawaiʻi. It is due to those two individuals that hula and the Kumulipo reemerged, symbols of our nationhood flourished (e.g., the construction of ʻIolani Palace and the Kamehameha Statue, the creation of the crown jewels, etc.), parliamentary democracy developed here, and our kingdom gained world attention and economic wealth. The perception of the outside world toward Hawaiʻi was largely formulated during this era. *E ō mai e Kalākaua, ke aliʻi.*

# Iā ʻOe e ka Lā: Around the World with King Kalākaua

Honolulu 1881. The smoky salons of the city are filled with rumors about King Kalākaua's next course of action. Over the past couple of months, the King had fought several political battles with the white business community, in particular over his right to appoint a cabinet of his choice. But now that he had survived these attacks, many were wondering what he would do next. It was always rather hard to tell what the King might do. Like his canoe-voyaging Polynesian ancestors before him, he had an adventurous spirit coupled with an idealistic, romantic, inquisitive, nationalistic, and flamboyant mind and soul. Kalākaua never ceased to surprise his political rivals. After months of suspense, the King announced to the legislature: "Now that my troubles are over, I mean to take a trip AROUND THE WORLD" (Dougherty 1992:147).

Indeed the King had had much to worry about. Since the day of his election in 1874, Honolulu had become a divided community. Divided among race. Divided among class. Divided among religion. But the one unifying symbol was the monarchy, though each section of Honolulu had a different idea of how much of a symbol the monarchy should be. King Kalākaua had gained a throne shaken by the passing of the Kamehameha dynasty, which the native Hawaiian people looked upon with nostalgia and adoration. Kalākaua also became the head of a monarchy that the small but wealthy American community in the islands viewed as headed by someone between the oppressive English King George III of the American Revolution and the savages who had eaten Captain James Cook. Furthermore,

King Kalākaua

King Kalākaua's prestige had been damaged by the outrage many native Hawaiians felt when the National Legislature elected him as sovereign over the popular Queen Emma. To add to this tapa cloth of troubles, his people, the native Hawaiian people, already decimated by disease, were continuing to die out as foreigners increased in population and political force throughout the island kingdom. Having lived through the British takeover of the islands in 1843, the King did not want to see a foreign flag fly above his own Hawaiian flag ever again. Kalākaua needed to rehabilitate his people and ensure the independence of his country. But how?

He decided that he would visit the exotic countries of the East, handpick people he felt were culturally compatible with his native Hawaiian people, and bring them to his realm. In this manner, the King felt that introducing more tolerant peoples to his kingdom would counterbalance the American Calvinist missionaries and their descendants, make Hawai'i a multi-ethnic nation, and thereby create a larger population loyal to Hawai'i and the Hawaiian people. In a speech to the legislature before departing the King said:

> Around this table are gathered people of many nations. In common with my predecessors, I desire the best welfare of all who gather under our flag in my dominions, and I believe that you who come from other lands, bringing with you the wealth, enterprise and intelligence of those lands, sympathize with me in my desire to protect my native Hawaiian people, and strengthen my nation.
>
> To do this we must work in harmony

> under the Constitution and Laws, and recognize cheerfully the fact that Hawaii as one of the family of nations must be governed in accordance with the ideas which control Constitutional Governments.
>
> We have many difficult questions to settle out of our peculiar situation, they demand the best statesmanship and patient investigation. I am in hopes, while absent, to gather some ideas which shall aid in their solution....
>
> If there have been mistakes in the past, let us profit by the lessons of experience, and with honesty of purpose let us press on to a future which I trust may be bright with prosperity and hopefulness. (Kuykendall 1967:228)

"Home" for many of the peoples of the Asia-Pacific region had become colonies of some faraway Western nation or, as in Japan and China, were facing tremendous cultural revolutions. Even European countries were facing internal problems, where commoners had few civil rights. What if the King could make these peoples see Hawai'i as a refuge and, furthermore, the Hawaiian monarch as more benevolent and democratic than their own rulers? That could give the Crown more political leverage and popularity. Still one further advantage: If native Hawaiians married these Asiatic peoples, might not their offspring inherit an immunity to the diseases that were killing off their full-blood Hawaiian relatives? The intermixing could create a new Hawaiian race that would be strong enough to maintain Hawai'i's nationhood in the face of foreign invasion. The King bluntly remarked to Colonel 'Iaukea, then Secretary of Foreign Affairs, that one of the goals of his trip was, in 'Iaukea's words, "to introduce British subjects and other nationalities to balance the predominant influence of the Americans, who by reason of the preponderance of United States interests in business were secretly working for the overthrow of the Monarchy" (Iaukea 1988:43), though this was not known beyond court circles.

The plantation owners, on the other hand, saw an advantage to themselves: since native Hawaiians were dying off, more workers were needed to tend the canefields. More labor meant more capital, more capital meant more production, which in turn meant that they could afford their homes in Mānoa and Nuʻuanu Valleys and their children's tuition to Punahou School and Oʻahu College, and to universities in the United States. After all, the King was already noted for his regal ease with dignitaries. Why not send him to dazzle them, thereby hopefully securing a favorable treaty that would bring in more laborers? This would also give the plantation owners a chance to get rid of the King for a couple of months and to try to favorably influence the next in line for the throne, Kalākaua's sister Princess Liliʻuokalani. It was a win-win situation for everyone.

Some of the more stingy Calvinist government officials (descendants of the first American missionaries to Hawaiʻi) saw the trip as expensive and extravagant, two words that would be used critically against Kalākaua throughout his reign. To appease these factions, the King selected two men closely tied to the missionary community to accompany him on his trip—Attorney General W. Nevins Armstrong (who would be given the title "Minister of State" for this occasion) and Chamberlain Charles H. Judd.

The famed prophet and high chiefess Nāhinu of Kauaʻi—who was the cousin of Kalākaua's Queen, Kapiʻolani—wrote a new chant to wish Kalākaua success and happiness in his journey and performed it for him. It was called "Iā ʻOe E Ka Lā E ʻAlohi Nei":

> Iā ʻoe e ka lā e ʻalohi nei
> Ma nā welelau o ka honua.
> Hōʻike aʻe ʻoe i kou nani,
> I ka mālamalama ʻoi kelakela.
> Nāu i noiʻi nowelo aku
> Pau nā pali paʻa i ka ʻike ʻia.
> ʻIke ʻoe i ka nani o Himela
> Ka hene waiʻolu lawe mālie
> Mauna i lohia me ke onaona,
> Kaulana ē ka nani me ke kiʻekiʻe.
> Kiʻekiʻe ʻo Kalani noho mai i luna.
> Nāu i ʻaʻe nā kapu o Kahiki.
> Hehihehi kū ana i ka huku ʻale
> I ke kai hālaʻi lana mālie.
> Kiʻina ʻia aku nā pae moku,
> I hoa kuilima nou e Kalani.
> Ma ia mau alanui malihini
> Āu i ʻōlali hoʻokahi ai.
> ʻO ka lama o ke ao kou kōkua,
> Hōkūloa nō kou alakaʻi.
> Lilo i mea ʻole nā ʻenemi,
> Lehelehe ʻeuʻeu hana loko ʻino.
> He ola ʻo Kalani a mau aku,
> A kau i ke ao mālamalama.
> Haʻina ʻia mai ana ka puana
> No Kalākaua nō he inoa.

> To you, O sun shining down
> Throughout the ends of the world.
> Show forth your beauty,
> The greatest of all lights.
> It is you who delve and seek
> Till the solid cliffs yield their secrets.
> You'll see the beauty of the Himalayas,
> The gentle slopes as you pass by,
> A mountain rich with fragrance,
> Famed for its beauty and height.

High above sits my royal chief,
You who tread the sacred places of
Kahiki,
Treading on the rising billows
And over the calm, tranquil sea.
Reach out to the other lands,
For companions to go hand in hand
with you,
Over those unfamiliar trails
That you undertake to walk alone.
The light of the day shall be your help,
The morning star your guide,
That your enemies be turned to naught,
The heartless ones with jabbering
mouths.
Long may you live, O heavenly one,
Till you reach the world of light.
This is the end of my chant
In honor of Kalākaua.

(Pukui 1995:128–131)

On the 20th of January 1881, Kalākaua
embarked on his journey, beginning with a
ten-day state visit to the cities of Sacramento
and San Francisco in California. In
Sacramento, he met most of the country's
prominent political leaders. General Upton, a
Civil War soldier, remarked that the King's
knowledge of military matters no doubt
exceeded that of most American militia
officers (Armstrong 1977:15). Not to be
outdone, several orators in the California
State Assembly predicted a Pacific united
under the rule of King Kalākaua, "the
Colossus of the Pacific" (15). In San Francisco,
a banquet was given at the Hang Fen Lou
restaurant by the Consul-General of the
Empire of China. The event was the costliest
dinner ever given in the 19th century by
Chinese in the United States (16). The
Consul-General praised Kalākaua for the fair
treatment of Chinese subjects in Hawai'i,
compared to the attitude in California,

where the State Legislature had just passed
the first Chinese Exclusion Act. Minister
Armstrong then turned to Kalākaua and
whispered, "You may be a pagan king, and I
the Minister of a pagan king; but our first
important experience in a foreign land is the
gratitude, expressed in this grand banquet,
to your government for its justice; and it is
done on the soil of a nation that deliberately does injustice to the Chinese" (17). After
many honors and dinners, the King and his
suite embarked for Japan.

It was at first decided that he would travel
incognito, simply as "Ali'i [Chief] Kalākaua,"
but the Japanese were informed by
diplomatic agents in California of the King's
intended visit (Kuykendall 1967:228). Much
to the King's surprise, as his steamer, the
Oceanic, entered Yedo (Tokyo) harbor, it
received a 21-gun salute from all vessels at
dock, the Hawaiian flag was hoisted next to
the red-and-white Japanese standard, and
"Hawai'i Pono'ī" was enthusiastically played
onshore. This was a king and he would be
received as such. Kalākaua was the first
foreign sovereign of any country to visit
Japanese soil.

While in Yedo, the King met with Emperor
Meiji and suggested several matters:
marriage between the King's niece (Princess
Ka'iulani) and Prince Higashifushimi no Miya
Yorihito (Komatsu); an Asian Federation of
States which the Emperor would head;
elimination of the unequal treaty provision
granting extraterritoriality to foreigners in
Japan; and emigration of Japanese to
Hawai'i.

To the marriage proposal, the King would
later receive a letter written by the Prince
himself stating:

Through the Reception Committee, I was informed of your generous kindness, in asking me, if it would be my happiness to be united to your Royal niece in marriage, I am at a loss to express fully my appreciation of this honour as I am still under age [Princess Ka'iulani was five-and-a-half and the Prince 15], I have consulted my father, and I am very reluctantly compelled to decline your distinguished proposal for the reason that I am already betrothed to my future companion in life; so I sincerely trust that your Majesty will not be disappointed at what duty compels me to do. (230)

A follow-up letter was then given by the Japanese Foreign Minister to King Kalākaua on behalf of Emperor Meiji that the emperor "has been led to say that your sincere desire to bring the relations of the Imperial and Royal Courts to one of a close friendship has deeply moved his heart.... In thus being compelled to decline your proposition my Sovereign has experienced a very great pain" (230).

To the second matter of an Asian Federation, the Emperor wrote:

I highly agree with Your Majesty's profound and far-seeing views. Your Majesty was also good enough to state that I might be the promoter and chief of this Federation. I cannot but be grateful for such expression of your love and confidence in me.

The Oriental nations including my country have long been in a state of decline and decay; and we cannot hope to be strong and powerful unless by gathering inches and treasuring foots

gradually restore to us all attributes of a nation. To do this our Eastern Nations ought to fortify themselves within the walls of such Union and Federation, and by uniting their power to endeavor to maintain their footing against those powerful nations of Europe and America, and to establish their independence and integrity in future. To do this is a pressing necessity for the Eastern Nations, and in so doing depend their lives.

But this is a mighty work and not easily to be accomplished, and I am unable to foretell the date when we shall have seen it realized....

In the face of the internal administration of my government being of such a pressing nature I have not a heart to turn my face from it, and leaving my country, to devote myself mainly to the work which more directly concerns other nations. In this is found the difficulty of my initiating at present the work of the Federation of Asian Nations....

In each laying out the course of the future policy to the other by interchanging our views, if it happily at a future time happen to help us, it cannot only be the fortune of Japan and Hawaii but also of whole Asia. (229–230)

While Emperor Meiji wholeheartedly agreed with the idea of an Asian Federation, he realized the realities of the world around him. There was much work that needed to be done within the empire. He himself was Japan's first constitutional monarch, and his constitution was barely 14 years old. At the same time, his country was busy

Westernizing and militarizing in the hopes of avoiding colonization like her Asian neighbors, who were slowly being plucked by European hands. Japan needed foreign investment and materials. Japan was not prepared for an embargo or war with the U.S. if they allied with Hawai'i, who was under the U.S. sphere of influence.

Although the majority of Kalākaua's proposals were declined, one important proposal was ratified—emigration. The Emperor had been wary that his subjects not toil in the same kind of conditions that the Chinese coolies in the United States were enduring. The King convinced the Emperor that should he ratify a treaty of emigration, Japanese subjects would be treated as if they were Hawaiian subjects, and they would be allowed to naturalize if they so desired. The Emperor consented and the treaty was ratified.

After meeting the Emperor and other important dignitaries, the King also toured Kobe, Osaka, Kyoto, and Nagasaki. Throughout his visit to Japan, he was fêted "as if he were the ruler of the greatest kingdom on earth" (228). Standing alongside the Emperor, he witnessed a 10,000-troop military review. The Emperor conferred upon Kalākaua the Imperial Order of the Chrysanthemum along with several hundreds of dollars' worth of gifts such as vases, kimonos, and other Japanese items much coveted in the West. The front pages of the Japanese newspapers were covered with articles about Hawai'i and its monarchy throughout the duration of Kalākaua's visit. Nightly fireworks displays were given in his honor. A steamer provided by the well-known Mishi-Bishi Company ("Mitsubishi" in modern spelling) took him from Tokyo to Nagasaki and Kobe (Armstrong 1977:79).

Kalākaua met most of the prominent political and religious leaders of the empire. He visited the Shinto temples of Shiba and learned how the Emperor was a descendent of the Gods (the Sun Goddess to be specific), much like Hawaiian rulers (85). He visited Buddhist temples and inquired about bringing priests to introduce Buddhism to Hawai'i (84). Didn't the Japanese themselves merge their old religion with Buddhism without conflict? In fact, it helped preserve their culture and provided a balance of ideas. The King also visited the Protestant Church of Yokohama, one of the first legalized Christian churches in Japan, received a copy of the New Testament in Japanese, and was reminded that the church was partially built by Hawaiian Christians (63).

After a month in Japan, Kalākaua was ready to depart. As he stepped onto his ship, a huge decoration with the word "ALOHA" spelled out in flowers was unveiled onshore and "Hawai'i Pono'ī" was played.

From Japan the King went to China (where he met with Viceroy Li Hung Chang and learned about Confucianism), British Hong Kong, then Siam (arriving in late March 1881). As the King's ship approached Bangkok, his retinue shouted, "This is Hawaii!" (119). Of all of the places the King was to see, Siam would be the most familiar to him, with its expansive coconut tree groves, lush green mountains, and sandy beaches. To Kalākaua's remark that Polynesians had Malay blood, King Chulalongkorn replied, "The Siamese are partly Malay; we are related" (126). While there a young Thai foreign affairs officer asked Armstrong, "Is it true that the civilisation of Europe is due to Christianity?" To the reply that such was the belief of church leaders, the Siamese officer said, "Then if

Christianity is the cause of European progress, is it also the cause of the fleets and armies with which they are ready to destroy one another?" (134–135). Another embarrassing question which had been posed while the royal suite was in Japan resurfaced when a Siamese Prince asked Minister Armstrong, "Is your King in the hands of foreigners? Why does he not bring his own people with him instead of white men [referring to Armstrong and Judd]? Does he do what you tell him to do?" (132). As in Japan, the King and his suite avoided the question.

From Siam, the King continued to Singapore, Johore, Malaya, and the British Indian Empire (including Pakistan and Burma). The Maharajah of Johore and the King compared common legends and common words (such as "api" in Malaysian and "ahi" in Hawaiian for "fire"; "alima" in Malaysian and "lima" in Hawaiian for "five"), concluding that Malays and Polynesians were "long-lost brothers" (144). (This expression would later be part of the Pan-Malaysian movement led by such imminent scholars as Dr. José Rizal, Professor Wenceslao Vinzons, and President Diosdado Macapagal (father of the current president of the Philippines). The idea of "long lost brothers" of a great Pan-Pacific Malay maritime civilization stretching from Malaysia to Hawai'i would become a major theme in the national liberation struggles of Southeast Asia until today.)

In British India and Burma, Kalākaua met many members of the British administration of those two colonies. In Calcutta, Minister Armstrong asked a colonial secretary of Bengal Province how 50,000 British soldiers kept 250 million Indians under British rule. The secretary replied, "They cannot agree among themselves; if they did, our rule

would end instantly" (159). Kalākaua was also given the rare honor of being brought into the caste system and made a Brahmin so that he might view more thoroughly the sacred Hindu shrines. Before leaving, the King, expressing a desire to secure a souvenir of India, selected a picture of Buddha and told his suite that this would remind him and his people that other great civilizations also worshipped idols like Hawaiians did (169).

As the King made his way to Egypt, he passed though the Holy Land of Palestine and viewed Mt. Sinai. Kalākaua asked, if the mountain was sacred to Christianity, why was it in the hands of the Muslim Ottoman Turks (who controlled much of the Middle East)? A British officer replied that Ottoman rule was not challenged because trade with Turkey was more important than religious sentiment. The King then remarked that it seemed Christians did not show respect for sacred places as he had been told (175). As a guest of the Ottoman Empire, Kalākaua was entertained by the Khedive (Viceroy), who showed the King the Pyramids, along with other ancient sites, including places that Egyptian Pharaohs, as well as Alexander the Great, Cleopatra, Mark Anthony, and Julius Caesar, had once lived in or visited. At several lodges in Cairo, Kalākaua gave impressive speeches reciting the history of Masonic fraternities. In a discussion with the King, the Khedive remarked:

> Europe will make drunkards of the Mussulmans [Muslims] within a century.... There is much good in Christianity, but if it prevailed in Asia, it would free the people from direct responsibility to God. Do the Christians of Europe obey the teachings of Christ? I have lived in England and I have not seen obedience.

There is more wickedness in London than in all of Asia Minor or Arabia and Egypt.... Christianity suits them, but Islamism is best for our people.... If Christianity is better for us, God will send it here; he knows best what we need, and he gives us what is best for us. (179–80)

While on the Khedive's steamer riding up the Suez, a funny incident occurred. As they approached the Canal station, the Khedive ordered a telegraph to be sent stating, "Prepare lunch for the King of the Sandwich Islands [the European name for the islands of Hawai'i]." The station's kitchen received the telegraph as "Prepare Lunch for the King. Sandwiches" (177). Needless to say, when they arrived the Khedive was very upset. Nonetheless, he continued to show Kalākaua the wonders of Egypt, including a tranquil ride up the Nile on a barge perhaps very similar to one used by Cleopatra herself.

From Egypt the King went to Rome, another city of antiquity. He was entertained in Italy and the Vatican, and was toasted by King Humberto, who pledged Italy's friendship and assistance to Hawai'i should it ever be required (Iaukea 1988:100). Queen Margherita of Italy had then turned to the King and asked how Italians and Catholics were treated in Hawai'i. The King responded that Italians were treated fairly and that a good many Hawaiians were devout Catholics, which pleased the Queen (Armstrong 1977:202).

Throughout his Italian tour, Kalākaua witnessed military reviews and was courted by many Italians wanting a souvenir from the King. He also called upon the Vatican for an interview with Pope Leo XIII in the richly painted chambers of the Holy See. The Pope

asked the King about the presence of Judd and Armstrong, to which the King replied that they were white Protestant Hawaiian subjects. One of the Cardinals in the room chuckled and replied, "Then they are in the opposition." Leaning towards the King, the Pope then asked, "Do my [Catholic] people in your kingdom behave well?" Kalākaua replied, "Yes, they are good subjects." The Pope then inquired, "If they do not behave, I must look after them. Why do you have a white Minister in your government?" The King, surprised at the question, deferred it to Minister Armstrong, who replied that Hawaiian kings appointed men based on merit rather than race. The Cardinal then asked, "Are there any Catholics in your government?" Armstrong simply answered, "No, the American Protestants entered the country before the Catholics did, and have kept control of public affairs; but no efficient Catholic is excluded from high office by reason of his faith" (208–209). After 20 minutes, the King kissed the Pope's ring and the audience was over. The King continued making diplomatic calls and visiting the many sites of Rome.

Since the royal party wanted to be in England during its summer months, they had to bypass France and go directly to England. The King met nearly every important government officer and royal family member in the British Empire, from Queen Victoria to Prime Minister Gladstone to the visiting Prince Imperial and Crown Princess of Germany to Princess Alexandria of Wales (considered to be one of the most beautiful women in the world). A good many of these British nobles and visiting German aristocrats had either visited Hawai'i or had heard stories about these curious islands that had at one time been under the British flag. Queen Victoria described in her diaries that

"King Kalikaua [*sic*] is tall, darker than Queen Emma [whom she had met some years earlier in London], but with the same cast of features…. He is a gentleman & pleasing & speaks English perfectly; he is of course a Christian" (Seiden 1992:116). The Queen, who for two decades had been in mourning for her husband, Prince Consort Albert, turned out for a garden party for the Hawaiian king, the first time she had attended a festive gathering since Albert's death.

While at a dinner banquet, Kalākaua had become distressed upon hearing about the plight of the Irish people and the open prejudice against them in English high society. (Queen Victoria herself, though "Queen of the United Kingdom of Great Britain and Ireland," openly disdained anything Irish.) Nonetheless, as part of the formalities of the banquet, when it was Kalākaua's turn to toast his hosts, he thanked the various personages he had met throughout the British Empire and said, "I have no political parties in my own country; there are no Land Leaguers there [referring to the Irish opposition party]. I would not permit such men to trouble my people." The banquet hall was filled with applause. The King sat down, rather pleased with himself, and looked at Minister Armstrong as if to say, "You see, I am able to take care of myself" (Armstrong 1977:237–238).

Irish nationalists did not take this lightly and a few days later the following article appeared in a Dublin newspaper:

QUASHEE ON HIS LEGS

The nominal ruler of Hawaii, who is a lineal descendent of Ho-Ki-Po-Kia-Wua-Ki-Frum, King of the Cannibal Islands, is on a visit to England in quest of subjects, and has been entertained at the Mansion House by that rabid nonconformist, Mr. Lord Mayor McArthur; this great grandson of the Anthropophagi indulged in a sneer at Ireland. We must take the liberty of giving him a figurative rap over the knuckles. (239)

Continuing with his journey, the King visited Ascot, the Tower of London, and Hastings, stopping at the jeweler of the British Royal Family to purchase two crowns, the ones he would use for his coronation. The King made such an impression upon the English that even "Punch" wrote verses about him:

He's really a most intelligent wight [wit],
Who's looked on many a wonderful sight,
And traveled by day, and eke by night,
O'er rivers and seas and dry lands;
But wrongly, it seems, his name we say,
And print it too, in a horrible way,
He ought to be called King Kalakua [*sic*],
This King of the Sandwich Islands. (242)

After leaving London, the King was whisked through Belgium (where he visited Waterloo), and traveled through the Teutonic empires of Germany and Austro-Hungary. In Berlin, a Swedish illustration appeared of Queen Victoria speaking to King Kalākaua and, referring to the ancient royal custom of kissing, bore the caption "Sire, you are a bad fellow; you bit me [alluding to cannibalism]—but since you are such a sweet thing you may kiss me again" (253).

The King toured northern Germany and presided over an impressive 7,000-troop military review, where, as throughout his travels, the Hawaiian Flag flew beside other national flags and "Hawai'i Pono'ī" was played. It was at one of these military parades that the King decided to model the now familiar blue Royal Guards uniforms after the Prussian Royal Army's uniforms. Most officers of the Prussian Royal Army, incidentally, were familiar with the melody of "Hawai'i Pono'ī" because it was a variation of the march "The Watch on the Rhine," the unofficial national anthem of Prussia.

Not without trouble, in Vienna the King was harassed by Austrian paparazzi when a young woman asked the King to dance with her while he was visiting the Prater. The King innocently accepted and they waltzed. Soon newspapers throughout Europe reported on Kalākaua's "Viennese [she was actually Danish] Mistress." Furthermore, she was a commoner, which horrified the conservative Viennese aristocracy. Later, many Austrian editorials were written in response to the criticism, praising the king for being a good-natured, enlightened, and liberal monarch, and a suitable model for a European ruler (257).

However, in all, the King's journey throughout Austria was favorable and thought provoking. In a letter to Lili'uokalani he wrote:

> Theatre's, Opera's, Racing and general holiday, the Jews Stores and warehouses all opened. Churches to[o] going on at the same time, without a disorder or disturbance to be heard among a population of over a Million. Can it possibly be that these light hearted happy people are all going to H—ll? All enjoying nature as nature's gift?

Surely not! But what a contrast to our miserable bigotéd [missionary] community. All sober and down in the mouth keeping a wrong sabbath instead of a proper Sunday. (Kalakaua 1881)

From Vienna, the King proceeded to Paris, toured various French sights, attended *Aïda* at the Paris Opera House, and watched a ballet performance. He also took the liberty of subscribing to *Le Figaro*, a famous French magazine, prompting a reporter to joke, "This will enable him, when he comes here to live as a subsidised monarch [referring to the number of deposed monarchs in France], to speak French and understand the chansons of the opéra bouffe" (Armstrong 1977:263). However, due to miscommunication, Kalākaua was not received immediately upon his arrival by the French Ministry of Foreign Affairs and was actually snubbed by the French government. The King made his only negative comment about a host country in Europe when he described the French Foreign Office as a "mean lot" (259). Perhaps Kalākaua exacted his revenge, for whenever the French played "Hawai'i Pono'ī," they were humbled—"The Watch on the Rhine" was the song that the Germans played when they victoriously marched into Paris during the Franco-Prussian War almost exactly a decade earlier.

Despite the bad press in Austria and the bad manners of France, of all cities the King saw, the cities of Vienna and Paris—the centers of European high society and music—caught his eye. In a letter to his sister, Princess Miriam Likelike, he wrote, "You ought to hear Strauss' band in Vienna. Oh! Exquisite music. The best I have ever heard. Vienna is one of the prettiest places we have visited but Paris seems to exceed all" (Dougherty 1992:151).

From France, Kalākaua traveled south to the Iberian courts of Spain and Portugal, where he negotiated a treaty with the Portuguese King, Dom Luis, for an increase of plantation workers to Hawai'i. Kalākaua watched a bull fight in the special stadium's Royal Box (usually reserved solely for the King of Portugal) and discussed exploration with the Queen, a lineal descendent of Vasco da Gama. Before leaving Portugal, the Kings of Portugal and Hawai'i embraced. Unknown to the King until he reached England were the fantastic stories circulating in the American press that the King was on his world tour to sell his kingdom. In fact, most of the major American officials were kept on top alert throughout the King's tour. U.S. President Garfield in a letter to his friend stated:

> The King has started on a voyage around the world, and it is feared he is contemplating either the sale of the Islands or some commercial treaty with European powers which would embarrass the United States. We shall probably soon have more delicate and important diplomatic work in that direction than at any previous time of our history. (Kuykendall 1967:239)

An editorial in *The New York Times* on 14 July 1881 declared:

> It is an open secret that Kalakaua, King of the Hawaiian Islands, is on a voyage around the world for the purpose of selling his kingdom…. If annexation ever arrives, it must take the Islands to the United States…the other Governments of the world should be notified that any attempt on their part to acquire the Sandwich Islands, by purchase or otherwise, would be regarded as an unfriendly act. (241)

The King immediately responded to these words with a press release: "My Kingdom is a constitutional monarchy, and the cession people talk of could not be effected in my absence or without a long discussion" (242). Another piece of information leaked out from the White House: After a meeting between U.S. Secretary of State James G. Blaine and Sir Edward Thornton, the British Minister in Washington, D.C., the minister wrote the following dispatch to his government in London and sent a copy to Honolulu, which found its way through the entire Hawaiian royal court. It read:

> Mr. Blaine…stated that whatever transactions His Hawaiian Majesty might enter into with a view to raising money, and whatever security he might give for the payment of such debts, the position of the Sandwich Islands was of such importance to the safety of the United States…that it would be justified in maintaining that no nation but the United States should exercise control over the Sandwich Islands which by their position almost belonged to this country [the U.S.].

> His last observance upon the subject was that such was the present state of the Islands that they must sooner or later come under the protection of the United States.

> The impressions which his remarks left upon my mind was that the United States Government, fearing that some complications with European Powers might be brought about by His Hawaiian Majesty during his present expedition, contemplates taking some early measures for securing to itself the entire control of the Islands. (239)

After reading the minister's statement, Queen Emma wrote an angry letter to the American diplomatic representative in Honolulu:

> The sudden and bold uncovering of America's long cherished wish (which they have always denied) to possess these Islands…has caused me great, great grief and anxiety…. I consider America is now our open enemy, and that to England would be our natural course to look for strengthening, and that as we have bounden friends in England and France, America cannot carry out her high-handed policy with regard to these Hawaiian Islands….
>
> The Native Hawaiians…are one with me in the love of our country, and determined not to let Hawaii become a part of the United States of America. We have yet the right to dispose of our country as we wish, and be assured that it will never be to a Republic! (242)

Also reading this dispatch was the then Princess Regent Lili'uokalani, who was deeply affected by it and sent a copy to her brother Kalākaua in Europe. In a dispatch to London, the British diplomatic representative in Honolulu wrote:

> Her Royal Highness the Princess Regent having shewn me much attention since her appointment as Regent of this Kingdom, and having manifested an earnest desire to draw closer the relations between Great Britain and the Hawaiian Government, having moreover expressed a hope that the Anniversary of Her Majesty Queen Victoria's Birthday would this year receive a "marked" celebration…I therefore gave an entertainment in honor of the day, at which, the Regent, Her Sister the Princess Likelike, my colleagues, some of the Cabinet Ministers and many others were present. The Princess Regent appeared to enjoy herself very much, and joined most cordially in the toast of "Her Majesty the Queen." (240)

Informed about these events at home and in America, Kalākaua crossed the Atlantic and visited the United States. In Washington, D.C., he was met by a new U.S. Cabinet, including the Acting Secretary of State, Robert R. Hitt, who inquired about the welfare of the Hawaiian people. The King responded, "What good do you think the Europeans and Americans have done there?...Captain Cook, and the fellows who came after him from New England, filled my people with disease and leprosy, and, besides, they forced rum on us…debauched our women…told our people to keep Sunday and stop dancing [hula]" (Dougherty 1992:151–152).

Making his way across the United States, the King boarded a steamer from San Francisco and headed back to his tropical kingdom. He now had the friendship of dozens of countries in the world and had acquired many of those countries' highest royal orders, various gifts, and countless memories. He was also the first monarch of any country to make a voyage around the world.

On the 29th of October 1881, the King arrived home to a thrilling reception, during which he greeted his people thus:

> Ua ka'ahele au ma luna o ka 'ili honua me nā moana,
> A 'Īnia mamao me Kina kaulana,
> Hō'ea i nā 'ae kai o Aferika a me nā

palena o Europa,
A hālāwai me ka ikaika o nā ʻāina a pau.

A iaʻu i kū ai ma nā ʻaoʻao o nā poʻo
aupuni,
Ka poʻe mana ma luna o lākou me ka
hiehie,
Hoʻomaopopo ihola au i ka ʻuka iki a
nāwaliwali o koʻu,
Me koʻu noho aliʻi i hoʻokahua ʻia ma
luna o kahi puʻu pele,
A ma kahi he miliona i hoʻokō i kā kēia
mau mōʻī,
He mau tausani wale nō ma lalo o koʻu
malu.

Akā ke ʻupu nei loko, naʻu ke kaena
hiki,
Aia he mau nani ma loko o nā pōʻai o
koʻu mau ʻae kai,
I ʻoi aku ka makamae i kā oʻu mau hoa
aliʻi.
ʻAʻohe oʻu kumu hopo ma loko o koʻu
aupuni.

He hiki ke hui me koʻu lāhui me ka weli
ʻole.
ʻAʻohe makaʻu noʻu iho, me ke kiaʻi paʻa
ʻole ʻia.
A naʻu ke kaena, he momi i hoʻouna ʻia
mai luna mai naʻu,
Eia me aʻu ke aloha pili paʻa o koʻu
lāhui kanaka.

I have traveled over many lands and
distant seas,
to India afar and China renowned.
I have touched upon the shores of
Africa and the boundaries of Europe,
and I have met the great ones of all
the lands.

As I stood at the side of heads of
governments,

next to leaders proud of their rule, their
authority over their own,
I realized how small and weak is the
power I hold.
For mine is a throne established upon a
heap of lava.
They rule where millions obey their
commands.
Only a few thousands can I count under
my care.

Yet one thought came to me of which I
may boast,
that of all beauties locked within the
embrace of these shores,
one is a jewel more precious than any
owned by my fellow monarchs.
I have nothing in my Kingdom to dread.

I mingle with my people without fear.
My safety is of no concern, I require no
bodyguards.
Mine is the boast that a pearl of great
price has fallen to me from above.
Mine is the loyalty of my people.

(Pukui and Korn 1973:153–155)

At last, the King was home. Kalākaua was
to reign for another decade, hosting a
coronation, reviving Hawaiian traditions,
completing ʻIolani Palace (which had been
under construction since 1879), and bracing
for serious changes in Hawaiʻi's history.
His sister Liliʻuokalani would be the last
Hawaiian monarch, thus ending the Golden
Age of Hawaiian Monarchy.

What were the results of King Kalākaua's
circumnavigation around the world? Because
of his trip, certain words and concepts related to Hawaiʻi (such as "aloha" and "hula")
entered the English language. Hawaiʻi was
no longer thought of as "cannibal islands."

It was now indeed a member of the family of nations, equal in standing to any.

Kalākaua reaffirmed the views the Chinese had of the Sandalwood Mountains—Hawai'i was not like racist America—and throughout his travels in China encouraged the Chinese to come to Hawai'i. His "heap of lava" was a just kingdom where all peoples regardless of race would be treated fairly, something that few nations in the 19th century could claim to do.

Kalākaua also understood more clearly the position of his kingdom in the family of nations. He was not only "Ali'i Kalākaua," but "King Kalākaua of Hawai'i," leader of a world-renowned Pacific island nation. His Hawaiian flag was saluted by the most powerful armies of the world, and "Hawai'i Pono'ī" was heard in the halls of Buckingham Palace, Versailles, and Schönbruhnn Palace. New treaties were signed and Hawai'i enjoyed "most favored nation status" with most European and Asian countries as a result of the King's visit. Kalākaua also announced through his world tour that his kingdom was not an appendage of Europe or America, but rather a country with an ancient civilization demanding that the world respect its sovereignty, its history, its culture, and its people. In so doing, he foreshadowed the anti-colonial revolutions of Southeast Asia of the 20th century and the coming of the Asia-Pacific Age of the 21st century.

## References

Armstrong, William N. 1977 [1903]. *Around the World with a King*. Rutland, VT: Charles E. Tuttle.

Dougherty, Michael. 1992. *To Steal a Kingdom*. Waimanalo, HI: Island Style Press.

Iaukea, Curtis Pi'ehu and Lorna Kahilipuaokalani Iaukea Watson. 1988. *By Royal Command*. Ed. Niklaus R. Schweizer. Honolulu: Hui Hanai.

Kalakaua [King]. 1881. Letter to his sister Liliuokalani. 10 Aug. Hawai'i State Archives. Honolulu.

Kuykendall, Ralph S. 1967. *The Hawaiian Kingdom, Volume III, 1874–1893: The Kalakaua Dynasty*. Honolulu: University of Hawai'i Press.

Pukui, Mary Kawena, trans. 1995. *Nā Mele Welo: Songs of Our Heritage*. Ed. Pat Namaka Bacon and Nathan Napoka. Honolulu: Bishop Museum Press.

Pukui, Mary K. and Alfons L. Korn, trans. and eds. 1973. *The Echo of Our Song: Chants & Poems of the Hawaiians*. Honolulu: University of Hawai'i Press.

Seiden, Allan. 1992. *Hawai'i: The Royal Legacy*. Honolulu: Mutual Publishing.

Photo by Lynette Cruz

Big Island Conspiracy at ʻIolani Palace,
12 August 1998 (Skippy second from right)

# *ioane*

Skippy Ioane • Skippy Ioane • Skippy Ioane • Skippy Ioane • Skippy Ioane

What puzzles me is religion and government. The de facto government came with a de facto god. They brought the god first. Then they brought the government. I feel that it's confusing for us to accept the god and not accept the government. If we going to go back to the de jure government, we should go back to the de jure gods.

## Samuela Texas

Samuela Texas call Mr. Pharaoh
Let the original people free
Missionary come with him and his vision
Mission him accomplish, him own me
Auwē, Auwē, Auwē

All the time before the day come
The night begins kanaka history
Sky the father and the earth is mother
Ke kinohi loa o nā Hawaiʻi

Annexation, constipation
Kanaka cities in a stolen nation
Tell the truth Sam, you stole the loot
Him say, No way! to the vato José
Him say, Do as we say, not as we do
We be da church if you be da fool

Fall down from the skies
Sail through the waters
Needed the gifts from the land and sea

Mālama kākou perpetual motion
Loa'a tomorrow for the keikis eat
Auwē, Auwē, Auwē

Lawa ka mea 'ai, time for the hiamoe
Go on down, lie down our bodies to sleep
Hale warm cause 'āina still love us
Papa remains under our feet

Fairy tales that you learn in school
Misinformation from the public education
Good ol' kanaka going do what he's told
Colonized down to his soul
Question not why he fighting the war
The pledge allegiance said him better than him
  been before
Came back home, all the bullets miss
Da blalas ua hala on the waiting list

1900's police evictions
Governor said, "It's an American thang"
Missionary laughing even after he passed away
Him hear kānakas in the courtroom sing
(What they singing?)
Auwē, Auwē, Auwē
(Take the burden off the people, brother)

Turn about, somebody sold us out
They said the rich had a snitch
With a kanaka's mouth
Could've been a boozer who's a macho loser
Could've been a winner who's a closet sinner
Fornicator, mind manipulators
Could've been da preacher or da preschool
  teacher
How can you see, peoples, you've been blind
Ya'll been set up way before your time
Can't find freedom with a looking glass
'Āina always been underneath your
Ass me no questions, Tell you no lies

Good gracious, this righteous jive,
Bill of Rights and the Big Five
We paying the bills, they got the jives

Them got democracy, we got survive
Auwē, Auwē, Auwē

Samuela Texas call Mr. Pharaoh
Let the original people free

*"Samuela Texas" was recorded by the Big Island Conspiracy on the CD entitled Reflective but Unrepentent (Ka'a Ka'a Records, 1999).*

## As the Story Goes /
## The Alibi in the Sky

Every sister's got a story
Every brother swings a tale
Some is quicker than ol' Br'er Rabbit
Some patient as a snail

They all need something that you got
You don't know it yet
But before the story's over
More than likely they'll get
You'll be Humpty-Dumpty up their sleeves
Drooling at the mouth
More 'n likely you believe
That the pilikia musta' been your fault

Leaving us humble to receive
Leaving us humble to receive
What an evil web we weave
When at first we practice
To deceive

Story has ol' George Washington
Chopping down a cherry tree
Moses and the Pharaoh arbitrating
Leave them kānakas in peace.

Now I weren't there, neither you
So truly I couldn't say
The facts bear witness
To the truth, to induce me to stay

Now I'm not here to mitigate
I've resurrected kanaka beliefs
But what puzzles me
Is the constitutional scriptures
From the 'ōpalatics of the thief

Leaving us humble to receive
Leaving us humble to receive
What an evil web we weave
When at first we practice
To deceive

The moral of the story
Is, What'n the hell you expect
Playing cards with a dealer
Who has tampered with the deck

You go out seeking judicial relief
And, hello, what you find
The one on the bench slamming on gavel
Is a perpetrator of the crime

Tita Pauahi always spoke to me
It's never safe to assume
The fragrance you thought to be justice
Was actually cheap toilet perfume

Leaving us humble to receive
Leaving us humble to receive
What an evil web we weave
When at first we practice
To deceive

John M. Kapena (Luna Hoʻoponopono) • John M. Kapena (Luna Hoʻoponopono)

## Ka Kakou Ai Hawaii

(*Ke Au Okoa* 15 Kekemapa 1870)

Ua olelo ka poe haole, "O ka barena ke kookoo o ke ola," a he mea kupono hoi ia kakou ka puana ana, "O ka poi ke kookoo o ke ola o kanaka Hawaii." Ma ka noho ana o kela lahui keia lahui o ka honua nei, ua hoolakoia mai e ka mana lani na ai a me na mea a pau loa e kupono ai no ka noho ana o kela a me keia kanaka o na lahui o ka honua nei. Ma ia hoolako ia ana mai no hoi, aole i ane kulike loa na ai i haawi ia mai no na pono o kanaka. O kekahi lahui, ua hoolakoia mai me na ili a me na hua o na laau ka lakou mau mea ai; a o kekahi lahui hoi, ua hoonohoia mai, aia ma ka waele a me ka mahi ana aku i ka honua e loaa mai ai na pomaikai e hanai mai ai i na pololi kino kanaka. He nui a lehulehu wale ae no hoi na mea a me na ano e hookanaho mai ai i ka houpo lewalewa.

Ano, ma ko kakou nei aina, he nui wale na lau nahelehele e hoopiha a e hoona mai ai i ka opu pololi a me ka houpo lewalewa o ke kino. Aka, aohe paha ai e ae, a ka opu Hawaii e ake nui loa ai mamua ae o ke kaunui ana aku e like me ka Poi, ka waiu a me ka meli i ke kanaka Hawaii. He mea makehewa no ia makou ka wehewehe ana no ke ano o ka Poi, oiai, aole e pau pono ma na huaolelo ke hoakaka mamua ae o ke kamaaina mau loa ana ia kakou mai ko kakou mau la opiopio loa mai; a i hoomaamaa loa ia mai e ko kakou mau kupuna mai kahiko mai. O ka Poi, ua like no ia me ka barena a me ka palaoa i na haole; he hoohalahala ke ake o na opu ke hoonele ia mai ia mea, a he mea kupono loa e like me ka makou i puana ae la ke kapaia, "O ka Poi ke kookoo o ke ola o ke kanaka Hawaii."

O ka hoao ana e hookahuli ae i ke ano o ka kakou ai mau mawaena ponoi o kakou nei he mea paakiki no ia, a aohe paha e hemo,

175

ina e imi ia kekahi ano *ukuhi* ana; koe wale no paha, ka nele loa ana o kakou i ka Poi ole. No ka mea, ua maa loa kakou mai kahiko loa mai i ka ai ana o ka Poi; a ua komo kona mau hunahuna hoonui a hooikaika iloko o ko kakou mau io na aa koko, ame he la no, ma na oni ana a pau loa o ko kakou mau olona a me na noonoo ano kanaka Hawaii. Owai ke kanaka Hawaii hiki ke hoopoina i kana poi uouo? Owai ka wahine i hooneleia no ka poi awaawa maikai me ka ia hou? Owai hoi ke keiki i hoomanao ole aia no ma na paipu a kona mau makua he mau kahina ai no kona paina ana? O ke kaunui ana i ka poi, me he mea la paha ua oi aku no ia mamua ae o ka paapaa ana o ka puu i ka wai; aia no a komo mai kioo, olu iho la ka maka poniuniu.

Ma ka nana ana no ko kakou ai Hawaii i keia manawa, ua pii ino loa kona kumukuai mai ko na makahiki i kaahope. I ka maiau ana nae no na kumu i pii ino loa ai o ke kumu kuai o ka ai, ua ane nalonalo no na kumu i pii ino ai; no ka mea, i keia manawa, he nui no ka ai e laweia mai nei i ka makeke i na kakahiaka a pau, koe ke Sabati. Eia nae, me keia nui no o ka ai, ua kalalea na kumukuai. Aole keia he kupono ke kapaia he wi no ka aina i ka ai, aka, he pii ano e wale ana no o ke kumukuai. Ma ka nana ana nae i ko keia wa me ko ka manawa he umi a keu aku na makahiki i hala aku nei; alaila, e ike ia no anei kahi i ano e ai. Me he mea la, ma ka nana ana, kekahi kumu paha o keia emi ana mai, ua hilinai aku ia ma ka hapa ana o ka poe mahiai i ka kakou ai Hawaii, i paiia mai ia hapa ana e ka lehulehu ana o kekahi mau oihana mahiai loaa e ae. Mamua aku o ka makahiki 1861, aole i ike ia ka hoopapau nui ana o na kanaka Hawaii ma ka mahiai raiki ana. Aka, i ke komo ana mai o ia oihana mahiai hou, ua hiolo kekahi hapanui o ka poe mahiai kalo ma ka mahi

ana i ka raiki. Ma ia loli ana o na kanaka mahiai kalo ma ia oihana hou, ua laweia kekahi poe mahiai ma ia mea, a ua hoopalaleha lakou i ka mahi ana o ke kalo no ka pii o na kumukuai o ka raiki. Aka, ma ia huli nui ana nae ma ia mea, ua ea mai ke kumukuai o ke kalo a mahuahua; a ua konoia ka poe i mahi i ka raiki e noho malalo o na kumukuai a ka poe mahiai kalo i hookau mai ai. Me he mea la, mai ia manawa mai i hoomaka nui mai ai ka pii ana o ka ai ma na kumu kiekie, a no keia mau makahiki elua, ua mau no ke kumukuai o ka Poi i ka hapalua o ka umeke. Ano, i keia manawa ma ke kaona nei, ua oleloia, ua oi ae ka makepono o ke ola ana ma na mea ai haole, mamua ae o ka ai Hawaii. Eia nae, aohe ka opu Hawaii e piikoi aku ana no ka ai haole, aia wale no ma ka ai Hawaii ke kaunui ana o kona mau manao; a he lohe makou e olelo pinepine ia nei, aohe maona pono i na mea ai haole, he la'ola'o wale no ka opu.

Nolaila, o keia pii ino ana o ke kumukuai o ka ai, he mea kupono no ia na ka lehulehu Hawaii e noonoo ai; oiai, ua puni like ma na mokupuni a pau keia pii ana o ke kumukuai, a he mea kupono no hoi ke noonoo pu ia me na kumu e hiki ai ke pale ae ia mau o ka pii ana; a e hoihoi hou ae hou i na kumukuai kaupono like.

NO TRANSLATION IS BEING PROVIDED FOR THIS ARTICLE.

Testimony Regarding Tuition
Waivers for Students of
Hawaiian Ancestry at the
University of Hawai'i

*In 1999, during the 20th session of the Hawai'i State Legislature, two historic bills relating to higher education of Hawaiian students went before the House and Senate: HB (House Bill) 704 and SB (Senate Bill) 456, both entitled "A Bill for an Act Relating to Tuition Waivers," sought to reduce the cost of education for Hawaiian students in the University of Hawai'i (UH) system in order to make higher education more affordable to Hawaiian students. Since the over 16,000 acres comprised by the University of Hawai'i campuses and field extension sites (including the Mauna Kea telescopes and observatories) sit on ceded lands, proponents of the Tuition Waiver Bills see this as one avenue for the State of Hawai'i to honor their responsibility to provide compensation to Hawaiians for the use of these lands. It has been widely documented and argued by many individual Hawaiians, social service agencies, educational institutions, and other native advocates that increased access to higher education*

*would not only benefit the individuals seeking higher education and their families, but would also benefit the Hawaiian community at large. By providing better opportunities for employment, a college education decreases the risk of welfare dependency; allows more Hawaiians to escape poverty and aspire to a higher standard of living; and reverses overwhelmingly negative trends and statistics, such as the overrepresentation of incarcerated Hawaiians.*

*HB 704 focused on two areas: (1) waiving tuition for 500 Hawaiian students in the University of Hawai'i system in addition to the tuition waivers currently granted to Hawaiian students; and (2) giving priority to Hawaiian students enrolled in Hawaiian-language courses or in education, and who are financially needy or participating in student recruitment programs. The bill was heard by House Education Committee members David Morihara (Chair), K. Mark*

Takai (Vice Chair), Ken Ito, Tom Okamura, Alex Santiago, David Stegmaier, and Bertha Leong. Committee members Dennis Arakaki and Bob McDermott were not present. Many Native Hawaiians testifying in support of this bill proposed adding two important amendments: (1) the deletion of the 500 maximum number of students for whom tuition would be waived to instead include all Hawaiians in the University of Hawai'i system; and (2) the deletion of the clause "financially needy."

SB 456 focused on amending the existing law passed in 1993 that mandated the UH to waive tuition for 250 Hawaiian students in addition to tuition waivers already being granted at the time to specifically provide that the Office of Hawaiian Affairs (OHA) and the UH Board of Regents, and not the State Legislature, take financial responsibility for the granting of tuition waivers. The Senate Education Committee members were David Ige (Chair), Norman Sakamoto (Vice Chair), Robert Bunda, Avery Chumbly, Matt Matsunaga, Rod Tam, and Sam Slom. The amendment stressed the special political relationship that Hawaiians have with both the Federal and State governments, as well as compliance with the UH Board of Regents' previously adopted Strategic Plan, which called for the recruitment and retention of underrepresented student populations, especially Hawaiians. However, this bill was problematic since it attempted to fold the tuition waiver issue into the negotiations then taking place between OHA and the State regarding ceded lands compensation, negotiations many Hawaiians protested.

The Tuition Waiver Bills were supported by Hawaiian organizations such as OHA, 'Īlio'ulaokalani, and the Hawaiian Civic Clubs; UH student organizations such as Kālai Pō and The Associated Students of the University of Hawai'i (ASUH); the faculty and staff of UH's Center for Hawaiian Studies and Hawaiian-language department; and numerous Hawaiian students, their families, and other concerned citizens. Several hundred 'ōiwi Hawai'i from across the pae 'āina (archipelago) presented testimony before the Legislative Educational Committees supporting these bills. The following are actual testimonies presented by some of these 'ōiwi Hawai'i before the House and Senate Education Committees during the months of February and March 1999 at the Hawai'i State Capitol. But because of the legislature's argument that it did not possess the kuleana (authority) to grant tuition waivers, as well as because of the current deflated economic situation and, some say, a continuing reluctance to fund Hawaiian programs, neither bill passed in that legislative session. Still, it seems certain that the fight will continue for tuition waivers for Hawaiian students at the University of Hawai'i.

# Testimony Regarding Tuition Waivers for Students of Hawaiian Ancestry at the University of Hawai'i

JON KAMAKAWIWO'OLE OSORIO

As a Native Hawaiian and a member of the faculty at the Center for Hawaiian Studies, University of Hawai'i-Mānoa, I would like to add my voice in strong support of an amendment to HB 704 that would award tuition waivers to all those of Hawaiian ancestry who wish to attend State-supported institutions of higher learning in the Hawaiian Islands.

As you know, the University of Hawai'i utilizes over 16,000 acres of Native trust lands known as the 5(f) Ceded Lands. These are lands that were the legal property of the sovereign Kingdom of Hawai'i and of the ruling monarch when the American government assisted a small group of conspirators in ousting the legitimate head of state and proclaiming a new government controlled by themselves. In addition to seizing control of the political apparatuses, the "Provisional Government" also pretended to have the authority to take ownership of over 2 million acres of the Kingdom's public and crown lands and proceeded to use them to further the growth of sugar and pineapple, agribusinesses under their control, through a 6-year period as a republic and a 60-year colonial possession of the United States.

Even the United States recognized that Native Hawaiians were entitled to a special consideration with regard to those lands and listed Hawaiians as one of five beneficiaries of the Ceded Lands in the Organic Act that formed the State of Hawai'i. To that extent, the Native people have been cheated of their due because the State did not even begin to recognize this obligation until the creation of the Office of Hawaiian Affairs in 1978, and since then has failed to compensate that agency with 20% of the revenues that the lands earn, as mandated by the Admission Act of 1959.

But I would argue that a 20% entitlement is an arbitrary number that does not truly address the fact that these lands were the legal property of the ruler and government of a constitutionally based, internationally recognized nation friendly to the United States, and that no Native Hawaiian ruler or representative has ever waived our rights to that land. When the "Provisional Government" stole that land, they did not somehow inherit the right to convey ownership to the Republic, and so to the United States, and so to the State of Hawai'i.

If the State of Hawai'i ever has to answer to the Native people for the improper and possibly illegal profiting from our land, would it not be better for the State to point to the ways in which it has benefited the Native to have the lands under the State's control? I believe very deeply that the ability of our people to educate ourselves is directly related to our ability to avoid homelessness, imprisonment, addiction, and violent behaviors, all of which are commonly perceived as afflictions of the Native. We are demanding that the State turn over the tools we need to better our situations in our own homeland. We believe that we can make this demand because we have a far better claim to the Ceded Lands than the State of Hawai'i can ever demonstrate.

Finally, while I acknowledge that the State has obligations to all residents in the

Archipelago, that fact does not allow the State to avoid a special political obligation to Native Hawaiians and the financial commitment that obligation entails. I do not imagine that tuition waivers for all people of Hawaiian ancestry would come without financial sacrifice, but we simply do not allow tenants to assume the right to use property without compensation. The State, like the Federal Government and Territory before it, used the lands of the Native Hawaiians without paying. There is, therefore, a debt, and like all debts can be negotiated.

So far some State legislators prefer to pretend that this issue is about University autonomy. It is not. The issue is simply that the lands of the Native people were improperly and illegally seized and used without compensation to the Native. Until the State of Hawai'i recognizes the need to negotiate with the Native people, we will continue to insist that 100% of the Ceded Lands are ours and the State's debt to us mounts with every passing day.

## M. HEALANI SONODA

Chair David Ige and Members of the Education and Technology Committee,

Aloha, my name is M. Healani Sonoda. I am a Hawaiian graduate student at the University of Hawai'i at Mānoa (UHM)

majoring in Pacific Island Studies, the Treasurer for the Native Hawaiian Student Union, Kālai Pō, at UHM, and the Chair of Ka Lāhui Hawai'i, East Kona district. As one of the few, fortunate recipients of Hawaiian tuition waivers over the past years, I was able to successfully attain a Bachelor's of Arts degree and am continuing on with my Master's. My journey into and through the University system was challenging, coming from a poor economic background and a people plagued with social, health, and political problems. Although we are categorized as "wards" of the State of Hawai'i and the State has taken and holds approximately 2 million acres of our land in trust for our "benefit," we have yet to see any dramatic improvements in our lives initiated by the State. Over the past decades Native Hawaiians have continually owned the worst statistics in Hawai'i, with a large portion of us living on the margins (in slums and decrepit housing), filling the prisons, stuck on financial assistance, struggling with terrible health problems (refer to native Hawaiian Data Book), and, more pointedly, unable to successfully infiltrate and gain equal representation in the State's higher education system, the University of Hawai'i. Although 20% of Hawai'i's population is comprised of Hawaiians and the University of Hawai'i controls 16,000 acres of valuable ceded Hawaiian lands, Hawaiians only make up 8.8% of the University of Hawai'i at Mānoa student population and received only 4% of all available tuition waivers at the UHM in the 1998–99 school year.

Having to overcome the most severe social, health, political, and economic challenges in the State in order to infiltrate Hawai'i's higher education system, we are understandably underrepresented. However, the economic challenge toward higher education can be relieved by the State through its agency, the University of Hawai'i, which generates millions of dollars of revenues from Hawaiian lands, by providing free higher education for all Hawaiians. Although the University of Hawai'i has utilized ceded lands for ninety-two years without any compensation toward Hawaiians for its use and has included Hawaiians as part of their missions and goals in their Master Plan—which reads "to recruit and find keys to the academic success of underrepresented student populations, especially Native Hawaiians"— Hawaiians remain underrepresented. Ignoring their financial obligation toward Hawaiians and ineffectively implementing their mission statement, the University has instead relieved the economic strain of foreign students from rich Asian countries such as Japan, China, and Indonesia by charging them in-state tuition rates, losing millions of dollars in revenues.

Having been one of the few Hawaiian students fortunate enough to have successfully completed the University system with the assistance of tuition waivers, I realize that higher education means much more than finding a good job after graduation. Education is a means of political empowerment, positive social reform and, of course, economic betterment, and by providing tuition waivers for Hawaiians the State will be taking a positive step toward the rehabilitation of the Hawaiian people while simultaneously beginning the retribution process concerning the University's financial obligation to Hawai'i's Native people.

## BERNICE AKAMINE

My name is Bernice Akamine and I have been working in the homeless Hawaiian beach communities across the state since 1997. I attend the University of Hawai'i as a full-time graduate art student. I am also the creator and president of a student-run arts organization that is dedicated to taking art out into the public sphere and has been in organization since 1998. I am a Native Hawaiian and a registered voter in the state of Hawai'i.

I am in support of SB 456 regarding Hawaiian Tuition Waivers and would like the bill amended at section 2, paragraph (a) to read as follows: "The University of Hawai'i shall waive all tuition fees for all Hawaiian students at all University of Hawai'i campuses." And to delete in section 2, paragraph (b), section (1) the words: "financially needy."

Working in the homeless beach communities within the state has opened my eyes to the consequences of the lack of education. Unfortunately, a large portion of these beach communities are Native Hawaiians with nowhere else to turn to and have arrived on the beaches as a last resort with little hope of creating a "better lifestyle" for themselves. The people of the beach communities are not able to afford an education for themselves or the children that they are raising on the beaches. Those five hundred tuition waivers that the senate is considering will not cover those families on the beaches and the other Native Hawaiians who will end up on the beaches should the state fail to live up to its moral and legal obligations to the Native Hawaiians, under the Hawaiian Homes Act and under section 5(f) of the Admission Act of 1959 in administering the "ceded" lands. We then see a cycle of poverty that is not decreasing, but increasing, as time goes on. That education is the key to raising the standard of living for a large portion of these communities is a given. It is no big secret that the economy in Hawai'i has taken a major downturn and that to be competitive in today's employment market one needs to have as much education as possible. If free higher education were offered to all Native Hawaiians they would then be better equipped to succeed in the 21st century.

## KAREN 'ULULANI VICTOR

At Ahu Tongariki on Rapanui, 1998

Chairpersons Morihara and Takai and Members of the Committee:

Aloha kākou. HB 704 requests that the University of Hawai'i waive all tuition fees for five hundred Hawaiian students in addition to the tuition waivers currently granted. I support this bill as a means to increase access to higher education for all Hawaiians and as a means to better the future of Hawai'i.

I am an extremely fortunate Hawaiian. Since both my parents had steady jobs, our family was financially stable enough to allow two of my three brothers and me to attend Kamehameha. This seemingly simple act granted me unprecedented access to educational opportunities that I would have never had if I remained within the public school system of my native Wai'anae Coast. At

Kamehameha, I leaped at the chance to learn as much as I could, to stretch my intellectual boundaries, and realize as much of my potential as was possible. I was in the top ten out of my class of four hundred. I was in orchestra and student government and traveled extensively as a result of my academic involvement. I was extremely fortunate to be allowed this chance to grow and develop, and I knew full well what a debt I owed to the foresight of one woman, Bernice Pauahi Bishop. Without her clarity of vision for the future of Hawaiian children, I would not be the person I am today. The same can be said, I'm sure, for thousands of other Kamehameha alumni.

But as I said, I am an extremely fortunate Hawaiian. Not every Hawaiian child has the good fortune to learn in such an enriching and supportive environment, and not every Hawaiian is allowed an opportunity for education. Sometimes this occurs because the individual in question is simply not motivated or interested; being Hawaiian doesn't automatically mean that one is gifted with superhuman intellect or drive. But most of the time, the pathway to knowledge and occupational opportunity and increased quality of life is barred by pure economics— there just isn't enough money.

For me, when it came time to graduate and move on to college, I was forced into the realization that I couldn't attend Harvard. I couldn't go to American University or Colorado College, my two favorite schools out of the five that I applied to and the countless others that clamored for my application. I couldn't go, even though I received partial scholarships and grants. I couldn't go because my family could not afford the staggering financial burden.

So I applied for the Regents Scholarship at UH–Mānoa. And, being the extremely fortunate Hawaiian that I am, I got accepted. And I've learned so much and grown so much thanks to this scholarship. But as I sat at that reception dinner and I looked around the tables at all my fellow Regent Scholars, I saw that I was the only Hawaiian there.

This phenomenon continued in many of my classes. In all except for Hawaiian Language, I was one of only a handful of Hawaiians among hundreds of other students. While there may be many factors involved here, I believe that the reason more Hawaiians aren't enrolled in higher education programs is, again, pure economics. I know many of my friends who would leap at a chance to attend school full-time instead of working three jobs to pay the rent and the bills *and* tuition.

I feel that tuition waivers should be made available to Hawaiians who are both financially needy and intellectually hungry. Why? Not because we're special or because we are more deserving of education than any other ethnic minority at UH, but because our people have a particular relationship with the United States government. Because our people have been denied access to a variety of opportunities as a result of that particular relationship. And because higher education for Hawaiians means a better educated Hawaiian community that is able to determine exactly how and where it wants to go rather than let its future be decided by outside forces like politics or economics.

I am an extremely fortunate Hawaiian. Because of the foresight of one person, I was granted access to education and the fulfillment of my intellectual thirst for high-er education. With the foresight of nine persons and the passage of HB 704, there will be a chance for 500 more Hawaiians and a new hope for the future of Hawai'i.

## P. KAMEHA'ILILANI WAIAU

Aloha pumehana nō kākou a pau loa, mai Hawai'i nui kuauli nani maoli i nā lehua a i Ni'ihau o Kahelelani, kaulana i nā pūpū, mai ko uka a ko kai, mai nā kūpuna a nā kamali'i, aloha kākou ē, aloha nō.

Eia au 'o Kameha'ililani Waiau, he kaikamahine no Papakōlea i uka o Pūowaina. He wahi hoa hele kula nō kēia i ke Kula Nui 'o Hawai'i ma Mānoa i ia mau makahiki 'ehiku i ka'a hope mai nei. Maopopo le'a maoli nō ia'u he mana a he kuleana ku'u wahi kūlana haumāna no ka 'ohana a pēlā pū me ku'u kaiāulu aloha. 'Oiai ua nele nui ku'u po'e 'ohana i ke kālā 'ole, 'o kēia ka makahiki 'elua wale nō a'u e hele kula nei ma ke 'ano he haumāna manawa piha. Me ke kōkua nui o ke kula 'o Kamehameha lāua 'o ka 'Aha Pūnana Leo, hiki ia'u ke holomua i nēia ala pono o ka na'auao e 'imi ai i kekelē B.A.

I ku'u wahi 'ohana, nui hewahewa nā kuleana o'u a o ku'u po'e mākua e hiki 'ole ai iā mākou ke uku i ke kumu kū'ai hele kula nui; e la'a ka mālama 'ana i ka hale a me nā po'e o loko, ko mākou ola kino, ka hānai maika'i 'ana iā mākou iho a pēlā pū me ka pu'u o nā pila he nui i ahu mai nei. Malama 'o kēlā ke kumu o ka holopono 'ole 'ana o ka hapanui o ku'u po'e lāhui.

No laila, eia nō mākou, 'o au me ku'u po'e 'aumākua, kūpuna, mākua a me nā keiki a'u e hahai mai ana, ke noi ha'aha'a nei iā 'oukou, e ku'u mau hoa o ka 'Aha 'Ōlelo, e nānā maika'i i nei pila ko'iko'i a e 'ae mai iā kākou e holomua ma ke 'ano he lāhui a me ke 'ano ho'i he aupuni. He waiwai nō a he pono ka hele kula nui 'ana no kā mākou po'e 'ōpio i kā mākou o noho wa'awa'a na'aupō lākou. E kāko'o mai!

## ELLABELLE CONSTANCE KILOLANI KAIAMA

Dear Senator David Y. Ige, Chair, and Members of the Senate Committee on Education and Technology,

Aloha, my name is Ellabelle Constance Kilolani Kaiama and I support the intent of Senate Bill No. 456 Relating to Tuition Waivers.

I speak as a private citizen of Hawaiian ancestry, as a mother of a bachelor's degree candidate in Hawaiian Studies at the University of Hawai'i at Mānoa and as a retired employee of the State of Hawai'i's Department of Public Safety, Corrections Division. As a mother of five I am all too

familiar with the social and economic challenges students face. The percentage of Hawaiians who enroll and complete degrees under the University of Hawai'i system is appallingly low and is a testament to the challenges which confront Hawaiians. This may be reflected in the fact that only one in five of my own children will have attained a 4-year degree.

The high cost of living in Hawai'i coupled with a relative lack of educational funding has set a spiral to Hawai'i's social woes. If you take into consideration the cost of housing one prisoner for a year in the State prison, you will find it is cheaper to keep him out of it by providing an educational benefit. Prison is a revolving door. The best of administrators don't have a handle on it because the problem is education—the lack of it. It is very easy to lock a person up and throw away the key, but all you do is compound the problem. The solution is education.

This bill would make a tiny but positive step towards improving the social and economic status of the native Hawaiian population, and Hawai'i as a whole, through higher education. Statistics reveal that Hawaiians make up the State's highest proportion of people receiving social services and welfare. We also form the majority of the State's incarcerated. S.B. 456 has the potential to open doors to higher education, which can provide Hawaiian youth with the vital tools needed for successful futures. Thus, the need to build more prisons would virtually disappear along with the burden on State social services and other governmental aid programs. The "aid" could then be applied toward a truly beneficial purpose, that being improved public education in Hawai'i. If the State's true intent is to *aid* its citizens, then it must switch its focus from incarceration to education. If the State is to be relieved of some of its economic burdens then it must concentrate on educating its youth who will become part of the fabric of an economically and socially sound society of the future. Senate Bill No. 456 proposes to waive tuition for *only* 500 Hawaiian students in the University of Hawai'i system. Calculations based on an academic year of undergraduate study for 500 students at a tuition of $1,500 per semester at the University of Hawai'i at Mānoa comes to $1,500,000. But divide this amount by 16,000—the approximately number of acres of ceded lands the UH occupies—and the resulting figure is a pale $93.75 per acre, an amount that hardly compensates for back rent and is substantially less than today's current land assessment values.

As written, S.B. 456 would give priority to those Hawaiian students who are enrolled in Hawaiian language courses, education, are financially needy, or participating in student recruitment programs. 500 tuition waivers is *a mere pittance* for the University's 92-year rent free occupation of over 16,000 acres of ceded lands. This fact alone warrants tuition waivers for *all* Hawaiians *without regulation* of study field. I recommend you change the bill to include *all* Hawaiians in *all* fields of study. Let's work to remove limitations, not increase them!

I urge you to SUPPORT Senate Bill No. 456 with the above recommended amendments. Mahalo.

## R. HŌKŪLEI LINDSEY

Senator Ige, Senator Hanabusa and Members of the Committees,

I am Hōkūlei Lindsey, the Vice President of the Associated Students of the University of Hawai'i at Mānoa (ASUH). ASUH is the elected student body, representing 10,000 undergraduate students at the University of Hawai'i at Mānoa (UHM). On behalf of ASUH, thank you for the opportunity to submit testimony in support of tuition waivers for Hawaiians within the University of Hawai'i system.

On January 25, 1999, after resounding testimony from students in favor of tuition waivers for students of Hawaiian ancestry, ASUH unanimously adopted Senate Resolution 12-99 entitled "Supporting Tuition Waivers for Hawaiians within the University of Hawai'i."

In this resolution, ASUH calls attention to the fact that in 1991 the UH Board of Regents adopted a Master Plan, which specifically states that one of its missions is to "recruit and find keys to the academic success of underrepresented student populations, especially Native Hawaiians." Tuition waivers for Hawaiians within the University system are one step toward meeting this stated goal.

In *Building a Rainbow*, a book about the history of buildings on the UHM campus, it is stated that after acquiring the crown lands upon which the Mānoa campus is now built, the Regents voted in 1911 to evict "about seven groups of Hawaiians." The University currently controls 16,000 acres of valuable 5(f) ceded lands of which Hawaiians are beneficiaries, but have never received any compensation in the University's ninety-two year history. Tuition waivers are one step toward compensation for the Hawaiian people.

ASUH also calls the Committees' attention to the fact that tuition waivers for students of Hawaiian ancestry are not based on race. They are, in fact, based on a special political relationship with the Federal and State governments established through the Hawaiian Homes Commission Act, Public Law 105-130, also known as the Apology Resolution, and Section 5(f) of the Hawai'i State Constitution. This relationship is similar to the trust relationship that exists between these governments and Indian tribes. Thus, programs that are preferential to Native Hawaiians, such as tuition waivers, are viewed as "rationally related to protecting or promoting self-governance, self-sufficiency, or native culture" and are, therefore, constitutional. The State of Hawai'i has a legal obligation to the Hawaiian people.

Finally, the education of Indigenous Peoples is not a new issue nor is it an issue limited to Hawai'i. At the United Nations in Geneva, Switzerland, the theme of the sixteenth session of the U.N. Working Group on Indigenous Populations, attended by over 700 Indigenous Peoples (including Hawaiians) and Nation-States (including the U.S.) in July 1998, was Indigenous Language and Education. In their intervention, the delegation from Hawai'i testified to the underrepresentation and lack of programs aimed at enrolling and retaining students of Hawaiian ancestry at the University of Hawai'i.

History warrants this issue. In Hawai'i, rent is overdue.

Senator Ige, Senator Hanabusa and Members of the Committees, thank you again for this opportunity to testify in support of Hawaiian tuition waivers.

## ALEXIS KEIKILANI MEYER

Keikilani (far left) and other university students on Bachman lawn, UH-Mānoa, challenging the accountability of the university to fulfill their mission statement to promote "diversity, fairness, and equity"

My name is Alexis Keikilani Meyer and I am in support of Senate Bill 456. I would also like to amend this bill at Section 2, paragraph (a) to read "The University of Hawai'i shall waive tuition fees for *all* Hawaiian students at all University of Hawai'i campuses."

I graduated from Kailua High School in 1975. After two failed attempts at attending college and 20 years of employment, I'm proud to say I received my A.A. from Windward Community College in 1997 and am currently attending UH-Mānoa. I am the first person to graduate from college in my family. I am 41 years old.

As an indigenous person of Hawai'i nei, I demand the wrong done to my people by the United States of America be corrected.

In 1993, we received an apology by the United States Congress, which acknowledged this fact: "The indigenous Hawaiian people *never* directly relinquished their claims to inherent sovereignty as a people or over their national lands to the United States."

As a student of Hawaiian ethnicity, I demand the opportunity to better myself by obtaining a higher education.

In 1991, the Board of Regents of the University of Hawai'i adopted a Master Plan which included the *implementation* of the recruitment and academic success of Native Hawaiians.

As a parent, I claim this right for my son and future generations of Native Hawaiians.

According to the United States Congress, the State of Hawai'i is responsible for the trust obligations stated in the Hawaiian Homes Act and the Admission Act of 1959. One of these obligations consists of 20% of the state's revenue from ceded lands being utilized for the *betterment* of Native Hawaiians. The key word is *betterment*, Chairman Ige and Committee members.

I ask you, has the State of Hawai'i *fulfilled* their obligation toward the betterment of Native Hawaiians? *I think not!* Hawaiians top the list in regard to *homelessness, welfare assistance, incarceration and illiteracy.* We've evolved from a self-sufficient people to a dependent people.

Now is the time for the United States of America, the State of Hawai'i and the

University of Hawai'i to *fulfill their political, social and financial obligations* to my people, the kānaka maoli.

Now is the time to do *more than* acknowledge the wrongdoing of the United States and the State of Hawai'i.

*Now is the time for action!*

*You*, as a legislative body, can *initiate* the start of fulfilling this political obligation to my people, the Native Hawaiians.

You can initiate *the betterment of Native Hawaiians* by giving us full tuition waivers throughout the University of Hawai'i campuses.

By passing Senate Bill 456, you declare that *now is the time* for a debt to be paid, for a state's political obligation to be fulfilled, for a native people to reclaim their self-sufficiency, *for the education and betterment of Native Hawaiians.*

## L. KU'UMEAALOHA GOMES

Aloha Senator Ige and members of the Committee on Education and Technology:

My name is Ku'umeaaloha Gomes, and I am the Director of Kua'ana Student Services at the University of Hawai'i at Mānoa, a recruitment and retention program for Native Hawaiians established in 1988. I am here today to testify as a member of the UHM Native Hawaiian Academic Advisory Committee, which is comprised of Native Hawaiian faculty and staff of the UHM, including representatives from the Ethnic Studies Program, Social Work, John A. Burns Medical School, College of Education,

College of Business Administration, Center for Hawaiian Studies and the Hawaiian Language Program, to name a few. The UHMNHAAC has as its mission: 1) Increasing the enrollment of Native Hawaiians in higher education; 2) Advocating for the hiring of Native Hawaiian faculty and staff in higher education, and especially on the UHM campus; and 3) Increasing the voice and visibility of Native Hawaiians, their issues and their history, through a curriculum designed and taught by Native Hawaiians that focuses on teaching Hawaiian language, Native Hawaiian history, and contemporary political issues.

This testimony is being written in support of SB 456, which calls for 500 tuition waivers to be awarded to students of Hawaiian ancestry enrolled at the University of Hawaiʻi.

A recent report completed by the Dean of Student Affairs and submitted to the University of Hawaiʻi's Board of Regents indicated that the UH system spends $14 million on its tuition waiver program per year, which includes tuition assistance to faculty and staff, graduate assistants and students. Of this amount, 900 Native Hawaiian students in the entire UH system are provided with financial assistance through tuition waivers.

The report projects that it would cost the University system anywhere from $5 million to $7 million per semester to provide tuition waivers for all Native Hawaiian students enrolled in the UH system. Currently, according to the UH Office of Institutional Research, there are a little over 6,000 Native Hawaiian students registered in the system; this includes full-time and part-time students. Recently the chancellor of Maui

Community College indicated that because 2/3rds of his students are Native Hawaiians, his system would not be able to absorb this cost, and to do so without additional funds would immobilize his entire operation.

From a business management perspective, in order to fulfill a request for tuition waivers for all Native Hawaiians enrolled in the UH system, without additional funds appropriated by the State Legislature, would mean that the University would have to make serious programmatic adjustments—perhaps closing the Richardson School of Law or the John A. Burns Medical School; scaling down some of its academic programs, getting rid of all of its student service and academic support programs...this scenario begins to get a little scary.

But the question here is not just one of cost, it is also very importantly about *the role of the University of Hawaiʻi in the education of Native Hawaiians!* This is a question that has to be answered not just by the University but also by the State government, including yourselves. Each citizen of this State has a right to access education. The role of the government of the State of Hawaiʻi is to assure that access to everyone. The situation of Native Hawaiians as a historical political group with a trust relationship with the State of Hawaiʻi is unique and cannot and must not be compared to other groups in Hawaiʻi. Native Hawaiian history dictates that revenues generated from Ceded Lands are to be used for the health and education of Native Hawaiians.

You and I both know that Native Hawaiians have historically shown up highest on welfare roles and incarceration lists. Child, domestic, alcohol and drug abuse are problems confronted by the Native Hawaiian community.

Over the years, Native Hawaiians have asserted the responsibility for improving the conditions in their community, working to establish various programs not only treatment-based, but more importantly those focused on prevention.

Education has been and continues to be a significant tool for the betterment of any society. Education allows individuals and groups of people to acquire skills that assist them in learning healthy behaviors. Education allows people to compete in the marketplace, to develop skills that allow them to be upwardly mobile. Education allows individuals to have pay scales to support families, taking them off of welfare roles. Education allows individuals to be able to have better jobs with incomes to afford healthy diets, consistent dental and medical care, and better housing. Education allows Native Hawaiians through their marketability to assist in improving the State economy by becoming good consumers and increasing their purchasing power.

I take this opportunity, while supporting SB 456, to also propose that the State Legislature recommend that the Office of the Governor and the Board of Regents of the University of Hawai'i work on a strategic plan to allow Native Hawaiians entering the UH system to have financial assistance through tuition waivers. I also propose as a first step that these entities recommend that the BOR clarify its definition of Native Hawaiians immediately so that in the future attempts by outside resources such as the Office of Hawaiian Affairs to fund scholarship programs for Native Hawaiians are not denied by the University of Hawai'i because of its archaic and incorrect definition of Native Hawaiians. Finally, I propose that this body support a mission for the University of Hawai'i that includes a commitment to the education of Native Hawaiians as the indigenous people and host culture of this archipelago.

In closing, I thank Senator Ige and his Committee on Education and Technology for allowing the voices of the people to be heard.

Kaimalino at one-
and-a-half years old
in Pīlaʻa, the place
"where he's from"

# *kaimalino*

Kaimalino Woo Andrade • Kaimalino Woo Andrade • Kaimalino Woo Andrade

I'm from waking up in the morning to the
   sound of the ocean,
I'm from living in a house that my dad built
   with his own hands,
I'm from having my closest neighbor living
   five miles away,
I'm from looking out my window and seeing
   a group of pigs just stroll on by,
I'm from walking around in the pasture,
   playing with the horses,
I'm from growing my own veggies and fruit,
I'm from eating papayas and avocados as a
   meal,
I'm from running around naked on the
   beach,
I'm from running away from cows,
I'm from running away from my sister's killer
   pet geese,
I'm from running away from home, goin'
   two blocks, and comin' back,
I'm from playing monopoly alone (and I still
   cheat),
I'm from being teased because I look haole,
I'm from being teased because I'm Hawaiian,

I'm from burning rubbish in the evenings,
I'm from stomping out flames with rubber
   slippers when my mom set the pasture on
   fire,
I'm from making fire every night with my
   brother for a hot bath,
I'm from listening to my dad play slack key,
I'm from falling asleep to the sound of the
   ocean.

Kaimalino today

190

# Kīlauea Imprint

*linda*

Linda Moriarty • Linda Moriarty • Linda Moriarty • Linda Moriarty

In May 1999, a garden of native coastal plants was created and dedicated at Kīlauea Point on Kaua'i's north shore to my late husband, Dan Moriarty, who was the manager of Kīlauea Point National Wildlife Refuge for many years. At the dedication ceremony, I read this poem, which I wrote for my children. It is to honor their father and the privilege our family had of living in such a beautiful place. In a Polynesian sense, it is also meant as an introduction of my children so others will know who they are in the context of where they were reared.

Until we moved to Honolulu for their high school years, my children lived at the Kīlauea Point Lighthouse, where they shared in the responsibilities of managing the wildlife refuge. They helped with bird banding, collected naupaka and 'ilima seeds for revegetation projects, and reared albatross chicks. There was no television and town friends rarely came to play, as the sheer cliffs near our house

struck fear in their parents. This wild, isolated peninsula with the beacon at the tip was home.

The isolation nurtured a closeness amongst us and to Kīlauea Point. Every fall, when the first cold, strong winds blew from the north, we all inherently knew that the albatross had returned to Kīlauea to nest.

# Kīlauea Imprint

(for my children)

I come from the fire of Pele, now calmed and
nurtured in the encircling arms of Mōkōlea
and Kīlauea.

I come from the constant winds of the north,
laden with salt.

I come from where the strong, cold winds
bring the albatross from the far ocean to raise
their love child.

I come from the waves that roll rocks and
climb cliffs.

I come from the gentle breeze of the summer,
calming after the winter tempest.

I come from the waves that hide fat 'opihi
from would-be suitors.

I come from the soft moan of the shearwater
and the hungry cry of their young.

I come from the mid-air dance of the
red-tailed tropic bird, seducing the gusting
wind to a tranquil lover's breeze.

I come from the rising sun reflected in the
'ilima at my feet.

I come from the protected cove where the
monk seal rest undetected amongst the
gray rocks.

I come from where āholehole glisten silver in
the foaming surf.

My home is framed in coco palms; my floor,
woven hala; my garden, naupaka.

My young ultimately fledge, stepping off the
cliff's edge onto the soaring updrafts.

They go far away, but someday return to
mate...Kīlauea imprinted!

# A Story Fo' Da Birds

David J. Imaikalani Wallace • David J. Imaikalani Wallace • David J. Imaikalani Wallace

There are many places I call home. Ho'olehua, Moloka'i, was my childhood home. There I learned how to be an independent person who valued honesty and hard work, and who honored my parents and akua. It is the land of my birth, a place where the iwi of my grandparents William and Ellen Wallace lay, along with those of my mother, Maggie Lei Wallace, who passed away in March 1999. I return frequently to Moloka'i to restore my mana and rid myself of the 'ōpala heaped upon my shoulders by the urban lifestyle I now live. My roots are strongly anchored in Moloka'i.

Another place I call home is Lā'ie, O'ahu. I spent most of my high school and young adult years living in Lā'ie with my sister Ziona, my brother Bill, grandpa John E. Broad, and a family friend, Dr. Guy Heder. Lā'ie was a safe, nurturing community where I was surrounded by family and lifetime friends. In this nurturing environment, I was given the encouragement to grow and develop into a young man. The first person to encourage me to write was Miss Ann Sheridan, my English teacher at Kahuku High School. Lā'ie is another place I visit to restore my mana and enjoy the companionship of family and true friends.

Finally, home is wherever my family and I happen to be living. Currently, that place is 'Aiea, O'ahu. What makes a place home is the safety and warmth that resides there, whether it's a tent down the beach or a mansion in Kāhala. Home is where family, love, mana, and akua intermingle and move about freely; a place where I can relax, heal, and enjoy peace of mind.

## A Story Fo' Da Birds

The first lesson a small farmer learns is never name an animal you plan to eat. My Dad learned that lesson the hard way after giving us kids the opportunity to name our first batch of chickens. They were Rhode Island Reds, and by the time they were pullets, each of them had a name.

One Saturday, without a word to us, Dad started a fire to heat some water. As he sharpened his hatchet, we approached him, curious. "Daddy," we asked in unison, "what you doin'???"

"Ahhh..." he replied, "jus' getting ready fo' take care da chickens, us all."

"So wat the hot wadda fo'wa?" asked Lei, my younger sister. "You going baffe 'em o' wat?"

"Ahhh...sumting li'dat... Why you guys no go inside da house, haa?"

Before Dad could say anything else, I asked, "So Daddy, wat da hatchet fo'wa?"

"Fo' cut da fiya wood...us all."

Seeing that our query into the matter was satisfied, Dad shooed us into the house, where Mom awaited us with some chores.

"No baada daddy today, haa, you guys," Mom said in a stern voice. "Jus' do yo' work, 'n no fool aroun'."

We raced through our chores, until our focus returned to Dad and our chickens. We had never seen a chicken taking a bath. Our curiosity led us to the back bedroom, where a small window proved a perfect vantage point to see what Dad was doing.

Dad was sitting on an old wooden folding chair, bending over a small tree stump. With one hand he held down Cluckie, our favorite chicken. With the other hand, he lifted his hatchet, struck Cluckie through the neck, then casually tossed the headless body to the ground, where it jumped, flipped, and spasmed as blood spewed into the air. "NOOO DADDY NOOO!!!" we yelled, pounding on the window. "NO KILL DA CHICKENS!!! NOT OUR CHICKENS!!! CLUCK-IEEEE!!!!"

We pushed through the window screen and spilled out into the yard, where we saw the carcasses of all our chickens, headless and soaked in their own blood. Stunned, we wept shamelessly as our parents tried to comfort us.

"Try fo' undastan', kids," Dad whispered. "We raise chickens fo' eggs and fo' eat."

"But dey owa' pets, Daddy," I sniffled.

"Dey not fo' pets, Kika," Mom said in a soothing tone. "Dis' kine birds, dey meat birds. We raise 'um fo' eat 'um. Plain an' simple."

But no matter what my parents said, comfort could not be found in their words, especially for a six-year-old boy. So Dad loaded up the birds into a large cardboard box and buried them in the back yard while we said a little graveside prayer.

For the following two months, we decorated the graves with bright-colored flowers every morning, and pulled the weeds from the grave as they sprouted. As the months drew on, however, our interests turned to new friends and pets and, slowly, weeds reclaimed the once hallowed ground.

Despite my early trauma, by the time I was 12, I had become a champion poultry farmer in the 4-H program. For two years, with the help of my Dad, I raised broilers that averaged over ten pounds each. I also developed a cleaner and more humane way of slaughtering a chicken. Using the clothesline in our yard, I would tie a chicken upside down until he blacked out. Then I would take a sharp metal rod, find the soft spot in the bird's upper palate, and strike his brain. There would be some wing flapping, but no jumping and flipping, like with the method Dad had used. Death was swift and painless. My method also insured that most of the blood drained from the carcass and no bruising occurred to the bird's flesh. A dressed and packaged bird coming from my roost looked like a medium-sized turkey.

I did not make the mistake Dad made: I did not give names to any of my birds.

After awhile, I stopped raising broilers and began raising pigeons instead. As my pigeon collection grew to over 60, I developed a binding relationship with two of my birds. They were a matched pair of blues who were always happy to see me. Both birds ate directly out of my hand and never minded a gentle stroke over the head. Often finding a perch on my shoulder or head, the two pigeons were king and queen of the coop. I spent countless hours with the pair, holding them, petting them, and teaching them tricks like ringing a bell and playing dead.

The entire flock were trained as high flyers, soaring into the clouds at my command. I often soared with them in my thoughts,

sometimes wishing for wings to complete the fantasy until, with two sharp toots on my whistle, I would call the entire flock zooming down out of the sky like dive bombers.

In a year's time, the pair of blues had sired six beautiful squabs that matured into powerful racers and hearty high flyers. All was well, until one day when I opened the cage door to see a huge rat scramble down from the nesting boxes and speed away through a hole in the wire. Quickly checking the cage, I discovered the headless bodies of my matched blues in their nest box. I gently removed the birds from the nest and found their squab, only a week old, hidden under the mother's wing. The baby bird, still alive, had a tiny nick on its tail. The rat had apparently attacked her, and her parents had come to her rescue. Tears streamed from my eyes as I carried the little family away from the coop. Near the site where Dad had buried all our chickens six years earlier, I dug a good-sized grave and placed the blues in it. I said a short prayer, covered the grave, and placed several flowers on top. As I turned away, the squab in my hand began to cry.

By the time Mom and Dad came home, I had tried everything I could to care for the baby bird. I had placed her in another nesting pair's nest, but she was attacked as an intruder. I had tried to feed her with an eyedropper, but she refused to open her beak. I was at wits' end when Dad opened the door, a welcome sight.

After hearing what had happened, Dad pondered and began to experiment. First he took a poi pounder and mashed a handful of corn into a fine powder. Then he added a drop of milk and some water to it to create a smooth, creamy liquid. In the meantime, the little squab was nibbling between my fingers, whistling softly. So I filled the eye-dropper full of the creamy liquid and slowly dripped the contents into her hungry, open mouth. It worked!!! The famished bird began feasting as though her stomach were a bottomless pit. Dad then put together an incubator out of an old cracker can and a light bulb. Then the incubator was taken to my room, where I was allowed to care for the bird.

For the next few months, I was both mother and father to the hungry, growing squab, who, like clockwork, would squawk out mealtime five times a day. Over a period of ten weeks, the growing bird metamor-phosed from cute, to grotesque, to ugly, to when she finally resembled an adult pigeon with long, pointed flight feathers and a necklace of soft blue-gray satin feathers. As her pin feathers and down disappeared, the squab began to leave the nest and, like a house cat, walk all through the house, squawking and begging for food.

One day, I overheard Nani, my youngest sister, call the squab "Weezy."

"Hey Nani," I said to her, "why you call my pigeon 'Weezy'?"

"'Cause it always stay wheezing," she replied. "See?"

At that moment, the bird began nibbling Nani's toes while calling out for food in a way that did sound like wheezing. This is how Weezy got her name.

Weezy grew into a very beautiful bird, taking on the affectionate nature of her mother. She was always nibbling at my ear

as she sat perched on my shoulder—her way of saying she wanted a kiss from me. Turning towards her, a quick peck on her beak satisfied us both. I guess you could say we loved each other.

When Weezy began to fly, I let her mix with the flock in some of their high-flying journeys. But no matter how high they soared, I could always single her out in the distance. As she matured and began spending more time with the flock, she paired up with a handsome brown-speckled male. But as soon as I came to the coop, Weezy devoted her entire attention to me.

One late afternoon in August, I released Weezy and the rest of the birds for their afternoon workout. An hour later, I blew my whistle to recall the birds. When the flock arrived, I looked for Weezy, but she was not among them. I quickly grabbed my bike and began circling the neighborhood, blowing my whistle. Nothing. I continued far into the night until Dad came looking for me.

"Son," Dad called from the pickup truck, "time fo' come home."

"But I gotta find Weezy!" I snapped back, starting to cry.

"Maybe she just resting o' got intercepted by one odda group o' pigeons," Dad said, attempting to calm me. "Come home, eat, go sleep, den tomorrow we go look fo' her."

Partly relieved, yet still worried, I followed him home.

Mom and Dad tried their best to calm me, but their words failed. Sleep was a restless and fleeting companion that night. A mixture of emotions flowed through me like winter surf crashing at Mo'omomi.

The next day, without eating breakfast, I ran to the pigeon coop, located 50 yards from the house. Weezy had not made it home. Taking an old chair, I positioned myself near the feed trough and blew my whistle for hours. Mom, Dad, and the rest of the family would come by the coop, give me snacks to munch on, and offer verbal support. Dad visited several other pigeon fanciers in the community, but to no avail. As time passed, a feeling of dread came over me.

The sun was just about to set in the western horizon when I suddenly heard the rustling of leaves from the nearby bushes. Thinking it was a rat, I grabbed a two-by-four and went to investigate. As I slowly crept towards a bush of sour grass, I froze in my tracks. There on the ground before me was Weezy, struggling to walk. Recognizing me, she seemed to find the extra energy to make one last push out of the bush. I carefully lifted her, while caressing her in my hands, and examined her body. To my horror, I found a large tear in her chest that had severed her right wing at the shoulder joint. The wound was so deep that the surfaces of her tiny, still-beating heart and intestines were dried due to the exposure. Someone had shot Weezy with a .22.

Weeping profusely, I ran into the house. "DADDY!" I screamed. "DADDY! SOME-BODY WENT SHOOT WEEZY!" The entire family ran to the dining area. I wrapped Weezy in my favorite T-shirt. She was suffering, struggling to stay alive.

"Let me see 'um," Dad whispered. He took the bird in his hands. "No look too good, boy," was all he said before he, too, shed some tears.

"But Daddy," I cried, "how can I make her get betta?"

"Son," Dad replied in a sober voice, "you been working wit' animals a while now, yeah?"

"Ahha."

"So you know sometimes you gotta do wat's bess fo' da animal, ha?"

"Ahha."

"So why you no give me Weezy now."

Understanding what Dad was trying to do for me, I gently protested. "Daddy, no need," I whispered. "She my bird, my responsibility."

Mom, Dad, and my sisters hugged me as I walked out of the house carrying Weezy in my hands, still wrapped in my shirt. I slowly took the long walk to the grave of Weezy's parents. Every step I took brought back memories of our friendship, a tear for every smile she gave me. I selected a spot near her parents and dug a shallow hole. Then, holding her between my hands in such a way that we could peer into each others' eyes, I kissed her good-bye. Her soul told me she understood. Placing my right hand over her head, a simple tug sent Weezy to eternal peace. Gently, I placed her into her grave, my tears falling on her small body, and covered her with soil and flowers. A heartfelt prayer was offered, a prayer that would make God weep. Then I turned from Weezy and returned to the warmth and safety of my home, where the love of my family awaited me.

*A Hundred Years after the
Pīkake Princess*

# hōkūlani

Arnold Hōkūlani Requilmán • Arnold Hōkūlani Requilmán • Arnold Hōkūlani Requilmán

## A Hundred Years after the Pīkake Princess

The procession moved slowly up Nuʻuanu Avenue and entered the black and gold iron gates of Maunaʻala—the "fragrant mountain" of past *aliʻi*, the Royal Mausoleum. The most prominent royalists were present in the procession, as were the surviving members of the Hawaiian Royal Family. This was no ordinary procession; this was for a princess, a person who was supposed to have become a queen one day. Men dressed in black suits and waving colorful *kāhili* walked alongside a black catafalque pulled by over 250 men also clad in black. Inside the catafalque was a *koa* coffin draped with a red-and-yellow feather cloak. Inside the coffin was the body of the frail 23-year-old princess, the hope of the Hawaiian people—Kaʻiulani, Crown Princess of the Hawaiian Kingdom, now on her way to join other family members in the

crypt of the Kalākaua Dynasty: her mother, Princess Miriam Likelike; and her uncle, King Kalākaua. A few years earlier, American marines had arrogantly smashed the Hawaiian crowns against a wall in the basement of ʻIolani Palace and stolen their jewels. Had they not, the royal crowns borne on a red velvet pillow would have preceded the catafalque. For many Hawaiians, the absence of the crowns reminded them of Kaʻiulani's words in 1898, after the forced annexation of Hawaiʻi to the United States:

> They [America] have taken away everything from us and it seems there is left but a little, and that little our very life itself. We [native Hawaiians] live now in such a semi retired way, that people wonder if we even exist any more. I wonder too, and to what purpose? (Seiden 1992:142)

Princess Ka'iulani

A year later, that "very little" of Ka'iulani was gone. Over 20,000 weeping Hawaiians, young and old, lined the sidewalks to watch the procession's movement. They wore traditional mourning clothes of the time: the women in white *holokū*, clutching handkerchiefs and wiping their tearing eyes; the men in black suits with white ribbons pinned above their left jacket pockets. Affluent men, white gloves partially tucked into their left jacket pocket, seized their top hats in grief. For this one day, Hawai'i's people were united beyond race or class for a single purpose: to pay their final respects to their beloved peacock princess. Aside from the periodic strains of crying, chanting, and wailing, all remained silent while the funeral march wound through the city.

In step behind the catafalque was another carriage—an empty black carriage pulled by two huge white stallions from the royal stables and driven by two liveried retainers of the Hawaiian Court. This carriage should have been ridden by Queen Lili'uokalani; however, she was in the American capitol of Washington D.C., continuing the fight for the rights of her people. This empty carriage not only symbolically represented the Queen, but reminded people of the now empty throne. With the death of Ka'iulani, no other royal family member remained who was legally approved by the House of Nobles to be the next heir. Ka'iulani would be Hawai'i's last Crown Princess, the last heir of the Kalākaua Dynasty.

After the procession ended its reverent march to Mauna'ala, palm bearers carried the coffin to the allotted vault next to Ka'iulani's mother in the Kalākaua crypt as a heart-rending *kanikau* (Hawaiian dirge) commemorating the princess's life was chanted. Ka'iulani's father, Archibald

Cleghorn, and her uncles Princes Kawananakoa and Kūhiō, among others, then sadly sealed the vault with a marble slab, her tombstone, and immediately "Hawai'i Pono'ī," the Hawaiian national anthem, was played. At that moment a light mist fell from the otherwise clear sky. Had things been different, had Ka'iulani outlived her aunt the Queen, these very men would have been among the first to officially proclaim, "The Queen is dead! Long Live the Queen! Queen Ka'iulani I, by the Grace of God, Queen of the Hawaiian Islands!" while "Hawai'i Pono'ī" was played for her coronation. An entirely different occasion.

As they sealed the tomb, Archibald Cleghorn no doubt recalled many memories of his daughter and how she might have been had she been given the chance to reign as queen. He, among many others, had remained vigilant at Princess Ka'iulani's bedside after she became ill a month earlier. On the night of her death, he had a "dream" that he woke up and saw his daughter dressed in a white *holokū* standing at the door of her room waving good-bye to everyone with her large, sad eyes looking about. She then turned to her father, waved to him, and cried out "Papa!" At that very moment, Ka'iulani's pet peacocks gave a loud, high-pitched wail, instantly waking Cleghorn from his "dream," and he knew that his daughter's mesmerizing brown eyes had closed for the last time. At 2:00 a.m. on 6 March 1899, the Heir Apparent to the Hawaiian Throne died of "inflammatory rheumatism."

Almost immediately after the official announcement of the passing of Princess Ka'iulani, a renewed sentiment for the plight of the Princess and her people, whose kingdom had been stolen from them, sprang forth. Newspapers from Sacramento to London and Paris carried articles and obituaries about the Hawaiian Crown Princess. One of the anti-royalist newspapers, the *Pacific Commercial Advertiser* wrote:

> Everyone admired her attitude. They could not do otherwise. Her dignity, her pathetic resignation, her silent sorrow appealed to all. The natives loved her for her quiet steadfast sympathy with their woe, her uncomplaining endurance of her own. The whites admired her for her stately reserve, her queenly display of all necessary courtesy while holding herself aloof from undue intimacy. It was impossible not to love her. (Zambucka 1976:153)

Many annexationists, who for the past five years had tried to spread horrible rumors about the Hawaiian Royal Family (including some about Princess Ka'iulani herself), had to accept the enchantment and sympathy the world had for Princess Ka'iulani. Letters poured into the hands of the white oligarchy in Honolulu, accusing them of causing Princess Ka'iulani's death. Some used profanity, while others put forth theories as to the real cause of her death. One particular letter written to Sanford Dole, the former President of the Republic of Hawai'i, arrived from Atlanta, Georgia, and contained 25 signatures expressing the general feeling against the men who had overthrown the Hawaiian government. The letter called the Dole regime "puppets" and denounced the Republic for "stealing the Princess' Royal inheritance" and "snatching away the Throne she was prepared all her life to occupy," and referred to the Provisional Government as "cheap adventurers who invaded the Hawaiian Islands just to make money...signed: Princess K's Friends in the South" (152).

Who was this person who could invoke such strong emotions? Who was this Princess Ka'iulani? Since the day she was born on the 16th of October 1875, Princess Ka'iulani was the pride of her family and her people. The then Princess Lili'uokalani wrote in her memoirs, "Princess Likelike brought boundless joy to the family and the nation by giving birth to a daughter. The hopes of all centered on this baby, Princess Ka'iulani" (Seiden 1992:138). Ka'iulani's full name—Victoria Kawēkiu Lunalilo Kalaninuiahilapalapa Ka'iulani—bore witness to that hope. Her first name, "Victoria" (for the British Queen), showed the close ties between Hawai'i and the British Empire. It also showed optimism that just as Queen Victoria had brought a second Golden Age to Britons, Ka'iulani might bring the same to her own people. After all, her parents were Princess Likelike (Kalākaua's sister) and Archibald Cleghorn (a Scotsman popular with Hawaiians), so she was "*hapa*," the blossom of two proud cultures, the new Hawai'i. The name "Lunalilo" (of the Kamehameha Dynasty and meaning "the highest of the highest") was given to her for yet another reason: Having only ruled for one year by that time, Kalākaua wanted to strengthen his rule by linking his dynasty with the popular kings who had reigned before him. King Lunalilo, also called the "Citizen King" or the "People's Sovereign," a man loved by the people, was to be her example. To further strengthen these ties, the newborn was *hānai*ed (adopted) by the wealthy Princess Ruth Ke'elikōlani (whom Ka'iulani would call "Mama nui"[1]). Lastly, "Ka'iulani" meant "the highest in the heavens" or the "sacred royal heights," for one day she would be the highest *ali'i* of the land, the Queen of Hawai'i.

Upon hearing of this royal birth, King Kalākaua ordered all church bells in Honolulu to toll a welcome to his new niece. He then sent out a proclamation giving the new child the title of "Her Royal Highness, Princess Ka'iulani." But while the proclamation was being circulated and the bells were ringing, the blue expansive sky revealed a bright morning star which was later covered over by dark rain clouds. A *hō'ailona* of things to come.

Pomp and circumstance early on became a part of Ka'iulani's normal everyday life. "Papa Mō'ī" and "Mama Mō'ī"[2] (Princess Ka'iulani's names for King Kalākaua and Queen Kapi'olani) wanted to ensure that the young princess received the proper training owed to her rank and future promise. In 1883, Ka'iulani attended the first of many public ceremonies—her uncle King Kalākaua's coronation. Princess Ka'iulani wore a light-blue corded silk dress with light lace trimmings and light-blue ribbons in her hair, and was followed by two retainers waving white hand *kāhili*, her personal symbol (Mrantz 1980:8), while her brown eyes charmed the multitude of dignitaries who attended this occasion. She was barely seven.

Much of Princess Ka'iulani's time, though, was spent with her parents at 'Āinahau, their palatial Victorian-style estate in Waikīkī. 'Āinahau had been given to Princess Ka'iulani by her Mama nui (Seiden 1992:138). Princess Ruth wanted to give her godchild a proper residence and deeded Ka'iulani a ten-acre plot to build a house and with enough land for Ka'iulani to play on. The princess, for her part, made good use of the land when young and had a good many animals around her, including a white pony named "Fairy" and several pet *pīkake*

(peacocks). Princess Ka'iulani was Archibald Cleghorn's fourth and last daughter, the three older girls—Helen, Rose, and Annie (who was closest to Ka'iulani)—being from his first marriage to a Hawaiian woman named Elizabeth (Mrantz 1980:6). But Ka'iulani was the only of his children who was a titled princess. In 1885, Gertrude Gardinier, Princess Ka'iulani's second governess, described the princess as "a fragile, spirituelle type, but very vivacious with beautiful large, expressive dark eyes. She proves affectionate; high spirited, at times quite wilful, though usually reasonable and very impulsive and generous" (Zambucka 1976:29).

The year 1887 proved to be a tragic one for the Kalākaua Dynasty. The usually very lively Princess Likelike began to withdraw from the public and her family. The slopes of Mauna Loa suddenly erupted with lava. Minister of the Interior Walter Murray Gibson recalled in his diaries: "The Princess Likelike said to be in danger—refuses food—affected by her native superstition that her death is required by the spirit of Pele of the Volcano. The King is angry with his sister on account of her obstinacy in refusing food" (Mrantz 1980:12). On February 2, Princess Likelike called her young daughter into her darkened bedroom and whispered to her that she had seen the future: Princess Ka'iulani would go away from Hawai'i for a long time, never marry, and never be Queen. The young girl ran out of the room, crying uncontrollably (Zambucka 1976:33). A few hours later, the red *akule* fish, a sign of the death of an *ali'i*, appeared at Honolulu Harbor. Princess Likelike was dead at 37.

In the same year, another kind of volcano erupted. Nineteenth-century Hawaiian politics was a constant tide of change and a battle of elements. The Hawaiian Kingdom struggled to maintain her independence while most of the world was being carved out and eaten by the West. Hawai'i was not immune to the advances of colonial powers nor to those inside the kingdom who wanted ultimate annexation to the United States of America. A young hot-headed attorney named Lorrin Thurston, a descendant of the first Protestant missionaries to Hawai'i, intensified his attacks on King Kalākaua. Many other "Mission Boys" also began to organize themselves against the "native monarchy." Kalākaua's two strongest supporters, his sister Lili'uokalani and his wife Kapi'olani, were in London representing Hawai'i at the Golden Jubilee of Queen Victoria. The King was left vulnerable, so that when he began to assert his authority against the leasing of Pearl Harbor to the United States, European and American business men formed militias and forced him to sign a new constitution at the point of the bayonet, the "Bayonet Constitution." The Crown was left crippled and weak. The majority of the native Hawaiian people couldn't vote in their own kingdom. The throne from which Ka'iulani would rule was undergoing severe internal changes.

While the nation was in an uproar over the latest political developments, Ka'iulani maintained her distance at 'Āinahau. In January of 1889, a frail poet arrived in Ka'iulani's life—Robert Louis Stevenson. During the next five months the Scotsman and the 13-year-old princess often sat under a banyan tree and discussed poetry, literature, art, and Europe (Zambucka 1976:37). This was a world radically different from the land in which Ka'iulani had been born and raised. Yet this was the world that was engulfing her and her people ever quicker and more completely.

The King decided that Ka'iulani was to be educated in England. He wanted to ensure that his niece be given a proper education, a British education. Under the new constitution, all the acts and proclamations of the King required the signature of a government minister. The King's new head minister, Lorrin Thurston, happily agreed to sign, since he believed this would keep the probable future heir far, far away from Hawai'i. The proclamation read:

> I, Kalakaua, King of the Hawaiian Islands do hereby give my consent and approval for my niece Her Royal Highness Princess Victoria Kaiulani, to leave the Hawaiian Kingdom and proceed to England on or about the month of May 1889, in charge of and under the care and control of Mrs. Thomas Rain Walker and be accompanied by Miss Annie Cleghorn.... Her return to the Hawaiian Kingdom to be during the year of Our Lord, One Thousand and Eight Hundred and Ninety. (41)

In May of 1889, Princess Ka'iulani chatted with Robert Louis Stevenson about poetry for the last time. Before leaving, the Scots poet wrote in Ka'iulani's autograph book:

> Forth from her land to mine she goes,
> The Island maid, the Island rose.
> Light of heart and bright of face,
> The daughter of a double race.
> Her Islands here in the Southern sun
> Shall mourn their Kaiulani gone.
> And I, in her dear banyan's shade,
> Look vainly for my little maid.
> But our Scots Islands far away
> Shall glitter with unwonted day,

And cast for once their tempest by
To smile in Kaiulani's eye.

Written in April to Kaiulani in the April
of her age and at Waikiki within easy
walk of Kaiulani's banyan. When she
comes to my land and her father's, and
the rain beats upon the window, (as I
fear it will) let her look at this page; it
will be like a weed gathered and
preserved at home; and she will remember her own Islands, and the shadow of
the mighty tree, and she will hear the
peacocks screaming in the dusk and the
wind blowing in the palms and she will
think of her father sitting there alone.
(38–39)

Stevenson wrote to his friend, "I wear the
colours of the little Royal Maid.... Oh, Low,
how I love the Polynesians!" (39). But
Ka'iulani and Stevenson would never
meet again.

During the few weeks preceding her
departure, Ka'iulani had visited dignitaries,
friends, and family to bid farewell. Her plans
were to go by sea from Honolulu to San
Francisco, then by train to Chicago and New
York City, and finally by ship to Great
Britain. It was a daunting trip for a 13-year-
old girl who had never known any land
outside of Hawai'i.

On the 10th of May 1889, Princess Ka'iulani
made her final visit to 'Iolani Palace,
where she hugged Papa Mō'ī, Mama Mō'ī,
Auntie Lili'u (her name of affection for
Lili'uokalani), and her father good-bye
before beginning her long journey to
England (42). As the ship sailed away, she
could hear the last verse of "Hawai'i Pono'ī"
being played at the harbor, and see the
countless people gathered at the wharf

waving their handkerchiefs good-bye to the
tearful, voyaging princess.

On June 18, Princess Ka'iulani arrived in
London, the largest city in the world in the
19th century. She toured famous sites: the
Tower of London, the Crystal Palace, the
National Art Gallery, and the British
Museum. The bright-eyed princess wrote letters back home to Papa Mō'ī and Mama Mō'ī
about her impressions of England. She
described Sir Walter Raleigh's cell in the
Tower of London as a "cave" and thought
about the many other notables who were at
one time unfortunate enough to be locked
away in the tower, including a few British
monarchs (44). In September, the Princess
wrote to Papa Mō'ī, "I am going to school in
the middle of September. The name of the
School is Great Harrowden Hall in
Northamptonshire," 68 miles north of
London (44). Great Harrowden Hall was a
school for young ladies of class, and was
housed in the 15th-century mansion of the
Barons (des) Vaux (45). Princess Ka'iulani
would spend the next two years of life being
educated there as a proper Victorian woman
of distinction. It was also the first school
Ka'iulani attended in her life.

Meanwhile at home, political turmoil rocked
the Hawaiian throne. Robert Wilcox and
some 200 red-shirted Hawaiians attempted
to overthrow the Bayonet Constitution and
return more power to the Crown. In a single
day, an American citizen militia (the very
ones who had forced the King to sign the
Bayonet Constitution) crushed the so-called
"Wilcox Rebellion of 1889." A couple of
months later, in October, the King wrote a
letter to Princess Ka'iulani to "be on guard
against certain enemies I do not feel free to
name in writing" (47). The startled princess
wrote back to her uncle, "I am quite at a loss

to know to whom you refer as 'not to be relied upon'—I wish you would speak more plainly, as I cannot be on my guard unless I know to whom you allude" (47). Shortly thereafter, on 20 January 1891, the King suddenly died of Bright's Disease while he was in San Francisco. Ka'iulani wrote to Auntie Lili'u:

> I have only just heard the sad news from San Francisco. I cannot tell my feelings just at present, but Auntie, you can think how I feel. I little thought when I said good-bye to my dear Uncle nearly two years ago that it would be the last time I should see his dear face. Please give my love to Mama Moi (Queen Kapiolani), and tell her I can fully sympathize with her.
>
> I cannot write any more, but Auntie, you are the only one left of my dear Mother's family, so I can ask you to do that little thing for me. (47–48)

In Honolulu, heralds and newspapers proclaimed the news: "The King is Dead! Long Live the Queen!" Auntie Lili'u was now "Queen Lili'uokalani I, by the Grace of God, Queen of the Hawaiian Islands." After the burial of her late brother, the new queen set to work organizing her government. After appointing a new cabinet, the Queen nominated Princess Ka'iulani as the Crown Princess, the immediate heir to the Hawaiian throne. The Queen recounts:

> On the ninth day of March, 1891, Princess Victoria Kaiulani, Kalaninuiahilapalapa Kawekiu i Lunalilo, daughter of my sister, Princess Miriam Kekauluohi Likelike and Hon. A. S. Cleghorn, was duly proclaimed heir apparent, and her nomination recog-

nized by the United States ship-of-war Mohican by a salute of twenty-one guns. (Liliuokalani 1990 [1898]:218)

Two months later, Queen Lili'uokalani addressed the 1892 legislative assembly for the first time and stated the goal of her reign:

> The decree of Providence and the Constitution of the Kingdom having called Me to occupy the Throne of Hawaii, it is my earnest prayer that Divine assistance may be vouchsafed to enable Me to discharge the duties of the exalted position to the advantage of My people and the permanent benefit of Hawaii.
>
> With the consent of the Nobles of the Kingdom I have appointed Her Royal Highness the Princess Victoria Kawekiu Kaiulani Lunalilo Kalaninuiahilapalapa as My successor…
>
> …[and] I shall firmly endeavor to preserve the autonomy and absolute independence of this Kingdom. (Lydecker 1918:180)

The shy 16-year-old princess was now formally "HRH Crown Princess Ka'iulani of Hawai'i" or "HRH Princess Ka'iulani of Hawai'i, the Heir Apparent." Ka'iulani's ascendancy to the throne seemed secure and probable. Yet, while there may have been much cause to celebrate for Ka'iulani, letters from home constantly provided bad news as men in and around the Court were plotting against the Queen to end the absolute independence of the Kingdom. Her aunt wrote to Ka'iulani:

> You have heard e'er this of the death of

your Uncle John [Prince Consort John Owen Dominis, the Queen's husband] from Mrs. Robertson.

I could not write at the time to tell you, for I was shocked.... It seems that we are having a series of sadness in our family for it is only seven months since my dear Brother died, when my husband was taken away—not that only but a short time before Uncle John's death the Queen Dowager Kapiolani had a stroke of paralysis and is likely to have another.

If it is the father's will in Heaven I must submit for the Bible teaches us "he doeth all things well". You and Papa are all that is left to me.

I shall look forward to the time when you finish your studies with all due satisfaction to your teachers, and then come home and live a life of usefulness to your people. My health is pretty good considering all that I have had to go through. (Zambucka 1976:51)

In February of 1892, Princess Ka'iulani wrote to her aunt about her change in schooling from Great Harrowden Hall to Brighton:

Thank you so much for your kind letter. It is very good of you to write to me, as I know how very busy you must be with State Affairs.

I am so glad to hear that Father is putting up a proper house at Ainahau. It has always been my ambition to have a house in Waikiki worthy of the beautiful garden.

I hope that you like my photographs.

I have left Great Harrowden Hall for good, Mr. Davies has kindly found a lady who will look after, and be sort of a mother to me while I am in Brighton. I believe Mrs. Rooke is a thorough lady.

I shall take lessons in French, German [the two languages of high European society], music and English, especially grammar and composition. I am anxiously waiting for the time to come when I may see you again. (53)

Princess Ka'iulani inherited the Kalākaua Dynasty's love of music. None of the Royal Family members were content to be simply patrons of music but were also musicians, composers, and singers. Ka'iulani wrote to her Aunt a month later:

I am taking lessons in music, singing, literature, history, French and German. I have such a nice lady for a singing mistress. She has taught me such a lot, and she says that I have a very sweet soprano voice—I think I must have inherited it from you. I am getting on pretty well with my music, and I am so fond of it. (56)

Princess Ka'iulani moved into her new room in Brighton and wrote to her aunt:

I hope that you will not think me impertinent in asking you for one of your photographs. I have not got one of you.

My room is very pretty but I think a few photos would improve it. At present I have only two—one of Mother and one of Father.

On my birthday Mrs. Rooke gave me "The Soul's Awakening", it is such a beautiful picture. I have always wished to have it, but I have never had enough money. It hangs opposite my bed so that the first thing I see in the morning is the girl's lovely face. I received quite a number of presents and such a lot of letters. I spent a very happy day in spite of being such a long way from home. (58)

On 30 January 1893, Ka'iulani received a shocking telegraph from Mr. Theo Davies, her former guardian: "QUEEN DEPOSED, MONARCHY ABROGATED, BREAK NEWS TO PRINCESS" (63).

Immediately, the Princess packed her things and told Mr. Davies, who was at the Hawaiian Embassy in London and about to leave for Washington D.C., that she would accompany him home to fight against annexation. She wrote him: "Perhaps some day the Hawaiians will say, Kaiulani you could have saved us and you didn't even try…. I will go with you" (63). A couple of days later, Princess Ka'iulani departed England and issued the following statement to the British Press:

Four years ago, at the request of Mr. Thurston, then a Hawaiian Cabinet Minister, I was sent away to England to be educated privately and fitted to the position which by the Constitution of Hawaii I was to inherit. For all these years I have patiently and in exile striven to fit myself for my return this year to my native country. I am now told that Mr. Thurston is in Washington asking you [America] to take away my flag and my throne. No one tells me even this officially. Have I done anything wrong, that this wrong should be done to me and my people? I am coming to

Washington to plead for my throne, my nation and my flag. Will not the great American people hear me…? (65)

Upon her arrival in New York City the Princess gave another moving speech to the American press who came to meet her on the wharf:

Unbidden I stand upon your shores today where I had thought so soon to receive a Royal welcome. I come unattended except for the loving hearts that come with me over the Winter seas. I hear that Commissioners from my land have been for many days asking this great nation to take away my little vineyard. They speak no word to me, and leave me to find out as I can from rumours of the air that they would leave me without a home or a name or a nation.

Seventy years ago, Christian America sent over Christian men and women to give religion and civilisation to Hawaii. Today three of the sons of those missionaries are at your capitol, asking you to undo their fathers' work. Who sent them? Who gave them the authority to break the Constitution which they swore to uphold?

Today, I, a poor weak girl with not one of my people near me and all these statesmen against me, have strength to stand up for the rights of my people. Even now I can hear their wail in my heart, and it gives me strength and courage and I am strong…strong in the faith of God, strong in the knowledge that I am right, strong in the strength of seventy million people who in this free land will hear my cry and will refuse to let their flag cover dishonour to mine! (65)

After a successful audience with President Cleveland and other leading American politicians in Washington D.C., Ka'iulani issued a farewell address to the United States before returning to Brighton:

Before I leave the land, I want to thank all whose kindness have made my visit such a happy one. Not only the hundreds of hands I have clasped nor the kind smiles I have seen, but the written words of sympathy that have been sent to me from so many homes, has made me feel that whatever happens to me I shall never be a stranger to you again. It was to all the American people I spoke and they heard me as I knew they would. And now God bless you for it—from the beautiful home where your fair First Lady reigns to the little crippled boy who sent his loving letter and prayer [to me]. (72)

In May of 1893, Princess Ka'iulani received a letter from her aunt:

I simply write to assure you that we are well and Papa seemed in good health but I think looks a little thin.

I hear from some parties that your house is looking fine, but Mr. Robertson says he has not ever seen it....

...I would simply like to add and say that should anyone write or propose or make any proposition to you in any way in regard to taking the Throne, I hope you will be guarded in your answer. [As early as January 1893, Sanford Dole thought that a regency should be

established for Ka'iulani with him as regent. Thurston refused the idea and a republican government was instituted instead.] The people all over the Islands have petitioned [literally] to have me restored and it would make you appear in an awkward light to accept any overtures from any irresponsible party, and the PGs [Provisional Government] are growing less and less, and I understand they will soon drop to pieces as the saying is, for want of funds to carry on the Govt. Mr. Spreckels will not help them or loan them any money and Bishop and Co. [the forerunner of Bank of Hawaii] would not loan them any money without Mr. Spreckels.... I will write you and acquaint you of all that transpires, and if you need be will advise you after consulting your father. (79)

Ka'iulani replied a month later on June 15:

I have never received any proposals from anybody to take the Throne. I have not received a word of any sort from anyone except my father. I am glad that I am able to say that I have not written to anyone about politics.

I have been perfectly miserable during my past four months. I have looked forward to '93 as being the end of my "exile". I have considered the four years I have been in England as years of exile. Now it seems as though things would never settle and I am simply longing to see you all—People little know how hard it is to wait patiently for news from home.... In the meantime "il fait attendre". (81)

Four days later, Ka'iulani received a letter from her father. As usual, the news from home was disturbing: "I have nothing to write that will please you. The PG have moved into the Palace which I think is a shame, but I hope the day is not far distant when they will have to go out for good—things look bitter, still we do not know what the US Govt will do" (82).

Realizing the impeccable impression of Hawaiians conveyed by Princess Ka'iulani while she was in the American capitol, the Provisional Government sought to destroy the reputation of the Queen and her family. The PGs began publishing their newspaper, *The Star*, and used that medium to attack the royal family, Hawaiian nationalists, and even Ka'iulani herself. At the same time, Lorrin Thurston, editor of the *Pacific Commercial Advertiser*, publically opposed the restoration of the Hawaiian throne. If native Hawaiians were to get back their sovereignty, he claimed, they would kick out all the *haole*s (Chapin 1996:102). Moreover, if America didn't take over Hawai'i, another nation would. John Sheldon, a non-native Hawaiian nationalist and one of the leading editors of the opposition paper the *Holomua*, responded "He [Thurston] Lies! and he knows it" and reminded people that his family had lived in the islands for four generations (102). Sheldon and many other nationalist writers were arrested and fined for their comments.[3] Cleghorn informed his daughter: "The newspapers here are simply dreadful. The Annexation Club are printing the most bitter things about us. I am glad you do not see the Star" (Zambucka 1976:84). In this "bitter" atmosphere, Princess Ka'iulani's correspondence from home began to look bleaker and bleaker as she grew more and more homesick.

However, Ka'iulani managed to keep abreast of all the propaganda being circulated, and of the actions of the Provisional Government as they became more totalitarian. Knowing that the population of Hawai'i was against them, the Provisional Government began converting churches for their military intelligence. In September 1893, Ka'iulani wrote to her aunt:

> How you must hate the sight of the Central Union Church. What a shame that a house of worship should be turned into a spy tower. I suppose it is wiser for you to remain in Washington Place, but how you must long to get away to some other place. If I was in your place, I am afraid I should pine away and die—I could not stand it—I am so tired of waiting—
>
> By the time this reaches you it will be my birthday. I hope that you will remember me away from my relations and friends. (84)

American President Grover Cleveland sent special envoy James Blount to Hawai'i to investigate the overthrow of the monarchy. Blount subsequently wrote a 2,000-page report clearing the Queen of wrongdoing and urging that the monarchy be restored. In December 1893, President Cleveland remarked in a Congressional speech that the overthrow was "an act of war" (Silva 1998:51) against a friendly nation, and he assured the Queen that he would not have the annexation treaty submitted during his term. Queen Lili'uokalani wrote to her niece at length about all that had transpired and asked Princess Ka'iulani to consider either marrying Prince David Kawananakoa or a certain unnamed Japanese prince who was visiting London at the time (Zambucka 1976:89–91). Being a romantic, and ever conscious of her status as a role model for her people, Princess Ka'iulani wrote back from London:

It is a very long time since I rec'd your kind letter. I have often tried to answer it, but have failed. I have thought over what you said in it about my marrying some Prince from Japan.

Unless it is absolutely necessary, I would much rather not do so.

I could have married an enormously rich German Count, but I could not care for him. I feel it would be wrong if I married a man I did not love. I should be perfectly unhappy, and we should not agree and instead of being an example to the married women of today I should become one like them, merely a woman of fashion and most likely a flirt. I hope I am not expressing myself too strongly, but I feel I must speak out to you and there must be perfect confidence between you and me dear Aunt.

I have been looking anxiously every day in the papers for news from home, but nothing seems to be happened. I wish things could be properly settled. It is such weary work waiting here not knowing what is happening. (92)

Tired of waiting, Ka'iulani left for Germany to get her mind off the state of affairs in Hawai'i. Much like her late uncle when he visited the country in 1881, Ka'iulani wrote glowingly to her aunt:

I was quite sorry to leave Germany, everyone had been so very kind to me there, and they have sympathized with us so much. During the last month of

my stay in Germany I went to Berlin and there I saw the grand Parade before the Emperor and Empress. It was really a sight worth seeing, there were nearly twenty thousand soldiers and the Emperor had a staff of 100 officers.

Berlin is a most interesting City, it is much more beautiful than London in regards private houses, squares and small parks, and all the chief streets are so wide and most beautifully kept. I visited all the palaces of the Emperors. (93)

In January of 1895, a nationalist rebellion broke out against the Republic of Hawai'i. The rebellion was crushed in two days by Republican forces who outgunned the nationalist forces. The Queen was arrested and brought before a military tribunal. The Republic found her guilty of "misprision of treason" (branding her a traitor) and fined her $5,000 and five years of hard labor (Liliuokalani 1990 [1898]:289). Instead of hard labor though, they decided to imprison her in a corner room of 'Iolani Palace for eight months. The Queen later said, "My crime was that I knew my people were conspiring...to throw off the yoke of the stranger and oppressor" (278). Not being able to correspond with the outside world, the musically gifted Queen Lili'uokalani sought solace during her imprisonment through music. She composed "The Queen's Prayer," one of her most famous hymns, and dedicated it to her niece, Princess Ka'iulani. In it, she asked God to forgive those who imprisoned her and let her nation be pure. But Princess Ka'iulani would not get to see this hymn until after Lili'u was released.

A friend of Ka'iulani described her during this time as "animated, capricious, headstrong, yes but her vivacity had a certain quiet sadness. Her eyes were too large above cheeks flushed hectically; but such a pride of bearing, love of companions and heartfelt loyalty of feeling for her native Hawaiians" (Zambucka 1976:94). On one of her trips to France, she met Nevison William de Courcy (son of the Count de Courcy) whom she nicknamed "Toby" and who would become her best friend. He was six years her senior and became a big brother to her. Often she called him "Father Confessor." Her letters to him reveal another side of Ka'iulani's personality:

My Dear Toby,

Very many thanks for yours of the 28th. I also heard from Sib that she had seen you—you both say the other was looking very pale and thin. Mon Ami qu'est ce qu'il-y-a? Surely you're not ailing! And I trust above all you are not suffering from mal au cœur. I have been very seedy. Papa was over in town, so he consulted the Dr. I have been suffering from too much worry!!! So I am to sleep a great deal etc. Evidently dancing is not harmful otherwise Papa would have prevented my going to a dance on Wednesday. Toby I feel so naughty, I have such a nice flirtation on pour le moment. Don't be shocked, and leave your lecture until we meet in Menton— it is too good to believe that I shall have the pleasure of seeing you soon—won't we talk! I have such piles to tell you.[4] (99)

Another letter written a few months later on 4 July 1897 states:

I have lived on milk for the past two months, and am not taking very much

exercise. Consequently I am growing fairly fat. I think I can stand a little more flesh on my bones, still I don't want to grow fat, it is so vulgar you know. Another reason I am growing stout, I have not been able to be up to any of my larks. I've quite got out of the way of flirting! I don't believe I could do it to save my skin. Now, don't laugh!

I am really feeling very much better, but have still to be very careful. I was so annoyed a few days back…I hate posing as an invalide….

…There is some talk of my going over to pay my revered Aunt a visit [Lili'uokalani was now staying in Washington, D.C., to continue fighting against annexation], but as yet things are extremely undecided. They talk of Annexation, but whether they will get it is quite another thing. However, things are in a very bad way out there, and I am pretty certain that we shall never have our own back again…. I am really rather sorry the way the whole things has finished up, much better to have a republic than to lose our nationality altogether…. I am very sorry for my people, as they will hate being taken over by another nation. (100–101)

In another letter to Toby written in the same year:

I am really ashamed of myself for having delayed so long in acknowledging your letter. I thank you very much for your kind wishes on my birthday—I laughed very much when I thought of my other birthday—what fun we had that night! … One of my young men came out to see me yesterday—I am supposed to be polishing him off—I can't make up my mind to do so yet—must have a little more fun as my fling is limited—I intend to get as much amusement this winter as I possibly can. There is a possibility of my being married in April to a man I don't care much for either way—rather a gloomy outlook—but "noblesse oblige".... Do you blame me if I have my fling now—better now than afterwards.

My engagement is a "great secret"—approved of by Mr. Davies and my Father—it is being kept secret for political reasons. Personally I think it wrong like this, as it is unfair to the men I meet now—especially if they take any interest in me....

I am not feeling at all fit, as I had two teeth taken out on my birthday. My jaw was fearfully cut up trying to remove the bits as they splintered. I have had a very bad time of it, as you may fancy. I hope I shall soon get one of your cheery letters, that is if you have nothing else to do. (102–103)

Whom Ka'iulani was "secretly engaged" to is still unknown, though many believe logically it was to her cousin Prince Kawananakoa, he being the only other eligible ali'i. Either way, in her words it was "rather a gloomy outlook." Toby was to keep all of her letters for the rest of his life (103).

After eight long years of "exile," Princess Ka'iulani said good-bye to her friends in Europe and began to make her journey home. While on the American East Coast, she paid her respects to her aunt in Washington, D.C.—this was their first meeting in eight years. Fondly they both recalled happier times, and upon leaving Washington, Lili'uokalani gave Ka'iulani a long letter explaining the dangerous current political climate:

Your short visit to me has been very pleasant, and we have not ceased to talk of you. I wish you could have stayed a month or two longer at least until the question of Annexation was settled. I think your presence here would have done some good, but as I knew that you and your father were both anxious to get home I naturally kept quiet.

Another reason was I had not the means to detain you which is another and most important point. During your stay I was glad to know that your heart and that of your father lay in the right direction that is you are interested in the cause of your people....

...Here is an opportunity for me to let you know something which I feel you ought to know—and leave it for your own good judgment to guide you in your decision. It has been made known to me that it is the intention of the members of the Republican Government of Hawaii to ask you to take the Throne of Hawaii in case they failed in their scheme of Annexation. That you should have nothing to say about the managing—that shall be theirs still, but you are to be a figurehead only. If you were to accept their proposition there would be no change whatever in the situation of the country for the good of the people or for all classes of men or for business advancements. You would only be in Mr. Dole's place, despised, and as he is now, in fear of his life.

You will have few followers who will love you, but it will only be the 2,600 who are now supporting Dole's Government and still have over 80,000 [*sic*] opposing you. It is through their mismanagement that their Government has not been a success. It is for this reason that knowing their instability they want to annex Hawaii to America…. If you decline to accept the position of Queen which will place you more in favour with the people, the Republic of Hawaii will fall through as even now they can barely maintain themselves, then there will be a call from the people for a "plebiscite",[5] then I say "accept it" for it is maintained by the love of the people….

…The people's wish is paramount with me, and what they say I abide by. Now my dear Child, for you are very dear to me, I hope you will act wisely for your own sake and be cautious in signing any documents that may present to you, reading over thoroughly and understanding it before hand—for they are greatest liars, and deceitful in all their undertakings and your young heart is too pure to see their wickedness. I mean the PGs. (113–114)

Mr. Davies, acting as Ka'iulani's chaperone, quickly responded to the Queen for the Princess that:

I take the liberty of saying that neither Mr. Damon or Mr. MacFarlane or anyone else has conferred with me in regard to putting forward claims on behalf of Princess Kaiulani to the Throne of Hawaii…. I am also certain that under no circumstances would the Princess Kaiulani have accepted the Throne except with the approval of Your Majesty and at the joint request of Hawaiians and foreigners. (114)

Utilizing her appeal to the American press and to correct some of the racist falsehoods being spread about the *ali'i* by members of the Republic of Hawai'i, Princess Ka'iulani made good use of her trip back to Honolulu through the United States. The American West Coast press was dazzled by the 22-year-old princess. An editorial in the *San Francisco Examiner*, for example, said:

A Barbarian Princess? Not a bit of it. Not even a hemi-semi-demi Barbarian. Rather the very flower—an exotic—of civilization. The Princess Kaiulani is a charming, fascinating individual. She has the taste and style of a French woman; the admirable repose and soft voice of an English woman. She was gowned for dinner in a soft, black, high necked frock, with the latest Parisian touches in every fold; a bunch of pink roses in her belt and a slender gold chain around her neck, dangling a lorgnette. She is tall, of willowy slenderness, erect and graceful, with a small, pale face, full red lips, soft expression, dark eyes, a very good nose, and a cloud of crimpy black hair knotted high. (111)

And a writer from the *San Francisco Call* wrote:

She is beautiful. There is no portrait that does justice to her expressive, small, proud face. She is exquisitely slender and graceful, holds herself like a Princess, like a Hawaiian—and I know of no simile more descriptive of grace and dignity than this last.

...Her accent says London; her figure says New York; her heart says Hawaii. But she is more than a beautiful pretender [meaning an heir to a throne] to an abdicated throne; she has been made a woman of the world by the life she has led. (111)

Finally on 9 November 1897, Ka'iulani arrived back home in Hawai'i, and she immediately wrote a letter to her aunt:

I must just send you a few lines to let you know of our safe arrival. Since we got here, we have been so busy, what with receiving and getting the house in order, I am fairly worn out.

Last Saturday the Hawaiians came out to see me. There were several hundred, and by six o'clock I didn't know what to do with myself, I was so tired. It made me so sad to see so many of the Hawaiians looking so poor—in the old days I am sure there were not so many people almost destitute.

...A great many of the haoles have called but I am at home for the first time tomorrow. I dread it as I am so very nervous. I have asked Mrs. Carter to help me receive....

I eat poi and raw fish as though I had never left, and I find I have not forgotten my Hawaiian. (119)

A few months later, on hearing that the treaty of annexation was going to fail in the U.S. Senate, Ka'iulani wrote a short note to her aunt on 5 January 1898:

Thank God Annexation is not a fact. The people here are not half so happy as

when I first came back. I find everything so much changed and more especially among the rising generation of Hawaiians and half whites. I think it is a great pity as they are trying to ape the foreigners and they do not succeed. (118)

A friend later said, "Kaiulani hid the bitterness in her heart from the public and strove to do what was expected of her" (120). Trying to keep her spirits high, Ka'iulani informed her aunt of what was happening in Honolulu:

Papa and I are going to stay with the Parkers [on the Big Island]...and I want to go away before the 4th of July festivities come off. I am sure you would be disgusted if you could see the way the town [Honolulu] is decorated for the American troops. Honolulu is making a fool of itself, and I only hope we won't be all ridiculed. (120)

In another letter Ka'iulani says that "the people of the Government are not particularly nice to me, excepting Mrs. Damon and Mrs. Dole. I think they are very sorry to see me here, especially since I give them no cause to complain" (120).

When she returned to 'Āinahau, she expressed her feelings about what Hawai'i was becoming:

Daily, we as a great race are being subjected to a great deal of misery, and the more I see of the American soldiers about town, the more I am unable to tolerate them, what they stand for and the way we are belittled, it is enough to ruin one's faith in God. (133)

Describing another incident to her aunt:

> Last week some Americans came to the house and knocked rather violently at the door, and when they stated their cause they wished to know if it would be permissible for the Ex-Princess to have her picture taken with them. Oh, will they ever leave us alone?... We live now in such a semi-retired way, that people wonder if we even exist any more. I too wonder, and to what purpose? (133)

After that event, Princess Ka'iulani sought every excuse not to return to Honolulu, often opting instead to stay at the Parker Ranch with her friend Eva Parker and her cousins Princes Kūhiō and Kawananakoa.

The year 1898 was one of the most horrible and shocking to the royal court. A new presidential administration was elected to the White House. Two chief promoters of annexation—William McKinley and Theodore Roosevelt—were now in power. In the early summer of 1898, war broke out between the Kingdom of Spain and the United States, and Americans went into an imperialistic frenzy. Then, in July of 1898, the U.S. Congress bypassed its own constitution and annexed the Hawaiian Islands by a simple joint resolution, insisting it needed Hawai'i as a coaling station for ships going to war in the Philippines (Silva 1998:65).

This news affected the Princess deeply, as it did many other Hawaiians. The Queen returned to Honolulu to see what she could do for her people. On August 12, the day of the formal transfer of sovereignty, members of the royal court gathered at Washington Place, closed the windows and took their last photograph together. The Queen sat in the middle on a sofa while Ka'iulani stood to the left of the Queen, next to Prince Kawananakoa. Like the other members being photographed, Princess Ka'iulani wore a formal black mourning gown adorned simply with a yellow feather lei.

During the following months after annexation, Ka'iulani became obsessed with death. Friends describe her moods as being "morbid." In the middle of January 1899, while on the Big Island, she rode her horse in a heavy downpour. Her friends called her to get out of the rain, but Ka'iulani replied, "What does it matter? What have I got to live for?" (Zambucka 1976:137).

On the 24th of January, the Honolulu newspapers circulated the news that "Princess Kaiulani is quite ill at the Parker home in Mana, Hawaii. Governor Cleghorn leaves for Mana on the Kinau today" (142). Ka'iulani's health improved slightly, but then began to fail again. The family physician, Dr. Walters, diagnosed the princess with "inflammatory rheumatism" with the complication of "ex-opthalmic goiter" (142). Cleghorn decided to take his daughter back to 'Āinahau, where on March 5, Ka'iulani's breathing became irregular. Her friends and family began to gather around her bedside.

Then, in the early morning of March 6, Her Royal Highness Princess Ka'iulani of Hawai'i, the Heir Apparent to the Hawaiian Throne, breathed her last and embarked on the final leg of her life's voyage.

Though she had lived a short life, she had witnessed the death of her mother, the stripping of power from her uncle, the betrayal of her aunt, and the outright theft of her nation by a country that had pledged to defend Hawaiian independence. Officially she died of "inflammatory rheumatism," but to many she died of heartbreak.

Today, a century after Ka'iulani's death, what may we say about her? More importantly, what lessons may be drawn from her example? In many ways, she was the prototype of modern Hawaiians—multi-ethnic, educated abroad, loyal to family, adaptable to her surroundings, though ever homesick for Hawai'i.

Ka'iulani felt that she belonged to two worlds. After all she was the child of two races. But she managed to feel just as much at ease playing in the ponds of Waikīkī as commenting on a new exhibit at the Paris Musée Des Beaux Arts. Abroad, she wore the most exquisite gowns, but once home wore colorful mu'umu'u. She spoke several languages; being particularly fluent in Hawaiian, English, German, and French. She was very attractive and had many gentlemen suitors, though nothing came of any of them other than some flirtations. Compared to other women of her age and position, she was considerably more progressive. Whereas many European aristocrats regarded commoners as somewhere slightly higher in value than cattle, Ka'iulani did not. During a time when people of a skin tone darker than Europeans were labeled as "heathens" and "noble savage" at best, Ka'iulani dared to call her people "a great race," a simple phrase, but not a popular European idea and not Victorian at all.

In some respects, Ka'iulani was much like her aunt, what the West would later call a "feminist." One must remember that Ka'iulani's *hānai* aunt was Princess Ke'elikōlani, a strongly traditional woman who reminded the young princess of Hawaiian women leaders and warriors like Manono, Ka'ahumanu,

and Queen Emma. This was in marked difference to the 19th-century Euro-American attitude, for example, where men could legally beat their wives and arranged marriages were the norm of especially upper-class ladies. Ka'iulani wholeheartedly disliked this Victorian view and vowed never to simply be a "woman of fashion and most likely a flirt." She would not marry a man she did not love.[6]

One of the things frequently mentioned about Ka'iulani was her remarkable beauty. Today we have hotels, songs, a line of *mu'umu'u*, a school, a street, portraits displayed in many places around Honolulu (a city, incidentally, she strongly disliked), and many other items bearing her name. Indeed, the name "Ka'iulani" itself renders the image of beauty, mystique, and enchantment. Ka'iulani was many of these things, but far more important to her, she would have liked to be remembered as a Hawaiian. When writing about her people, she never expressed being nervous or uncomfortable around them. On the contrary, she ate poi and raw fish with them and often lamented how she wished she could do more. Since the first week of her arrival back in Honolulu, she engulfed herself in many charitable and social projects for her people, including with the Hawaiian Relief Society and as the vice-president of the Hawai'i Chapter of the Red Cross (121). She did all she could for her people.

Following her return to Hawai'i in 1897 right up till the end of 1898, she entertained many of the men who had overthrown her government, but this was not because she had accepted or forgiven American rule. Indeed, she was deeply resentful of what had happened and, even more resentful at the sight of American troops. She was doing all she could to help her people gain as much as they could under the circumstances. The U.S. could easily have classified Hawaiians along with blacks and Native Americans insofar as granting them citizenship with limited voting rights and establishing an apartheid form of government, such as in the American South, as many Republican officials wanted. Ka'iulani was well traveled and was fully aware of government-supported racism. It is much to the credit of the lobbying skills of the Royal Family and the many other Hawaiian leaders that Hawaiians were given a special status and a (slightly) more liberal government than other American colonies, such as the Philippines and Puerto Rico. Ka'iulani's love of Hawai'i was greater than her hatred of America.

There is much to be learned from Ka'iulani and, even a hundred years from now, there still will be much to be remembered about her. Perhaps she said it best: "I must have been born under an unlucky star—as I seem to have my whole life planned out for me in such a way that I cannot alter it" (103). But we are fortunate that that star appeared at all, that we as a nation were able to glimpse its radiance for that one brief moment, a shining beacon during our people's blackest of nights.

**Notes**

[1] Possibly "Māmā nui."

[2] Possibly "Pāpā Mō'ī" and "Māmā Mō'ī."

[3] John Sheldon and another editor held the record for the most arrests and incarcerations—eight times under the PG/Republic government, the same number of opposition papers for which Sheldon was editor. He was staunchly royalist and prided himself in the number of times he was tried by the PG. When Sheldon was arrested shortly after his comment, the *Gazette* wrote that the editors "are enjoying a long-needed term of rest.... The editors are passing their vacations in Oahu Prison" (Chapin 1996:103).

[4] Since the news of the overthrow, Princess Ka'iulani had been suffering various illnesses (Zambucka 1976:131). Menton is on the French Riviera, and Ka'iulani spent her holidays there when her father was in Europe since it was much warmer than England (100).

[5] As noted in Public Law 103-150 (in 1993), there were no plebiscites or referendums taken for the establishment of the Republic or for annexation. The Queen constantly reminded American political leaders of that fact and urged that a plebiscite be taken to prove the will of the people, which no doubt would have been to restore her to the throne.

[6] Ka'iulani's words on marriage and her speeches to the American and European press (i.e. "I, a poor weak girl") echoed another famous monarch familiar to Ka'iulani—Queen Elizabeth I—who had led England from the status of a third-world nation to a first-world global power. Both women would never marry but, unlike Elizabeth, Ka'iulani would additionally never rule as a political monarch, but rather a princess reining in the hearts of her people, much like another more contemporary English royal, Diana Princess of Wales.

## References

Chapin, Helen Geracimos. 1996. *Shaping History: The Role of Newspapers in Hawai'i*. Honolulu: University of Hawai'i Press.

Liliuokalani, Queen. 1990 [1898]. *Hawaii's Story By Hawaii's Queen*. Honolulu: Mutual Publishing.

Lydecker, Robert, comp. 1918. Roster Legislatures of Hawaii 1841–1918. Honolulu: The Hawaiian Gazette.

Mrantz, Maxine. 1980. *Hawaii's Tragic Princess: Kaiulani, The Girl Who Never Got to Rule*. Honolulu: Aloha Graphics and Sales.

Seiden, Allan. 1992. *Hawai'i: The Royal Legacy*. Honolulu: Mutual Publishing.

Silva, Noenoe. 1998. "Kanaka Maoli Resistance to Annexation." *'Ōiwi: A Native Hawaiian Journal* 1 (Dec.)

Zambucka, Kristin. 1976. *Princess Kaiulani: The Last Hope of Hawaii's Monarchy*. Honolulu: Mana Publishing.

*Bereaved Daughter-in-Law*

*City Pastoral*

*Junkie*

*Holy Ground*

*Queenie*

Māhealani in 1989 with her youngest daughter,
Eōmailani, and oldest granddaughter, Tasia-Marie

# kamau'u

Māhealani Kamau'u • Māhealani Kamau'u • Māhealani Kamau'u • Māhealani Kamau'u

## Bereaved Daughter-in-Law

We die soon enough—
Brides reunited in Christ,
Men gone to ether, flame,
Or vaulted in, whatever.
In that final agony
Heroin and a good beer
Might do for some;
For others,
A contemplation on the Divine,
I don't know.
My husband once told me
About coming upon
Young lovers on a hill
At twilight
Beside Kewalo's surf
After bringing the nets in;
I guess the dusky hill,
The surf's languor,
The innocents,
Long black hair down
Her slender back, astride,

Caught him by surprise.
He left quickly
Unnoticed and embarrassed;
He told me about it later
When words
Were awkward
Between us. I blushed
Feeling he somehow imagined us there.

Yesterday mom died.
Her soul was routed through
The Mormon tabernacle
By Times Supermarket.
She once scolded me
For my irreverent poems,
And raged when
I turned her son in
For his demons.
"What kind of Hawaiian are you!"
Her recriminations stung
But yesterday
I kissed her face and
Caressed her hands;

For love of her
Queues formed at the coffin
Out the great hall, around the corner,
Down the city block—
So many tears,
And mine the least among them,
Feeling unworthy to approach even
Moe kapu,
Prostrate;
Yet she would always have me
Take my place
As family.
Mom, please accept our gifts,
Your son's carved *palaoa,* my leis,
Forgive us,
Help us work out our love
And I know you understand now
I can't help
The poems.

*(lei) palaoa* is a pendant, traditionally associated with
royalty and made of whale-tooth ivory

# City Pastoral

Filigree of trees
Heavy laden and
Chandeliered with rain;
Moon warmth all over sky,
The city sleeps.
Park bench souls snore
Under newspaper eaves;
Ghosts scuttle among leaves,
Alley doorways,
Remnant patches of grass.
The Swing Club
With its Blues Band of Love,
Smith's Union Bar and
The Orchid Ballroom
Are emptied out,
Their patrons gone
To a farther hill
And landscape.
I am the unwashed reprobate,
Bag lady, all the rest—
Mere condensate of mud
Flung across arc of asphalt,
Eddying along guttered sidewalks
Coursing to sea.
I have known the moon,
Its winds,
Cloud formations;
I have seen
Star bursts across skies,
A tiny bud's radiance,
Morning's welcoming sunrise.

## Junkie

When will the silver-chained hands
Rich veined and held unsteady
For a further infusion
Of needle's gold
Be lifted
To receive
The clear benediction
Of trees, ocean, wind?

## Holy Ground

O Moon,
Lift the brittle white dust,
The red augury of tears;
Call forth the sea,
Enchant its blue heart—
Form this place holy,
And holy again.

# Queenie

My name is Queenie
I am a direct lineal descendant
Of Queen Ka'ahumanu
I just found this out
I researched the Archives
Everywhere I did my research
I never found this out
Until one day I talked to
That lady—you know her
Always hanging around there—
She knows all about
The genealogies
She told me, "Queenie,
That boy Martin
You know him
He's a big shot
That's Auntie Katie's boy
From Kaua'i
They related to you
They have information
About your genealogy
When I talked to them
I went to Kaua'i
And I found out
About being royal blood
I just cried
I couldn't tell anybody
Who could I tell?
I just cried, I tell you
I went into the forest
By myself
And I cried
To the trees
They understood
Our kūpuna
Received me
And they went understand me
Who else could I tell?
Nobody
I tell you
I cried and cried
So you see

What I am telling you
Is the truth
My ancestors were ali'i
They were of
The royal class
That's why I
Cannot put up
With squatters
On my land
Who are these people?
They have no rights!
They don't belong
On this land
This is my land
I tell you
This is a place
Where the King himself
Used as a retreat
The King himself!
Where you can find
Anybody who can say
That their tūtū
Was invited
Into the compound
Of the ali'i?
You cannot find that
But I can remember
This place
Since I was a child
A little girl
When was low tide
My tūtū man
Would carry me
On his shoulders
To that island
Who the hell
Are these people
To come here and squat?
They're nobody!
They're commoner class
I am an ali'i
I tell you the truth
If my tūtū man were
Alive today, they would never,

They would never, treat me
This way!
Who are these people?
What right do they have here?
They don't own this land
This land belongs to my family
They had a
What you call
Condemnation
Actually
I got no beef with
The state
The federal went take 'em
First during the war
Then they went give 'em
To the state
What right did they have to
Take our land?
Fuck the United States!
Fuck them all!
My friends tell me,
"Queenie, you get all the rights
You should fight for the island
You know that belongs to you"
And I tell them, "I know"
I tell you true
I not going rest
Until I get justice
Who are these people
To come here and
Act like they own the land?
My grandfather sued for
The island—
Incomplete, he died
They did a fraud
My grandfather was
The first to put in
His claim
When my tūtū died
Nobody dared touch
That island
When I speak
It comes out
Spiritually

My name is Queenie
I like to declare war
On the United States
And I tell them too
When I say this
They must be thinking
Wow, she must be a communist
But the U.S.
Know they cannot
Get away with this
They know Queenie
Can prove the genealogy
They know I'm
Going to bring the lawsuit
Even the Campbells
Cannot prove anything
You know what my real name is?
Kahuionālanikūpihea
It hurts, it still hurts
But I will carry this fight
Until I die
They take one look at me
I look so dumb
I speak pidgin English
I want to act mean too
Like my kings and queens
In a spiritual way
When I meditate or chant
Things come out right for me
But I tell you
The way I feel
I like kill somebody
I like kill all of them
They trying to make
The Hawaiians mentally ill
You know my friends tell me
Queenie, let's go down there
And blow everything up.

# *Notable Hawaiians*

Notable Hawaiians • Notable Hawaiians • Notable Hawaiians • Notable Hawaiians

*When the second issue of 'Ōiwi: A Native Hawaiian Journal was being conceptualized in 1999, it was difficult to ignore the number of "best of" lists which were being announced on almost a daily basis. It seemed as if we couldn't get enough—What were the most important books of the millennium? The one hundred most significant events? The best and worst dressed movie stars? While sometimes humorous, thought-provoking, and/or controversial, the categories were also nearly endless. Yet all the hoopla was difficult to ignore. After all, there was one question not being addressed in the general media at both the local and national levels: Who were the most notable Hawaiians of the 20th century? After all the attention given over the years to issues of Hawaiian sovereignty, native gathering rights, and endless statistics on Hawaiian health, education, and social problems, what did we know of the contributions individual Hawaiians had made to society? While*

*newspaper and magazine articles, television news reports, and an occasional book profile highlighted a few Hawaiians now and then, no one had taken account at any length of Hawaiians who were admired by and who inspired other Hawaiians.*

*We began discussing this idea amongst ourselves: Whom did we consider noteworthy and important? Whom were we inspired by in our personal, spiritual, and professional lives? These conversations were enthusiastic and spirited. Yet something was missing. What was it? Oh yes—the voice of the people. We decided that instead of imposing our own ideas of who was inspirational and noteworthy, we would ask the Hawaiian community: "Who do you, the Hawaiian people, feel are the most inspirational and notable Hawaiians of the 20th century, and why?" To help get the word out, Honolulu Star-Bulletin staff writer Pat Omandam wrote an article entitled "Who were the*

most notable Hawaiians?" (5 July 1999:A-3),
and the Office of Hawaiian Affairs ran a
small blurb in the August 1999 issue of their
paper, Ka Wai Ola o OHA. We also put the
call out through email and word of mouth.

Because we wanted the list to be as
broad-based and all-inclusive as possible, the
"ground rules" for nominations were quite
simple. In order to be nominated, the person
had to: (1) have been living (but not
necessarily have been born) in the 20th
century; (2) be of Hawaiian ancestry (any
blood quantum); and (3) have made a
significant contribution to the Hawaiian community or community at large; or have exem-
plified Hawaiian culture or lifestyle in their
familial, spiritual, and/or professional life. All
we asked of those who nominated someone
was that they, too, be of Hawaiian ancestry.

Over the next months, we tracked down
leads, encouraged people to put down in
words the reasons for their nominations, and
did some background research. Every
reasonable effort was made to insure
that the information was factually correct.
Because the information provided varies,
there is a disparity in length and detail
between entries. Some of the people
nominated are controversial in that there is
disagreement about whether their activities
or achievements were beneficial or harmful
to the Hawaiian community. Yet others
might not typically be considered
"notable"—they were not famous, did
not receive accolades, and did not perform
history-moving feats; but they served as mentors, sources of inspiration, and role models
for their families or small communities. What
comes through in all the nominations is the
sense of personal presence and influence
that has made these Hawaiians "notable."

The list is alphabetical by family name (with
the exception of the initial collective entry of
Nā Haumāna Hanohano o ke Kula Kaiapuni),
followed by the categories we felt best
describe the area of achievement:

arts & humanities—traditional, modern, and
Western forms of artistic expression.

business & industry—including agriculture
(traditional and modern), fashion,
restaurateurs and food industry, tourism,
computers, and others.

community leadership—covering a wide
range of areas, from sovereignty and
environmental activism, to social welfare
and building community pride.

(Hawaiian) culture—with emphasis on
traditional practitioners of such arts as hula,
lā'au lapa'au, lomilomi, fishing, taro farming,
chant, and religion.

education—educators in State-related as well
as in independent programs and
institutions.

entertainment—performers in the tourist
industry and commercial sectors.

government service—in city & county, state,
federal, and international capacities where
they are not holding political office but have
contributed towards the general good of the
Hawaiian community.

health & medicine—health care professionals,
such as doctors, nurses, administrators, social
workers and social service agencies, and community outreach workers.

(Hawaiian) language—those who have
concentrated on 'ōlelo Hawai'i in their work.

law—*those working within the legal system as judges, attorneys, police officers, and related positions who have contributed significantly to the Hawaiian community, or who exemplify Hawaiian achievement.*

mana wahine—*this term could be loosely translated as "woman power!" and refers here to Hawaiian women who have excelled in their fields.*

military service—*in all branches and levels of the military. Despite strong criticism by segments of the Hawaiian community in regard to the detrimental effects of the U.S. military in Hawai'i, others consider such service an honor that benefits the Hawaiian community, or a new expression of Hawaiian patriotism and warrior spirit.*

politics—*those who have held political office, from community boards to Congress, as well as those who have actively campaigned for and championed Hawaiian rights through community activism.*

religion—*leaders in traditional Hawaiian and non-Hawaiian spirituality.*

sports—*athletes who have excelled in foreign-introduced sports such as football, volleyball, golf, and sumo wrestling, or in such traditional Hawaiian sports as surfing, swimming, and canoe racing.*

"Hawaiian firsts"—*pathbreakers in various areas of life.*

*The Hawaiians named here represent a wide and diverse spectrum of the Hawaiian community: there are kāne (men) and wāhine (women), kūpuna (elders) and 'ōpio (youth), individuals and hui (groups), Hawaiians from all islands of the pae 'āina (archipelago) as well as from Moku Honu (the North American continent). Some are still living, while others have passed on. Some have spent their entire lives on one island or in one rural community, while others have traveled the globe. Some have advanced in Western education, while others have little or no Western education.*

*A truly comprehensive list of this kind would be the size of an encyclopedia. But in an effort to include all those nominations that were sent to us, yet about whom more time was needed to gather information, we will continue this list as Part II in the next issue (volume 3) of 'Ōiwi.*

*When the 20th century began, our population had been decimated by foreign diseases, our sovereign government had been overthrown, our language banned, our choice to pursue our traditional culture and practices forcibly wrested from us. As the 21st century dawns, there is renewed hope and promise that we can undo at least some of the wrongs: Hawaiian-language immersion schools have been established across the pae 'āina; Hawaiian sovereignty is no longer just a vague dream, but is being worked out in real, concrete ways; and Hawaiians once again have taken pride in our resolve to continue customary cultural practices such as taro farming, gathering from the land and sea, and long-distance canoe voyaging. In the face of the great adversities of the past century, the fact that we are still here makes us all notable. But we have not merely survived. Hawaiians have contributed so much to the world, and have so much more to contribute. In the words of our ancestors: I mua ē, i mua ā, i mua aku nō, a ki'ina i ka lei, ka lei o ka lanakila, go forth, go forward, go forward indeed, and grab hold of the lei, the lei of victory.*

KUʻUALOHA HOʻOMANAWANUI
COMPILER

## Notable Hawaiians of the 20th Century

### Part I

***Nā Haumāna Hanohano o nā Kula Kaiapuni***—*language, Hawaiian firsts.* Two decades ago, a small group of mostly Hawaiian parents had a dream: that their children could grow up speaking Hawaiian as their first language. They worked tirelessly to make that dream come true by lobbying the legislature to change the Hawaiʻi law that, despite Hawaiian being an official language of the state (along with English), continued to uphold the 1896 ban on the teaching of Hawaiian in the Department of Education (DOE). They lobbied for funding for the pilot Hawaiian immersion program; for expansion of the program from kindergarten only to K-12th grades; and for teachers, equipment, curriculum, and campus space. We pay tribute to their efforts by honoring the class of 1999 of Nā Kula Kaiapuni, the DOE Hawaiian Language Immersion program, the first students in over a century to graduate from a Hawaiian language-based educational institution. We wish these four young men and seven young women and their families the best in their future: (from Ke Kula Kaiapuni ʻo ʻĀnuenue in Pālolo, Oʻahu) Kaimalino Woo Andrade, Hōkūnani Fox, Kini Kaʻakimaka, ʻĀnela Maunakea Lopez, Kāhea Naʻauao, and Kaliko Palmeira; and (from Ke Kula Kaiapuni ʻo Nāwahīokalaniʻōpuʻu in Keaʻau, Hawaiʻi) Kekuamanohā Burgess, Kananinohea Kawaiʻaeʻa, Kauikeōlani Naniʻole, Hulilau

Wilson, and Kalimahana Young. *E ola mau ka ʻōlelo Hawaiʻi!*

***Eddie Aikau***—*community leadership, sports* (born 4 May 1946; died 17 March 1978). From the late 1960s through the 1970s, Eddie Aikau was a lifeguard stationed at Waimea Bay on the North Shore of Oʻahu. Although quiet and humble, he distinguished himself time after time by venturing into the ocean at its most out-of-control moments to make seemingly impossible rescues of people who misjudged the ocean's power. Hundreds are alive today only because of Aikau's remarkable abilities and willingness to immerse himself in horrendous conditions that would keep most lifeguards out of the water.

When he wasn't making rescues, the ocean was Aikau's playground. When he was a teenager, as a newcomer to giant surf, he startled experienced bigwave masters one day when he began surfing the largest waves of the year at Waimea. In the months ahead, while he continued to leave onlookers speechless with daring rides, it became clear to everyone that Eddie Aikau, a full-blooded Hawaiian, had an amazing relationship with the sea. The ocean in all its moods brought him immense joy and peace. People still talk about his bright grin, which projected like a lighthouse beacon from his dark face whenever he streaked across monstrous Waimea waves.

In March 1978, the Polynesian voyaging canoe *Hōkūleʻa* departed from Oʻahu on her second voyage to Tahiti despite signs of bad weather. Eddie, then 31 years old, was on board as a crewmember. Several hours after departure, about 12 miles off of Lānaʻi in the Kaiwi channel, one of the most treacherous stretches of ocean in the world, the canoe encountered 12-foot high swells and gale force winds, and swamped. Eddie, with only his surfboard, paddled towards the island for help. But despite the most extensive air and sea search in the state's history, he would never be seen again.

Eddie Aikau is regarded as a hero in the Hawaiian community for his brave and selfless actions. Polynesian Voyaging Society head navigator Nainoa Thompson said of him, "Eddie was totally intense and strong, but he was also a very caring man. He loved his culture. He loved the canoes. He was a total Hawaiian. He stood out. I will always remember a crew meeting before the trip. Eddie brought his guitar and he was playing music. We were talking in the back, just the two of us, and he told me that what he wanted most in the world was to see Hawaiki rise up out of the ocean. After Eddie's death, we could have quit. But Eddie had this dream about finding islands the way our ancestors did and if we quit, he wouldn't have his dream fulfilled. Whenever I feel down, I look at the photo of Eddie I have in my living room and I recall his dream. He was a lifeguard...he guarded life, and he lost his own trying to guard ours. Eddie cared about others and took care of others. He had great passions. He was my spirit."

Eddie Aikau has since been memorialized through a big wave surf contest on O'ahu that is held every winter, but only when swells reach a minimum of 25 feet. Although the contest is officially known as "The Quicksilver In Memory of Eddie Aikau Big Wave Invitational," to surfing aficionados worldwide it is known simply as "The Eddie."

James Jones, a regular participant in "The Eddie," has said of Aikau, "There's thousands of people who are great surfers or have other terrific talents. But how many people use their talent the way that Eddie did, to help other people? There are situations on the North Shore where it's likely that a lifeguard will perish if he tries to rescue someone. You can't require a lifeguard to risk his life like that. You couldn't pay someone enough. But Eddie would go all the way to help. It didn't matter [who it was]. No one would tell him, no one would ask him, but Eddie would go. I saw it many times." That simple phrase "Eddie Would Go" is still seen on bumper stickers in Hawai'i more than 20 years since Eddie's passing. In a time of overnight sensations and stars around the world battling with each other for recognition, Eddie Aikau remains a symbol of strength, courage, and aloha to the Hawaiian community, including Hawaiian youth who weren't even born when Eddie disappeared. The Hawaiian rap group Sudden Rush also pay tribute to Eddie in the *mele* (song) "Think About It" with the words, "Mahalo, braddah Eddie."

While man-made memorials may crack and crumble, the legend of Eddie Aikau remains as indestructible and inspiring as the sea. When huge waves make their inevitable return to Waimea Bay, and surfers, in Eddie's honor, courageously launch themselves from the ocean's tallest peaks, the world will be reminded that when the seas became unruly and lives were in danger, when others stepped back in fear, Eddie would not turn away. Eddie would go. To the day he died, Eddie would go.

(Note: Parts of this entry were excerpted from: "Eddie Would Go, Has Gone, and Is Still Going" by David Aldo Ciaffardini, *Hawaii Magazine* (December 1996):59-62;

and the website of the Polynesian Voyaging Society at http://leahi.kcc.hawaii.edu/org/pvs/nainoa80tahiti.html.)

**Abraham Akaka**—*community leadership, religion.* One of the most beloved Hawaiian spiritual leaders of all time, Kahu Abraham Akaka was born on 21 February 1917 in Pauoa valley on the island of O'ahu, the fourth of seven children of a Hawaiian-Chinese father (Kahikina Akaka) and a Hawaiian mother (Annie Akaka). A 1934 graduate of McKinley High School, Akaka went on to receive a bachelor's degree at Wesleyan University in Illinois.

Akaka often spoke of his inspiration in choosing to dedicate his life to God through Christian service. When he was 22 years old, he attended a World Conference of Christian Youth in Amsterdam, The Netherlands. The mix of cultures and ethnicity working together for peace on earth through Jesus Christ made a big impression on the young Hawaiian. Upon returning to Hawai'i, he spent a year doing youth work at Kawaiaha'o Church, before going off to the Chicago Theological Seminary to pursue his calling as a Christian minister. There he received his Bachelor of Divinity degree, the first Native Hawaiian to receive a graduate degree in theology from a major American university. It was while he was in Chicago that he met his future wife Mary Louise Jeffery. After they returned to Hawai'i and were married, they began many years of service at 'Imiola Congregational Church, a small Hawaiian church in Waimea on the island of Hawai'i. They also served at small rural Hawaiian churches on Maui and later at Haili Church in Hilo before eventually settling on O'ahu, where for nearly 30 years Kahu Akaka would preside over Kawaiaha'o Church, the oldest Hawaiian Protestant church on the island.

While some Hawaiian Christian ministers and congregations have shunned Hawaiian culture and frowned upon its inclusion in the church, Akaka embraced it. Besides continuing and encouraging the traditional practice of utilizing the Hawaiian language during worship service, including the singing of Hawaiian hymns, the reading of Scripture, and the recitation of prayers all in Hawaiian, Akaka also instituted new traditions, such as Ali'i Sunday, which is the celebration of the lives of the Hawaiian Royalty on the Sunday before their birthdays. This was also a time when Hawaiian issues could be presented and goals articulated. Even before it was popular or widely accepted, Akaka encouraged the acceptance of hula in the church, a practice which had been banned by the American Calvinist missionaries a century before. He used Hawaiian metaphors regularly in his sermons, and upheld Hawaiian values for all to embrace, such as *aloha kekahi i kekahi*—love one another. Akaka believed that his life was guided by the precept of God first, others second, yourself third. "The great need today," he is often quoted as saying, "is for a new kind of godly [person], the [person] of aloha. The church should help prepare people to live creatively. Hawai'i is a laboratory proving what can be done."

One of his most famous metaphors was centered around the *'ukulele*, where each string represented a different culture and people: "The four strings are white, black, yellow, and brown, like the people of the world. Harmony lies in tuning the instrument and accepting the fact that each string needs to sound differently. To force conformity would make them uncomfortable, because they are made to sound differently, and shouldn't sound alike. God is the one tuner."

Akaka has been called the most influential and widely known Hawaiian since Kamehameha the Great. *Newsweek* magazine once described him as "having the charm of a beachboy and the force of Billy Graham." Greatly respected and liked by many, he has had many honors in his long career, such as serving as a Regent for the University of Hawai'i system from 1960–1961. In 1964 he addressed 17,000 people at the famed Hollywood Bowl's Easter Sunrise Service in California. In 1970 during a visit to Hawai'i, President Richard Nixon attended one of Akaka's services to give thanks for the safe return of the ill-fated Apollo 13 mission. Nixon was so impressed with Akaka's sermon that he invited him to the White House to speak. Kahu Akaka also developed a close friendship with the Reverend Martin Luther King Jr. when he participated in a civil rights symposium in Hawai'i. As the first chairman for the Hawai'i Advisory Committee to the U.S. Commission on Civil Rights, he and two others went to Washington to lobby for the passage of a strong civil rights bill in 1964. He gave the blessing for Hawaiian statehood in 1959, a speech in which he coined the term "Aloha State" for Hawai'i; this speech was included in A. Grove Day's collection of Hawaiian lit-erature called *A Hawaiian Reader* (Appleton, 1959). He carried the ashes of legendary surfer Duke Kahanamoku out to sea at the Duke's funeral, and said of this fellow Notable Hawaiian that the Duke "represented the ali'i nobility in the highest and truest sense—concern for others, humility in victory, courage in adversity, good sports-manship in defeat. He had a quality of life we are all challenged and inspired to emulate." (See the entry on Duke Kahanamoku.)

Akaka fought against attempts by the state to desegregate The Kamehameha Schools and force the institution to hire non-Protestant teachers. He also fought against passage of Hawai'i's land reform law. He was involved in many civic groups, including the Friends of Kamehameha Schools, which he founded.

Kahu Akaka has been recognized for his years of great service to Hawai'i through such awards as Father of the Year (1958), the Ke Ali'i Pauahi Award (1963), Grand Marshall of the Aloha Week Parade (1977), Ambassador of Aloha for the Aloha Week Festivals (1981), and the first recipient of the Nā Po'okela Award (1987) during the Year of the Hawaiian Ho'olako celebration. In 1986 he was inducted into the McKinley High School Hall of Honor for distinguished alumni in the areas of humanitarian service, professional work, civic and patriotic contributions, and government service. That year he was also the first non-medical person to give the annual lecture to the American Psychiatric Association/National Institute of Mental Health Annual Conference in New York City. In 1991 he was honored by the Historic Hawai'i Foundation, along with *kupuna* Irmgard Aluli as Kama'āina of the Year, and in 1995 he received the Kūlia i ka Nu'u award for outstanding community service.

Despite officially retiring from Kawaiaha'o Church in 1984, Kahu Akaka continued to serve Hawai'i's communities in a variety of ways. He presided over a myriad of services, such as weddings, funerals, baptisms, and blessings. He was the voice of prayerful aloha at graduations, groundbreakings, and grand openings. He was sought after both in Hawai'i and abroad for lectures, sermons, and other activities. Through it all, Akaka set up a relief foundation that was dedicated to help the needy, provide scholarships to uplift native Hawaiians, assist Kawaiahaʻo Church programs, and promote world peace. This foundation was financed in part by honoraria for his services. He also set up a special scholarship for Hawaiians aspiring to answer the call of the ministry called the Abraham K. Akaka Fellows Chicago Theological Seminary Scholarship program.

Kahu Akaka passed away from this life on 20 September 1997 at the age of 80. The Very Reverend Joseph Bukoski III, judicial vicar for the Catholic Diocese of Honolulu, called him "an extraordinary and great man...[with] deep spirituality and faith, which was solidly and firmly connected to his Hawaiian roots. He perpetuated the aloha of God. We admire his gentle and gentleman ways. He truly blessed many lives, but most importantly as a cleric he brought the love of God in a tangible way to many people. There's a dignity of who he was and what he did. It is with fond memory that we bid him aloha ʻoe."

**Alfred Unauna Alohikea**—*arts & humanities (music), politics* (born 10 September 1884; died 15 September 1936). A farmer by trade who was also a talented composer and musician, Alfred Alohikea was a renowned composer who settled in Hanalei valley on the island of Kauaʻi, raising taro and pigs between gigs. He is most noted for his compositions "Hanohano Hanalei," "Nāmolokama," "Kai Hāwanawana," and the ever popular *mele aloha* (love song) "Pua Līlia." In addition to his musical career, Alohikea was elected to the Territorial House of Representatives for the island of Kauaʻi in 1928. He was known to have composed campaign song lyrics, traveling through the taro fields on the back of a

flatbed truck, serenading the workers with his campaign promises while they worked. It paid off, because he never lost an election. (For more information see *Hawaiian Music and Musicians* by George S. Kanahele (University of Hawaiʻi Press, 1979) and the video *Words, Earth, and Aloha* by Eddie Kamae.)

**Irmgard Kealiʻiwahinealohanohoka-haopuamana Farden Aluli**—*arts & humanities (music), culture, language* (born 7 October 1911, Lahaina, Maui; died 4 October 2001). A talented musician and composer, Irmgard Aluli has inspired generations of Hawaiians with her compositions, such as "E Maliu Mai" and "Puamana," just two of the 400-plus songs she is credited with having written (not all of them published). She has worked as a teacher and in real estate, but her real calling has been music. From a large and musically talented family (she has ten brothers and sisters, not to mention musically inclined parents, aunts, uncles, cousins, daughters, and granddaughters), Aluli was a member of the Annie Kerr Trio, one of the most popular female groups of the 1930s. For many decades she performed with her daughters Kaneʻeaulani, Mihana, and Aima as the group Puamana. In 1998, she was inducted into the Hawaiʻi Music Hall of Fame, the same year she was honored with the Hōkū's Lifetime Achievement Award. She passed away in October 2001, just two months after she was honored as a Living Treasure by the Prince Kūhiō Hawaiian Civic Club. Niece Manu Meyer wrote, "Aunty Irmgard is not only talented and gracious, she has survived a tremendous past to inspire all of us nieces, children, and grandchildren to live a kind life, and sing a good song." (For more information see *Hawaiian Music and Musicians* by George S. Kanahele (University of Hawaiʻi Press, 1979).)

**Noa Emmett Aluli**—*culture, medicine, politics.* As a co-founder of the Protect Kahoʻolawe ʻOhana (PKO), Dr. Emmett Aluli is admired for his devotion since the 1970s to the cause of returning Kahoʻolawe to Hawaiians, for his dedication to native Hawaiian health, and for his 1981 pioneering "Molokaʻi Heart Study," which inspired other physicians to further the study of the native Hawaiian diet, including the link between traditional foods (such as fish and poi) and native Hawaiian health. Cousin Manu Meyer wrote, "Emmett has been my role model. He has believed in Kahoʻolawe as no one I know. His work in this field and in the area of land and healing reminds me of our grandfather. His dedication was never clearer than when we walked up to Moaʻula on his birthday, and he was running up with Lono. Emmett extends what his uncle Joseph Nāwahī wrote and believed about aloha ʻāina."

**Noa Webster Aluli**—*law, politics.* A lawyer by profession, Noa Aluli was devoted to the idea of healing and invigorating the Hawaiian people by bringing us back to the land. In 1914, along with Prince Jonah Kūhiō, John H. Wise, and the Reverend Akaiko Akana, Aluli was a founding member of the ʻAhahui Puʻuhonua o Nā Hawaiʻi (Hawaiian Protective Association), devoted to uplifting the Hawaiian people through social work and education. He also collaborated on the Hawaiian Homes Act of 1920.

**Alfred Aholo Apaka**—*arts & humanities (music), entertainment* (born 19 March 1919, Honolulu; died 30 January 1960). One of the most well-known singers ever to come out of Hawaiʻi, Alfred Apaka began singing early on, in a chorus at Roosevelt High School, as well as in Mormon church choirs. In 1938, he began his professional career at the Royal Hawaiian Hotel (with Don McDiarmid) before traveling to New York's Lexington Hotel to sing with Ray Kinney in 1940. He traveled around the U.S. continent throughout the 1940s and '50s, and appeared on Bob Hope's NBC radio show with Dorothy Lamour in 1952. He continued performing in Hawaiʻi at the Hawaiian Village with Benny Kalama in 1955, and served as the hotel's entertainment director until his untimely death in 1960. (For more information see *Hawaiian Music and Musicians* by George S. Kanahele (University of Hawaiʻi Press, 1979).)

**William Auld**—*community leadership.* William Auld was born on 7 August 1842 in Honolulu, where he resided all his life, mainly at Pālama. He was a steadfast *aloha ʻāina*, and served as secretary of Hui Kālaiʻāina during the anti-annexation struggle. He was selected as one of four delegates entrusted by the people to travel to Washington, D.C., to present the anti-annexation petitions to the Senate of the United States Congress. He was a personal friend of ka Mōʻīwahine Liliʻuokalani. Mōʻī Kalākaua appointed him High Priest of the Hale Nauā secret society. Mr. Auld was also a thirty-second degree Mason, holding membership in several lodges. He was an authority on Hawaiian *moʻolelo* (stories), *mele* (songs), traditions, and religion of the *poʻe kahiko* (people of old).

**Billie Beamer**—*community leadership, education, law, politics, sports.* Billie Beamer has been an educator, administrator, assistant professor at the University of Hawaiʻi, director of the U.S. Census, golf professional, chairperson of the Department of Hawaiian Home Lands, independent video producer, radio commentator, assistant director of Parks, and an Office of Hawaiian

Affairs trustee. She is, as one person wrote, "without a doubt the most notable native Hawaiian who has both given her all to the native Hawaiian community and has set the example for native Hawaiians and all of the children of Hawai'i to follow. She was a noted athlete, successful businesswoman, and a respected speaker and author. Even during her later years of discomfort due to serious health problems, she continued to be a faithful servant to the native Hawaiian community and all of Hawai'i. Just recognition of Billie Beamer is long overdue." (For more information see *The Royal Torch* by Billie Beamer (Billie and Billie Publishing, 1989).)

**Richard Kekuni Blaisdell**—*community leadership, health & medicine, politics*. Dr. Richard Kekuni Blaisdell is the rarest of all men, a Renaissance man of unparalleled respect and integrity. "Kekuni," as he likes to be called, balances living in two very different worlds, and he makes it look easy. He is one of Hawai'i's best physicians, specializing in blood disorders, and is also a Native Hawaiian activist who has been at the forefront of the Hawaiian sovereignty movement for the last 20 years.

Kekuni recalls his days at The Kamehameha Schools (class of 1942): "I refused to be bleached. They wanted us to be like every-one else, to de-Hawaiianize us. I was lucky, I had a teacher, Donald Mitchell, who came from Missouri to teach. He fell in love with our homeland and people and culture. He taught us to be proud of our culture and to live it. I was being trained to be an electrician, but he encouraged me to become a doctor." Years later, Kekuni helped care for his mentor as he was dying.

Following his graduation from The Kamehameha Schools, Kekuni entered the

University of Redlands in California during World War II. From there he went to the University of Chicago School of Medicine. He interned at Johns Hopkins University in Baltimore, Maryland, and did part of his residency at Tulane University in New Orleans, Louisiana. Kekuni joined the U.S. Army while he was interning at Johns Hopkins and became part of the U.S. Army Medical Corps. During the early years of his medical career, Kekuni worked in a research lab in Lawrence, Kansas, and in the Department of Pathology at Duke University in North Carolina.

In 1959, Kekuni was invited to Japan to do research on atomic bomb survivors. His extraordinary work there was only the beginning of his brilliant medical career. In 1966, Kekuni returned to Hawai'i, where he not only helped to start the University of Hawai'i Medical School, but he also became the first Kanaka Maoli professor of medicine. He was also instrumental in founding the Native Hawaiian Physicians Association. Throughout his career, Kekuni has won national recognition for his research in blood disorders, but he brushes aside the accolades he has received for his work. His brilliance is only equaled by his modesty.

Since the early 1980s, Kekuni has lobbied Congress at the national level to set up a health care system for Hawaiians. The passage of the Native Hawaiian Health Care Act in 1988 was the first step in addressing the myriad health needs of the Hawaiian community.

In addition to being a physician, Kekuni was also a founding member of Ka Pākaukau, a pro-sovereignty organization. Ka Pākaukau is working towards United States' recognition of the inherent sovereign right to self-determination of the Hawaiian people, and supports the return of all Hawaiian land. Physician, political activist, and visionary, Kekuni Blaisdell embodies the blending of ancient and modern traditions, and challenges us to live up to our hopes for the future.

**Gladys Kamakakūokalani Ainoa Brandt**—*community leadership, education, mana wahine*. Former principal of The Kamehameha School for Girls, University of Hawai'i Regent, and co-author of the article "A Broken Trust," regarding the illegal actions of the Bishop Estate trustees, Gladys Brandt has dedicated her life to the education of Hawaiian youth and the people of Hawai'i. As a UH Regent, "Aunty Gladys" was instrumental in getting built the Center for Hawaiian Studies. Although UH policy states that no building can be named for a living person, the Center was unofficially named in her honor for several years before being officially dedicated in 2002.

**Abigail Kuaihelani Maipinepine Campbell**—*community leadership, mana wahine, politics*. A descendant of Maui *ali'i* Kahekili, Abigail Campbell was the President of Hui Aloha 'Āina o nā Wāhine, the Women's Patriotic League, which supported the men's organization Hui Aloha 'Āina o nā Kāne in their work to prevent the annexation of Hawai'i to the United States. She was married to James Campbell. Her daughter Abigail Wahiikaahuula married David Kawananakoa.

**David E. K. Cooper**—*community leadership, military service*. David E. K. Cooper is a Native Hawaiian-Caucasian born and raised in Waikāne, O'ahu, and is a 1959 graduate of The Kamehameha School for Boys. Among other important executive positions, he also served as the first chairman of the

Congressionally established 15-member Federal Advisory Committee on Minority Veterans. He is a frequent speaker on issues affecting Pacific and Asian Americans and minorities and has had a number of articles published in various publications. He completed a successful career in the U.S. Army, retiring as a brigadier general, and has received Distinguished Alumni Awards from The Kamehameha Schools and the University of Hawai'i, for whom he is a UH Alumni Association representative. One person wrote, "David Cooper is a tireless worker on behalf of the Hawaiian people."

**Wendall and Mariah Davis**—*community leadership, religion*. 'Anakala Wendall is the reverend for Kahikolu Congregational Church in Kealakekua, Hawai'i. One person wrote, "[Kahu Wendall and Mariah Davis] give their life to helping Hawaiian communities. They are both talented musicians that could easily be making money in our local music industry, but instead they dedicate their time and energy to keeping the Hawaiian culture alive."

**Beadie Kanahele Dawson**—*community leadership, law*. A Honolulu businessperson for many years before pursuing a career in law, Beadie Dawson was at the forefront of the recent Bishop Estate controversy. Prior to this, Beadie worked as deputy attorney general, in part settling claims for Hawaiians on the Department of Hawaiian Home Lands waiting list.

In addition to her legal profession, Beadie has continued to remain very active on numerous boards, including the Friends of 'Iolani Palace, the Queen Lili'uokalani Children's Center Advisory Council, the Native Hawaiian Bar Association, Hawaiian Historical Society, Historic Hawai'i

Foundation, Hui Hānai, and the University of Hawai'i Medical School. She has made her mark on each of these organizations through her leadership, vision, and tenacity.

Perhaps her most important contribution toward the betterment of native Hawaiians and our Ali'i Trusts was the role she played as the attorney for the students, parents, and alumni of The Kamehameha Schools/Bishop Estate comprising Nā Pua a Ke Ali'i Pauahi. During the critical early stages of the KSBE trustee controversy, Beadie represented the direct beneficiaries of The Kamehameha Schools at a time when no other attorney in Hawai'i was willing to challenge the powerful Bishop Estate. She first convinced the members of Nā Pua to believe that they were in fact the beneficiaries of the trust and as such had the legal right to hold the trustees accountable for their actions and wrongdoings. She helped them form their organization and prepared their Petition to Intervene in the controversy. When she stood up in court on behalf of the direct beneficiaries, she rattled the cages of the secretive trustees as never before, and opened the door for the authors of the now famous "A Broken Trust" article and subsequent attorney general investigation which lead to the resignation or dismissal of all the trustees.

**Dana Naone Hall**—*arts & humanities (literature), community leadership, politics.* One person wrote, "I have known Dana Naone Hall since about 1995, when I asked her for help for a project I was doing in an environmental studies class. Since then I have formed a close bond with her, working with her in projects that related to the kanu hou 'ana i nā iwi kūpuna [reinterment of Hawaiian bones], the efforts to stop the runway extension of the Kahului airport, the

maintenance, support, and improvement of the Hawaiian Language Immersion programs on Maui, and a number of other issues. She and her husband, Isaac, have provided a powerful voice for the Hawaiian community in their roles as advocates for Hawaiian rights. Dana is also a noted Hawaiian writer, and she has contributed to such collections as *Ho'omānoa: An Anthology of Contemporary Hawaiian Literature* (Ku Pa'a, 1989) and *Hawai'i: Return to Nationhood* (International Work Group for Indigenous Affairs, 1994), as well as editing a collection called *Mālama, Hawaiian Land and Water* (Bamboo Ridge Press, 1985). She also helped produce a video on kalo farming entitled *Back to the Roots* (1994). She was also one of the key figures in the protests against the Ritz Carlton on Maui, who had disinterred over 1,000 iwi kūpuna in the construction of their hotel. Her commitment to the Hawaiian people and to the protection of our 'āina is steadfast and unwavering."

**Kapua Wall Heuer**—*community leadership, culture.* Big Island native Kapua Wall Heuer has spent most of her 87 years on horseback. Growing up on her family ranch "Māhealani" in Kona, she roped wild cattle, hunted sheep, and participated in cattle drives from sun up to sun down. She was an original *pā'ū* rider in Anna Perry Fiske's "Old Hawaii on Horseback" pageant through the 1970's, and again when the pageant was revived in 1998. In 1994, she was the Pā'ū Queen in the Merrie Monarch Parade, and continues to participate annually in both the Merrie Monarch and Aloha Week festivities as a *pā'ū* rider.

A 1932 graduate of Punahou School, Kapua worked for Hawaii Meat Company before eventually marrying and returning to Kona, where she raised her family and continued

Kapua Wall Heuer

her lifelong love of the *paniolo* lifestyle. She was active as a 4-H leader and a 4-H judge. She still rides her 32-year-old mare, Olomana, regularly. In 1999 she was inducted into the Paniolo Hall of Fame, which is sponsored by the O'ahu Cattlemen Association. She was one of the first ten members, and was the only female *paniolo* so honored.

Granddaughter Christy Lassiter wrote, "My Nana represents a time in Hawai'i's history in which the romantic life of the cowboy was in full operation and survival skills on the mountain meant more than money. My Nana used to hunt sheep up on Hualalai, rope cattle at Keauhou and Kukaiau Ranch, and mingle with Honolulu society. She could be a grand lady or switch to being a cowgirl without even blinking an eye. When she was a little girl, she crossed the 'Alenuihāhā [the channel between the Big Island and Maui] on the Humu'ula in order to attend Punahou. She is now 87 years old and is receiving well-deserved attention for her interesting and exciting life. She is outstanding because she lived the life of turn of the

century Hawai'i, and will no doubt lead us on in great style to the next century."

***Martha Poepoe Hohu***—*arts & humanities (music), community leadership*. (See the biographical essay in this issue entitled "Legacy of Music, Legacy of Love: The Gifts of Aunty Martha Kaumakaokalani A'oe Poepoe Hohu" by great-grandniece Leslie Stewart.)

***Papa David Ka'alakea***— *community leadership, language, religion* (born 8 December 1919, Kīpahulu, Maui; died 9 December 1998, Paukūkalo, Maui). Papa Ka'alakea began a humble life in Kīpahulu, becoming a *paniolo* (cowboy) and raising a family, until 1953, when a trip to the doctor resulted in a diagnosis of tuberculosis. He was sent to the Kula Sanitarium and placed in the ward for terminal cases. During this time, after a visit from his deeply spiritual father, Ka'alakea had a vision; days later, the tuberculosis was gone. He believed that this was a calling from God into the ministry, an endeavor he soon pursued. Ka'alakea is one of those Hawaiians who was able to balance his great faith and love of the Christian God with his Hawaiian culture, not forsaking one for the other. A Pentecostal minister for Jesus Is the Way Church in Kīhei, Maui, Ka'alakea also held fast to the Hawaiian language, in which he had been raised but hadn't spoken much after he became a young man. It was after his father's visit to the hospital, where they prayed in Hawaiian, that Ka'alakea recommitted his life to the Hawaiian language at the same time that he made a commitment to God. He encouraged others to do the same, and worked to keep alive cultural traditions.

He was involved with other Maui cultural leaders and activists, such as Kahu Charles

Maxwell, Les Kuloloio, and Dana Naone Hall, in the protest against the removal of Hawaiian bones from Honokōhau, Maui. In a *Maui News* article by Valerie Monson written shortly after Papa Ka'alakea's death, Les Kuloloio said, "I will always see him walking the trail, doing his ministry on the slopes of Kīpahulu, Kaupō, Hāna, Honua'ula. His spirit and presence with our kūpuna will always be there when I need him. He was my kahu." Fellow Maui native Dana Naone Hall, in the same article, said, "Kahu was always there to accompany us on our spiritual and cultural journeys. The way he lived, his examples and teachings have made a difference in our lives. He has helped make me who I am."

One person wrote, "I only met Papa Ka'alakea a couple of times, but in those times that I did meet him he was a man of great warmth, aloha, and spiritual strength. He was very unassuming—ha'aha'a—but you could tell he stood upon a kahua [foundation] that was pa'a pono [solid in righteousness]. Anytime I heard anyone speak of him, and it was quite often, he was characterized by his love of God, his love of his people, and his great service to the community as a spiritual leader. He was an inspiration to all who knew him." (For more information and photos of Papa Ka'alakea see the website of Charles Maxwell at http://www.moolelo.com, and the 1998 video *Hawaiian Voices: Bringing Past to the Present* by Eddie Kamae.)

**Kū and Nālei Kahakalau**— *community leadership, culture, education, language, politics*. Long-time Hawaiian advocates and community activists Kū and Nālei Kahakalau are pathbreakers in the field of Hawaiian education. One former student wrote, "I personally know that their family, including their beautiful daughters, have dedicated

their lives to helping the children of Hawai'i succeed in life. A Hawaiian Academy, Kanu o ka 'Āina, at Honoka'a High School is a school within a school started by Kū and Nālei. This academy teaches everything that students need to succeed in life and continue their education, but from a Hawaiian perspective. From their first year [1997–98 school year] they started with only grades 10–12 and only 50 students. In the '98–'99 school year, there were over 80 students; in the 2000–01 school year, the Academy will expand [it has since become an independent charter school] to include grades K–12. This program is unbelievable; I was part of the first graduating class, and there were only 5 of us! I learned so much in just that one year than from all the rest of my high school years. What I enjoyed the most is how we learned the ancient traditions of our Hawaiian ancestors when at the same time we were very modernized. This past year the Academy was very fortunate to receive enough grants and support from our local Hawaiian organizations that they were able to have their own mini computer lab. The work that this family has done and is continuing to do to better the lives of Hawaiians is UNREAL."

**Duke Paoa Kahanamoku**—*community leadership, politics, sports*. Perhaps the most recognizable Hawaiian figure of the 20th century, "the Duke" was more than an Olympic Gold medalist, Hollywood actor, Goodwill Ambassador, and sheriff of Honolulu. As Annie Kilbey Silva recalled, "Duke embodied such grace and dignity. When he entered a room he had such elegance and humility. Despite all of his fame and fortune, he never failed to make a person feel that they were special. He truly embodied what it meant to be Hawaiian."

Duke Kahanamoku was born on 24 August 1890 on the estate of high chief Abner Pākī in Honolulu. Duke swam daily while growing up near Waikīkī. His powerful physique and natural athleticism were ideal for swimming. He later refined his swimming technique as a member of the Hui Nalu Canoe Club, which he helped form in 1908.

On 12 August 1911 Hawai'i held its first Amateur Athletic Union (AAU) sanctioned event for swimming. Without AAU recognition, swimmers could not compete on the U.S. continent and be eligible for the Olympics. Since Honolulu had no adequate swimming pool, the races were held in Honolulu Harbor. Duke startled the audience by winning the 50-yard freestyle in 24.2 seconds, beating the old record by 1.6 seconds. His winning time of 55.4 seconds in the 100-meter freestyle obliterated the old record by an incredible 4.6 seconds. Duke spent the next year competing on the U.S. continent and was chosen for the 1912 Olympic team. Duke finished off his Olympic debut in Stockholm with a gold medal for the 100-meter freestyle and a silver medal in the 4 x 200-meter freestyle relay. Duke was the gold medal favorite for the Berlin Games of 1916, but the competition was canceled due to World War I. The world will never know how many gold medals Duke would have won at those games.

During wartime, Duke swam in meets in Hawai'i and on the U.S. continent, helping to promote swimming. Swimmers from Hawai'i dominated the U.S. swim team at the 1920 Olympics in Antwerp, Belgium. On Duke's 30th birthday, he won the gold medal for the 100-meter freestyle in a world record time of 1:00.4, followed by his teammates Pua Kela Kealoha and Bill Harris. Duke also went on to help his Hawai'i teammates

win the 4 x 200-meter freestyle relay. At those Olympics, Hawai'i swimmers won a total of seven Olympic medals. In 1924 Duke was back at the Olympic Games held in Paris, France, and this time he brought along his 19-year-old brother, Sam. The 34-year-old Duke's reign as 100-meter freestyle champion came to an end in Paris, but it took an Olympic record by Johnny Weismuller to beat him. Duke's little brother Sam finished the American 100-meter freestyle sweep by finishing behind the Duke with the bronze medal.

Duke won medals, trophies, and worldwide fame as a swimmer, but he surfed purely for the fun of it in the era before surfing became the competitive sport of today. Although no spectacular video footage records his legendary longboard surfing, memorials and museums in Australia, California, Florida, New York, and Hawai'i pay tribute to his influence on the sport of surfing all over the world.

In his lifetime, Duke saw surfing grow from the pastime of a handful of enthusiasts to a multibillion dollar sport enjoyed by people around the world. By the end of Duke's extraordinary life, anywhere there were waves, there were surfers. Fifty million people watched the televised Sunset Beach first annual Duke Kahanamoku Invitational Surfing Championships in 1965. Yet the man known as the International Father of Modern Surfing never won a major surfing championship and never won money from it. He simply surfed for the love of it.

On 22 January 1968 the world bid its last farewell to Duke Kahanamoku. Thousands of people attended Duke's funeral on the shores of Waikīkī Beach. A flotilla of 14 canoes paddled out to scatter Duke's ashes. Throughout his remarkable life, Duke Kahanamoku had earned a slew of world records for swimming, including three Olympic gold medals. He also had performed minor roles in 30 Hollywood movies, rescued eight fisherman from a capsized launch off the California coast in 1925, and served 26 years as the sheriff of Honolulu. His accomplishments were many, but what Duke is most remembered for is the grace and dignity with which he lived. He was in every sense of the word a true Hawaiian.

***Jacob Iakopa Kaio Jr.***—*arts & humanities (music), community leadership, culture, sports, Hawaiian firsts.* Jacob Kaio was born in 1953 and grew up in Lāʻie, Oʻahu. His family raised taro, surfed, fished, and spoke Hawaiian. After Hawaiʻi became a state, his family moved to town, and by the age of nine he had started paddling canoe for the Waikīkī Surf Club. He was the first 16-year-old to ever cross the Molokaʻi channel, be in a senior men's crew, and place first in a canoe race. He grew up in the club, and eventually became a coach. He met his future wife of over 19 years while paddling canoe, and they presently live in Waimānalo.

Jacob Kaio has been recognized by the Celtic culture as the first Hawaiian in the world to play the bagpipes. In June 1999 he became the first Hawaiian to reach the level of Pipe Major in America for a bagpipe band. He currently leads the Honolulu Pipes and Drums of Hawaiʻi, which is sponsored by the Honolulu Police and Fire Departments.

His interest in the bagpipes began when he was nine. While paddling the Ala Wai Canal, he heard a lonely sound on the banks of the canal and tracked it down. Upon finding the piper, he learned that the gentleman was a

marine, and was leaving the islands. How could he ever learn the instrument? As fate would have it, years later he married a Scotswoman. One day, his in-laws invited him to a Scottish party, where then Pipe Major Lawrence Coleman asked if anyone

Jacob Iakopa Kaio Jr.

was interested in learning the bagpipes for free. "FREE!" thought Jacob. Too good to be true. After five years of playing, in which he won numerous awards, medals, and trophies from across the states, Jacob succeeded Lawrence Coleman, becoming the first Hawaiian to ever play or lead in the pipes.

***David Kalauokalani (Keawe)***—*community leadership, politics.* David Kalauokalani (whose last name is sometimes given as "Keawe"), was the President of Hui Kālaiʻāina during the anti-annexation petition drive at the end of the last century. He was among those who took the petitions to Washington, D.C., and lobbied successfully to have the annexation treaty killed in the U.S. Congress. (Congress subsequently annexed Hawaiʻi by way of the Newlands Resolution, illegal under both U.S. constitutional and international law.) He was co-founder and president of the Independent Home Rule Party.

**Moses Kalauokalani**—*culture*. Along with Richard Paglinawan, Moses Kalauokalani is one of the very few known ʻŌlohe Lua (Lua Masters) for Pā Kuʻi A Lua. Together with Noelani Mahoe, one person wrote, "these three leaders have dedicated much of their lives to educate Hawaiians about their culture and the nearly lost Hawaiian [martial] art of lua. Their aloha for our people is shown greatly. Whether or not you choose to recognize them as Hawaiians of the century, they are indeed Hawaiians of the century in the hearts of all their students." Moses is also the great-grandson of David Kalauokalani. (See the entries on Richard Paglinawan and Noelani Mahoe.)

**Lilikalā Kameʻeleihiwa**—*culture, education, language, politics*. Lilikalā Kameʻeleihiwa is the director of the Center for Hawaiian Studies at the University of Hawaiʻi at Mānoa. Trained as a historian and fluent in Hawaiian, she is also an expert on Hawaiian cultural traditions and in the Hawaiian sovereignty movement, and served as co-scriptwriter of the 1993 award-winning documentary *An Act of War: The Overthrow of the Hawaiian Nation*. Her books include *Nā Wāhine Kapu: Divine Hawaiian Women* (ʻAi Pōhaku Press, 1999); *He Moʻolelo Kaʻao o Kamapuaʻa: A Legendary Tradition of Kamapuaʻa, the Hawaiian Pig-God* (Bishop Museum Press, 1996); and *Native Land and Foreign Desires: Pehea Lā e Pono Ai?* (Bishop Museum Press, 1992).

She has served as protocol officer and crew member for the double-hulled Polynesian Voyaging Canoes *Hōkūleʻa* and *Hawaiʻiloa*, and wrote the first year-long course on Traditional Navigation offered at any university in the world. Since 1987, she has written another dozen courses in Hawaiian history, mythology, and culture for the Center for Hawaiian Studies.

**Dennis Keiki Puʻuhonua "Bumpy" Kanahele**—*community leadership, politics*. Bumpy's active support of Hawaiian land rights, self-determination, and self-governance for over 20 years has made him one of Hawaiʻi's most well-known advocates for independence. Frontline civil resistance has cost him his freedom on several occasions, but he used his time in prison to educate incarcerated Hawaiians on U.S. Public Law 103–150, the so-called "Apology Bill." After his probation was ended on 22 February 1999, he said, "I'm now working within the system to change the system." From his appointment to the Governor's Advisory Commission on Hawaiian Sovereignty in 1993 to his election in 1999 as a delegate to a Native Hawaiian convention, he is widely recognized throughout Hawaiʻi as a consistent voice for the just restoration of Native Hawaiian rights, gaining the respect of Hawaiians and non-Hawaiians, as well as the state's political and business leaders.

Presently, Bumpy is involved with the establishment of the first Native Hawaiian owned and controlled bank under the Community Development Financial Institution (CDFI) program. He sees this as a first step in the economic stabilization of Hawaiʻi. This bank would facilitate self-help programs and micro-enterprises to promote economic growth in the Hawaiian community. A tax-free economy, free health care, and affordable housing are all possible in Bumpy's vision of an independent Hawaiʻi.

Bumpy is currently a member of the International Indian Treaty Council, Waimānalo Neighborhood Board, and

Waimānalo Health Center. Bumpy's direct, honest approach and positive vision make him a dynamic public speaker who has brought clarity on the issues of Hawaiian sovereignty throughout Hawai'i and America.

As executive director of Aloha First—a 501(c)(3) non-profit corporation established in 1996 to restore and maintain the Native Hawaiian culture—Bumpy works tirelessly to perpetuate Pu'uhonua o Waimānalo village. Visits to the village are welcomed physically and virtually via the internet. (For more information visit the website at http://www. hawaii-nation.org.)

**Pualani Kanaka'ole Kanahele, Edward Kanahele, and Nālani Kanaka'ole Zane**— *community leadership, culture, language, politics.* For their many contributions to Hawaiian culture, language, and education, Noe Noe Wong-Wilson wrote, "Aunty Pua and Uncle Ed [who passed away 16 February 2000] have dedicated themselves to further-ing Hawaiians through education and understanding of our culture. They give tirelessly to the Hawaiian community and, most importantly, to their students. Through the Edith Kanaka'ole Foundation, they move forward the work of Aunty Pua's mother, the late Aunty Edith Kanaka'ole. As educators and instructors at Hawai'i Community College, they keep Hawaiian thought and tradition alive, and teach us our culture in a manner unique even in these modern times.

"Aunty Pua and her sister, Nālani Kanaka'ole, are kumu hula of the world-renowned Hālau o Kekuhi. They and the hālau have won numerous awards and honors for their work in Hawaiian chant and dance. Aunty Pua and Uncle Ed's work

goes well beyond the hālau. They are responsible for developing major projects like the Kalo Restoration Project in Waipi'o Valley and developing a curriculum for waste management based on Hawaiian practices and principles. They were co-chairpersons for the 1999 World Indigenous Peoples' Conference on Education, a historic gathering of native peoples held in Hilo, Hawai'i. In addition, they are often found at the forefront of significant Hawaiian movements, like the efforts to defend our gathering rights and stop further develop-ment on our sacred Mauna Kea.

"Edward and Pualani Kanaka'ole Kanahele are quiet and humble people who, along with their family, have greatly enhanced the lives of Hawaiians and should be recognized for their contribution."

Along with her work for the Edith Kanaka'ole Foundation, Aunty Pua is a founding member of 'Īlio'ulaokalani, a non-profit organization dedicated to the preservation of Native Hawaiian gathering rights and related issues.

In 1998, Aunty Pua received the Governor's Award for Distinguished Achievement in the Arts. In her honor, her student of Hawaiian language and culture Leilehua Omphroy composed the following *mele inoa* (name song), and together with other students chanted it to their *kumu* (teacher) as "a makana of their aloha." In regard to the title of the *mele*, Leilehua says, "The lei is a gift from the land and Pua is a gift also, because she is from the land. She gave me of her knowledge and I wanted to express to her how I felt about it, even in the simple Hawaiian that I knew. I wanted to give her something back, something from inside more valuable than something you can buy."

Lei Pualani

Eō e Pualani, ku'u kumu kūpono
Nani 'oe i nā pua o nā moku o Hawai'i
Haku au i lei pua nani
He ho'onani kēia nou e Pualani.

Pua 'a'ali'i o Ka'ū
'O Ka'ū hiehie i ka makani
Lūlū 'ia ka hua ma ka 'āina
He 'a'ali'i kū makani 'oe.

Pua hīnano o Puna
'O Puna paia 'ala i ka hala
Ka māliko me ka 'a'ala
Onaona ka 'āina iā 'oe.

Pua lehua o Hilo
'O Hilo i ka ua kani lehua
Makalapua ka lehua me ka mana
Ho'ohala 'ia ka na'aupō me kou 'ike.

Pua 'awapuhi o Waipi'o
'O Waipi'o 'āina o nā 'aumākua
Ulu nā pua o ka wā ma mua
Ho'opili 'oe i ka wā kahiko me kēia ao.

Haku i lei kukui o Kohala
'O Kohala i ka unu pa'a
Eia ka lei mālamalama
Ho'omālamalama 'oe na mākou.

Wili 'ia ka lei hinahina o Kona
'O Kona ka 'āina o Keolonāhihi
He lei ho'ohihi nui 'ia
He makamae 'oe na mākou.

'O kā mākou lei pua nani
Pua nani o Hawai'i
'O kā mākou lei poina 'ole
Lei Pualani, Pualani Kanahele.

**Herb Kawainui Kane**—*arts & humanities
(art), community leadership, education.* Herb

Kane is widely known as a contemporary Hawaiian painter and artist who has spent most of his career depicting and recreating traditional Hawaiian historical scenes, gods, and landscapes. Such research and vision also helped bring into existence the *Hōkūle'a* (which he designed and named), the first Polynesian-inspired double-hulled voyaging canoe built in modern times, under the auspices of the Polynesian Voyaging Society, which he co-founded with Ben Finney and Tommy Holmes in 1973. His dream would inspire the building of other canoes, such as *Hawai'iloa*, and voyages to all parts of the Polynesian triangle and other areas of the Pacific. Kane was educated at Chicago University and the Art Institute of Chicago, and lived in Wisconsin for many years before returning home to Hawai'i in 1971. His work appears in many state buildings around the islands, and can also be seen on various postage stamps for the United States (6), Marshall Islands (18), French Polynesia (4) and the Federated States of Micronesia (6).

Kane was one of 16 Hawaiians selected as *po'okela* (master) in his field in the 1987 Year of the Hawaiian celebration. He has also been honored with a Living Treasure of Hawai'i award. He currently resides in south Kona on the island of Hawai'i. (For more information see Kane's publications *Voyage: the Discovery of Hawaii* (Island Heritage, 1976); *Pele: The Goddess of Hawai'i's Volcanoes* (Kawainui Press, 1987); *Voyagers* (WhaleSong, 1991); and *Ancient Hawai'i* (Kawainui Press, 1997). Kane is also featured in a segment of the 1987 video *E mau ana ka ha'aheo* (Enduring Pride) produced by Heather Giugni under Juniroa Productions.)

**James Keauiluna Kaulia**—*community leadership, politics.* James Kaulia was born on 16 August 1860 at Hōlualoa, Kona, Hawai'i. His parents were G. W. and Eva Laioha. When he was three years old, he was adopted by G. and Mikala Ahia. The family moved to Honolulu, where young Kaulia attended Kawaiaha'o district school and Kehehuna school. He married Maraea Malaihi in 1879. In the same year, his mother, Mikala Ahia, married Asa Kaulia. James became his adopted son and took his name. James studied law while working in the sheriff's office in Hilo under J. L. Kaulukou and S. K. Kāne. When Joseph Nāwahī founded Hui Hawai'i Aloha 'Āina (Hawaiian Patriotic League) after the overthrow in 1893, Kaulia served as secretary. After the death of Nāwahī in 1896, Kaulia was elected president of the Hui. He led the Hui in the massive anti-annexation petition drive in 1897. He was one of four delegates selected to take the petitions to Washington, D.C.; the others were David Kalauokalani, William Auld, and John Richardson. Their efforts succeeded in defeating the 1897 Treaty of Annexation. In 1900, Hui Aloha 'Āina (under Kaulia) and Hui Kālai'āina (under Kalauokalani) merged, becoming the Independent Home Rule Party, and Kauila became its vice-president. He died in 1902 at the young age of 42 at his home at Kaumakapili Church, after spending the morning helping prisoners at the jailhouse in Honolulu assert their civil rights.

**Brian Lopaka Keaulana**—*community leadership, government service, sports*. A lifeguard for Honolulu County Department of Parks and Recreation since 1978, Brian Lopaka Keaulana received a Medal of Valor in 1993, for heroically rescuing a tourist from a sea cave along Farrington Highway after the man was swept off the road by an unexpected wave. Brian is heavily involved in the Junior Lifeguard programs, aimed at giving career guidance to youth on the Wai'anae coast. He is a world-renowned surfer, known

especially for his big-wave riding prowess. He is an invitee to the Eddie Aikau Competition at Waimea, and an expert canoe and tandem surfer, as well as a coordinator of water stunts for Hollywood productions. Brian is the oldest son of the famous big-wave surfer Buffalo Keaulana.

**Curtis Kekoa**—*community leadership, law, military service*. A full-blooded Hawaiian, Curtis Kekoa is one of many Hawaiians who has served in the United States military forces, continuing the proud warrior heritage of our Hawaiian ancestors. Now in his 80s, Mr. Kekoa retired as a full colonel in the United States Air Force after 30 years of military service. Acting at times as lead pilot for the Wing (54 B-17 bombers), Colonel Kekoa flew 20 combat missions over Europe during World War II. Each mission usually involved over 1,000 airplanes. The aircraft losses from such bombing missions were staggering, often running as high as 30 percent. Colonel Kekoa was declared a hero, and during his military career he received such awards as Legion of Merit, Distinguished Flying Cross, Bronze Star, Air Medal with seven oak leaf clusters, and the Meritorious Service Medal. He also flew 100 jet combat missions in the Korean War and was the Director of Operations of the Royal Thai Air Force Advisory Group (JUSMAGTH-AI) during the Vietnam War.

Following his distinguished military service, Colonel Kekoa attended law school, graduating from the University of Southern California School of Law. He served as an attorney in Hawai'i from 1978 to 1991. During this time, he became chairman of the Ad Hoc Committee for a Hawaiian Trustee to the Bishop Estate. In 1972 this Committee spearheaded the first movement to place a Hawaiian on the Board of Trustees for The

Kamehameha Schools/Bishop Estate. The Committee represented 20 different Hawaiian entities and enlisted support by meeting with groups on O'ahu, Maui, and the island of Hawai'i. Arising from the Committee's efforts was the landmark case *Kekoa et al. v. Supreme Court of Hawaii and Board of Trustees*, which challenged the Supreme Court justices' failure to appoint a Hawaiian trustee to the Bishop Estate. The outcome of the Committee's efforts resulted in the appointment of "Papa" Richard Lyman, followed by other Hawaiian trustees.

**Jacob Keli'ikipi**—*sports, Hawaiian firsts*. Like many Hawaiians, Jacob Keli'ikipi loved adventure. He was the first Hawaiian bullfighter...yes, bullfighter. He fought in Aguascalientes, Mexico, as a *novillero* [apprentice matador]. As a Kona native, he most certainly would have been familiar with wild cattle roaming the slopes of Hualalai, but few Kona kids venture as far as Mexico to tackle the bulls. What an inspiration!

**Samuel Pailthorp King**—*community leadership, law*. Samuel P. King, son of Samuel W. King (see below) was the first Federal District Judge of Hawaiian ancestry. A graduate of Yale University and Law School, he served as an attorney in Hawai'i for over 50 years and in many other capacities helping the Hawaiian community. Most recently, he co-authored the article "A Broken Trust," which launched a full-scale investigation into the Bishop Estate, resulting in the unprecedented removal and replacement of all five Bishop Estate trustees. Samuel P. King showed leadership qualities from his youth: as a teen he won a national speech contest and a trip to Europe. He served as a naval officer in World War II, despite not having the use of one eye. One person wrote, "He is

a man of great integrity, who has spent his entire life trying to make Hawai'i a better place. Throughout his life he has encouraged other Hawaiians to strive for excellence and to make their way proudly in the world as Hawaiians."

**Samuel Wilder King**—*government service, politics, Hawaiian firsts*. Samuel Wilder King was the first Hawaiian governor of Hawai'i prior to statehood, appointed in 1953. He fought for statehood for many years, because he felt that, as a territory, Hawai'i was being unfairly represented as a second-class member of the United States. He was the first Native Hawaiian graduate of the U.S. Naval Academy at Annapolis, and the second commissioned Navy officer of Hawaiian ancestry (the first was Victor Houston). He served in both World War I and World War II, and was Hawai'i's elected delegate to the United States Congress for many years (he left Congress before being elected for a fifth term in order to rejoin the Navy in World War II). It is interesting to note, too, that he never lost an election.

Samuel Wilder King also served as a trustee of the Bishop Estate, and was a pioneer in fee simple real estate in Hawai'i. One of his most important deeds was ensuring the rights of Japanese Americans in Hawai'i during World War II by not allowing the Federal government to put Japanese who were American citizens into work camps. Instead, he and Joe Farrington convinced the government that a curfew for the entire territory would provide enough safety for Hawai'i. As a result, most of Hawai'i's Japanese kept their land and property, as well as their freedom, in marked contrast to those living on the U.S. continent.

**Napu Kong**—*community leadership, culture*. One person wrote, "Aunty Napu

Kong, who I have known all of my life, lives at the bottom of the Koʻolau mountains in Kahaluʻu, on Oʻahu. She is the most generous and giving person I know. She is involved in so many Hawaiian organizations that perpetuate the Hawaiian culture, and what I love most about her is that if you ever need help with anything, fundraising, lūʻaus, support, sometimes you don't even have to say anything and she is right there helping. I would say that she is one of the unspoken ones, the ones who are never heard of, but work so hard. She is also a Kupuna at one of the elementary schools on Oʻahu. You should see her, it's the middle of summer and she is already planning on what to share with the children, she gets so excited, her face just lights up. She is a Hawaiian of the Century."

**Jesse James Walani Kuhaulua**—*sports, Hawaiian firsts.* A Maui native, Jesse Kuhaulua was the first foreigner in Japan to enter the world of sumo wrestling, Japan's national sport. Jesse Kuhaulua's journey to becoming the first non-Asian sumo wrestler in the history of the sport was not an easy one. When he was in the second grade, he was hit by a car. Even though the accident damaged both Jesse's legs, it did not weaken his determination to make the Baldwin High School football team. During his four years at Baldwin, he helped his team win four straight Maui championships and became an all-star tackle in his senior year. His football coach at Baldwin, Larry Shishido, recommended that Jesse try sumo to strengthen his legs. Jesse then joined the Maui Sumo Club and trained under coach Isamu Ogasawara.

Jesse practiced hard and his efforts paid off. After being noticed by Japanese sumo coaches training in Hawaiʻi, Jesse was invited in February 1964 to wrestle against Japan's top sumo wrestlers at an exhibition in Honolulu. He gave a solid performance, making such an impression that famed stablemaster Takasago invited him to join his stable in Tokyo. Soon after, 19-year-old Jesse was in Japan and starting a new life.

Jesse's transition into Japanese culture was a challenging one to say the least. His athletic ability was only surpassed by his mental fortitude. He learned a new language, adapted to the harsh winters, and silenced his critics who predicted his failure. He assumed the ring name of Takamiyama Daigoro ("mountain of the lofty view"), after the renowned champion of the 19th century and the founder of Takasago stable.

In 1967, Jesse became the first non-Asian wrestler to earn a salary. His greatest accomplishment was in July of 1972 when he became the first non-Asian to win a tournament, earning the victory of the Emperor's Cup at the 15-day summer tournament in Nagoya. The historic win was recognized by U.S. Ambassador Roger Ingersoll, who walked up to the sumo ring and read a letter of congratulations from President Richard Nixon. The message signified the first time that English had been officially spoken in a sumo ring.

During his illustrious career from 1964 to 1984, Jesse reached sumo's third highest rank of *sekiwake* (junior champion) and made numerous records, including a streak of 1,231 consecutive matches in the *makuuchi* (elite) division and the most career matches at 1,653. In 1980 Jesse applied for Japanese citizenship and assumed the new name of Daigoro Watanabe, to reflect his wife's maiden name. Upon his retirement in 1984, the Japanese Sumo Association gave him the name Azumazeki Oyakata. In 1986 Jesse made history again when he became the first non-Asian wrestler to open his own stable, Azumazaki Beya.

Jesse Kuhaulua's stellar career led the way for many sumo hopefuls, including Chad Rowan (Akebono), who went on to capture Japan's highest sumo title of *yokozuna* (grand champion). (See the entry on Chad Rowan.) The dignity and grace which personifies his style and gentle demeanor has earned Jesse the respect not only of the Japanese people, but of the Hawaiian community as well.

***John Keola Lake***—*community leadership, culture, education, language.* An educator by profession, John Lake has for more than 30 years taught courses at St. Louis High School in Honolulu, such as social studies, English, Spanish, and Hawaiian Studies, a course he introduced there in 1965. He also started the Hawaiian-language program at Chaminade University in the 1970s, where he still teaches during the summers. In the 1970s and 1980s, he taught hula and chant through the Hawaiian Music Foundation, eventually starting his own Hawaiian Academy, which is currently housed at the Center for Hawaiian Studies at the University of Hawai'i-Mānoa campus. For his dedication to Hawaiian culture and arts, he was honored with a Living Treasure of Hawai'i award in 1987.

Kumu Lake is recognized in Hawai'i as a leading figure in the re-establishment of the deepest ritual practices that re-instill meaning to our most sacred sites and works. His efforts to reinvigorate the *heiau* of Pu'ukoholā at Kawaihae in Kohala on the island of

Hawai'i is a continuing and powerful act of devotion that has led to the training of a growing cadre of practitioners of the art of *oli* (chant) and *hana kūpono* (appropriate protocol). This new generation of Hawaiians is thereby empowered to learn, understand, appreciate, preserve, and promulgate their cultural heritage, meaningfully unifying their rich past with an equally rich present. Kumu Lake has on many occasions assisted with the selection and delivery of powerful protocol to mark events of great significance. The reunification of the descendants of the families of Kamehameha and the vanquished chief Keōua Kū'ahu'ula at Pu'ukoholā 200 years after Keōua's sacrifice there was perhaps one of the most remarkable of these. Many lives have been profoundly touched by this single event, with ramifications that stretch far indeed. Kumu Lake serves on many advisory boards, including those of the National Park Service in Hawai'i and the Bernice Pauahi Bishop Museum. He has provided for the cultural needs of the staff of Outrigger Hotels many times in the past, and assisted with the cultural training and development of the concept of the Hawaiian sense of place and its role in defining the uniqueness of the Hawaiian experience.

One student wrote, "I have described Kumu Lake to other people as a sort of living day Hawaiian Santa Claus! He is the jolliest person I know, always pleasant and pretty much optimistic. He has the ideal personality! He trained in the traditional style, and dedicated himself to the continuity of the Hawaiian arts, to share with people of all heritages. He maintains a hālau that teaches dance, chant, language, protocol, and various related arts.

"Particularly to me he is like a father; Kumu Lake has so much knowledge in so many subjects, he speaks many different languages fluently and with such love and skill in each one. Yet he is so extremely humble about all that he knows. He shares wholeheartedly with those close to him, with others reaching for his closeness, and to strangers from every walk of life that he embraces, without hesitation. He is the perfect example of a Hawaiian living today and still embodying the presence of his ancestors from all ancient times before. An example of that is his religion. Many people ask how he can be such a strong Catholic and a strong Hawaiian cultural practitioner. He just said the other night that he answers that by saying, 'I was born Hawaiian first! I respect and look to Him in so many aspects of life. I hold God dear, as well as everything.' Kumu Lake teaches me so many aspects of life, especially religion, since I am Catholic as well. I hold God dear as well as everything Kumu Lake teaches me about Hawaiian ancient times and respecting all the spirituality of it all. Kumu Lake is the only kumu I know that sincerely wants to share all of his knowledge with any that respectfully want to learn. He has taken on students that just wanted to learn, and maybe couldn't pay him. He would always say, 'Come!' He also will find a way to do things for his haumāna [students] when they need help. He will sew things himself, block print them, make leis, make hula implements, etc. Other kumu I know don't do these things! With Kumu Lake, no matter how hard things are, he always will teach his haumāna to make things for them-selves because he knows how. He will teach, do, and learn whenever needs be; to me, he can do almost ANYTHING!!!"

***Jacqueline Lokelani Lau***—*culture.* Caroline Leilani Lau wrote: "My sister is the reason that I am proud to be Hawaiian. Slow learner that I am, when she was alive,

mostly, we didn't get along. Maybe it was because she was about six years older, but I sense that it might have been all that mystery between us that both draws me to her and confused me when I was a child. As far as her formal accomplishments go, she was Kapalapala Queen while she attended the University of Hawai'i and picked up a few other assorted trophies. Jacqueline Lokelani also danced with 'Iolani Luahine when it was frowned upon to be associated with such 'dark forces.'

"The hula was not revered in the fifties while I was growing up: the stated goal of the territory was to become the 50th state. Everything was *haole* or wannabe *haole*, except for the 'underground' multi-ethnic forces. In those days, my eldest Chinese aunt on my mother's side would drive out to Wai'alae when it was just a dirt road and chicken farms to buy what she called 'non-injection chicken.' Upon returning home, one by one she would slit the jugular veins while saving the blood as I held the struggling feet fighting for life. My mother had me fingerprinted and identified because she was afraid I would be kidnapped. You might say fear and pretending to be *haole* was a big part of life with my parents in those days.

"Strangely, I really don't know my sister very well. It was as though her body could be in the same room as mine and yet it was as if she wasn't real. Maybe this is what keeps our relationship growing, because now that I am 53 and she has been dead for a long time, we only have a spiritual life to reconcile and overcome differences. As I lived each year beyond her own 34 years on earth, sometimes I feel cheated that we have no history of sharing our adult lives with each other. Where is my sister? I can't even remember the sound of her laughter. But I do remember that young, smooth body, her passion for hula and her attraction to dream.

"Though I am a writer, purposefully, I am not fancy-dancing on the page because Jacqueline to me represents the ordinary Hawaiian like the sacrificed chicken—struggling to be alive with honor in the face of adversity. As I successfully went along with the wannabe *haole* attitude and crowd, my sister chose to be proud she was Hawaiian and Hakka. Since no one volunteered to explain anything to me, I just didn't understand my parents or my sister while growing up. It's painful to reflect on my childhood and have no memories of the family smiling together doing this or that at this or that occasion.

"Some people have even accused me of not being Hawaiian, and while it upsets me to pull out my birth certificate and name family members who would scoff at the idea that I am not, it is a weird feeling having been raised in Mōʻiliʻili which has a limited conscious Hawaiian history—as opposed to Waiʻanae, which is my favorite *ahupuaʻa*. Not Hawaiian enough, not Chinese enough—imagine my confusion at 48 when as I sat in my cousin's back seat of the car, she calmly told me that our Hawaiian grandmother's last name was Machado! Wow: the mystery of my childhood growing up near to my Hawaiian family and only being exposed to them once during my cousin's wedding.

"I guess I am writing to nominate my sister Jacqueline Lokelani Lau as a notable Hawaiian because she is like the poster girl who was and is somebody real beneath the romantic popular image. Not that the hula poster girls are or were impostors, but that my sister, in her great beauty as a dancer,

never achieved success as appreciated by Western standards. Over the years, Lokelani, named after my Tūtū Rose, has developed into a symbol for the psychic pain that manifests in the bodies of Hawaiians. Unlike the Japanese who were conquered by 'us' Americans, Hawaiians were not permitted to speak our natural tongue. In terms of hermeneutics (interpretation) and linguistics (structure of speech), there are some powerful implications, most of which are unfavorable. As I write about my sister and my impressions, this is not intended as confession, as there is no shame or bad deed which we shared: in my comings and goings among Hawaiians in California, unless one is attached to a *hālau*, many Hawaiians still feel bad about being Hawaiian. If they are not dancing or singing in a group, somehow, they are ashamed. Hey! A Hawaiian does not have to sing or dance to be Hawaiian. Generally, Hawaiians love to sing and/or dance but it is not essential to the perception of our being that mandates this unspoken edict. In terms of *hoʻoponopono* as we approach the millennium, as the *Kumulipo* is not static—because that would contradict the laws of nature upon which it is based, my wish for all Hawaiians is that we participate in a ceremonial *hiʻu wai*—wherever we are—to pray and include all *kānaka* in our prayers that we be healed from any and all scars of the past, discard the behavioral and cognitive imprints that misled our lives and once again *nānā i ke kumu*, return to positive wisdom which has been passed down in the families for generations but might have been neglected for reasons beyond our knowledge or control. Let the *makaʻāinana* stand tall and be counted. Let there be no divisions among who may or may not look or act Hawaiian but simply is Hawaiian and may be secretly still ashamed of not measuring up to an ambiguous standard. Let the future be represented by our purified hearts and actions. Let Lokelani Lau, an unknown hula dancer, be a formal symbol of a Hawaiian consciousness that deserves recognition because she lived—so determinedly Hawaiian."

*Kwai Wah Lee*—*community leadership, culture, education, language*. While many people are familiar with the Hawaiian Studies/Kupuna Program run by the Department of Education (DOE), few people, if any, have given a thought as to when, why, and how this program originated. According to the 75th Keaukaha Homestead Anniversary History Book, the program is only one of many community-based accomplishments of Keaukaha Homesteader Kwai Wah Lee. In 1969, then PTA President and Curriculum Committee Chairperson Kwai Wah Lee led a historical movement at Keaukaha Elementary School: the introduction and establishment of the first Hawaiiana Program for all grade levels, including a community night-school program. This was the beginning of the Hawaiian Studies/Kupuna Program that would eventually be adopted at elementary schools throughout the state. This initiative began as a community-based effort called Project IMUA. The objectives of the program were, in part, (1) to develop an interest in Hawaiian history, language, and culture; (2) to encourage self-expression through hula, Hawaiian language, and native music and arts; (3) to stimulate the creativity of Hawaiian youth through hands-on arts, crafts, games, and implement making utilizing native material; and (4) to develop leadership among the junior population of the Keaukaha Homestead through employment and summer programs. This project became a joint effort between the

DOE and the Keaukaha Homestead Association, and included such esteemed community members as Edith Kanaka'ole (Project Coordinator), Maile Akimseu, Abbie Napeahi, and Eleanor Ahuna. Kwai Wah Lee served as the Keaukaha-Pana'ewa Homestead Association President at this time.

It was during this period that Kwai Wah successfully led the fight to preserve the Keaukaha Hawaiian Homestead lands by protecting the residential neighborhood against the County of Hawai'i's plans to evict homesteaders to expand the Hilo Airport and turn the entire Keaukaha region into a light industrial park. Major portions of the Keaukaha Homestead around the Ewaliko, Krauss, Lyman, and Ka'uhane Avenues would have been eliminated, which would have resulted in the eviction of 172 Hawaiian families from approximately 50 acres of Hawaiian Home Lands. Kwai Wah was one of the first to question the County's power to do such planning and land grabbing, particularly without the consent of the Department of Hawaiian Home Lands. While many Hawaiians before and since have fought valiantly (and sometimes successfully) against illegal land deals, there is a particularly interesting twist to Kwai Wah Lee's story.

When Kwai Wah was president of the Keaukaha Homestead Association in 1970, he felt compelled to educate himself about the history of the 1920 Hawaiian Homestead Act, in order to be better prepared to fight Hawai'i County's plans to evict the Keaukaha Homesteaders. First he wrote to then Hawai'i Senator Hiram Fong, asking for assistance in locating Prince Jonah Kūhiō Kalaniana'ole's speech before Congress in 1920 which led to the establishment of the Homestead Act. Next Kwai Wah and other association leaders went to Honolulu to seek legal advice. While visiting attorney Stanley H. Roehrig, Kwai Wah noticed a large book in the trashcan. He asked Mr. Roehrig about it, who gave it to him, saying it was just "an old book." Kwai Wah had been a high school drop out, but he set his mind to reading the entire book, hoping it could educate him on legal matters pertaining to the situation at hand. It did, as this law books was the basis for his newly acquired knowledge of law in relation to the Hawaiian Homes Commission, Department of Hawaiian Home Lands, and Federal jurisdiction. Armed with legal knowledge, Kwai Wah unveiled the illegality of Hawai'i County's rezoning plans for the Keaukaha and Pana'ewa Homesteads.

Kwai Wah's perseverance created a firestorm in the media, with local headlines reading "Authority to Change Zoning is Challenged" and "DHHL Land Rezoning Said Illegal." Following this near catastrophe, he tried to get authorization for a Federal investigation of the Department of Hawaiian Home Lands, but the Keaukaha Homestead membership failed to come through. While this prompted Kwai Wah to resign as Association President, he continued, in his own way, to support Hawaiian rights and educational efforts, including supporting the college education of his five children. Furthermore, Kwai Wah's actions prompted the first inventory of Hawaiian Home Lands, resulting in a 1973 finding that there was a "substantial disparity" (approximately 13,622 acres) between present lands and those originally set aside in the Hawaiian Homestead Act.

**Queen Lili'uokalani (Lydia Lili'u Loloku Walania Kamaka'eha)**—*arts & humanities (literature, music), community leadership, culture, language, politics*. The last reigning

*ali'i* of the independent Hawaiian nation, Queen Lili'uokalani is a beloved symbol for Hawaiian people, even today. She has left two enduring legacies: first, her extensive collection of musical compositions, most of which have just recently been published in a beautiful collection by Hui Hānai; and second, her trust, commonly known as the Queen Lili'uokalani Children's Trust, to benefit Hawai'i's children. She is nominated for her tireless and unending attempts to restore the independence of the Hawaiian nation, her grace and dignity under tremendous pressures, and her commitment to peace and to *ka lāhui Hawai'i*, the Hawaiian people. (For more information see Lili'uokalani's autobiography *Hawaii's Story by Hawaii's Queen* (Mutual Publishing, 1990), and *The Queen's Songbook* (Hui Hānai, 1999).)

**Ivan M. Lui-Kwan**—*community leadership, law*. Ivan Lui-Kwan is one of the many Hawaiians who have committed themselves to the cause of improving the health of native Hawaiians. In his former capacity as executive vice president and chief operating officer of the Queen's Health Care Systems, he collaborated with other non-profit and community-based organizations across Polynesia to establish stronger relationships between Hawaiians and other Polynesians, from whom he believes we could learn more about ourselves and our cultural heritage. In his vision of Queen's role as a community builder, he also advocated for investment in community health centers in areas with greater health needs. Ivan Lui-Kwan has his degree in law, and worked on behalf of the native Hawaiian community for many years prior to his involvement with the Queen's Health Care System. His son Kalama wrote, "He has made significant contributions to the native Hawaiian community as an attorney and also, during those same years, as an activist for political leaders that he believed would service the Hawaiian community. There are many people who would be better able than me to speak about these contributions. The reason I am nominating him is because, as my father, he has impressed upon me the Hawaiian value of selflessness. Now that I am 29 and a lawyer myself, I can see the sacrifices that he made to ensure that my brother and I had the best possible opportunity to learn and grow emotionally, spiritually, physically, and intellectually. In high school, he spent countless hours in his law office to support me and my brother, but still made time to attend my track meets and basketball and soccer games. I am sharing my feelings for him in this forum because I believe that while his professional contributions to Hawaiians should be sufficient to earn him a place on your list, they also reveal a selfless dedication to his peers that does not come at the expense of his children."

**Tandy Ka'ohu MacKenzie**—*arts & humanities (music)* (born 10 March 1892, Hāna, Maui; died 9 November 1963). A native of Hāna, Maui, Tandy MacKenzie was the first of a handful of Hawaiians who took their musical talents outside Hawaiian music and into the realm of opera. A Kamehameha graduate (class of 1910), MacKenzie left Hawai'i soon after finishing high school to pursue his passion for opera, eventually achieving a reputation as a world-class operatic tenor. MacKenzie studied music in Toronto, New York, Paris, and Milan and appeared in operas such as *La Bohème, Äida, Tosca, Cavalleria Rusticana, Rigoletto, Il Travatore*, and *Pagliacci*. He sang in many places, from Honolulu to Czechoslovakia, from Paris to Tokyo, and was honored as one of the few singers allowed to sing in

Italian (rather than German) in Munich at the State National Theater. He appeared in several Hollywood movies: *San Francisco, Anthony Adverse, Going to Town*, and *There's Magic in Music*. He was also a recording artist for Columbia Records, recording Hawaiian songs such as "Nā Lei o Hawai'i" and "'Imi Au Iā 'Oe." Towards the end of his life, he worked as a voice instructor. Tandy MacKenzie demonstrated the spirit of adventure that many Hawaiians have in pursuing his passion for music outside Hawaiian parameters, but in such a Hawaiian way. (For more information see the biography *Tandy* by Jean S. MacKenzie (Island Heritage, 1975); the phonograph of the same name (Island Heritage, 1976); and *Hawaiian Music and Musicians* by George S. Kanahele (University of Hawai'i Press, 1979).)

**Archibald Scott Mahaulu**—*community leadership, law*. Judge Archibald "Archie" Scott Mahaulu was the district magistrate of the Waialua, O'ahu, district from 1900 to 1916 and the first magistrate to occupy the Waialua courthouse when it opened in 1913. (The courthouse, which is located in Hale'iwa, was recently restored and is now managed by OHA.) He was educated at 'Iolani School and first worked as a law clerk for the law firm of Lorrin Thurston and F. M. Hatch. In later years, Thurston was to have the dubious distinction of being the leader of the Annexation Movement (and was instrumental in overthrowing Queen Lili'uokalani and the Hawaiian government). In 1885, Archie Mahaulu worked for the Department of the Interior under King Kalākaua, and in that same year was commissioned as a second lieutenant in the Queen's Own—the bodyguard unit of Queen Kapi'olani. In 1886, he became a captain in the Queen's Own. He was a good friend and golf partner of Prince Jonah Kūhiō

Kalaniana'ole and at times accompanied Kūhiō on his neighbor island trips. As a friend of Kūhiō, he was a staunch Republican and, it is said, quite an orator.

In his lifetime, he held other positions as well: police captain, boys' probation officer, deputy tax assessor and collector of the Waialua District, and assistant lay pastor of the Waialua Protestant Church. His grand-niece wrote, "If I were asked the question, 'If you could invite anyone to dinner, who would you invite?' My answer would be, 'My grand uncle Archie.' Just think of all the fascinating stories he could share with us at the dinner table! Tales of both rogues and royalty."

**Noelani Mahoe**—*culture*. An 'Ōlohe Haka for Pā Ku'i A Lua, Noelani Mahoe, along with Richard Paglinawan and Moses Kalauokalani, is one of three leaders of the Pā who, as one person wrote, "have dedicated much of their lives to educate Hawaiians about their culture and the nearly lost Hawaiian [martial] art of lua." She is also a talented singer, and co-author of *101 Hawaiian Mele*. (See the entries on Richard Paglinawan and Moses Kalauokalani.)

**Thomas Kananiokeaupunimālamalama Maunupau Jr.**— *community leadership, culture, language*. Laulani Teale wrote, "Uncle Tom Maunupau was an important kupuna who passed away in December 1998. He was the son of Tom Maunupau Sr., a very early Kanaka Maoli rights advocate (from the 1930s) and scholar, who was instrumental in the struggle for Papakōlea, amongst other things. (Side note: He brought President Roosevelt to Papakōlea, the only time I know of since Cleveland that an American President has come here to be involved in a Kanaka Maoli struggle). Uncle

Tommy (Jr.) was the classic embodiment of the humble and powerful aloha spirit. He loved everybody; he had no enemies except oppression itself. He advocated and taught 'ōlelo Hawai'i everywhere: in the prisons, at bus stops, at OHA, at sovereignty gatherings, at parties, etc. He could always be seen riding the bus in his baseball cap and misfitting clothes, striking an educational conversation with someone he'd just met, with a masking taped-up 'ukulele and a book full of songs, language lessons, and sovereignty articles. He fiercely advocated for Kanaka Maoli rights and against the theft of our lands, culture, and government, with no malice whatsoever. He was extremely articulate and down-to-earth; internationally renowned professors were blown away by him. He attracted and taught many young people from around the world and formed a band (I was in it) called Uncle Tommy's Aloha 'Āina Gang, which performed at many sovereignty gatherings and cultural functions. He was a Hawaiian Advisory Council member (even though he disagreed with too much working 'in the system')."

**Charles Kauluwehi Maxwell**—*community leadership, culture*. A native of Maui who currently resides in Pukalani, Charles Kauluwehi Maxwell has been a champion for Hawaiian culture and rights for many decades. A retired (disabled) police officer, he is married to *kumu hula* Nina Boyd Maxwell, and is currently a Hawaiian Cultural and Spiritual Consultant and Hawaiian Storyteller at the Maui Ocean Center. In addition, he has taught and lectured on Hawaiian culture and related issues at schools, colleges, and universities throughout the Hawaiian islands as well as in Alaska. He has also appeared on many local and national television shows and documentaries, from *Sam Choy's Kitchen* to *Good Morning America*.

He started his mission for Hawaiian rights in the early '70s, and was closely involved in regaining control of Kaho'olawe from the U.S. military. He was instrumental in getting T-shirt vendors out of sacred 'Īao valley, and for stopping the wanton and thoughtless mass slaughter of sharks after a woman was fatally injured by a tiger shark in waters off Olowalu in 1991. Through his efforts, the state established a task force on shark hunting, of which he was a part; his involvement helped educate Hawaiians and the general public about the role of 'aumākua (ancestral family guardians) that sharks have in Hawaiian culture and traditional society. In 1996, the *Honolulu Advertiser* chose him as one of ten people who "made a difference in Hawai'i." In 1998, just prior to the death of Kahu David Ka'alakea, he was passed Papa Ka'alakea's spiritual torch and blessed with his *hā* in the traditional manner, and is now an ordained Christian minister. (See the entry on Papa David Ka'alakea.)

Commenting on his achievements and how he has been such an inspiration to others, his daughter wrote, "He has been involved in many issues, from Kaho'olawe to the reawakening of Hawaiian rights; he has fought for protecting our 'āina, our iwi, our Kānaka Maoli, our 'aumākua, and for insuring these inherit rights will benefit the keiki of today and the next millennium. He is a person who goes against the tide rather than with it. By doing this his voice and his mana'o is heard by all. He is not one waiting in the wings, but is in the front line like a warrior always ready to defend the rights of the Hawaiian people. He has taught me that you can't just talk about something you don't agree with—you must do something about it. Take a stand and make a difference."

Of "Uncle Charlie" one person wrote, "Wow! Such energy, heart, and wisdom all rolled into a delightful boyish charismatic persona. A living treasure." Another said, "He has made many attempts to let people know who and what the Kānaka Maoli are and what we stand for, and most of his attempts that I can remember have been successful. In my mind he has never let the Hawaiian people down. He has a tough head on his shoulders, which at times might frighten people, but they know his compassion and passion for the Kānaka Maoli is what occupies his heart, and that attitude is what leaves a lasting impression on people. They always remember that he means business for the Hawaiian people." (For more information visit the website of "Uncle Charlie" Maxwell at http://www.moolelo.com.)

**Edward McCorriston Sr.**—*community leadership, law*. An editorial in the *Maui News* dated 29 December 1945 states, "Maui County suffered [a] distinct [loss] during the past week with the demise of Judge Edward McCorriston of Molokai. Judge McCorriston was almost a storied figure in the life of Molokai. His prodigious hospitality has been a watchword that has spread even to the Mainland United States. For almost a quarter of a century he has been the district magistrate on Molokai, and dispensed justice as he saw it, without fear or favor. Truly a figure who will be mourned by hundreds, yea, thousands of friends everywhere."

Another editorial from *The Native Son* (a local newspaper which ran from 1939 to 1950) says, "In the passing away of this Native Son, the island lost one of its most well known community workers. He was known to all as the 'Mayor of Kaunakakai' as he was noted for greeting visitors at his little court house in the Island capitol city on many occasions. He was liked by all. As a jurist he made his decision after careful study and was noted for his honesty. As a community worker he pitched right in whenever his services could be of some help to the community. He was a strong backer of The Native Son and was responsible in getting many of the Friendly Island citizens to become members of this paper's large family."

Judge Edward McCorriston

Judge McCorriston is also one of the signers of the recently uncovered anti-annexation petition which circulated in 1897, a petition which was signed by virtually every adult of Hawaiian ancestry alive at the time.

Of Judge McCorriston, one granddaughter wrote, "I was only five years old when he passed away, but all my life I have heard stories about his kindness, honesty, and fairness, not to mention his ongoing hospitality. My grandmother would tell me stories of how he would bring strangers

home for dinner, after court adjourned. He once locked up his own son because he had broken the law. Even today, the mention of his name, Eddie McCorriston, sparks fond memories among the kūpuna of Hawai'i nei."

***George Nā'ope***—*culture (hula), language.* A respected and accomplished chanter, *kumu hula*, and "father of the Merrie Monarch Hula Festival," Uncle George Nā'ope has spent most of his life perpetuating Hawaiian culture and language through the art of hula. Nā'ope founded the Merrie Monarch Hula Festival in 1961, which is still one of the main cultural events in the islands, with thousands of competitors and spectators from around the world flocking each April to Hilo, Hawai'i, for this prestigious event. One person wrote, "Uncle George Nā'ope is the first person who came to mind [to nominate], because of his knowledge and his willingness to share his knowledge with everyone, most of all our Hawaiian children. Even at his age, he still flies around the world perpetuating the Hawaiian culture." One of his former students said that "his greatness is twofold: the wealth of knowledge that he has and his willingness to share that knowledge."

***Emma 'A'ima and Joseph Kaho'oluhi Nāwahī***—*community leadership, law, politics.* Joseph Nāwahī passed away in 1896, and technically isn't a "Hawaiian of the 20th century," but it is difficult not to include him in this list because of the foundation he laid, along with his wife, Emma, of native Hawaiian anti-annexation protest, and because of how they fought tirelessly for Hawaiian independence. The two married on 17 February 1881, and had two sons, Albert and Alexander. Together they founded Hui Aloha 'Āina, the Hawaiian Patriotic League, of which Joseph was president. Emma was a member of the central executive committee of the women's branch of the Hui, and was instrumental in organizing and gathering signatures for the anti-annexation petition. In 1895 Emma and Joseph started the anti-annexation newspaper *Ke Aloha Aina*, which Emma continued to publish after her husband's death until 1910.

In Mrs. Nāwahī's speech at the Hui meeting in Hilo in 1897, she said, "The United States is just—a land of liberty.... Let us tell them— let us show them that as they love their country and would suffer much before giving it up, so do we love our country, our Hawai'i, and pray that they do not take it from us. Our one hope is in standing firm— shoulder to shoulder, heart to heart.... In this petition, which we offer for your signature today, you, women of Hawai'i, have a chance to speak your mind." Hundreds of people signed the petition that day.

Emma was born in Hilo, Hawai'i, on 28 September 1854. Her mother was Kahaole'au'a, and her father was Tong Yee, a successful Chinese businessman in the sugar industry in Hawai'i (so she was *hapa-Pākē* (half-Hawaiian, half-Chinese)). Upon her birth, she was honored with a *mele inoa*, a name chant, which was later performed for Vivian Mader of the Bishop Museum by the noted chanter J. 'Ilālā'ole. She was a member of the Daughters of Hawai'i, the Hilo and Honolulu Ka'ahumanu Society, Hale o nā Ali'i, Hilo Women's Club, the Haili Church, and was also an honored life member of the American Red Cross. She remained active in many activities until her death in 1935.

Joseph K. Nāwahī(okalani'ōpu'u), a native of Puna, Hawai'i, was brought up by missionary David Lyman and his wife, and was educated at their Hilo Boarding School. He himself became an educator who later taught there, as well as at Lahainaluna in Maui and the Royal School in Honolulu. A brilliant man and a talented painter, Joseph Nāwahī found his career in law and politics. He was a member of the Hawai'i legislature for 20 years, from 1872–1892, and was one of the electors who made Lunalilo king. He passed away in San Francisco in 1896. Great-grandniece Manu Meyer wrote, "They taught me more about our history of resistance. Joseph taught me more about land as my mother. They, of course, resisted American control of Hawaiian lands and Emma was instrumental in bringing together the petition against annexation." (For more information see *Kū'ē: The Hui Aloha 'Āina Anti-Annexation Petitions, 1897–1898* (Noenoe Silva and Nālani Minton, 1998); Noenoe Silva's "Kanaka Maoli Resistance to Annexation," and "Na Lima Kakauha Maluna o ka Pua-I o Kekahi Lahui (Strangling Hands on the Throat of a Nation)" in *'Ōiwi* vol.1; and for the lyrics and translation of Emma's *mele inoa*, see *Nā Leo Hawai'i Kahiko, the Master Chanters of Hawai'i, Songs of Old Hawai'i* (Bernice Pauahi Bishop Museum, Department of Anthropology, 1981).)

***Paleka Ono (nui)***—*community leadership, law*. (See the biographical essay in this issue entitled "Stolen Lands and Other Stories of Paleka Ono (nui)" by granddaughter Patricia Piilani Ono Nakama.)

***Richard Kekumuikawaiokeola Kapule Pagliniwan***—*community leadership, culture, education* (born 26 April 1936, Pālolo, O'ahu). Raised in rural Waiāhole on the windward side of O'ahu, Richard Pagliniwan is a graduate of McKinley High School. He attended the University of

Richard Kekumuikawaiokeola Kapule Pagliniwan

Hawai'i-Mānoa, where he obtained a B.A. and an M.A. in Social Work. He worked for five years in such institutions as the Queen Lili'uokalani Children's Center (QLCC), the Queen Emma Foundation, and the Salvation Army. He worked for 28 years in the public sector in various positions, such as a researcher for the Hawai'i Housing Authority and as deputy director for both the Department of Social Services and Housing (DSSH) and the Department of Hawaiian Home Lands (DHHL). He was also the administrator for the Office of Hawaiian Affairs (OHA) for several years. For over 15 years he was a chair and member of the State Historic Sites Review Board, and is currently employed as a Project Leader and Cultural Specialist with the Queen Emma Foundation. Richard Pagliniwan is a practitioner and trainer of the Hawaiian family reconciliation process known as *ho'oponopono*. He is also an instructor and practitioner of the Hawaiian martial art of *lua*, and studied under noted lua master Charles Kenn.

One person wrote, "Richard Pagliniwan has dedicated much of his life to educate Hawaiians about our culture and the nearly lost art of lua. His aloha for our people is shown greatly." Another said, "He is an individual of pure honesty, true integrity, a real 'people' person, not one to be corrupted. He is a community problem solver and developer, troubleshooter, and a hands on leader."

***Abraham Pi'ianai'a***—*education, Hawaiian firsts*. Abraham Pi'ianai'a has been an educational role model for Hawaiians for decades. The first Hawaiian to receive a master's degree in Pacific Island Studies from the University of Hawai'i, in 1954, he went on to be the first director of the Hawaiian Studies Program, a position he held until 1985. In a 16 June 1953 article by Clarice B. Taylor for the *Honolulu Star-Bulletin*, she wrote, "All Hawaiians may take pride in Mr. Piianaia's accomplishments, for he is a symbol of the coming of age of the Hawaiian. They may be proud of the fact that Mr. Piianaia, a descendant of the old priests who were Hawaii's intellectuals, is demonstrating a desire for scholarship shown by his alii ancestors, one of whom was a true 'hidden' alii."

***Kawaipuna Prejean***—*community leadership, culture, education*. One person wrote, "Kawaipuna Prejean, the great but largely unknown warrior, musician, and teacher who originally instigated the Kaho'olawe movement, the Native Hawaiian Legal Corporation, and the U.N. decolonization struggle, as well as the 1992 struggle to protect Hālawa Valley (O'ahu) and expose the crimes of Bishop Museum and the state Department of Transportation in the H-3 project. He died while fighting this battle, on his 49th birthday. Kawaipuna traveled all over the world to fight for Kanaka Maoli rights, and not in luxury—he often slept in cars or on people's floors and made no money from all his work; he lived in or near poverty for most of his life. He was also a great frontline musician who inspired people all around the earth with his music and spirit. He made many crucial connections with indigenous leaders all around the world, including Bill Means and Rigoberta Menchu. Throughout his busy life he always made time to educate, support, and encourage young people like me and to practice hands-on aloha 'āina. Just about everybody who ever met him has some funny and/or amazing story to tell." (For more information see *Hawai'i: Return to Nationhood* by Ulla Hassager (International Work Group for Indigenous Affairs, 1994).)

**William S. Richardson**—*community leadership, law.* Former Chief Justice of the Hawai'i Supreme Court, William Richardson helped determine that traditional native Hawaiian customs should be "the law of the land."

William S. Richardson rose through the ranks of Hawai'i's judicial system to become one of the most controversial judges in our history. As chief justice of the Hawai'i Supreme Court from 1966 to 1982, he drew a line in the sand in favor of the public. Richardson swept aside a century of legal precedents in the field of property rights, including the notion that, in the court's own words, "The Western concept of exclusivity is not universally applicable in Hawai'i."

The Richardson court helped expand Native Hawaiian rights to access private and public lands for cultural practices. It awarded new land created by lava flows to the state, instead of to nearby property owners. It broadened the rights of citizens to challenge land court decisions. In its most controversial and criticized decision, the Richardson court reached back into the history of the Hawaiian monarchy and duplicated how the *ali'i* determined water rights. In a stunning decision, his court declared that water that had been fought over by two Kaua'i sugar plantations for 50 years belonged to neither of them; it belonged to the public.

A "local boy" of Hawaiian, Chinese, and *haole* ancestry, Richardson graduated from Roosevelt High School and the University of Hawai'i, and earned his law degree from the University of Cincinnati. He served in World War II with the 1st Filipino Infantry Regiment. He fought for statehood, served as Hawaii Democratic Party Chairman from 1956 to 1962, and was lieutenant governor under Governor John A. Burns before becoming chief justice. When Richardson retired from the bench, he served as a Kamehameha Schools/Bishop Estate trustee from 1983 to 1992.

The University of Hawai'i School of Law is named in his honor, a testimony to the courage and conviction of a man who stood for justice.

**Puanani Rogers**—*community leadership.* Puanani Rogers is a long-time community activist from Kaua'i. She has been the *po'o* for Ka Lāhui Hawai'i on Kaua'i for at least six years, and has been relentless in her opposition to everything from telescopes to Star Wars. She supports Hawaiian land occupation and has protested at countless evictions. She has also taken part in cultural exchanges with the indigenous Maori people of Aotearoa and the native Ainu people of Japan.

**Chad Rowan**—*sports*. A Waimānalo native and 1986 graduate of Kaiser High School, Chad Rowan is the first foreign born (not from Japan) *sumotori* to earn the rank of *yokozuna*, the highest ranking title in sumo, the national sport of Japan. Recruited out of high school by Hawai'i native and sumo great Jesse Kuhaulua, Chad Rowan—or Akebono, as he is known in the sumo world—was the first of many other local wrestlers to seek success in the *sumotori* ring. In 1998 he participated in the opening ceremonies of the Winter Olympics held in Nagano, Japan. He has been honored in the traditional Hawaiian style with at least two *mele inoa* (name songs): "Tengoku Kara Kaminari" (Thunder from Heaven) on Israel Kamakawiwo'ole's CD *E Ala Ē* (Big Boy Records, 1995) and "Akebono, Waimanalo Warrior" on Del Beasley's *World's Got to Choose* (Tropical Records, 1995).

**John Rupert Rowe**—*military service* (born 1892). On 13 July 1918, John Rupert Rowe had the dubious honor of being the first American of Hawaiian ancestry to be killed in action at the Aisne-Marne River in Europe during World War I. His name is memorialized at the Waikīkī War Memorial and Natatorium. He is also honored at the American Legion Headquarters on the Ala Wai, where a building—John Rupert Rowe Post 17—is named after him.

**Rebecca Waiānuenue Kahuli Hale Rowe**—*Hawaiian firsts*. Rebecca Hale was a pure Hawaiian who married Robert Joseph Rowe and is the mother of John Rupert Rowe (see above). The couple had 15 children, three of whom fought in World War I. Only two returned home. Thus Rebecca Rowe has the sad distinction of being the first Hawaiian Gold Star mother, an honor bestowed upon a woman whose child is killed in a military conflict. World War II would call back to action the two Rowe brothers who had fought in the first World War. Their mother died on 13 March 1945, before the war ended, and didn't get to see her two sons return home from war.

**David Kekaulike Sing**—*community leadership, education*. As the director of the Nā Pua No'eau program, a federally funded enrichment program for gifted and talented Native Hawaiian youth which encourages Hawaiian children to raise their educational standards through various programs, David Sing has worked tirelessly with Hawaiian communities across the *pae 'āina* (Hawaiian archipelago) to increase opportunities for Hawaiian youth in education. He is currently coordinating the Native Hawaiian Education Association for Hawaiian educators working in all levels of education. Colleague Manu Meyer wrote, "David has always cultivated his own mind, his own philosophy, his own humor. I have learned more about the art of visioning, collaborating, and trust through him. He has been the only Hawaiian at the University of Hawai'i in Hilo who has been a consistent and effective advocate for our Hawaiian people." Of "Uncle David" one student said, "Nā Pua No'eau came about as a vision of Dr. David Sing some ten years ago. This program has helped numerous Hawaiian children, including myself, pursue and attain dreams and goals by providing us with the confidence and opportunities to do so. His vision has become a reality, and the Nā Pua No'eau program that began in the little town of Hilo in 1989 has now expand-ed to Maui, Moloka'i, O'ahu, and Kaua'i. Programs integrating education and Hawaiian cultural values are held year round on all these islands, giving our *keiki* a chance to better themselves while at the same time improving the Hawaiian population overall."

**William Wallace Mokahi Steiner**—
*community leadership, Hawaiian firsts.*
William Wallace Mokahi Steiner was born 16
November 1942 in Honolulu, Hawai'i, but as
a child grew up in Oregon and on a cattle
ranch in Idaho.

In 1967 he returned to Hawai'i to pursue
advanced degrees at the University of
Hawai'i and to reunite with his Hawaiian
side of the family. After graduation he
traveled extensively, conducting research for
the Atomic Energy Commission on atomic
bomb effects and in the genetics of beneficial biological control agents. In 1995 he
returned to Hawai'i to accept a position as
first director of the Pacific Island Ecosystems
Research Center, one of 17 U.S. Geological
Survey Biological Resource Division Centers
responsible for conducting research
concerning conservation issues for
Department of the Interior agencies such
as the U.S. Fish and Wildlife Service and the
National Park Service. Much of the Center's
work deals with endangered Hawaiian
species of plants and animals. In 1996, Dr.
Steiner organized the first intern program
designed specifically for biology students of
Polynesian descent, for which he won a
prestigious Outstanding Performance Award
from the U.S. Department of the Interior. His
efforts resulted in a collaboration with the
University of Hawai'i-Hilo campus where
Native Hawaiian students may earn summer
credit for their work while simultaneously
earning a salary, gaining experience in
conservation biology, and developing
contacts with State and Federal agencies
that may help them gain jobs in biology
after their matriculation. Other agencies,
Chaminade University, the Community
College system of Hawai'i, and others have
since joined this effort to make it a truly
robust and well-grounded opportunity for

study and research of natural sciences and
island ecosystems for native sons and
daughters of Hawaiian descent.

Dr. Steiner's research efforts have resulted in
many firsts in the field of science, helping to
identify new species and better target
populations for biological control. He was
also a member of a research team that
helped establish the existence of endangered Hawaiian plants and animals on
Kaho'olawe and which also established
animal restoration guidelines for the island.
He has served as a scientific consultant to
the U.S. Department of Defense, the Hawai'i
Department of Land and Natural Resources,
the Department of the Interior, and various
overseas agencies and foreign governments,
and is a member of the State of Hawai'i's
Endangered Species Committee and an
adjunct scientist of the Bishop Museum. On
a personal level, Dr. Steiner runs an organic
farm in Missouri, is self-taught on the guitar,
and has written more than 100 songs. He

William Wallace Mokahi Steiner

259

also writes poetry and has published over a dozen poems.

One person wrote, "In many ways, his story is a classic one for this century. In other ways, he is very unique. Either way, he is a product of two cultures whose values are often at odds with one another, just as they are within this man. Yet he has charted a course through his life that has led him to work for the well-being of the natural environment, especially for the protection of environmental biodiversity of the Hawaiian islands. In Bill Steiner, the small Idaho community recognized someone special and awarded him in the areas of athletics, civics, and scholarship. He is notable not only because of his contributions to education, science, and government, but also because of his expressions for the joys and tragedies of life through his songs and poems. He crosses cultural boundaries in these arenas as well. His poems are often about science, and his songs are archives of the regions and peoples of where he has lived. He has closely observed and commented on many aspects of the natural and human experience during this last half of the 20th century. He is a poet who writes of science, a paniolo in Idaho's Owyhee County who worked with horse-drawn equipment and now works with top-notch scientific technology and information systems, a person disciplined in the American work ethic who has a Hawaiian sense of humor and love of life, a scientist who feels Pele beneath his feet, a man who feels the tug of two very different ancestors in his heart. I believe he sets a good example for those who will follow in the 21st century."

**Nainoa Thompson**—*community leadership, culture.* Twenty-five years ago, little did Nainoa Thompson know that his dream of navigating the Pacific Ocean would have such a profound impact on Hawaiian and Polynesian communities across the Pacific and on other peoples around the world. Born and raised on the island of O'ahu, Nainoa grew up listening to the stories of his ancestors told to him by his Hawaiian grandmother. As a Hawaiian youth in a Western-dominated education system, the stories of his *kūpuna* conflicted with that of his formal education. Out of this conflict came the desire to prove that his ancestors did indeed navigate the vast Pacific Ocean without instruments, an achievement few felt was possible before the voyage of the *Hōkūle'a* proved it to be true.

The Polynesian Voyaging Society (PVS) was thus founded in 1973 by Herb Kawainui Kane, Tommy Holmes, and Ben Finney. The *Hōkūle'a*, the first Polynesian double-hulled, long-distance voyaging canoe to be built in modern times, was launched under the auspices of PVS on 8 March 1975. It was navigated by Micronesian master navigator Mau Piailug over 2,000 miles of open ocean from Hawai'i to Tahiti, proving to the world that such feats were possible without the aid of modern Western navigational equipment. Nainoa joined them as a crewmember in Tahiti and sailed on the second leg of the voyage back to Hawai'i.

The second attempt from Hawai'i to Tahiti in 1978 met with tragedy—soon after leaving Hawai'i, the canoe capsized in rough seas about 12 miles off of Lāna'i and crewmember Eddie Aikau was lost at sea (see the entry on Eddie Aikau). It could have been the end of the *Hōkūle'a*, but Nainoa, along with other PVS and crew members, felt that if they stopped voyaging, Eddie's death would have no value. "I believed that voyaging inspired our Hawaiian community and gave us all pride," Nainoa said. "I believed we had to continue. It was Eddie's inspiration that kept us together during those hard times." For the next several years, Nainoa trained with Mau Piailug to prepare himself to navigate the next voyage, to Tahiti in 1980.

Over the past two and a half decades, Nainoa has received countless awards, recognition, and honors for his contributions to voyaging, Hawaiian culture, education, and environmental issues. In 1995 he was named Educator of the Year by the National Education Association.

Currently, Nainoa is the head navigator of the Polynesian Voyaging Society, a former regent for the University of Hawai'i system, and a Bishop Estate trustee. As such, he has continued his personal dream as well as that of PVS to continue educating Hawaiians and others around the world. Some of Nainoa's accomplishments over the past two and a half decades include:

• participating in numerous voyages of the *Hōkūle'a* (and later of the *Hawai'iloa*) after 1980: 1985–1987 (Aotearoa); 1992 (Rorotonga); 1995 (Marquesas, American West Coast, British Columbia); 1999–2000 (Rapa Nui).

• sponsoring numerous educational programs for youth across the state, such as 1992's No Nā Mamo (For the Generations) Voyage for Education, which created a historic live satellite link between the *Hōkūle'a* (which was sailing from Rorotonga in the Cook Islands back to Hawai'i), the space shuttle *Columbia* (which was orbiting the earth on one of its many missions), and Department of Education classrooms across the state. Even more significant on a local and personal level is that fellow Punahou

Alumni Charles Lacy Veach was one of the astronauts on board the *Columbia*. During one live session, a Hawai'i student asked the question, "What are the similarities and differences between canoe and space travel?" Veach responded that "both are voyages of exploration; the Hōkūle'a in the past, and the Columbia in the future." To that Nainoa added, "We feel both are trying to make a contribution to mankind—theirs is in science and technology, ours is in culture and history. Columbia is the highest achievement of modern technology today, just as the voyaging canoe was the highest achievement in its day."

• inspiring the building of more canoes, namely the *Hawai'iloa*, the first canoe built in modern times with tradition materials. The lack of Hawaiian resources, such as *koa* logs, led to a relationship with the Tlingit people of Alaska, who donated two 400-year-old spruce logs for the building of the canoe hulls. This lack of resources also inspired PVS's Mālama Hawai'i (Caring for Hawai'i) environmental protection program, which has participated in activities such as planting thousands of *koa* seedlings on the Big Island in numerous reforestation projects.

• contributing to the revival of canoe building and navigation throughout the Pacific. Inspired by the *Hōkūle'a*'s accomplishments, the Sixth Pacific Arts Festival, held in Rorotonga in the Cook Islands in 1992, was dedicated to Polynesia's great voyaging heritage. A call was put out to nations across the Pacific to build their own canoes and sail to the festival, which many of them did. Some of the canoes built in Hawai'i and across the Pacific besides *Hawai'iloa* include the *Makali'i* and *E Ala* (Hawai'i), *Te Aurere* (Aotearoa), *Takitumu* and *Te Au o Tonga*

(Rorotonga), *Tahiti Nui* and *'A'a Kahiki Nui* (Tahiti).

Nainoa himself would be quick to point out that his accomplishments were not something that he achieved alone. "It's not a one-man show. I just do the navigation," he once said during an interview. He is quick to give credit to other key figures in his life—his family; Herb Kawainui Kane, Tommy Holmes, and Ben Finney, co-founders of the Polynesian Voyaging Society; Mau Piailug, from whom he learned the art of navigation; and the countless number of others, from crew members to community members, who helped him achieve his dreams and accomplish his goals. But as the first Hawaiian since the 14th century to navigate thousands of miles across the vast Pacific Ocean on a traditionally designed canoe and using only traditional navigational techniques, Nainoa has become a symbolic leader to many Hawaiians today. Not surprisingly, in a *Honolulu Advertiser* poll, Nainoa had the highest favorable rating of Native Hawaiian leaders, despite never holding political office.

While claiming retirement from navigating future voyages, Nainoa continues to train new navigators and crewmembers for the *Hōkūle'a* and her growing *'ohana* of canoe siblings. Nainoa has thus had more time to focus on his other interests, namely educational and environmental issues. For example, Nainoa has been a visible spokesperson for the Polynesian Voyaging Society and *Honolulu Star-Bulletin*'s literacy campaign, "Literacy is a Lifelong Voyage." He has also spoken to thousands of school children and community groups across Hawai'i and on the continent on caring for the environment. His Mālama Hawai'i message has stressed the need for everyone to get involved in caring

for our islands, our earth, our ocean. (For more information see *Voyage of Rediscovery: A Cultural Odyssey through Polynesia* by Ben Finney (University of California Press, 1994).)

***Haunani-Kay Trask***—*arts & humanities (literature), community leadership, culture, education, mana wahine, politics.* As a political scientist and Native Hawaiian, Haunani-Kay Trask has dedicated her life to the issue of Hawaiian rights, self determination, and sovereignty, particularly for land rights, including international work at the United Nations. Under her leadership, the Center for Hawaiian Studies at the University of Hawai'i at Mānoa came into being. She also served as co-scriptwriter of the 1993 award-winning documentary *An Act of War: The Overthrow of the Hawaiian Nation*. Besides her political work, Trask is an accomplished and internationally recognized poet. (For more information see her publications *From a Native Daughter* (Common Courage Press, 1993; revised ed. University of Hawai'i Press, 1999); *Light in a Crevice Never Seen* (Calyx Books, 1996); and *Night is a Sharkskin Drum* (University of Hawai'i Press, forthcoming 2002).)

***Mililani Trask***—*community leadership, law, mana wahine, politics.* Attorney Mililani Trask, along with the Trask family (including sister Haunani-Kay Trask), has dedicated her life to fighting for Native Hawaiian sovereignty. She was a trustee for the Office of Hawaiian Affair and for many years she served the Hawaiian people as founder and *kia'āina* (governor) of Ka Lāhui Hawai'i ("The Hawaiian Nation"), the largest entity in the forefront of the struggle for self-determination.

**Puanani Van Dorpe**—*arts and humanities (art), culture.* Pua Van Dorpe is widely considered to be the leading authority on *kapa*, Hawai'i's ancient bark cloth, and is recognized as the person responsible for the rebirth of that art. In 1989, she led a team of *kapa* makers who reinterred the remains of 1,018 ancestors in *kapa* after they had been dug up during the construction of a new hotel on Maui. In 1990 she was named a Living Treasure of Hawai'i. In 1995 she made the *kapa* that was used to wrap Father Damien's right hand for its return from Belgium to Moloka'i. In the last two decades, her entire life (seven days a week, eight to eleven hours a day) has been dedicated to making, dying, researching, and cataloguing *kapa*.

**Robert William Kalanihiapo Wilcox**—*community leadership, education, politics* (born 1855, Maui; died 1903). Robert Wilcox, best known for his Royalist views and for his attempted restoration of the Hawaiian monarchy, was a school teacher on Maui when his political career began. He was elected to Kalākaua's Legislative Assembly in 1880, supporting such bills as tax relief for large Hawaiian families, and developing hospitals and roads on all the islands. King Kalākaua sent Wilcox to Italy for military training. Prior to his attempt to restore the monarchy in 1895, Wilcox fought to restore Kalākaua's power in 1889. As the leader of the Home Rule Party, Wilcox was elected as the first delegate to Congress in 1900. Although the position did not come with voting power, he did introduce pro-Hawaiian legislation that reflected his vision of Hawai'i as a modern American state which would be governed internally by educated Hawaiians. Along with his second wife, Theresa Laahui Cartwright, Wilcox ran several newspapers, including the post-

annexation *Home Rula Repubalika*. (For more information see *Unconquerable Rebel: Robert W. Wilcox and Hawaiian Politics, 1880–1903* by Ernest Andrade (University Press of Colorado, 1996).)

**John Henry Wise**—*community leadership, culture* (born 1869, Kohala, Hawai'i; died 1937). John H. Wise Sr. was a prominent figure in Hawaiian politics, education, and religion. His parents were Rebecca Nāwa'a of Hawai'i and Julius A. Wise of Hamburg, Germany. He entered the first class of The Kamehameha Schools in 1887. His interest in religion took him to Ohio, where he graduated from Oberlin Theological seminary in 1893. Upon his return home, Wise reckoned with the overthrow of the Hawaiian Kingdom. Based in Honolulu, he was initially associated with the Hawaiian Board of Missions. However, upon learning about their support of and participation in the overthrow, Wise resigned. He later devoted himself to Kamakuamauloa Church, where he acted as pastor. In 1895, Wise and Prince Jonah Kūhiō, along with Robert Kalanihiapo Wilcox, played an active role in planning an armed insurrection to restore the Queen to the throne. He was charged with treason, along with many others, and served a year in prison as part of his sentence. Wise refrained from telling the full story of his role, the involvement of others, and the detailed plans for the insurrection until the 1930s, when all of the other participants were no longer living.

After his prison sentence, Wise worked for a couple of years as a carpenter in both Kohala and Honolulu. In 1898 he married Kauahi Kawai, daughter of Peke (w) and J. Kawai (k) and they had ten children, six daughters and four sons whose descendants continue to flourish today. Wise devoted himself to Hawaiian political advancement within the American system. By 1900, he was Hawai'i's delegate to the Democratic National Convention in Kansas City. In 1901, he became the Hawaiian-language interpreter for the territorial House of Representatives, and eventually made clerk of the House during a special session of the legislature in 1904. From 1907, Wise also translated documents for the archives and was later renowned as an authority in 'ōlelo Hawai'i. He worked as clerk of the territorial Senate in 1911 and 1913. In 1914, along with Prince Kūhiō, Noa Aluli, and the Reverend Akaiko Akana, Wise was a founding member of the 'Ahahui Pu'uhonua o Nā Hawai'i (Hawaiian Protective Association), devoted to uplifting the Hawaiian people through social work and education.

In 1915, while Wise was traveling in Seattle, Washington, on behalf of union laborers, he was elected to the Senate for a four-year term. Wise is credited with having helped draft the earliest version of The Hawaiian Rehabilitation Resolution, which was introduced to the territorial legislature in 1919. Wise was also one of the members of the territorial legislative committee who traveled to Washington, D.C., in order to bring the proposal to Congress (where Kūhiō presented it as a bill). Throughout the debates which led to the formation of the Hawaiian Homes Commission Act of 1920, Wise remained firmly committed to the inclusive definition of "native Hawaiian" as up to 1/32 ethnicity (firmly opposing the highly exclusive 50% blood quantum rule) because more Hawaiians were entitled to the crown lands that would be utilized for the homesteading plan. In late 1923, President Coolidge appointed Wise Director of Prohibition for the Territory.

Beside his involvement in politics, Wise's love for football (since his college days) persisted. In his later years, he lectured on topics dealing with Hawaiian religion and taught Hawaiian language at the University of Hawai'i. He was also a member of the Order of Kamehameha, Hale o Nā Ali'i, and Chiefs of Hawai'i.

**Elizabeth Kahiku Johnson Young—**
*culture, education, language, Hawaiian firsts* (born 15 April 1901, 'Ewa, O'ahu; died 30 September 1972). Elizabeth Young, *pūpū a'o 'Ewa* (a native of 'Ewa, O'ahu), traces her lineage to La'amaikahiki, son of voyaging chief Mō'īkeha. One of La'amaikahiki's three wives was from Pu'uloa, where Elizabeth Kahiku's paternal grandmother, La'amaikahi-ki Wahine, was born about 1836, and subsequently raised along the banks of Waiawa stream, near the sacred pond of Pā'au'au. This was also the place occupied by Kamehameha's friend and ally, Don Francisco de Paula Marín, and his descendants. La'amaikahiki Wahine married Ambrose Peters Johnson.

Elizabeth's parents were Pedro Johnson and Pa'ahana Hopu, known later as Hana Palaniko. Pedro Johnson was a *paniolo* (cowboy) who, along with his brother John, accompanied Ikua Purdy to Cheyenne, Wyoming, where Purdy attained fame in the National Rodeo Finals held there. Elizabeth's mother's name is well known to lovers of Hawaiian music: she is Pa'ahana, *"ke kaikamahine noho kuahiwi,"* the young girl who fled to the Wahiawā uplands, where Pedro Johnson found her surviving in the wild on *'ōpae*, guavas, and the like. Pa'ahana was a descendent of Thomas Hopu and Puakea Nāhakuali'i. Thomas Hopu, an 'Ewa native, stowed away on an American ship bound for Boston in order to escape Kamehameha's

Elizabeth Kahiku Johnson Young, at her Kalapana home passing out 'ulu to the Kīlauea Military Camp dependents

forces when they invaded Oʻahu. Young's daughter wrote, "According to my mother, there were five sisters in the family who were being hunted down along with the ʻohana by Kamehameha's warriors in a conflict of aliʻi succession." In Boston, Hopu befriended Henry ʻŌpūkahaʻia and returned to Hawaiʻi as a missionary with Hiram Bingham and the first company of missionaries to Hawaiʻi in 1820 (after Kamehameha's death) as a replacement for ʻŌpūkahaʻia, who was too ill to make the long journey. (ʻŌpūkahaʻia later died in New England, and was buried in Cornwall, Connecticut).

Although Elizabeth Young did not hold political office, she spent much time lending her support to other political hopefuls, and campaigned for the likes of Benjamin Dillingham, Senator Doi, and Senator Richard "Papa" Lyman, who later became a much-loved and respected trustee of The Kamehameha Schools/Bishop Estate.

She became involved in cultural activities on the island of Hawaiʻi, assisting George Nāʻope and Dotty Thompson in bringing the very first Merrie Monarch Festival to life. She also assisted in expanding the Aloha Week Festival activities in Hilo, becoming the first chanter in both events.

Young spent many years teaching Hawaiian language, culture, and chant in formal and informal settings. She was an instructor at Kapoho Elementary School and at Hilo Community College, where in 1972 she composed a *mele* for the commencement exercises there. Young also lectured at Kīlauea Military Camp, where she "addressed tourists, military officials, and even astronauts."

She was an informant to Mary Kawena Pukui in her work compiling entries for the *Hawaiian Dictionary*, and was sought out by other scholars for her valued knowledge of history, legends, and lore. She was a cultural consultant to Hawaiʻi Volcanoes National Parks Superintendent Alan MacDonald, and shared her knowledge of ʻEwa with Kamokila Campbell's Lanikūhonua Culture Center. She was called upon to perform the blessing at the commencement of the restoration work of Kamehameha's sacred *luakini heiau* of Puʻukoholā.

Elizabeth's daughter wrote, "In the rural communities of ʻOpihikao, Kapoho, Kalapana, and Pāhoa she was widely known as a gracious host with a ready meal, a generous friend to the needy and a wise and trusted advisor, interceding on many a kanaka's behalf with this or that and with untangling the bureaucratic red tape in Hilo or Honolulu, bridging the gap between the country folk and the American bureaucracy. Although she was a member of various Christian organizations—Kalawina, Catholic, and Mormon—she never relinquished her traditional beliefs and kept on practicing the ceremonies and rites of the ancestral religion." Upon her death in 1972, the Aloha Week Festival court in Hilo left her chanter's space open in her honor.

**Notable Hawaiians who may be appearing in Part II:**

Judge James Aiona
Dr. Patrick Aiu
Senator Daniel Akaka
Kaniala Akaka
Bernard Akana
Maile Akimseu
Debbie Akiona
Yuklin Aluli
Haunani Apoliona
Papa Henry 'Auwae
Helen Desha Beamer
William "Bill" Blaisdell
Hayden Burgess (Pōkā Laenui)
Mervina Cash-Kaeo
Sam Choy
Michael Chun
Ho'oipo DeCambra
Emma DeFries
Annie Mikala Cockett Enfield
Eric Enos
Venus Holt Gay
Dorothy Kahananui Gillett
Kamehaitu Helelā
George Jarrett Helm
Don Ho
Calvin Ioane Hoe
George Holokai
John Dominis Holt IV
Victoria Holt-Takamine
Richard and Sol Ho'opi'i (The Ho'opi'i Brothers)
Mamo Howell
Gabriel "Pele" I
David Michael Kaipolaua'eokekuahiwi Inciong
Rubellite Kawena Johnson
'Īmaikalani Kalāhele
Jonah Kūhiō Kalaniana'ole
Eddie Kamae
Dennis Kamakahi
Israel Kamakawiwo'ole
Edith Kanaka'ole

Danny and Sonny Kaniho
Sol Kaopuiki
Elizabeth Kauahipaula
Thomas Kaulukukui Jr.
Genoa Keawe
Elizabeth Lindsey
'Iolani Luahine
Aaron Mahi
Ted Makalena
Kaiakapu Malule
Kahu James Kimo Mersberg
Harry K. Mitchell
James Kimo Mitchell
Lokalia Montgomery
Judge Clifford Nakea
Lyons K. Naone Jr.
Lolena Nicholas
Soli Niheu
Jonathan Kamakawiwo'ole Osorio
Gabby Pahinui
Māhealani Pai and the Pai 'ohana
Hinano Paleka
Alvina Park
Irene Cockett Perry
John Pia
Mary Kawena Pukui
Ikua Purdy
Keali'i Reichel
Ernest Richardson
Emma Sharpe
Noenoe Silva
Oswald Stender
Rell Sunn
Myron Pinky Thompson
John Waihe'e
No'eau Warner
Charlie Wedemeyer
Jenny Wilson
Kau'i Zuttermeister

# Kunihi ka mauna i ka lai e,

O Waialeale la i Wailua,

Huki i luna ka popoo ua o Kawaikini,

Alai ia ae la e Nounou,

Nalo ka ipu haa,

Ka laula ma uka o Kapaa e,

I paa i ka leo, he ole ka hea mai,

E hea mai ka leo—e."

*Steep stands the mountain in the calm*

*Waiʻaleʻale there at Wailua*

*The heavy rain of Kawaikini*

*Reaches up to the heavens*

*Obstructed by Nounou*

*Kaipuhaʻa is hidden*

"Kunihi ka mauna i ka lai e

O Waialeale la i Wailua

Huki iluna ka popo ua o Kawaikini

Alai ia aela e Nounou

Nalo Kaipuhaa

Ka laula mauka o Kapaa—e

I paa i ka leo, he ole ka hea mai

E hea mai ka leo—e."

"Kunihi ka mauna i ka lai—e

O Waialeale la—e i Waialua

Huki ae la iluna ka papa o Anokawailani

Alai ia ae la e Nounou

Nalowale Kaipuhaa

Haa i ka laula

Haa ka ipu, haa makai o Kapaa—e

Haa ka ipu, haa mauka o Kapaa—e

Mai paa i ka leo

He ole ka heahea mai."

*"Kūnihi ka mauna i ka laʻi ē*

*ʻO Waiʻaleʻale lā, i Wailua;*

*Huki aʻela i ka lani,*

*Ka papa ʻauwai o Kawaikini;*

*Ālai ʻia aʻela e Nounou,*

*Nalo Kaipuhaʻa,*

*Ka laulā, ma uka o Kapaʻa ē;*

*Mai paʻa i ka leo.*

## *He ʻole ka hea mai ē!"*

The broad plains above Kapaʻa

Humble in the expanse

The gourd is low, low below Kapaʻa

The gourd is low, low above Kapaʻa

If the voice is withheld,

No greeting will come;

The voice calls.

**"Kunihi ka mauna i ka laʻi e,**
**O Wai-aleale, la, i Wai-lua;**
**Huki iluna ka popo ua o Ka-wai-kini;**
**Alai ia aʻe la e Nounou,**
**Nalo ka Ipu-haʻa,**
**Ka laula ma uka o Ka-paʻa e.**
**I paʻa i ka leo, he ole e hea mai.**
**E hea mai ka leo, e!"**

"Kunihi ka mauna i ka laʻi e—

O Waialeale la i Wailua

Huki ae la ka lani kapapa-ua Kawaiki

Alai ae la paa Nounou

Nalowale ka laula mauka

Makai o Kapaa e—

Mai paa i ka le—o

He ole ka hea ma—i."